The Court of Justice of the European Communities

Jurisdiction and Procedure

ENGLAND:	BUTTERWORTH & CO. (PUBLISHERS) LTD. LONDON: 88 Kingsway, W.C.2
AUSTRALIA:	BUTTERWORTH & CO. (AUSTRALIA) LTD. SYDNEY: 20 Loftus Street MELBOURNE: 473 Bourke Street BRISBANE: 240 Queen Street
CANADA:	BUTTERWORTH & CO. (CANADA) LTD. TORONTO: 1367 Danforth Avenue, 6
NEW ZEALAND:	BUTTERWORTH & CO. (NEW ZEALAND) LTD. WELLINGTON: 49/51 Ballance Street AUCKLAND: 35 High Street
SOUTH AFRICA:	BUTTERWORTH & CO. (SOUTH AFRICA) LTD. DURBAN: 33/35 Beach Grove
U.S.A.:	BUTTERWORTH INC. WASHINGTON, D.C.: 7300 Pearl Street, 20014

The Court of Justice of the European Communities

Jurisdiction and Procedure

By

EDWARD H. WALL, M.A. (Cantab.)

of Lincoln's Inn, Barrister-at-Law

With Forewords by

JUDGE CHARLES-LÉON HAMMES

*President of the Court of Justice
of the European Communities*

and

THE RT. HON. LORD WILBERFORCE, P.C.

Lord of Appeal in Ordinary

**LONDON
BUTTERWORTHS
1966**

©

BUTTERWORTH & CO. (PUBLISHERS) LTD.
1966

Printed in Northern Ireland at The Universities Press, Belfast

To

VALENTINE LOGUE

this book is gratefully dedicated

Preface

In the Spring of 1957 the High Authority of the European Coal and Steel Community honoured me with an invitation to spend some days in Luxembourg in order to see at first hand the working of the Court of Justice of the Community and of the Legal Service of the High Authority itself. As it happened, my visit was made within a day or two of the signing in Rome of the new treaties for the setting up of the European Economic Community and the European Atomic Energy Community, for both of which the Court was in due course to become the judicial institution, with, as a consequence, a great increase in the volume and variety of its already considerable work. I recall being greatly struck at that time by the fascination and delicacy of the task being performed in Luxembourg of reconciling, for the purposes of application of the Coal and Steel Community Treaty, legal concepts differing somewhat as between one member country and another but relating to similar factual problems in them all. Of this process of reconciliation perhaps the outstanding example at that time was in respect of the concept of the misuse of its powers by a public authority. *Détournement de pouvoir* of the French needed to be reconciled with *Ermessensmiszbrauch* of the Germans and corresponding concepts in the other four member countries. That was but one example. But if all law has a natural tendency to be fissiparous and centrifugal, part of the fascination of the general task now being performed was its concern, not with fission, but with fusion—for a purpose unprecedented.

By 1957 the process of reconciling not only the languages but, much more difficult, the essence of the notions they expressed, was already far advanced. Linguistic hesitations might conceivably, in the very early years, have provoked a Frenchman into exclaiming, in reversal of the accepted order of the assertion: *"Tout ce qui n'est pas français n'est pas clair"*; or a German to murmur, though with no thought turned on *Die Lorelei*: *"Ich weisz nicht was soll es bedeuten"*; or an Italian to ask: *"Che vuol' dire in latino?"* But if any such hesitations, if they had ever existed, there was now no trace. The process of reconciliation of both languages and concepts was already resulting in a new organic whole.

My task is to interpret the results of this process to date, so far as the jurisdiction and procedure of the Court are concerned, to the English lawyer and, indeed, I would hope to any lawyer who is within the sweeping generic embrace of what the Continental Europeans fondly describe as "Anglo-Saxon law". The concepts familiar to the latter are more different, though not irreconcilably so, from those of the European Community countries, than those of any one of these countries in relation to the other five. Many of the legal concepts of Continental Europe, however, though not identical with those of "Anglo-Saxon law" are expressed by means of technical words that are virtually identical with the words used by the latter—they have the same etymological origins and often are spelt the same or sound little different. To ensure clarity I have wherever necessary either used a paraphrase, or inserted an explanation after the continental expression.

French is the only official and authentic language of the first in date of the three European Communities, that of Coal and Steel. French, German, Italian and Netherlands are all official and authentic languages of the two later Communities, the Economic Community and Euratom. The translations of the Rules of Procedure of the Court, of the Instructions to the Registrar, of the Articles of the Coal and Steel Community Treaty and of the Statute of the Court annexed thereto, are taken from the draft (1964) revised translations, prepared, and very kindly made available to me before publication, by the British Foreign Office. For the English translation of the two later Treaties I have made use of the (unofficial British Government) versions published by Her Majesty's Stationery Office in 1962, suggesting such amendments therein as appeared to me desirable.[1] The translations from the Court's Official Law Reports (*Recueil de Jurisprudence*) are my own. I have in all cases compared the renderings in the four Community languages, before translating into English, though where any shade of meaning was in doubt, I have, in respect of the Coal and Steel Community only, placed greatest reliance on the French.

The provisions which govern the jurisdiction and procedure of the Court did not all acquire the force of law at the same time. Upon the original Coal and Steel Community Treaty with its annexed Statute of the Court there followed the Rules of Procedure of the Court, the two later Treaties, the revised Rules of Procedure and the Instructions to the Registrar. Frequently, on a given aspect of the Court's work the Statute amplifies the Treaty, or the Rules of Procedure amplify one or other, or both, of these. The inter-relation is important, with the consequence that much cross-reference in the present work is essential. I have nevertheless sought to arrange the material so as to make it possible to follow the course of any proceedings before the Court in progressive sequence from beginning to end, without losing sight of the whole context at any one point in the progression, or making it impossible for the user of the book to obtain an overall impression of the work of the Court.

While, therefore, the method and form (and, I trust, the language) of the book should seem familiar to the English or "Anglo-Saxon" practitioner or academic lawyer, the legal concepts may frequently appear novel. In preparing the presentation of these I have not fought shy of the Continental European doctrinal writers, whom the sheer novelty of the subject has prompted to great activity. To many of them I must acknowledge my indebtedness. But in presenting the material I have eschewed theory and have relied throughout on the judgments or dicta of the Court itself or on the submissions of the Advocates General. All decisions of the Court up to the Spring of 1965 which have an important bearing on the subject-matter have been cited or referred to in the text.

In conclusion, I gratefully acknowledge the kind encouragement and great assistance I have received from the President and other Judges of the Court itself, from the Registrar, the Deputy Registrar, and the Attaches to the Judges, from the leading members of the Legal Services of the Communities both in Brussels and Luxembourg, from several of the leading practitioners of different nationalities whose practice takes them frequently to the Court, and from the Librarian of the Court. To my grateful indebtedness to a number of doctrinal commentators, some of whom I have not had the privilege of meeting in person, I have already referred. The consideration and care with which my Publishers have prepared my manuscript for the

---

[1] The documents made available to me by the British Foreign Office have been published in slightly amended form, since this book went to press, by Her Majesty's Stationery Office. The extracts from these documents and from the H.M.S.O. publications of 1962, all of which are Crown Copyright, are reproduced in this book by permission of the Controller of Her Majesty's Stationery Office. Extensively revised translations of the E.E.C. and E.A.E.C. Treaties are expected to be published by Her Majesty's Stationery Office in 1966.

press and seen it through the various stages leading to publication have been of the highest order.

I wish especially to thank Lord WILBERFORCE and Judge HAMMES for the great interest they have taken in my book and for the honour they have each done me in so kindly contributing a Foreword.

Judge HAMMES—in a vein contrasting, no doubt deliberately, with that of the body of the book—has devoted, I am aware, much time and care to sketching in his Foreword the philosophy underlying the work of the Court, of which, having been a member from the beginning, he speaks from such a wealth of experience. I am greatly indebted to him for thus providing what is in effect a complement to my work.

E. H. W.

12 NEW SQUARE,
LINCOLN'S INN.
December, 1965.

Foreword

BY JUDGE CHARLES-LÉON HAMMES

It is one of the most outstanding characteristics of the European Communities that they have brought into being their own particular legal order, resting on institutions and principles of which the purpose is both to give enduring form to communities of independent States and to eliminate the rivalries and tensions between them that have existed for centuries, by the pooling of the economic assets of a large part of the European continent.

The salient feature of this new legal order is the autonomy of its law-making and enforcing processes. Such functions were hitherto the exclusive privilege of States; their exercise was a prerogative right, deriving from sovereignty, to which no authority other than the State itself could lay claim.

But the resulting homogeneity of law, confined as it was within national frontiers, revealed itself increasingly unsatisfactory and inadequate as the expansion of economic life and the needs of human society progressively spilled over the frontiers of individual Nation States. As they did so, they raised problems of growing complexity, requiring their own specifically designed solutions, thus leading finally to the abandonment, in their isolation, of the legal orders of individual Nations. For, as the principles and rules of such national legal orders, independent in their origin and sovereign in their application, come into conflict with other, equally sovereign and independent, rules, each similarly pursuing particular ends, the antagonisms that ensue brook no deferment of their topical solution, whether it be on the basis of customary rules or on that of agreement by convention.

It is this problem—or, I would prefer to say, this void—that classical International Law has sought to solve or to bridge. International Law differs from Municipal Law in its source, being not the creation of a single sovereign power, but of the wills of several States acting jointly to arrive at a solution. Thus it often represents no more than a compromise between mutually opposing demands, the conciliation of which may impose limits on each demand or may require a median way between conflicting interests *inter partes*, that is to say between States alone.

These two spheres of law—Municipal Law, because of the exiguous nature of its domain—International Law, because of its lack of direct adaptation to the needs of individuals—were both inadequate to meet the challenge of the evolving new European order. This order requires a direct response to the conflicting demands which are no longer demands of States themselves but of the subjects, individual or corporate, of which they are comprised. These demands are created by the progressive abolition of economic frontiers as these become increasingly meaningless through the extending range of human needs and interests.

This communitarian approach to specific problems—limited incidentally to the economic and social fields—conferred upon the legal concepts governing these fields a greater emphasis than do national legal orders, and had to provide the substratum of a legal system aimed at establishing co-operation and solidarity in the domain of production and trade, at all cost, in good times and in bad. The process of the pooling of needs and resources had to be matched by a body of governing rules of correspondingly common application.

It is, in point of fact, the institutionalizing of these factors—their rationalization and translation into positive form—as a system of principles and rules varying in the detail of their definition according to the degree of economic evolution attained, and, as a direct consequence of the aims pursued by the Community Treaties, either superimposed on, or juxtaposed with, the national legal system of the Member States, which has brought into existence a Power manifesting itself through forms which are not—or, at least, are not exclusively—those traditionally sanctioned by the constitutional practices and attitudes of Nations. In its exercise, this Power reaches beyond its economic mission to embrace the general task of promoting the common interests of the national groups over which it has sway; yet, in doing so, it respects the particular characteristics and requirements of all and each of these groups, for their independence and autonomy is to remain intact and free from interference.[1]

Formerly, rules of law—in any circumstances at all comparable to the present—have been brought into existence by way of amendments or additions to the body of law of individual States. Juxtaposed with each national system, these rules have operated as a "national law for use in external relations" in accordance with principles which are hybrid in origin; the reception of the rules themselves into the national systems was by no means free from complications (I have in mind the dualist doctrine of International Law); furthermore, these rules were inoperative as far as their direct application to States' nationals is concerned (they were, in short, classical International Law). In place of such rules, thus created, has come now a new concept of law, in the form of an institutionalized "supranational" Power, sanctioned ultimately by the consent of those subject to its authority, and by their confidence in its being appropriately exercised in accordance with the requirements of the shrinking world of today—a Power possessing full legal competence within the scope assigned to it for making binding rules, of its own motion, unassisted by other law-making powers established singly in the Member States.

What is this phenomenon?

We are witnessing an inflection of one of the long-term cycles which it is believed can be traced in the evolutionary movement of legal orders, which, like economic cycles, pass through successive phases. Thus, there has been a passage through the universality of Roman law; through its dichotomy, in the Christian era, rooted in the distinction between the temporal and the spiritual; through the phases in which these exchanged roles, in their subordination the one to the other; the period of law-making monopoly of the Nation States; and, now, the dislocation of law resulting from the exercise of certain sovereign or regalian prerogatives by an independent Power.

Within the compass of the Communities, the integration of the tasks to be performed was to lead to the setting up of law-making machinery superimposed upon the national legal systems, handing down principles of obligatory force binding on all persons of the Communities within its jurisdiction, regardless of the individual legal order to which, nationally, they are subject.

Teleologically, the establishing of such institutional machinery, while satisfying the concrete needs of the new communities, in a Europe divided by historical, psychological and even ethnographical atavisms, had to avoid any chimerical idea of unification, and to derive its motive force from the interests placed in common.

---

[1] See the general introductory provisions of the Treaties (E.C.S.C., Articles 1–6; E.E.C., Articles 1–6; E.A.E.C., Articles 1 and 2, *post*).

A common policy which is directed at the solution of the great problems that surpass the strength of individual Member States had to be reconciled with the aspirations of each of these individual Communities. Delicate problems arise in attempting to demarcate the spheres of jurisdiction of the Nation States and the Community respectively. In the area where the two legal orders intersect or overlap each other, once the extent to which one or the other is eclipsed has been ascertained, the effect of Community rules depends in the first place on the possibility of their direct execution, on their self-executing character. The immediate and direct impact of such rules on the rights and duties of the persons who are subject to them tends to confer upon them a pre-eminence over the national laws, which by implication they thus abrogate. But the matter is complicated by virtue of the fact that implicit abrogation is not corroborated except by reference to the objectives of the Community, while the residuary law continues to derive its force from the national legal orders.

The antinomies between inter-State law and municipal law are regulated in classical International Law by the principle that the direct applicability of International Law, in the absence of explicit conventional provision to the contrary, is exceptional. The Treaties establishing the Communities determine this question in no more than a few instances (see, for example, the E.C.S.C. Treaty, Article 65(4)(a)) but the Court of Justice of the Communities has evolved a case law clearly contrary to the traditional solution, basing itself both on the finality of Community law as evidenced by the Treaties, and on the abandonment, by the Member States, to the Community, of the exercises of certain of their sovereign prerogative rights, including, partially, the right to legislate.

It thus comes about that a schism begins to appear in the positive law of each of the Member States. On the compact body of the internal legal orders, a collection of rules is grafted which is continually expanding in scope as integration develops and prospers. Just as the pathological multiplication of cells destroys living bodies by strangling their physiological functions, the growth of law-making by the extra-national authorities will, in the areas in which it operates, paralyse and ultimately annihilate the national legal orders, which will find themselves replaced by a new system better related to the aims being pursued.

The reconciliation of these antinomies in the etymological sense of the word (one law resisting another law) will be facilitated by the slowness with which the economic and political problems of the Communities evolve. For it is a dominant characteristic of the Communities that the Treaties confine themselves to defining the general objects at which they aim, while leaving to the Institutions they establish the achievement of these objects by appropriate measures taken with the ad hoc means at their disposal.

The task of reconciliation is rendered more difficult, on the other hand, by the fundamental difference which underlies both the conception and the application of the two legal orders in question. Alongside the Continental national systems of law, built up over many centuries into an ordered whole, there is now growing up a new pragmatic "experimental" law, which is a strange phenomenon in this continental Europe where all legal thinking is so much attuned to the Cartesian method. For that reason the antinomies relate not only to the conflicts between specific rules of law but extend to the whole purview and conception of the nature of the general law to which their solution should conform. On what has been called the "battlefield for antinomies"[2] there stand arrayed against each other the classical lawmaking

---

[2] Professor Lemar Tammalo, Sydney, in *"Les Antinomies du Droit"*, Brussels, 1965.

process which develops a rule of law with the assistance, and from the starting point, of traditional constitutional principles, on the one hand, and, on the other hand, a process of making laws that are deliberately functional, frequently designed for a particular contingency, conceived in the spirit of a community order in course of formation, and inspired with the resolve to bring to perfection the great concept which holds within itself the salvation of Europe.

It is to the Court of Justice of the European Communities, an Institution which is independent both of national and of Community authority, that the role has been assigned of freely deciding *in concreto* the spheres of application of the respective legal orders, in accordance with its mission of "ensuring that the law is observed in the interpretation and implementation" of the Treaties (see E.C.S.C. Treaty, Article 31; E.E.C. Treaty, Article 164 and E.A.E.C. Treaty, Article 136). It is by decisions in individual cases, made with regard to what is reasonable—a method akin to that of the Anglo-Saxon tradition—that the Court, through the resultant body of prescient case law, must seek to rationalize what is permitted by the law of the Treaties with that which general public interest prescribes, thus enabling varying legal orders to be assimilated, within this pragmatic system, into Community law.

Seen against the general background of the foregoing summary reflections, the excellent study which Mr. Wall has prepared provides an exposé of Community law which is both apt and exhaustive and, through its judicious commentary, draws revealing comparisons and furthers that mutual understanding which is indispensible.

The work is, of course, primarily designed for the legal practitioner, for whom it will constitute a most complete and practical authority on the work of the Court of Justice of the European Communities.

He will indeed be faced in an increasing measure with practical legal problems—complex in matter and wide in scope—arising from the new network of economic inter-relation between Member States of the Communities and third countries.

On the scientific level, this development is already providing new subject matters for Comparative Law and the general study of Political Science.

CHARLES-LÉON HAMMES

Foreword

By the Rt. Hon. Lord Wilberforce, P.C.

It is most encouraging that, in spite of the great disappointment of January 1963, the interest of English lawyers in the legal institutions and practices of the European Communities so far from fading, seems to be on the increase.

This book should add a fresh stimulus to it.

The European Court of Justice continues to grow in stature: it is evidently one of the key creative organs of the three European Communities. Nobody who is interested in the progress of legal institutions can afford to neglect it. We have had access to its decisions: now Mr. Wall helps us to understand the exact basis for its varied jurisdiction, which he analyses under twenty three different headings, and its procedural working. And of course as we study its procedure we get to know much more about the substance of its achievement.

It would be a mistake to regard the present book merely as an act of faith in the future of British participation in Europe—though I for one would be glad to accept it as such. But, quite independently, it constitutes a comparative study into the working and integration of a large economic unit which is of interest and benefit to all who believe in the development of regional institutions. Perhaps most important of all it gives us an insight into the operation of continental administrative law and into its creation by European judges from which, if we will, we can learn so much with advantage to ourselves. As well as commending the care and thought which Mr. Wall has put into the arrangement of his book, I would like to take the opportunity of congratulating Messrs. Butterworths for having commissioned it.

WILBERFORCE

Table of Contents

Table of Treaties

(including Statutes of the Court, Rules of Procedure and Instructions to the Registrar)

Figures in heavy type indicate the pages on which the text of the Article is set out

Table of Cases

In the following table the abbreviation "R." refers to the French edition of the official Court law reports—"Recueil de Jurisprudence"

Introduction

I

A not inconsiderable amount of literature is now available in the English language dealing either with the economic principles embodied in the Treaties setting up the three European Communities or with the substantive legal form in which these principles are cast—whether this results from the Treaties themselves, from domestic law making by the Member States in execution of the Treaties, or from the evolving case law of the Court of Justice of the Communities.

The present work is concerned, not with the substantive law thus created or evolving, but with the central judicial machinery of the Communities, that of the Court of Justice. This was created to administer the law of the Treaties either directly, through its own unappealable decisions, or indirectly through decisions of an interpretative nature constituting a unifying influence in respect of application of the Treaties by the judicial authorities of the individual Member States.

Economic regionalism and its attendant legal integration is the order of the day. This study of the central judicial machinery of one regional grouping may assist in highlighting the legal elements that have needed to be harmonized, or unified, as between six States showing considerable similarities as well as considerable differences in their individual legal techniques, and thus be of service for comparative purposes in other regions.

II

What is now the Court of Justice of the European Communities originally came into existence in 1952. It was created to ensure the observance of law in the interpretation and implementation of the Treaty establishing the European Coal and Steel Community, and was created by the same Treaty. The other Communities (the European Economic Community and the European Atomic Energy Community) did not then exist, indeed they had probably barely been thought of. But when they were set up by the Treaties signed in Rome in the spring of 1957 the function of the Court of Justice was enlarged so that it might carry out, in respect of the two later Communities, a similar task to the one upon which it was already engaged.

The first Community, that of Coal and Steel, was designed to create a common market throughout the six Member States, in the specific industries of coal, steel (and scrap). It derived its driving force from the central executive authority which the Treaty established—the High Authority with its seat in Luxembourg. It is the High Authority which gives the Community its material shape, in the form of the common market for coal and steel. Very considerable powers were vested in it to enable it to do so. In addition to offering advice or suggestions it can give instructions and orders not only to the Member States of the Community but also, *directly*, to industrial undertakings in coal and steel situated in the Member States. Thus, the High Authority is placed in a position to do more than formulate and recommend policy for the Community. It exercises direct control within the Member States over the day to day execution of policy. This, from the legal point of view, is perhaps the most novel feature in the Treaty.

The makers of the Treaty were anxious to ensure that whilst the powers thus conferred could be freely exercised, that must always be done with due observance of the law of the Treaty. Therefore, Member States and industrial undertakings were both given, by the Treaty, rights of recourse to the Court of Justice in order to secure annulment of acts of the High Authority which could be demonstrated to infringe that law.

The jurisdiction conferred by the Treaty on the Court extended, of course, far beyond these and related administrative matters, for example to such widely different types of question as disputes between Member States arising from the Treaty and disputes between the Community and its employees. But because of the powerful administrative position in which the High Authority was placed, and more particularly because of its novel power of direct action in respect of industrial undertakings within the Member States, it is not surprising that a very large proportion of the cases decided by the Court in relation to the Coal and Steel Community have been cases of administrative law in which the High Authority has been defendant.

The task of the European Economic Community established in 1958 is somewhat different. It is to create a common market amongst the six Member States not in one clearly defined sector of industry, but for virtually the whole range of economic activities. The Treaty provided the Community with a central executive authority (the Commission) in some ways not unlike the High Authority, but it was clear from the outset that because of the diversified nature of the task confronting the Community much of the actual execution of policy would have to be left to the Member States themselves. The driving force of the Economic Community does not derive so completely from the central executive as does that of the Coal and Steel Community. It is provided by the Member States as well.

From the point of view of ensuring the observance of law in the interpretation and implementation of the Economic Community Treaty, there are, in consequence, already clear portents that although, with certain modifications resulting from experience, the administrative law features of the Coal and Steel Treaty are retained, the cases which the Court of Justice will be called upon to decide will tend to be of a different category. Mainly they will be references from the Courts of Member States for interpretation by the Court of Justice of provisions in the Treaty that are in issue before them. These will include references for a ruling as to whether a given provision or provisions of the Treaty is or are self-executing and as to whether they directly create and vest rights in private parties in the Member States, without legislation or even bare acknowledgment by the latter being required. Since 1961 cases of this kind have begun to come before the Court. They are thought likely to increase in number.

III

The expressions administrative jurisdiction and administrative law have in continental Western Europe a more precise connotation than in England, although the essential problem there as here is the control of the legality of the exercise of public or governmental authority. Administrative law in continental Europe consists in a body of principles largely distinct from the civil (that is, private) law and administered for the most part by special administrative courts equally distinct from the ordinary judicial tribunals. In England the control of the legality of the exercise of statutory powers, for example,—which brings into play certain concepts, such as that of ultra vires, similar to those of continental administrative law—is a function of the ordinary courts, and the law administered in such circumstances is not regarded as distinct or separable from the general body of English law. When the originators of the Community idea came to consider upon what principles of law they might provide for the control of the legality of the exercise of its Treaty powers by the executive authority of the Community they had ready to hand a clearly distinct source of inspiration upon which to draw. That was particularly true of the administrative law and jurisdiction of France, partly at least owing to the emergence there, at an appreciably earlier date than in the other five Community countries, of a separate tribunal, the Conseil d'Etat, to adjudicate in disputes between private parties and the State. The administrative case law developed by that tribunal may well have been an historical accident, for the reformed Conseil d'Etat of the Napoleonic period was not at the outset intended to do more than obviate the obstruction of the very centralised administrative programme put into operation following the revolution, that would have resulted if objectors to the programme had been allowed recourse to the ordinary judicial tribunals for this specific type of litigation. In the event, it was the very existence of the Conseil d'Etat as a separate judicial institution that facilitated the evolution, more rapidly after 1870 and even more so after 1900, of a body of administrative case law untrammelled by civil law concepts and affording very considerable protection of private interests against those of the State.

The influence of that judicial thinking was felt throughout Western Europe, particularly in Belgium, Italy and Holland. In Germany also, broadly similar principles of administrative law administered in special courts took shape spontaneously—and exercised during one period a considerable influence in Holland. In Luxembourg, a Conseil d'État on modern lines was finally established in the 1850's; an independent conception deriving much of its particular originality from the contrasting sources—successively, the public law of France, of the Netherlands, and, since 1830, of autonomous Belgium—upon all of which the Grand Duchy had been either obliged or led to draw, as a consequence of its political history. In Belgium, Italy and Holland, moreover, there were indeed in existence, at the time of the Community negotiations in 1950, bodies with the same name as the French Conseil d'Etat, though in the last two they had not the same span of judicial action. The Belgian Conseil d'Etat was established in 1946, with intentional similarity to the French and no doubt partly for the reason that the existence of a separate tribunal to adjudicate in this branch of the law would bring even greater definition and coherence into the body of administrative law already developed by the ordinary courts. But whether or not there were or had long been separate administrative courts in the negotiating countries, it was clear that there existed in each of them a body of distinct principles of administrative law sufficiently alike the one to the other to make it possible for a Community court to build up its own administrative case law, using them, in conjunction with the Treaty provisions, as a starting point, without encountering any major stumbling block in the form of divergencies between them. When it came to formulating in the Treaties (in Article 33 of the E.C.S.C. Treaty, Article 173 of the E.E.C. Treaty and Article 146 of the Euratom Treaty) the four grounds on the basis of which action might be brought against the executive power in the Community by Member States or private parties, this was done *expressis verbis* by the use of the classical concepts of the law evolved by the French Conseil d'Etat: "lack of powers", "violation of basic procedural rules", "misuse of powers", while the fourth (listed third in the Treaty) "infringement of the Treaty or of any rule of law relating to its implementation" was no more than the adaptation for the particular purposes of the Treaty of the "breach of the law" of French administrative law. A detailed commentary on these grounds will be found in the body of this work. Suffice it here to make the point that though French administrative law has provided the verbal inspiration—and indeed much more than the verbal inspiration—for these grounds, it is not incumbent upon the Community Court to have regard to French law more than to that of the other member countries for purposes of interpretation where these grounds are invoked in any given case before it.

Besides these particular grounds, other administrative law features appearing in the Treaties owe their direct inspiration perhaps primarily to French administrative law. There is the classic distinction between the exercise of "full jurisdiction" by the Court (see Article 172 of the E.E.C. Treaty) and the "jurisdiction to annul" the act of the executive power on the basis of the four grounds just referred to. The latter jurisdiction can make a dead letter of the administrative act complained of, and the declaration to that intent is effective throughout the Community in respect of all, governments and private parties alike. But it cannot go further than that. In the exercise of "full jurisdiction", however, the Court is empowered to review an administrative decision and amend it. The Court's ruling is binding, legally, only on the parties to the action—though its effect may in practice be all prevading.

It is the purported exercise of governmental authority or public power which, in continental European legal thinking, characterises an "administrative act" and the expression is there a term of art throughout. It is distinct from the lay meaning of any such expression as an "act of the administration". The distinction is important, for while a purported administrative act brings the executive power which makes it within the domain of administrative law in respect of it, the same executive power may if it chooses conduct its legal operations in the sphere of private law instead, as, for example, where it makes a contract in respect of the lease of property to itself.

In the European Community Treaties the term "administrative act" is not expressly used. But it is frequently employed in practice as denoting the means by which the executive power can give its binding instructions to Member States or private parties (recommendations or decisions in the E.C.S.C. Treaty; directives, regulations, or decisions in the E.E.C. and Euratom Treaties). That is to say, in its legal substance it connotes an act purported to be done in the exercise of the governmental authority conferred by the Treaty upon the executive power in the Community. It is only with "administrative acts" in this strict sense that the administrative law provisions of the Treaties are concerned. Thus it becomes apparent to the English reader that in continental Europe the distinction between public law on the one hand (in which administrative law bulks largely) and private law on the other, can not only be made but requires to be made. That distinction will be met with, in terms, in the European Community Treaties, in which it is expressly recognised that the executive power may act either in public law, or in private law. The most important result of this distinction is that, under the Treaties, where the Community executive power acts in private law, it may sue or be sued (for example, upon its contract) before the ordinary courts of Member States (unless a clause in the contract requires submission of any dispute arising therefrom to the Community Court). Where however the executive power purports to carry out an administrative act, adjudication on any dispute arising with regard to that must be by the Community Court. It will be realized that in regard to its purported administrative acts, the executive power is always in the relatively favourable position of defendant before the court. That is still true where the executive power has failed to act in implementation of a duty incumbent upon it under the Treaty. For in such a situation there must first be elicited from it, as in comparable circumstances in administrative law in the member countries individually, a decision not to act, against which decision an action may then and only then be brought at the court.

At this point it is convenient to note that the bringing of proceedings at the Community Court has no automatic suspensory effect upon the enforcement of the administrative act appealed against. This principle is also applied in the administrative law systems of the six original member countries. The reason for its existence there as in the Communities is obvious enough; it aims to avoid the control for legality impeding unduly the normal course of administration. The Community Court has jurisdiction, however, if it considers it proper in the circumstances so to do, to order a suspension of enforcement of the administrative act in dispute. It seems likely that this power will be sparingly and jealously exercised. Clearly, in weighing up the circumstances in order to decide whether a suspension should be ordered, the Court can have no alternative but to have regard to the facts in the light of which the administrative act has been determined upon. At this point it would therefore enter upon very delicate terrain. For the assessment of the facts appertains in the first place to the executive power for the purpose of carrying on the administration. As, in the national context, French theory neatly puts it, control of the desirability and expediency of the administrative act (*le contrôle de l'opportunité*) must be kept distinct from control for legality (*le contrôle de la légalité*) of the same act exercised by the administrative court. The extent to which that distinction can be strictly adhered to in practice will be a valuable leitmotif for the study of the developing administrative case law of the European Court, as it already is for the administrative law that has evolved in the continental European countries.

But though it has been convenient to introduce into the present discussion the question of the disengagement of law and fact, in the setting of administrative law, through the Community Court's power to grant a suspension of enforcement of an administrative act, this is not, of course, the only or the most important field in which this general problem is encountered in the Communities. More should now be said about it. It would be accurate to state that by 1950, at the time of the first Community negotiations, administrative law had evolved in the six countries a considerable way in the direction of judicial assessment of the same facts, for the purpose of the control of legality, as had already been assessed by the executive power for the purpose of determining the "*opportunité*" of the administrative act itself. That evolution had evoked in some the thought that the pendulum might be swinging too far in the direction of the judge-administrator in the long term movement away from the administrator-judge. Undoubtedly that thought was one element in the general debate concerning the question whether or not the Community Court should be entrusted with the task of assessing and appreciating the facts, that is to say, not only of recognising the existence of material facts, but of evaluating their legal import. There were other elements tending against the conferring of such a function on the Court, such as unsatisfactory experience of courts handling economic matters and the undesirability of reviewing a second time the facts that would already have been investigated under the most careful scrutiny, as the Treaty envisaged, by the executive power assisted by a consultative council. As against those arguments a second school of thought was against any restriction of the power of the Court, adducing in support of that view the artificial and arbitrary nature, as shown by the experience of the final courts of appeal in the negotiating countries, of the separation of law and fact. The upshot was the E.C.S.C. Treaty provision: "the court's enquiry into the case may not cover the evaluation of the situation, resulting from economic facts and circumstances, in the light of which such decisions or recommendations were taken". The E.E.C. and Euratom Treaties contain, however, no similar provision. There is little doubt that its omission is in keeping with the position regarding the reviewability of facts by an administrative tribunal in the internal law of the six countries, though this is only of incidental importance; its omission is certainly in keeping with the experience of the limitations upon the applicability of such a general provision, in the pioneer E.C.S.C. Treaty, that are automatically imposed by the inevitable exceptions to it implicit in the Treaty itself. Thus, where the Court exercises "full jurisdiction" in reviewing a fine imposed on a Member State or an enterprise by the executive power (the High Authority) it must perforce form its own appreciation of all the facts in determining how far a decision imposing the fine is to be modified. Again, as has been shown, one of the grounds on which its "jurisdiction to annul" may be exercised is the "misuse of powers" (*détournement de pouvoir*) by the executive. Where a claim is brought on this ground (or on the ground that the High Authority has patently misinterpreted the provisions of the Treaty or any rule of law relating to its implementation) the Treaty confers jurisdiction on the Court to evaluate the economic situation, as an exception to the general principle referred to above. But the additional difficulty confronting a judicial examination of a claim brought on this ground is that it involves the subjective motives which led the executive power to exercise authority for purposes other than those for which it was conferred, and these motives are hardly separable from the facts which actuated them.

It should be noted, however, that "*détournement de pouvoir*" may tend, in litigation before the European Court, because of the difficulties of proving a subjective analysis, to recede in importance as compared with "infringement of the Treaty or of any rule of law relating to its implementation", listed in the Treaties as an alternative ground for annulment—but frequently different rather in method than in essence, involving positive rather than subjective considerations in relation to the same facts. "*Détournement de pouvoir* affecting them" early became prominent in litigation under the E.C.S.C. Treaty because it was the only ground provided for in the Treaty upon which undertakings could bring a claim for annulment of a *general* decision of the High Authority. No decision of the Court annulled a High Authority decision on the ground of *détournement de pouvoir*—at any rate expressly on that ground. In the later Treaties *détournement de pouvoir* has not been singled out as the only ground upon which private parties may claim the annulment of administrative acts ("Regulations") comparable to the "general decisions" of the E.C.S.C. Treaty, but in practice it seems that these can really be assailed only by the Member States (R. Vol. VIII, pp. 977 *et seq.*). The tendency for *détournement de pouvoir* to be overtaken in importance, as the ground on which annulment of an administrative act is sought, by "infringement of the law", has latterly been apparent in the setting of French internal law where "*détournement de pouvoir* had attained a high degree of importance. This tendency is not out of step with administrative law in the other five countries of the Six.

Further exceptions to the principle of non-reviewability by the court of the situation resulting from economic facts and circumstances arise where the State specially petitions the court because of "fundamental and persistent disturbance" in its economy likely to be brought about by a given action or inaction of the executive power (Article 37 of the E.C.S.C. Treaty); or where an industrial concentration is the subject of litigation on the ground that it is contrary to the Treaty (Article 66). There are one or two other exceptions of lesser importance.

IV

It will have become apparent at this stage to the reader that administrative law in continental Europe is essentially judge made. The administrative courts do not proceed on the basis of any code and, given that jurisdiction is conferred upon them either generally or by particular statutes, the law they apply is principally of their own making. In its administrative law aspect the work of the Community Court is in much the same position except that it proceeds from the starting point of the Treaty, in which certain grounds on which an action will lie are, as has been shown, specifically indicated, and some administrative law principles (such as "full jurisdiction" or the non-suspensory effect of proceedings before it) are embodied—the grounds and principles alike being inspired by the national systems. These are, however, no more than a starting point, their interpretation and application, like the rest of the Treaty, being entrusted to the Community court in its task of ensuring the observance of law in respect of it. The same is true of the other aspects of the jurisdiction of the court besides the administrative. There is therefore no doubt that the case-law developed by the court will be—is indeed already becoming—together with the relevant Treaty, the most important statement of the law of whichever of the three Communities may be in point.

That being so, two questions will immediately suggest themselves to the English reader. First, what is the function, if any, of precedent, either in the formation, or in its application in Member States, of Community case-law? Secondly, on what sources may the Community court draw, other than on the Treaty itself, in its task of ensuring the observance of law in its interpretation and application? Some indications regarding the second question have already been incidentally made, but it will be preferable to defer further consideration of both of them to enable some illustration to be given first of the extent in practice of judicial law making by the Community court. For the purposes of this introduction one outstanding example will suffice.

The E.C.S.C. Treaty provides (Article 33) that a claim for annulment of decisions or recommendations of the High Authority (on the four grounds previously discussed) must be brought within one month from the date of notification or publication of the same. If that is not done, no other means are made available by which decisions or recommendations may be impugned. This limitation applies equally to Member States and to undertakings or associations of undertakings, the latter being given by the same Article the right of claiming on the same grounds against *individual* decisions or recommendations concerning them or against *general* decisions or recommendations which they deem to involve a "misuse of powers affecting them". It follows that a general decision, such as one requiring undertakings to conform to a stated practice subject to a fine in the event of non-compliance, might be legally unobjectionable and irresistible as far as an undertaking was concerned, if there was no possibility of invoking the ground of misuse of powers: This would normally be the case, because the legally well-advised High Authority would certainly refrain from intentionally taking action in respect of a given undertaking by a misuse of powers in a general decision, having ready to hand in any event the possibility of using an individual decision addressed to that particular undertaking in order to achieve the desired end. After the lapse of one month the general decision would be no longer impugnable. There was a certain body of European

Continental opinion to the effect that undertakings were in this respect left
with inadequate remedies by the Treaty. However that may be, suppose the
undertaking fails to comply with the general decision and is fined in consequence. The fine is an individual decision—in the parlance of administrative
law it is an administrative act just as was the general decision from which it
derives its authority. Now it is an accepted principle that a claim against a
fine lies to the "full jurisdiction" of the court, and in the E.C.S.C. Treaty
this is provided for in Article 36. The same article goes on to provide moreover that in support of such a claim the applicant may invoke the irregularity
of the (general) decision, non-compliance with which is the reason for the
fine, on the same four grounds of Article 33 (that is, the four grounds for
annulment) which by that Article are open to Member States or to undertakings in respect solely of an individual (and not a general) decision. Thus
there is opened up to the undertaking the possibility of invoking the grounds
for invalidity of a general decision which in the first place were available
to it only in respect of an individual decision, and to invoke them, moreover,
after the prescribed time limit of one month for bringing an action to annul.
The technical expression (though it is not used in any of the three Treaties)
for this use of the four grounds of Article 33 is "exception of illegality"
(*l'exception d'illégalité*). Assistance to private parties *vis à vis* the executive
power was to this extent provided by the E.C.S.C. Treaty itself in any event.

But the court has developed the matter further, widening the principle
of Article 36, originally limited to fines, to a general principle, and recognising a claim of exception of illegality against any general decision or recommendation whenever an individual act based on it is the subject of appeal.
When the two later Treaties were being negotiated the time was ripe for
inclusion therein (Article 184, E.E.C. Treaty; Article 156, Euratom Treaty,)
of a provision that any party may claim the exception of illegality against a
regulation of the Council or Commission, the wording therein used being
its "inapplicability". (A regulation is the equivalent of a general decision
under the E.C.S.C. Treaty.)

It will be appreciated that the claim for exception of illegality, being
comprised in an appeal in regard to which the court exercises "full jurisdiction", can from the technical point of view result only in a judgment *in
personam inter partes*. The judgment is, in form, a declaration that the general
act or regulation successfully appealed against is "inapplicable" (that is,
to the party claiming). The constant practice of the court in this matter
was doubtless largely responsible for the use of the expression "inapplicability" in the two later Treaties, it not having been present in the E.C.S.C.
Treaty in distinguishing this appeal. Though the act or regulation is thus
not annulled by the court's judgment the effect in practice may be much the
same as if it were. For since it would be likely to prompt other parties in
similar circumstances to claim an exception of illegality on the same grounds,
it may well follow that the Community Institution (Council or Commission
as the case may be) may conclude that it would be wiser to proceed to a new
administrative act free of legal taint.

V

It is now time to offer some observations on the meaning and function of
precedent in relation to Community law. Accustomed as is the English lawyer
to a legal system in which the principle of *stare decisis*, whereby judges of
lower courts ensure that a decision of a superior court in a similar case must
be followed if it is not distinguished (and the final court of appeal is "bound"
by its own decisions) he will need to find how to discover his bearings in a

system where the rule does not apply. Does its absence mean that no such concept as precedent exists at all? To seek an answer to that question in terms of Community law involves a consideration of the position regarding it in the internal legal systems of the member states, for the threefold reason that these provided some of the inspiration for what is embodied in the Treaties, that the general principles of their law(s) are a recognised source of Community law in interpretative amplification of the Treaties, and finally, that upon their attitude to it there may depend in part their attitude to, and the mechanics of, the internal recognition and enforcement within their jurisdiction of judgments of the Community Court.

The English lawyer who has had to deal with an issue of private law directly involving the law of a continental European state will have discovered something of the true meaning and the limitations of the notion that the degree of certainty conferred in English law by the operation of precedent is there provided instead by a code. For though there is undoubtedly an element of truth in the notion, the existence of a code does not absolve the continental lawyer from taking into account the decisions of the courts in their application of the code. Decisions, in particular of higher courts, will be of persuasive authority and will be so most of all where a trend is established by a court of final appeal in deciding in the same sense a number of cases turning on the same point. Such a trend is of well nigh conclusive authority. The French expression for it is a *"jurisprudence constante"*, which is readily usable or translateable in the other continental countries. It may be of interest to make passing reference to the fact that the supreme civil court of France (the Cour de Cassation, which adjudicates on a vastly larger number of cases in a year than the House of Lords) has for a considerable time made use (though not slavish use) of a card index for assembling readily a line of previous decisions it has made involving the point now at issue.

Thus, while the principle of *stare decisis* is not followed in continental Europe it would be inaccurate to suggest that all notion of judicial precedent is there inexistent. Perhaps, rather than by approaching the understanding of it through an attempt to distinguish the binding nature of English precedent from that of the persuasive force of judgments in continental law, a more practical way is to seize on the difference between the English individual case precedent method and the continental trend method—that is the "precedent" created by several decisions in the same sense. The importance of the trend method has been mentioned in its relation to codified civil law. It will be appreciated that its importance was and is all the greater in administrative law, where there was in fact no code, in any of the member states of the Communities. No authoritative statement, in the form of a treatise, for example, of French administrative law as applicable by the Conseil d'Etat exercising judicial function, would ever have been possible failing the stabilising force of *"jurisprudence constante"*. Nor would there have been available such a concise formulation of the grounds for annulment of an administrative act, as was embodied, to the satisfaction of all signatory states, in the E.C.S.C. Treaty, and later adopted in the other two Community Treaties. The Community Court, in applying them, thus starts with a provision that has a suggestion of codification about it, which was lacking in the administrative laws of the Member States from which it derives. But substantially the Community Court has no legal code to administer, for the Treaties in all else but their jurisdictional articles, are statements not of lawyers' law as is a code, but of economic principles to be brought either immediately or progressively into operation in establishing three communities with varying economic functions. That is a measure of both the difficulty and the importance of the role of the court, for the case law it develops takes its place alongside the Treaties as the law of the Communities. What is the effect upon that development of the absence of the principle of *stare decisis* in relation to the previous decisions of the court itself? Like the International Court at the Hague, this is a special court with particular functions and not a supreme appellate court at the head and in control of a hierarchy of tribunals, as in a national system. As already shown, it has no direct link with the tribunals of Member States, except in the reservation to its exclusive jurisdiction as against Courts of final appeal of preliminary points, of interpretation only, in issue before them. It has, unlike the International Court, little advisory jurisdiction as such. Like the International Court it stands very much by itself, and like it, too, it has already shown a distinct tendency to refer to and to follow its own decisions, though it is not bound to do so. As a result, there emerges a *"jurisprudence constante"* with respect to particular questions of law, which may on occasion, as has been shown in regard to the *"exception d'illégalité"*, be more than a gloss on the Treaty and even develop the law beyond the strict wording of the latter.

Given the habits of legal thought in the original six Member States such a development by a *"jurisprudence constante"* in the law of the Treaty becomes an element in Community law on which reliance can be placed. It could even be thought of as "binding" upon them, that is, of such persuasive authority that it can hardly be contravened—certainly until the Court breaks with the trend established, which is likely to be the rarest of phenomena. Such would be a natural mental reflex in continental Europe. The example given, however, relates to the manner in which the Court's jurisdiction can be invoked and exercised under the E.C.S.C. Treaty rather than to its substantive provisions, so that on further analysis "binding" might in this case seem to be too comprehensive an adjective and "permanently available as a legally enforceable procedure" a better expression. Indeed, the wider and important question arises, whether in respect at any rate of the substantive provisions in the Treaties, the interplay between case law and the written law, such as is normal in continental European countries, ceases to a considerable extent to fulfil its usual role and gives way to a system approaching in some measure the *stare decisis* principle, though not of course expressed as such in the Treaties themselves. Consider for example, the position under the E.E.C. Treaty where the jurisdiction of the Community Court in respect of the interpretation of the Treaty (Article 177) is interlocked with that of the tribunals of the Member States under a duty to apply the Treaty. On the reference to it by the latter of a preliminary point of interpretation, it is clear that the Community Court must disengage that point from the issues in the particular dispute that occasioned its reference, for it must avoid determining the dispute itself, to do which it has (under Article 177) no jurisdiction. The interpretation determined upon by the Community Court obviously is directly binding on the national tribunal from whence it was referred, but is not this individual decision on a point of interpretation one that will stand whenever the same point arises again? The Court itself is of that opinion.

The question extends further. Interpretation is one part only of the Court's function of "ensuring the rule of law in the interpretation and implementation of the Treaty". But all implementation must be related to interpretation, as is abundantly clear, for example, where a claim for annulment of a purported act of implementation is brought upon the ground of infringement of the Treaty. The need to proceed from interpretation to the determination of the legality of the act of implementation then stands revealed. Where the act is annulled as being based on what the court finds to be a mistaken interpretation of the Treaty, it would seem to be unlikely that the Community Institution responsible would use the same interpretation a second time. The practical effect at least would be a permanent statement of the law by virtue of a single judgment. Now, there is some reason for supposing that an individual judgment in exercise of the Court's exclusive jurisdiction to interpret may not only be binding on the national tribunal from which the point was referred in deciding the particular issue in which it was raised, but have in practice a wider and more permanent authority valid wherever the Treaty is applicable. For, whenever—and wherever—the point arises again, and is truly the same point not capable of bring distinguished, it would seem natural to expect a very considerable hesitancy on the part of the national tribunal and the parties before it to refer to the Community Court for an interpretation. But would the same tendency follow an individual judgment, involving a point of interpretation, given by the Community Court in the exercise of its jurisdiction to annul, where the same indistinguishable point is the determining factor in a dispute before a national tribunal. In such a situation the national tribunal is not responsible in any way, as it is under Article 177 of the E.E.C. Treaty, to the Community Court. Will a national tribunal on the continent tend to look for a *"jurisprudence constante"* before it accepts the persuasive authority of the Community Court's decision in the matter, or will it take into consideration primarily the relationship of the constitutional law of its own country to Treaty law, concluding, where the former specifically indicates the internal supremacy of the latter (as it does in Holland) that an individual judgment of the Community Court is in a sense so part and parcel of the Treaty that it should be followed, though not "binding" in the narrower legal sense? Developments in respect of this important question relevant most of all to the E.E.C. Treaty must await events.

CHAPTER

1

The Task of the Court

"The Court of Justice of the European Commities" is the correct title for what is commonly referred to as "the European Court". There is one Court (see Chapter 3); but there are three Communities, each es ablished by Treaty, in respect of each of which, severally, it is the task of the Court to adjudicate. Its adjudication is in fulfilment of the general role assigned to it in identical terms by each of the Treaties: "The Court shall ensure that the law is observed in the interpretation and implementation of this Treaty" (E.E.C. 164, E.A.E.C. 136, E.C.S.C. 31). The purpose of this Chapter is to set out the essential features of the three Communities, the European Economic Community, the European Atomic Energy Community and the European Coal and Steel Community, so that the task of the Court may be seen in its general context. The Communities are dealt with, in the above order, below:

I. THE EUROPEAN ECONOMIC COMMUNITY

A. ESTABLISHMENT

The European Economic Community is immediately established upon the entry into force of the Treaty.

E.E.C. 1

By the present Treaty, the High Contracting Parties establish among themselves a European Economic Community.

"... The present Treaty ...". E.E.C. 239 provides:

"The protocols which are to be annexed to this Treaty by common agreement between the Member States shall form an integral part thereof". By the Final Act of the Intergovernmental Conference on the Common Market and Euratom of 25th March 1957, the E.E.C. Treaty—with 13 annexed Protocols and the Convention relating to certain institutions common to the European Communities—were enacted, and included in that Final Act was the decision of the Conference to prepare at a later date the Protocol on the Statute of the Court of Justice of the European Economic Community and the Protocol on the Privileges and Immunities of the European Economic Community which were to be annexed to the E.E.C. Treaty.

Entry into force.

The date was 1st January, 1958, by virtue of the provisions of E.E.C. 247 that the Treaty should "... come into force on the first day of the month following the deposit of the instrument of ratification by the last signatory State to do so".

Duration. E.E.C. 240 provides:

"This Treaty is concluded for an unlimited period".

Territorial Application. E.E.C. 227 provides:

1. This Treaty shall apply to the Kingdom of Belgium, the French Republic, the Federal Republic of Germany, the Italian Republic, the Grand Duchy of Luxembourg and the Kingdom of the Netherlands.

2. With regard to Algeria and the French overseas departments, the general and special provisions of this Treaty relating to:

— the free movement of goods,
— agriculture, save for Article 40 (4),
— the liberalisation of services,
— the rules of competition,
— the protective measures provided for in Articles 108, 109 and 226,
— the institutions,

shall apply as soon as this Treaty comes into force.

The conditions under which the other provisions of this Treaty are to apply shall be determined by unanimous decision of the Council [*as to which see post, p.* 19], on a proposal of the Commission [*as to which see post p,* 21], at the latest two years after this Treaty comes into force.

The institutions of the Community shall, within the framework of the procedure laid down in this Treaty and, in particular, of Article 226, devote attention to facilitating the economic and social development of the regions concerned.

3. The overseas countries and territories listed in Annex IV to this Treaty shall be the subject of the special arrangements for association described in Part IV of this Treaty.

4. The provisions of this Treaty shall apply to the European territories for whose external relations a Member State is responsible.

Languages of the Treaty. E.E.C. 248 provides:

"The present Treaty, drawn up in a single original in the French, German, Italian and Netherlands languages, all four texts being equally authentic, shall be deposited in the archives of the Government of the Italian Republic which shall transmit a certified copy to each of the Governments of the other signatory States".

Revision of the Treaty. E.E.C. 236 provides:

"The Government of any Member State or the Commission may submit to the Council proposals for the revision of this Treaty.

If the Council, after consulting the Assembly [*as to which see post, p.* 18] and, where appropriate, the Commission, expresses an opinion in favour of the calling of a conference of representatives of the Governments of Member States, such conference shall be convened by the President of the Council for the purpose of determining by common agreement the amendments to be made to this Treaty.

Such amendments shall come into force after being ratified by all Member States in accordance with their respective constitutional requirements".

"**... The high contracting parties ...**" namely, the King of the Belgians, the President of the Federal Republic of Germany, the President of the French Republic, the President of the Italian Republic, the Grand Duchess of Luxembourg, the Queen of the Netherlands.

". . . establish among themselves a . . . Community". "Establish" is in the present tense, for the Community—in its legal essence—is established immediately upon entry into force of the Treaty (with the annexures, as to which see under "the present Treaty . . .", *ante*, p. 13). The nexus of legal relationships knitting together multilaterally the Institutions of the Community, the Member States of the Community and the natural or legal persons within the ambit of the Treaty, is in complete existence at the moment of ratification of the Treaty. Natural and legal persons are within the ambit of the Treaty by virtue of doing (or contemplating) some act within the scope of the provisions of the Treaty if (a) they are nationals of one of the Member States; or (b) they are resident within one of the Member States; or (c) (conceivably) they are present within one of the Member States; or (d) though neither (a), (b) or (c) applies, the act produces (or would produce) some consequences within one of the Member States. In some instances the Treaty Articles (*e.g.* E.C.S.C. 33, *post*, p. 89), providing rights of action at the Court, limit to a specified category the natural or legal persons who may avail themselves of such rights. This matter is dealt with under each relevant Treaty Article in Chapter 2, *post*, p. 57. The sum total of the rights and obligations of the natural and legal persons in the ambit of the Treaty, of the Institutions of the Community and of the Member States, *inter se*, forms the nexus of legal relationships referred to above. That nexus is the personal law of the Community. Some of that law is executory in the sense that further measures having the force of law are necessary for its application in detail to be ascertained. The phrase "Community law", as commonly used, embraces that personal law—with which the Community was born, and which conditions its existence—and also the law which the Community creates by its own legislative operations (as to which see under ". . . by establishing a Common Market . . ." *infra*) and other elements, among which the more important are the case law of the European Court and law made by individual Member States for Community purposes.

The following two questions, for example, relate to the personal law of the Community, rather than to the wider "Community law": Article 85 of the E.E.C. Treaty, setting out some of the Treaty's "Rules of Competition" prohibits certain agreements between undertakings, and decisions by associations of undertakings, and declares they "shall be automatically null and void". This is a translation of *"sont nuls de plein droit"*, which is in the present tense and leaves no room for doubt that such agreements and decisions *are* a nullity. Though these words could not put the Treaty into full effect without the implementing Regulation to determine which particular agreements and decisions were in fact caught by the provisions of the Article, they nevertheless became effective in law as from the entry into force of the Treaty (see judgment in case 13/61 R. Vol. VII at p. 103). This question, which remained acute in the Community until the passing of the implementing Regulation No. 17 in March 1962, never, however, came before the Court. The second question illustrates the novelty in law of the personal law of the Community, involving, as it has how been decided by the Court to do, the direct and immediate conferment by the Treaty itself of subjective rights on private parties within its ambit. The Court so held in answering in the affirmative in the same terms the question first raised in case 26/62 and repeated in the consolidated cases 28/62, 29/62, and 30/62 (the "Tariff Commission cases"):

"Whether Article 12 of the E.E.C. Treaty has internal effect [*i.e., in the Member States—Author*] in the sense alleged by the plaintiffs, in other words whether private persons, relying on this article, can claim individual rights which must be upheld by the Courts" [*of the Member State to whose jurisdiction they are subject—Author*].

B. Means for Fulfilling the Task

The means for fulfilling the task (Fr. "mission") of the Community are established progressively.

E.E.C. 2

It shall be the task of the Community, by establishing a Common Market and progressively approximating the economic policies of Member States, to promote throughout the Community a harmonious development of economic activities, a continuous and balanced expansion, an increased stability, an accelerated raising of the standard of living and closer relations between its member States.

"... by establishing a Common Market ...". The Common Market is not brought directly into existence by the Treaty, but is to be established by the Community which the Treaty creates (see E.E.C. 8, Appendix, *post*). "Establishing a Common Market and "progressively approximating the economic policies of Member States" are the means by which the Community is to carry out its task (Fr. "*mission*"), which is "to promote throughout the Community a harmonious development of economic activities, a continuous and balanced expansion, an increased stability, an accelerated raising of the standard of living and closer relations between its Member States". For the shaping of these means and for the carrying out of the activities of the Community set out in E.E.C. 3 (*infra*) executive and legislative powers are conferred upon certain Institutions of the Community (see E.E.C. 4, *post*, p. 17 and, thereunder, Provisions Common to Several Institutions, especially E.E.C. 189). The exercise of such legislative or rule-making powers brings into existence a body of Community law, over which, together with the personal law of the Community (referred to in the comment "establish among themselves a ... Community" under E.E.C. 1, *ante*, p. 15), the Community Court exercises supervision. The expression "Community law" is commonly used to embrace both these aspects of the law with which the Court is concerned (and other elements besides, see under "establish among themselves a ... Community" *ante*, p. 15).

C. The Activities of the Community

E.E.C. 3

For the purposes set out in the preceding Article, the activities of the Community shall include, under the conditions and in accordance with the time-table envisaged in this Treaty:

(*a*) the elimination, as between Member States, of customs duties and of quantitative restrictions in regard to the import and export of goods, as well as of all other measures having equivalent effect;

(*b*) the establishment of a common customs tariff and of a common commercial policy towards third countries;

(c) the abolition, as between Member States, of obstacles to the free movement of persons, services and capital;

(d) the inauguration of a common policy in the field of agriculture;

(e) the inauguration of a common policy in the field of transport;

(f) the establishment of a system ensuring that competition in the Common Market is not distorted;

(g) the adoption of procedures permitting the co-ordination of the economic policies of Member States and the correction of instability in their balances of payments;

(h) the approximation of their respective national laws to the extent required for the Common Market to function in an orderly manner;

(i) the creation of a European Social Fund in order to improve the possibilities of employment for workers and to contribute to the raising of their standard of living;

(j) the establishment of a European Investment Bank to facilitate the economic expansion of the Community by opening up fresh resources; and

(k) the association of overseas countries and territories with a view to increasing trade and to pursuing jointly the task of economic and social development.

The eleven activities (Fr. "*l'action*") of the Community listed in this Article are not exhaustive. Some of them primarily involve consequential action by Member States in their own respective legislative fields. Others depend principally upon executive action by the Community Institution concerned (E.E.C. 4, *infra*). Others again, especially (f), of which Articles 85–89 of the Treaty are in part implementation, involve legislative action by Community Institutions (E.E.C. 4, *infra*), while, in turn, Regulations resulting from such action may, in their application to particular cases, be subject to review by the Community Court (as in the case, for example, of Regulations No. 17, which see under (c) The Commission, E.E.C. 155, —"exercise the powers conferred on it by the Council to ensure effect being given to rules laid down by the latter". (*post*, p. 22).

D. The Four Institutions of the Community

They are (a) the Assembly (see *infra*); (b) the Council (see *post*, p. 19); (c) the Commission (see *post*, p. 21) and (d) the Court of Justice.

E.E.C. 4

1. The achievement of the tasks entrusted to the Community shall be ensured by the following institutions:

—an ASSEMBLY,
—a COUNCIL,
—a COMMISSION,
—a COURT OF JUSTICE.

Each institution shall act within the limits of the powers conferred upon it by this Treaty.

2. The Council and the Commission shall be assisted by an Economic and Social Committee acting in a consultative capacity.

"The achievement of the tasks entrusted to the Community . . .". The expression "tasks" (Fr. *"tâches"*) would seem to embrace the task (Fr. *"mission"*) defined by the words following "to promote" in E.E.C. 2 (*ante*, p. 16) together with the non-exhaustive list of "the activities" (Fr. *"l'action"*) of E.E.C. 3 (*ante*, p. 16).

"Each Institution . . . within the limits of the powers conferred upon it . . .". The Community's Institutions form the subject of Part V of the Treaty (Articles 137–209). The four Institutions are the Assembly, the Council, the Commission, the Court of Justice. The first three of these are commented on, in that order, immediately below under (a), (b), and (c). The Court of Justice in its organizational aspects is dealt with in Chapter 3 of this work). (For the purposes of the Court's Rules of Procedure the European Investment Bank is treated as an Institution of the Community, see Chapter 2, *post*, p. 152; see also p. 78.)

(a) The Assembly

The Assembly, has advisory and supervisory powers (see E.E.C. 137, *infra*). Its formal measures (Fr. *"actes"*) must be published (see comment under E.E.C. 137, *infra*) but are not open to challenge on any ground before the Court of Justice. Nor are any other of its measures.

E.E.C. 137

The Assembly, which shall consist of representatives of the peoples of the States united within the Community, shall exercise the advisory and supervisory powers which are conferred upon it by this Treaty.

The Assembly holds an annual session in October, and may meet in extraordinary session at the request of a majority of its members or of the Council or Commission (E.E.C. 139). Members of the Commission may attend all meetings and, at their request, must be heard on behalf of the Commission; the Commission must reply orally or in writing to questions put to it by the Assembly or its members; the Council must be heard by the Assembly in accordance with its rules of procedure (E.E.C. 140). Except where otherwise provided for in the Treaty the Assembly acts by absolute majority of the votes cast (E.E.C. 141) and so adopts its rules of procedure which, *inter alia*, define what is a quorum and make provisions regarding the publication of its "formal measures" (Fr. *"actes"*) (E.E.C. 141 and 142). These *"actes"* are not however susceptible of challenge on any ground before the Court of Justice, nor are any of the Assembly's measures which do not come into the category of "formal". If the Assembly passes a vote of censure, by a two-thirds majority of the votes cast, and representing a majority of the members of the Assembly, "the members of the Commission shall collectively resign their office" (E.E.C. 144). Certain provisions of the Treaty require the Council to consult the Assembly before taking a decision (see under (b) The Council, comment on E.E.C. 145, "have power to take decisions" (*post*, p. 20)). The Council may by a unanimous decision amend the number of the members of the Commission (by virtue of E.E.C. 157, which see under (c) the Commission, *post*, p. 21.

E.E.C. 138

1. The Assembly shall consist of delegates who shall be nominated by the respective Parliaments from among their members in accordance with the procedure laid down by each Member State.

2. The number of these delegates shall be as follows:

Belgium	14
France	36
Germany	36
Italy	36
Luxembourg	6
Netherlands	14

3. The Assembly shall draw up proposals for elections by direct universal suffrage in accordance with a uniform procedure in all Member States.

The Council shall unanimously decide on the provisions which it shall recommend to Member States for adoption in accordance with their respective constitutional requirements.

By the "Convention relating to certain Institutions common to the European Communities", annexed to the Treaty, provision was made (by Article 1 of the Convention) for a single Assembly to exercise the powers and competence respectively conferred by the Treaties on the Assembly of E.E.C. and the Assembly of E.A.E.C., and (by Article 2) for it to exercise also the powers and competence conferred upon the "Common Assembly" established by E.C.S.C. 21. (The same Convention also made provision for a single Court of Justice for the three Communities (see Chapter 3, *post*, p. 180) and (by Article 5) for a single Economic and Social Committee to exercise "the duties respectively conferred upon the Economic and Social Committee by the Treaties establishing" E.E.C. and E.A.E.C.).

(b) *The Council*

The Council in order "to ensure the achievement of the objectives laid down in" the Treaty has a general executive duty to ensure "that the economic policies of the Member States are co-ordinated", and (to that end) is invested with a power of decision (as to which see under E.E.C. 145, *post*, p. 20). Legally, its role is identical with that of the E.A.E.C. Council (see *post*, p. 40).

As from January 1st, 1966, a single body is to exercise the functions of the Councils of E.E.C., E.A.E.C. and E.C.S.C. From the same date the functions of the Commissions of E.E.C. and E.A.E.C. and of the High Authority of E.C.S.C. are also to be exercised by a single body. The legal powers of each of the three Councils and the legal powers of each of the two Commissions and of the High Authority will however remain as at present with regard to their respective Communities. The merger of the six existing bodies into two was provided for in a Treaty signed at Brussels on the 8th April, 1965, by Ministers of the Six Member States. The unified body to exercise the functions of the E.E.C. and E.A.E.C. Commissions and of the

E.C.S.C. High Authority will consist of fourteen members for the first three years (France, W. Germany and Italy will have three each; Belgium and Holland two each; Luxembourg one).

E.E.C. 145

To ensure the achievement of the objectives laid down in this Treaty, and in accordance with the provisions thereof, the Council shall:

—ensure that the economic policies of the Member States are co-ordinated;

—have power to take decisions.

"... **have power to take decisions** ...". This is a translation of *"dispose d'un pouvoir de décision"*, which, it is suggested, would have been better rendered into English as "invested with a power of decision" (as has been done in the introductory comment to (b) the Council, *supra*). For the word "decision" in this Article must not be read in any limitative sense that results from the technical meaning of "decision" in E.E.C. 189 (which see, under "Provisions common to several Institutions", *post*, p. 26) but primarily as contrasting the executive functions of the Council with the advisory and supervisory powers of the Assembly. The Council's power of decision is exercised through regulations, directives and decisions (which are binding) and it may also formulate recommendations or opinions (which are not) (see E.E.C. 189 under "Provisions common to several Institutions", *post*, p. 26 and compare comment "have power to take decisions" under (c) the Commission, E.E.C. 155 *post*, p. 22). Potentially, one of the most important provisions for the taking of a decision (in the technical sense of E.E.C. 189) is that of E.E.C. 235:

"where action by the Community appears necessary to achieve one of the objectives of the Community, within the framework of the Common Market, and where this Treaty has not provided for the necessary powers of action, the Council shall adopt the appropriate provisions by a unanimous decision, after consulting the Assembly".

Decisions, together with regulations and directives (though not recommendations and opinions) are acts which are within the jurisdiction of the Court to annul on specified grounds (see Chapter 2, "Legality of Acts", *post*, p. 83). Not all decisions of the Council need be unanimous (see E.E.C. 148, *infra*).

E.E.C. 148

1. Except where otherwise provided for in this Treaty, the Council's resolutions shall be reached by a majority of its members.

2. Where the Council's resolutions are required to be reached by qualified majority, the votes of its members shall be weighted as follows:

Belgium	2
France	4
Germany	4
Italy	4
Luxembourg	1
Netherlands	2

The following majorities shall be required for the adoption of resolutions:

—twelve votes in favour where the Treaty requires them to be taken on a proposal of the Commission,

—twelve votes in favour, cast by at least four members, in all other cases.

3. Abstentions by members either present or represented shall not prevent the adoption by the Council of decisions which require to be unanimous.

The Council, when it acts on a proposal of the Commission, may only adopt amendments to that proposal by unanimous decision and the Commission is free to amend its original proposal at any time before the Council reaches a decision, especially if the Assembly has been consulted on the proposal in question (E.E.C. 149). The Council makes its own rules of procedure, which may provide for the establishment of a committee of representatives of Member States, whose powers and duties are determined by the Council (E.E.C. 151). The Council may request the Commission to undertake studies which the Council considers desirable for the achievement of the common objectives, and to submit proposals (E.E.C. 152). The Council lays down the statute of the Committee provided for in the Treaty, after receiving an opinion from the Commission thereon (E.E.C. 153). The Council by qualified majority vote determines the salaries, allowances and pensions of the President and members of the Commission, and of the President, Judges, Advocates General and Registrar of the Court of Justice, and by the same majority determines any allowances to be granted in lieu of remuneration (E.E.C. 154).

(c) The Commission

The Commission, "in order to ensure that the Common Market works efficiently and develops satisfactorily" has the particularized executive duty "to ensure that the provisions of the Treaty and the measures taken by the Institutions by virtue of the Treaty are carried out". The Treaty provides to that end that it shall "formulate recommendations or give opinions", be invested with a power of decision, and "exercise the powers conferred on it by the Council to ensure effect being given to rules laid down by the latter" (in respect of all the above matters see E.E.C. 155, *infra*). Legally, the rôle of the Commission is identical with that of the E.A.E.C. Commission (for which see *post*, p. 42; and compare also with the High Authority of E.C.S.C. in the comment under E.C.S.C. 8, *post*, p. 51). As from January 1st, 1966, a single body to be known as the Commission of the European Communities is to exercise the functions of the E.E.C. Commission, the E.A.E.C. Commission and the E.C.S.C. High Authority (see paragraph beginning "As from January 1st, 1966", *ante*, p. 19).

E.E.C. 155

In order to ensure that the Common Market works efficiently and develops satisfactorily, the Commission shall:

—ensure that the provisions of this Treaty and the measures taken by the institutions by virtue of this Treaty are carried out;

—formulate recommendations or give opinions on matters within the scope of this Treaty, if it expressly so provides or if the Commission considers this necessary;

—have power itself to take decisions and in the circumstances provided for in this Treaty participate in the shaping of measures taken by the Council and by the Assembly;

—exercise the powers conferred on it by the Council to ensure effect being given to rules laid down by the latter.

"—**have power . . . to take decisions**" as in the case of E.E.C. 145 (see under (b) the Council, *ante*, p. 19) these words are a translation of "*dispose d'un pouvoir de décision*" which, it is suggested, would have been better rendered into English as "dispose of a power of decision" (as has been done in the introductory comment to (c) the Commission, *supra*). For the word "decision", in this Article, must not be read in any narrower sense that results from the technical meaning of "decision" in E.E.C. 189 (which see, under Provisions common to several Institutions", *post*, p. 26) but as embracing "regulations", "directives" and "decisions" in the technical sense of E.E.C. 189. "Recommendations" and "opinions" in the technical sense of E.E.C. 189 are acts the Commission is empowered to take by virtue of the immediately preceding sub-paragraph of E.E.C. 155. (Cp. the judgment at *post*, pp. 84–86.)

"—**exercise the powers conferred on it by the Council to ensure effect being given to rules laid down by the latter.**" An example of the operation of this process is the following: In implementation of the provisions of E.E.C. 85 and 86 (directed against restrictive business practices) the Council issued Regulation No. 17 (amended by Regulation No. 59 of 3rd July 1962) of which Article 24 (*post*, p. 24) authorized the Commission "to lay down implementing provisions" relating to that Regulation. In exercise of these specific powers conferred by the Council the Commission issued its own Regulations 25 and 153 (which act was also, of course, a particular exercise of the general power conferred directly on the Commission by E.E.C. 189 (which see, under Provisions common to several Institutions, *post*, p. 26) to issue regulations in the discharge of (its) duties and in accordance with the provisions of this Treaty). In so doing the Commission in fact exercised executive powers, specifically conferred, of a rule-making character. Executive powers that are more free of legislative characteristics are the powers of investigation of the Commission conferred by Regulation No. 17 Articles 14(1) and (3) (*post*, p. 24).

But the Commission exercises also powers of a judicial character specifically "conferred on it by the Council to ensure effect being given to rules laid down by the latter" in the same Regulation No. 17, that is, the powers conferred by virtue of Article 9 "Competence" of the same Regulation (*post*, p. 23). The Commission's decisions, in exercising its "sole competence", by virtue of Article 9, "to declare Article 85, paragraph 1, inapplicable pursuant to Article 85, paragraph 3, of the Treaty, though judicial in essence, are decisions of an executive Institution of the Community, and are "decisions", of the Commission, in the technical sense of E.E.C. 189 (which see, under Provisions common to several Institutions, *post*, p. 26). As decisions of an executive Institution, they are, as Article 9 (*post*, p. 23) provides, "subject to review . . . by the Court of Justice . . ." (in the prescribed conditions of E.E.C. 173—see Chapter 2, *post*, p. 83). This is the confirmation, in the Regulation, of the legal position that results directly from the Treaty and is indicated in the first part of a clause in the Preamble (*infra*) to Regulation No. 17: "Considering that all decisions taken by the Commission under the present Regulation will be subject to review by the Court of Justice . . .", (as to the concurrent jurisdiction of the commission and national courts, see *post*, p. 139).

A further type of decision which the Commission may take by virtue "of the powers conferred on it by the Council to ensure effect being given to rules laid down by the latter", is less wholly judicial. It is exemplified twice in Regulation No. 17, in Articles 3, *infra* and 16 (Appendix, *post*). These, again, like those considered in the preceding paragraph of this comment, are decisions in the technical sense of E.E.C. 189 (which see under Provisions common to several Institutions, *post*, p. 26) and are thus reviewable by the Court in the prescribed conditions of E.E.C. 173 (see Chapter 2, *post*, p. 83) as indicated in the first part of the clause in the preamble (*infra*) to Regulation 17, referred to in the preceding paragraph of this comment. But the decisions which the Commission is empowered by the Council to make by virtue of Regulation No. 17, Article 16 (Appendix, *post*) are brought (by Article 17 of the Regulation, *post*, p. 24) within the jurisdiction of the Court in a way that the decisions of the Commission authorized by Article 3 (*infra*) of Regulation 17 are not. This, also, is indicated in the clause in the Preamble (*infra*) to Regulation 17 which makes clear, by the use of the words "it is moreover desirable to confer on the Court of Justice . . . full jurisdiction . . .", that the Court would have no jurisdiction of the nature conferred by Article 17 of the Regulation (*post*, p. 24) by the sole operation of the treaty, and unless it were specifically conferred. (See Chapter 2, *post*, pp. 78 *et seq.*) The relevant portions of Regulation 17 (referred to *supra*) are as follows (unofficial translation):

Regulation 17 (Extracts)
Penultimate Clause in Preamble
Considering that all decisions taken by the Commission under the present Regulation will be subject to review by the Court of Justice, under the conditions defined in the Treaty, and that it is moreover desirable to confer on the Court of Justice, under Article 172, full jurisdiction as to the merits in respect of decisions by which the Commission imposes fines or penalties . . ."

Article 3.—Ending of infringements
If, acting on request or of its own volition, the Commission finds that Article 85 or Article 86 of the Treaty is being infringed it can, by means of a decision oblige the undertakings or associations of undertakings concerned to put an end to the said infringement.

A request to this effect may be submitted by:
(a) Member States
(b) Natural and legal persons, who show a justified interest. (*cf.* in Chap. 2 under "any natural . . . appeal" (*post*, p. 84) and Chap. 4 under "Parties" (*post*, p. 212).

Without prejudice to the other provisions of the present Regulation, the Commission, before taking a decision of the type mentioned in paragraph 1, may address recommendations to the undertakings or associations of undertakings concerned with a view to ending the infringement.

Article 9.—Competence
Subject to review of its decision by the Court of Justice, the Commission shall have sole competence to declare Article 85, paragraph 1, inapplicable pursant to Article 85, paragraph 3 of the Treaty.

The Commission shall have competence to apply Article 85, paragraph 1, and Article 86 of the Treaty, even if the time-limits for notification laid down in Article 5, paragraph 1, and Article 7, paragraph 2, have not expired.

As long as the Commission has not initiated any procedure pursuant to Articles 2, 3 or 6, the authorities of the Member States shall remain competent to apply Article 85, paragraph 1, and Article 86 in accordance with Article 88 of the Treaty, even if the time-limits for notification laid down in Article 5, paragraph 1, and Article 7 have not expired.

Article 11 (5)

Where the undertaking or association of undertakings does not supply the information required within the time-limit set by the Commission, or supplies incomplete information, the Commission's request for information shall be made by means of a decision. This decision shall specify the information requested, fix an appropriate time-limit within which it is to be supplied and specify the sanctions applicable under Article 15, paragraph 1, sub-paragraph (b), and under Article 16 paragraph 1, sub-paragraph (c), and shall indicate that there is a right to institute proceedings against the decision before the Court of Justice.

Article 14 (1)

(1) In carrying out the duties assigned to it by Article 89 and by provisions laid down pursuant to Article 87 of the Treaty, the Commission may conduct all necessary investigations into the affairs of undertakings and associations of undertakings.

For this purpose the Commission's duly appointed servants shall be invested with the following powers:

(*a*) to examine the books and other business documents;
(*b*) to make copies of, or extracts from the same;
(*c*) to ask for verbal explanations on the spot;
(*d*) to have access to all premises, land and vehicles of undertakings.

(2) . . .

(3) Undertakings and associations of undertakings must submit to the investigations ordered by a decision of the Commission. The decision shall state the subject and purpose of the enquiry, fix the date when it is to begin and call attention to the sanctions provided for under Article 15, paragraph 1, sub-paragraph (c), and Article 16, paragraph 1, sub-paragraph (d), and shall indicate that there is a right to institute proceedings against the decision before the Court of Justice.

Article 17.—Review by the Court of Justice

The Court of Justice shall have full jurisdiction as to the merits within the meaning of Article 172 of the Treaty to adjudicate on proceedings instituted against a decision of the Commission fixing a fine or a penalty; it may cancel, reduce or increase the fine or the penalty imposed.

Article 24.—Implementing provisions

The Commission shall have authority to lay down implementing provisions concerning the form, content and other details of applications submitted pursuant to Articles 2 and 3 and of the notifications provided for in Articles 4 and 5, and to lay down those concerning the hearings provided for in Article 19, paragraphs 1 and 2.

E.E.C. 156

The Commission shall publish annually, not later than one month before the opening of the session of the Assembly, a general report on the activities of the Community.

E.E.C. 157

[*As to the powers of the Court in respect of this Article, see Chapter* 2, post, pp. 168 *et seq. E.E.C.* 157 *is identical with E.A.E.C.* 126, post p. 43.]

E.E.C. 158

The members of the Commission shall be appointed by mutual agreement between the Governments of Member States.

Their term of office shall be for a period of four years. It shall be renewable.

E.E.C. 159

Apart from death and retirements in rotation, termination of appointment of a member of the Commission shall occur by voluntary resignation or compulsory retirement.

A vacancy thus caused shall be filled for the remainder of his term of office. The Council may unanimously decide that such a vacancy need not be filled.

Unless he is compulsorily retired in accordance with the provisions of Article 160, a member of the Commission shall remain in office until his successor's appointment.

E.E.C. 160

[*As to the powers of the Court in respect of this Article, see Chapter* 2, post, p. 169. *E.E.C.* 160 *is identical with E.A.E.C.* 129, post, p. 44.]

E.E.C. 161

The President and the two Vice-Presidents of the Commission shall be appointed from among its members for a term of two years in accordance with the same procedure as that laid down for the appointment of members of the Commission. Their term of office shall be renewable.

Save where the whole Commission is replaced, the Commission shall be consulted before such appointments are made.

In the event of resignation, compulsory retirement, or death, the President and the Vice-Presidents shall be replaced for the remainder of their terms of office in accordance with the provisions of the first paragraph of this Article.

E.E.C. 162

The Council and the Commission shall consult together and shall decide on their methods of collaboration by mutual agreement.

The Commission shall adopt rules of procedure to ensure that both it and its administrative services operate in accordance with the terms of this Treaty. It shall ensure that its rules of procedure are published.

E.E.C. 163

The Commission shall reach its conclusions by a majority of the number of members provided for in Article 157.

A meeting of the Commission shall only be valid if the number of members laid down in its rules of procedure are present.

E. Provisions Common to Several Institutions

E.E.C. 189

The Council and the Commission shall, in the discharge of their duties and in accordance with the provisions of this Treaty, issue regulations and directives, take decisions and formulate recommendations or opinions.

Regulations shall have general application. They shall be binding in every respect and directly applicable in each Member State.

Directives shall be binding, in respect of the result to be achieved, upon every Member State, but the form and manner of enforcing them shall be a matter for the national authorities.

Decisions shall be binding in every respect upon those to whom they are directed.

Recommendations and opinions shall have no binding force.

E.E.C. 190

The regulations, directives and decisions of the Council and of the Commission shall be fully reasoned and shall refer to any proposals or opinions which this Treaty requires to be obtained.

E.E.C. 191

The regulations shall be published in the Official Journal of the Community. They shall come into force on the date provided for in them or, failing this, on the twentieth day following their publication.

Directives and decisions shall be notified to those to whom they are addressed and shall take effect upon such notification.

E.E.C. 192

Decisions of the Council or of the Commission which include a pecuniary obligation on persons other than States shall have the enforceability of a Court judgment (*titre exécutoire*).

Enforcement shall be governed by the rules of civil procedure in force in the State in the territory of which it takes place. The order for its enforcement (*formule exécutoire*) shall be stamped on the decision, without more verification than that the document is authentic, by the national authority which the Government of each Member State shall designate for this purpose and which shall be notified to the Commission and to the Court of Justice.

When these formalities have been completed at his request, the party concerned may proceed to enforcement by applying directly to the authority which is competent according to domestic law.

Enforcement may only be suspended by a decision of the Court of Justice. Provided always that the proper method of enforcement shall be a matter for the domestic courts.

As to the suspension of enforcement of an administrative act (referred to in paragraph 4 of this Article) see Chapter 2, *post*, p. 158. As to the stay of execution of a judgment of the Court itself (a judgment is also an act of an Institution of the Community) see Chapter 2, *post*, p. 177.

F. Expenses of the Institutions

The expenses of the Institutions are to be "set out in separate sections of the budget, without prejudice to special arrangements for certain common Institutions" (E.E.C. 202, paragraph 4). "The administrative expenses of the single Assembly, the single Court of Justice, and the single Economic and Social Committee shall be divided equally between the Communities concerned" (Convention relating to certain Institutions common to the European Communities, Article 6).

G. The Setting up of the Institutions

This is the subject of E.E.C. 241–246 inclusive, which provisions are now executed.

H. The Economic and Social Committee

This is the subject of the provisions of E.E.C. 193 to 198 inclusive.

I. The Obligations of Member States

E.E.C. 5

Member States shall take all measures, whether general or particular, appropriate to ensure the carrying out of the obligations arising out of this Treaty or resulting from the acts of the institutions of the Community. They shall assist the latter in the achievement of its tasks.

They shall abstain from any measures which could jeopardise the attainment of the objectives of this Treaty.

Obligations upon Member States. These are of two kinds: Those "arising out of this Treaty", that is to say, either where the Treaty provisions impose immediate obligations or are executory (*e.g.* E.E.C. 8, Appendix, *post*) and those "resulting from the acts of the Institutions of the Community", that is either the acts of the Council or Commission that have binding force (see E.E.C. 189 under Provisions Common to several Institutions, *ante*, p. 26), or the judical acts of the Court of Justice (see in Chapter 4, *post*, "Judgments", pp. 254 *et seq.* The Court of Justice has jurisdiction in respect of a claim, that a Member State is failing to carry out its obligations, brought by another Member State or by any of the other parties forming part of the legal nexus which is the Community (see E.E.C. 1, *ante*, p. 13), that is, the Institutions and any natural or legal person, in the conditions prescribed by the Treaty (see Chapter 2, *post*, p. 62).

J. Collaboration of Member States and the Institutions

E.E.C. 6

1. Member States shall, in close collaboration with the institutions of the Community, co-ordinate their respective economic policies to the extent necessary to attain the objectives of this Treaty.

2. The institutions of the Community shall take care not to prejudice the internal and external financial stability of the Member States.

K. The Personality and Legal Acts of the Community

E.E.C. 210

The Community shall have legal personality.

By virtue of its legal personality the Community may treat with non-Member States and other international persons (and see E.E.C. 228, *post*, p. 33).

E.E.C. 211

The Community shall in each of the Member States enjoy the most extensive legal capacity accorded to legal persons under their domestic law; it may, in particular, acquire or dispose of movable and immovable property and may sue and be sued in its own name. For this purpose the Community shall be represented by the Commission.

"... **The most extensive legal capacity** ..." A feature of some continental legal systems, unknown in English law, is that there may exist differing degrees of personality as between persons that are creatures of law. The expression *"la petite personnalité"* is thus, for example, common in France. The capacity of a legal person, as distinct from an individual, is related to the degree of personality which that person enjoys. E.E.C. 211 confers the most extensive legal capacity, vis à vis the domestic laws of the Member States, upon the Community, as represented by the Commission.

L. The Contractual and Tortious Liability of the Community

E.E.C. 215, Para. 1

The contractual liability of the Community shall be governed by the law applying to the contract in question.

The law governing the contractual liability of the Community is determined by the application of the principles of private international law, and consequently may be the law of a Member State (see comment to E.E.C. 183, *infra*, and comment, p. 155.

M. The Relation of the Community to the Internal Law of Member States

E.E.C. 183

Subject to the powers conferred on the Court of Justice by this Treaty, cases to which the Community is a party shall not for that reason alone be excluded from the jurisdiction of national courts.

Where a case to which the Community is a party is not excluded from the jurisdiction of national courts, the law governing the contractual liability of the Community may fall to be determined by the application of the principles of private international law of such forum (see E.E.C. 215, *ante*, p. 28 and "The 'proper law' . . . contract", *post*, p. 155).

N. The Privileges and Immunities of the Community

E.E.C. 218

The Community shall enjoy the privileges and immunities essential to its work in the territories of the Member States, as shall be provided for in a separate Protocol.

The privileges and immunities enjoyed by the Community and set out in the Protocol required by E.E.C. 218, are the consequence of the conferment upon the Community (by E.E.C. 210, *ante*, p. 28) of legal personality, and (with a very small number of additions) are the equivalent of the privileges and immunities customarily granted by a Sovereign State to the diplomatic missions of other States upon its territory. The privileges and immunities of the Community are, by virtue of the Treaty alone, enjoyed only in respect of Member States of the Community. By virtue of the Protocol (Article 16) the customary diplomatic immunities are granted by the Member State in whose territory the Community has its seat to the missions of non-member countries accredited to the Community. (As to the jurisdiction of the Community Court see *post*, p. 175).

The relevant Articles of the Protocol are set out below:

Protocol (Extracts)

Article 1

The premises and buildings of the Community shall be inviolable. They shall be exempt from search, requisition, confiscation or expropriation. The property and assets of the Community shall not be the subject of any administrative or legal measure of constraint without the authorisation of the Court of Justice.

Article 2

The archives of the Community shall be inviolable.

Article 3

The Community, its assets, income and other property shall be exempt from all direct taxes.

The Governments of Member States shall, wherever possible, take the appropriate measures to remit or refund the amount of indirect taxes or sales taxes included in the price of movable or immovable property where the Community makes, for its official use, major purchases in the price of which taxes of these types are included. Provided always that these provisions shall not be so applied as to distort conditions of competition within the Community.

No exemption shall be granted in respect of taxes or other charges which amount to charges for public utility services.

Article 4

The Community shall be exempt from all customs duties and prohibitions and restrictions on imports and exports in respect of articles intended for its official use; articles so imported shall not be disposed of whether in return for valuable consideration or not, in the territory of the country into which they have been imported, except under conditions approved by the government of such country.

The Community shall also be exempt from any customs duties and any prohibitions and restrictions in imports and exports in respect of its publications.

Article 5

As regards their official communications and the transfer of all their documents the institutions of the Community shall enjoy in the territory of each Member State the treatment granted by that State to diplomatic missions.

Official correspondence and other official communications of the institutions of the Community shall not be subject to censorship.

Article 6

Passes in a form to be laid down by the Council and which shall be recognised as valid for travel purposes by the authorities of the Member States may be issued to members and servants of the institutions of the Community by the presidents of these institutions. Such passes shall be issued to officials and servants under conditions laid down by the terms of service provided for in Article 212 of this Treaty.

The Commission may conclude agreements for these passes to be recognised in the territory of third countries as valid travel documents.

Articles 7, 8 and 9 . . .

Article 10

Representatives of Member States taking part in the work of the institutions of the Community, as well as their advisers and technical experts shall, during the exercise of their duties and during their travel to and from the place of meeting, be accorded the customary privileges, immunities and facilities.

This Article shall also apply to members of the consultative organs of the Community.

Article 11

In the territory of each Member State and whatsoever their nationality, the officials and other servants of the Community referred to in Article 212 of this Treaty:

(a) shall, subject to the provisions of Articles 179 and 215 of this Treaty, be immune from suit and legal process in respect of acts done by them in the course of the performance of their official duties, including their spoken or written words; they shall continue to benefit from such immunity after their duties have ceased;

(*b*) shall, together with their spouses and the members of their families dependent on them, not be subject to immigration restrictions or to formalities for the registration of foreign persons;

(*c*) shall, in respect of currency or exchange rules, be accorded the same facilities as are accorded by custom to the officials of international organisations;

(*d*) shall have the right to import, free of duty, from the country of their last residence or from the country of which they are nationals their furniture and effects at the time of first taking up their post in the country concerned and the right to re-export, free of duty, their furniture and effects, on the termination of their duties in that country, subject in either case to the conditions deemed necessary by the government of the country in which this right is exercised;

(*e*) shall have the right to import free of duty their motor car for their personal use, purchased either in the country of their last residence or in the country of which they are nationals on the terms ruling in the latter's home market, and to re-export it free of duty, subject in either case to the conditions deemed necessary by the government of the country concerned.

Article 12

Subject to the conditions and in accordance with the procedure laid down by the Council acting on proposals submitted by the Commission within one year of this Treaty coming into force, the officials and servants of the Community shall be liable, for the benefit of the latter, to a tax on the salaries, wages and emoluments paid to them by it.

They shall be exempt from national taxes on salaries, wages and emoluments paid by the Community.

Article 13

In respect of income tax, of capital tax, of death duties and the application of conventions on the avoidance of double taxation concluded between Member States of the Community, the officials and servants of the Community who, solely by reason of the exercise of their duties in the service of the Community, establish their residence in the territory of a Member State other than the country where they have their residence for tax purposes at the time of their entry into the service of the Community, shall be considered both in the country of their actual residence and in the country of residence for tax purposes as having maintained their residence in the latter country provided that it is a member of the Community. This provision shall also apply to a spouse, to the extent that the latter is not gainfully employed and to children dependent on and in the care of the persons referred to in this Article.

Movable property belonging to persons referred to in the preceding paragraph and situated in the territory of the country of actual residence shall be exempted from death duties in that country; it shall, for the assessment of such duty, be considered as being in the country of residence for tax purposes, subject to the rights of third countries and to the possible future application of the provisions of international conventions on double taxation.

Any residence acquired solely by reason of the exercise of duties in the service of other international organisations shall not be taken into consideration in applying the provisions of this Article.

Article 14

The Council shall, by means of a unanimous decision, on a proposal which the Commission shall submit within one year of this Treaty's coming into force, lay down rules governing security benefits for officials and servants of the Community.

Article 15

The Council, acting on a proposal of the Commission and after the other institutions concerned have been consulted, shall determine the classes of officials and servants of the Community to whom the provisions of Articles 11, 12, second paragraph, and 13 shall apply in whole or in part.

The names, positions and addresses of officials and servants included in such categories shall be communicated periodically to the governments of Member States.

Article 16

The Member State in whose territory the Community has its seat shall grant the customary diplomatic immunities to the missions of third countries accredited to the Community.

Articles 17, 18 and 19 . . .

Article 20

Articles 11 to 14 inclusive and Article 17 shall, subject to the provisions of Article 3 of the Protocol on the Statute of the Court of Justice concerning immunity from suit and legal process of judges and advocates-general, apply to the judges, the advocates-general, the Registrar and the assistant rapporteurs of the Court of Justice.

Article 21 . . .

O. Saving of Existing Systems and Incidents of Ownership

E.E.C. 222

This Treaty shall in no way prejudice existing systems and incidents of ownership (*propriété*).

P. The General Relationship of Member States to the Community: Internal and International Security

E.E.C. 223

1. The provisions of this Treaty shall not adversely affect the following rules:

(*a*) No Member State shall be obliged to supply information the disclosure of which it considers contrary to the essential interests of its security;

(*b*) Any Member State may take whatever measures it considers necessary for the protection of the essential interests of its security, and which are connected with the production of or trade in arms, munitions and war material; such measures shall, however, not adversely affect conditions of competition in the Common Market in the case of products which are not intended for specifically military purposes.

2. During the first year after this Treaty comes into force, the Council shall, by a unanimous decision, determine the lists of products to which the provisions of paragraph 1 (*b*) shall apply.

3. The Council may, by a unanimous decision, on a proposal of the Commission, amend the said list.

E.E.C. 224

Member States shall consult one another with a view to taking in common the necessary steps to prevent the operation of the Common Market from being affected by measures which a Member State may be called upon to take in case of serious internal disturbances affecting law and order (*ordre public*), in case of war or serious international tension constituting a threat of war, or in order to carry out undertakings into which it has entered for the purpose of maintaining peace and international security.

E.E.C. 225

[*For text see post*, p. 69.]

E.E.C. 226

1. If, during the transitional period, serious difficulties, which might persist, arise in one sector of the economy or if there are difficulties which may result in a region suffering grave economic hardship, a Member State may request authority to take protective measures in order to rectify the position and adapt the sector concerned to the economy of the Common Market.

2. At the request of the State concerned, the Commission shall, by emergency procedure and without delay, determine the protective measures which it deems necessary, indicating specifically the circumstances in which, and the manner in which these are to be given effect to.

3. The measures authorised under paragraph 2 may include derogations from the rules of this Treaty, to such an extent and for such periods as are strictly necessary in order to achieve the objectives referred to in paragraph 1 of this Article. Priority shall be given in the choice of such measures to those which will least disturb the operation of the Common Market.

Q. Agreements Between the Community and Non-Member
States or International Organizations

E.E.C. 228

1. Where this Treaty provides for the conclusion of agreements between the Community and one or more States or an international organisation, such agreement shall be negotiated by the Commission. Subject to the powers conferred upon the

Commission in this respect, such agreements shall be concluded by the Council after the Assembly has been consulted where required by this Treaty.

The Council, the Commission or a Member State may, as a preliminary, obtain the opinion of the Court of Justice as to the extent to which the agreements contemplated are compatible with the provisions of this Treaty. An agreement which has been the subject of an adverse opinion by the Court of Justice shall only come into force under the conditions laid down in Article 236.

2. Agreements concluded under the conditions laid down above shall be binding on the institutions of the Community and on Member States.

The Community has legal personality (see E.E.C. 210, *ante*, p. 28). As to the preliminary opinion of the Court of Justice see Chapter 2, *post*, p. 163).

E.E.C. 237

Any European State may apply to become a member of the Community. It shall address its application to the Council which, after obtaining the opinion of the Commission, shall give a unanimous decision thereon.

The conditions of admission and the adjustments to this Treaty necessitated by it shall be the subject of an agreement between the Member States and the applicant State. Such agreement shall be submitted for ratification by all the contracting States in accordance with their respective constitutional requirements.

E.E.C. 238

The Community may conclude with a third country, a union of States or an international organisation agreements creating an association embodying reciprocal rights and obligations, joint actions and appropriate forms of procedure.

Such agreements shall be concluded by the Council by a unanimous decision and after consulting the Assembly.

Where such agreements involve amendments to this Treaty, such amendments shall first be adopted in accordance with the procedure laid down in Article 236.

R. Saving Provisions for E.A.E.C. and E.C.S.C.

E.E.C. 232

1. The provisions of this Treaty shall not affect the provisions of the Treaty setting up the European Coal and Steel Community. This applies in particular to the rights and obligations of Member States, to the powers of the institutions of the said Community and to the rules laid down by the said Treaty for the operation of the common market for coal and steel.

2. The provisions of this Treaty shall not derogate from the provisions of the Treaty establishing the European Atomic Energy Community.

II. THE EUROPEAN ATOMIC ENERGY COMMUNITY

A. Establishment

The European Atomic Energy Community is immediately established upon the entry into force of the Treaty (with annexed Protocols and Conventions).

E.A.E.C. 1.—First paragraph

By the present Treaty the High Contracting Parties establish among themselves a European Atomic Energy Community (Euratom).

"... The present Treaty ..."—. Annexures. E.A.E.C. 207 provides:
"The Protocols which are to be annexed to this Treaty by common agreement between the Member States shall form an integral part thereof"

Entry into force. E.A.E.C. 224 provides:
"This Treaty shall be ratified by the High Contracting Parties in accordance with their respective constitutional requirements. The instruments of ratification shall be deposited with the Government of the Italian Republic.
This Treaty shall come into force on the first day of the month following the deposit of the instrument of ratification by the last signatory State to do so. If, however, such deposit is made less than fifteen days before the beginning of the following month, this Treaty shall not come into force until the first day of the second month following the date of such deposit".

Duration. E.A.E.C. 208 provides:
"This Treaty is concluded for an unlimited period".

Territorial application. E.A.E.C. 198 provides:
"Except where otherwise provided for, the provisions of this Treaty shall apply to the European territories of Member States and to non-European territories under their jurisdiction.
They shall also apply to the European territories for whose external relations a Member State is responsible".

Languages of the Treaty. E.A.E.C. 225 provides:
"The present Treaty, drawn up in a single original in the French, German, Italian and Netherlands languages, all four texts being equally authentic, shall be deposited in the archives of the Government of the Italian Republic which shall transmit a certified copy to each of the Governments of the other signatory States".
(See also, *post*, pp. 204–206).

"The high contracting parties ...". The comment under this heading in respect of E.E.C. (*ante*, p. 14) applies *mutatis mutandis* to E.A.E.C.

"Establish among themselves ... a Community ..." The comment under this heading in respect of E.E.C. (*ante*, p. 15) applies *mutatis mutandis* to E.A.E.C. The natural and legal persons who are affected by the Treaty are however more strictly defined in E.A.E.C. than they are in E.E.C.; E.A.E.C. 196 provides:

"For the purposes of this Treaty and except where otherwise provided therein:

(*a*) "Person" shall mean any natural person who carries out the whole or part of his activities in the territories of Member States within the field specified in the relevant chapter of this Treaty;

(*b*) "Undertaking" shall mean any undertaking or institution which carries out the whole or part of its activities under the same conditions, whatever its public or private legal constitution and status"

B.   MEANS FOR FULFILLING THE TASK

The means for fulfilling the task of the Community are developed progressively.

E.A.E.C. 1.—Second paragraph

It shall be the task of the Community to contribute to the raising of the standard of living in Member States and to the development of exchanges with other countries by creating the conditions necessary for the speedy establishment and growth of nuclear industries.

" ... by creating the conditions necessary for the speedy establishment and growth of nuclear industries ..." For the creation of these conditions and the shaping of the means involved therein (set out in E.A.E.C. 2, *infra*) executive and legislative powers are conferred upon certain Institutions of the Community (see "D.   The Four Institutions . . . ", *post*, p. 38 and "E.   Provisions common to several Institutions", especially E.A.E.C. 161, *post*, p. 46). As to the results of the exercise of such powers see, *ante*, p. 16, . . . by establishing . . . Market . . ."

C.   THE ACTIVITIES OF THE COMMUNITY

E.A.E.C. 2

In order to fulfil its task, the Community shall, in accordance with the provisions laid down in the present Treaty:

(*a*) develop research and ensure the dissemination of technical information,

(*b*) establish uniform safety standards to protect the health of workers and of the general public and ensure their application,

(*c*) facilitate investment and ensure, particularly by encouraging individual efforts on the part of undertakings, the creation of the basic facilities necessary for the development of nuclear energy in the Community,

(*d*) ensure that all users in the Community receive a regular and equitable supply of ores and nuclear fuels, (*e*) make certain, by appropriate control measures, that nuclear materials are not diverted to purposes other than those for which they are intended,

(*f*) exercise the right of ownership conferred upon it with respect to special fissionable materials,

(*g*) ensure wide commercial outlets and access to the best technical methods by the creation of a common market in specialised materials and equipment, by the free circulation of capital for investment in the field of nuclear energy, and by freedom of employment for specialists within the Community,

(*h*) establish with other countries and international organisations any relationships likely to promote progress in the peaceful uses of nuclear energy.

The eight activities ((a) to (h)) set out in E.A.E.C. 2 are the subject of the detailed provisions of Title II of the Treaty "Provisions designed to encourage progress in the Field of Nuclear Energy", under the following Chapter headings: I. Development of Research (Articles 4–11); II. Dissemination of Information (Articles 12–29); III. Health Protection (Articles 30–39); IV. Investments (Articles 40–44); V. Joint Undertakings (Articles 45–51); Supplies (Articles 52–76); VII. Security Supervision (Articles 77–85); VIII. System and Incidents of Ownership (Articles 86–91); IX. The Nuclear Common Market (Articles 92–100); X. External Relations (Articles 101–106).

These eight activities and tasks are to be carried out in general by the supervisory, advisory and executive Institutions of the Community (see E.A.E.C. 3, *post*, p. 38) subject to the legal control over them exercised by the Court of Justice, itself an Institution of the Community. In this aspect of its nexus of legal relationships E.A.E.C. is identical with E.E.C. For the second activity listed in the preceding paragraph of this comment, however, "Dissemination of Information", provision is made in E.A.E.C. 17–25 (for text of the Articles 17–21, see Chapter 2, *post*, pp. 171–174) for the dissemination of information not otherwise at the disposal of the Community by, *inter alia*, "the granting of Liscences by Arbitration". As part of that provision there is established an Arbitration Committee. The Court of Justice, by virtue of the Treaty, exercises jurisdiction over the formal legality of its decisions much as if the Arbitration Committee were an Institution of the Community (see E.A.E.C. 3, *post*, p. 38) and not merely an accessory organ. E.E.C. has no exactly comparable feature to the Arbitration Committee of E.A.E.C. though it also has an accessory organ, the European Investment Bank (as to which see *ante*, p. 18). The Court's jurisdiction over decisions of the Board of Governors of the Bank is, however, wider than that over the formal legality of the decisions of the Arbitration Committee of E.A.E.C. (compare the difference in Chapter 2, *post*, pp. 152 *et seq.* and pp. 171–173).

The carrying out of the above eight activities by the Institutions brings the Commission especially into particular relationships with Member States, in respect of which the jurisdiction of the Court of Justice may be invoked (see Chapter 2, *post*, pp. 70–71). Thus, the Commission makes recommendations to Member States with regard to the level of radio-activity in the air, water and soil. Non-compliance by Member States with these recommendations may result in an application to the Court. A record is maintained of ores, source material and special fissile material used or produced, and inspectors recruited by the Commission obtain and verify that record, reporting any infringement to the Commission. If a Member State does not comply with a directive from the Commission to put an end to the infringement the matter may be referred immediately to the Court of Justice (see Chapter 2, *post*, p. 71). Where persons or undertakings infringe the obligations imposed by the Chapter of the Treaty dealing with Security Supervision the Commission may impose sanctions. These may be appealed against to the Court (see Chapter 2, *post*, pp. 81–82). In respect of the external relations of Member States, or persons or undertakings, of the Community, the Court of Justice may rule as to the compatibility of agreements or conventions with the provisions of the Treaty (see Chapter 2, *post*, pp. 163 *et seq.*). The Commission may send inspectors into the territories of Member States (E.A.E.C. 81) to "exercise supervision over ores, source material and special fissile material and to ensure that "these are not diverted from their intended uses as declared by the users", and that "the provisions relating to supplies and any special obligations with regard to supervision assumed by the Community in an agreement concluded with a non-member country or an international organization are observed" (E.A.E.C. 77). In respect of supervisory measures taken or intended by such inspectors where there is opposition to such a measure, or danger in delay in its being carried out, two possible situations involve not the Court of Justice as such, but the President of the Court (see Chapter 2, *post*, p. 176: "President of the Court to decide as to warrant for enforcement of supervisory measure or to give subsequent approval of Commission's written order to proceed with a supervisory measure", *post*, p. 176).

For the legal authority and method by which the Commission carries out the above activities see under (c) the Commission, *post*, p. 42.

D. The Four Institutions of the Community

The four Institutions of the Community carry out its tasks. They are: (a) the Assembly (see *post* p. 39); (b) the Council, (see *post*, p. 40); (c) the Commission (see *post*, p. 42) and (d) the Court of Justice.

E.A.E.C. 3

1. The tasks entrusted to the Community shall be carried out by the following institutions:

> —an ASSEMBLY,
> —a COUNCIL,
> —a COMMISSION,
> —a COURT OF JUSTICE.

Each institution shall act within the limits of the powers conferred upon it by this Treaty.

2. The Council and the Commission shall be assisted by an Economic and Social Committee acting in a consultative capacity.

"Each Institution shall act within the limits of the powers conferred upon it . . .". The "Institutional Provisions" are the subject of title III (Articles 107–170) of the Treaty. The Assembly, the Council, and the Commission are treated below under (a), (b) and (c) respectively.

The fourth Institution, the Court of Justice, is in its organizational aspects the concern of Chapter 3 *post*, pp. 180 *et seq.*

(a) The Assembly

The Assembly has advisory and supervisory powers. The following Articles make provisions for its organization and functioning.

E.A.E.C. 107

The Assembly, which shall consist of representatives of the peoples of the States united within the Community, shall exercise the advisory and supervisory powers which are conferred upon it by this Treaty.

E.A.E.C. 108

1. The Assembly shall be composed of delegates who shall be nominated by the respective Parliaments from among their members in accordance with the procedure laid down by each Member State.

2. The number of these delegates shall be as follows:

Belgium	14
Germany	36
France	36
Italy	36
Luxembourg	6
Netherlands	14

3. The Assembly shall draw up proposals for elections by direct universal suffrage in accordance with a uniform procedure in all Member States.

The Council shall lay down by unanimous vote the provisions which it shall recommend to Member States for adoption in accordance with their respective constitutional rules.

By Articles 1 and 2 of the "Convention relating to certain Institutions common to the European Communities" annexed to the Treaty, a single Assembly "composed and appointed as provided for in . . . E.A.E.C. 108" exercises "the powers and competence . . . conferred upon the Assembly" by the Treaty and also the powers and competence of the Assembly provided for in E.E.C. 138. (As to this Convention see comment under the European Economic Community, E.E.C. 4, "Each Institution within the limits of the powers conferred upon it", *ante*, p. 17).

E.A.E.C. 109

The Assembly shall hold an annual session. It shall meet automatically on the third Tuesday in October.

The Assembly may meet in extraordinary session at the request of a majority of its members or at the request of the Council or of the Commission.

E.A.E.C. 110

The Assembly shall appoint its President and its officers from among its members.

Members of the Commission may attend all meetings and shall, at their request, be heard on behalf of the Commission.

The Commission shall reply orally or in writing to questions put to it by the Assembly or its members.

The Council shall be heard by the Assembly under the conditions which the Council shall lay down in its rules of procedure.

E.A.E.C. 111

Except where otherwise provided for in this Treaty, the Assembly shall act by means of an absolute majority of the votes cast.

The quorum shall be laid down in the rules of procedure.

E.A.E.C. 112

The Assembly shall adopt its rules of procedure by a vote of the majority of its members.

The formal measures taken by the Assembly shall be published in accordance with the conditions laid down in its rules of procedure.

E.A.E.C. 113

The Assembly shall discuss in open sessions the annual general report submitted to it by the Commission.

E.A.E.C. 114

If a motion of censure on the activities of the Commission is tabled in the Assembly, no vote may be taken thereon until at least three days after it was tabled and this vote shall be by open ballot.

If the motion of censure is carried by a two-thirds majority of the votes cast, representing a majority of the members of the Assembly, the members of the Commission shall collectively resign their office. They shall continue to carry out current business until their replacement in accordance with the provisions of Article 127.

(b) The Council

The Council has "powers of decision", and the general executive duty to co-ordinate the activity of the Member States and that of the Community. Legally its role is identical with that of the E.E.C. Council (*ante*, p. 19).

As from January 1st, 1966, a single body is to exercise the functions of the E.E.C. Council, the E.A.E.C. Council and the E.C.S.C. Council (see paragraph beginning "As from January 1st, 1966, *ante*, p. 19). The following Articles make provision for its organization and functioning.

E.A.E.C. 115

The Council shall exercise its prerogatives and its powers of decision in accordance with the conditions provided for in this Treaty.

It shall take all measures within its competence to co-ordinate the activity of Member States and that of the Community.

The word "decision" is not here used in the technical and limitative sense of E.A.E.C. 161 (which see on *post*, p. 46. See also comment on E.E.C. 145 under "The European Economic Community", *ante*, p. 20).

E.A.E.C. 116

The Council shall be composed of representatives of the Member States. Each Government shall delegate to it one of its members.

The office of President shall be exercised for a term of six months by each member of the Council in rotation according to the alphabetical order of the Member States.

E.A.E.C. 117

Meetings of the Council shall be called by the President acting on his own initiative or at the request of a member or of the Commission.

E.A.E.C. 118

1. Except where otherwise provided for in this Treaty, resolutions of the Council shall be passed by a majority of its members.

2. Where the Council's resolutions require a qualified majority, the votes of its members shall be weighted as follows:

Belgium	2
Germany	4
France	4
Italy	4
Luxembourg	1
Netherlands	2

The following majorities shall be required for the adoption of resolutions:

—twelve votes in favour where the Treaty requires them to be passed on a proposal of the Commission;

—twelve votes in favour cast by at least four members in all other cases.

3. Abstentions by members either present or represented shall not prevent the adoption by the Council of resolutions which require to be unanimous.

E.A.E.C. 119

When the Council acts, pursuant to this Treaty, on a proposal of the Commission, it may adopt amendment to that proposal only if it is unanimous.

As long as the Council has not reached a decision the Commission may amend its original proposal, particularly in cases where the Assembly has been consulted on such a proposal.

E.A.E.C. 120

Where a vote is taken, any member of the Council may act as proxy for not more than one other member.

E.A.E.C. 121

The Council shall lay down its rules of procedure.

These rules of procedure may provide for the establishment of a committee composed of representatives of Member States. The Council shall determine the duties and powers of that committee.

E.A.E.C. 122

The Council may request the Commission to undertake any studies which the Council considers desirable for the achievement of the common objectives, and to submit to it any appropriate proposals.

E.A.E.C. 123

The Council shall by qualified majority vote fix the salaries, allowances and pensions of the President and members of the Commission, and of the President, Judges, Advocates-General and Registrar of the Court of Justice. The Council shall also fix, by the same majority, any allowances granted in lieu of remuneration.

(c) *The Commission*

The Commission, "in order to ensure the development of nuclear energy within the Community", has the particularized executive duty "to watch over the enforcement of the Treaty and of the provisions adopted by the Institutions of the Community in pursuance thereof". It formulates recommendations, expresses opinions and takes decisions (within the definition of those expressions in E.A.E.C. 161 (which see under "Provisions common to several institutions", *post*, p. 46). It also exercises "the powers conferred on it by the Council to ensure enforcement of the rules laid down by the latter". Legally its role is identical with that of the E.E.C. Commission (*ante*, p. 21) but is to be contrasted with that of the High Authority of E.C.S.C. (for which see under E.C.S.C. 8 *post*, p. 51). As from January 1st, 1966, a single body to be known as the Commission of the European Communities is to exercise the functions of the E.E.C. Commission, the E.A.E.C. Commission and the E.C.S.C. High Authority (see paragraph beginning "As from January 1st, 1966", *ante*, p. 19). (As to the particular relationships with Member States into which the Commission is brought in the fulfilling of its particularized executive duty see the third paragraph of the comment on E.A.E.C. 2, *ante*, p. 37).

The following Articles make provision for the organization and functioning of the Commission:

E.A.E.C. 124

In order to ensure the development of nuclear energy within the Community, the Commission shall:

—watch over the enforcement of this Treaty and of the provisions adopted by the institutions of the Community in pursuance thereof:

—formulate recommendations or express opinions within the spheres defined by this Treaty, where the latter expressly so provides or where the Commission considers it necessary;

—under the conditions provided for in this Treaty possess its own power of decision and participate in the shaping of measures taken by the Council and the Assembly;

—exercise the powers conferred on it by the Council to ensure enforcement of the rules laid down by the latter.

E.A.E.C. 125

The Commission shall publish annually, not later than one month before the opening session of the Assembly, a general report on the activities of the Community.

E.A.E.C. 126

1. The Commission shall consist of five members, each of a different nationality, who shall be chosen on the grounds of their general competence having regard to the special subjects of this Treaty, and whose independence can be fully guaranteed.

The number of members of the Commission may be amended by the Council, acting unanimously.

Only nationals of Member States may be members of the Commission.

2. The members of the Commission shall perform their duties in entire independence, in the general interest of the Community.

In the performance of their duties, they shall neither seek nor take instructions from any Government or other body. They shall refrain from any action incompatible with the nature of their duties. Each Member State undertakes to respect this principle and not to seek to influence the members of the Commission in the performance of their duties.

The members of the Commission may not, during their term of office, engage in any other paid or unpaid occupation. When entering upon their duties, they shall give a solemn undertaking that, both during and after their term of office, they will respect the obligations resulting therefrom and in particular their duty to exercise honesty and discretion as regards the acceptance, after their term of office, of particular appointments or benefits. In the event of any breach of these obligations, the Court of Justice, on the application of the Council or of the Commission, may, according to the circumstances, rule that the member concerned either be compulsorily retired in accordance with the provisions of Article 129 or forfeit his right to a pension or other benefits in lieu thereof.

As to the powers of the Court in respect of this Article see Chapter 2, *post*, pp. 168 *et seq.*

E.A.E.C. 127

The members of the Commission shall be appointed by mutual agreement between the Governments of Member States.

Their term of office shall be for a period of four years. It shall be renewable.

E.A.E.C. 128

Apart from retirement in rotation, or death, the duties of a member of the Commission shall be terminated in individual cases by voluntary resignation or by compulsory retirement.

A vacancy thus caused shall be filled for the remainder of the term of office. The Council, may unanimously decide that such a vacancy need not be filled.

Except in the case of compulsory retirement under the provisions of Article 129, a member of the Commission shall remain in office until provision has been made for their replacement.

E.A.E.C. 129

If any member of the Commission no longer fulfils the conditions required for the performance of his duties or if he has been guilty of serious misconduct, the Court of Justice, on the application of the Council or of the Commission, may compulsorily retire him.

In such a case the Council may unanimously decide to suspend the member provisionally from his duties and may make provision for his replacement pending the ruling of the Court of Justice.

The Court of Justice may on the application of the Council or of the Commission provisionally suspend the member from his duties.

As to the powers of the Court in respect of this Article see Chapter 2, *post*, pp. 168 *et seq.*

E.A.E.C. 130

The President and the Vice-President of the Commission shall be appointed from among its members for a term of two years in accordance with the same procedure as that laid down for the appointment of members of the Commission. Their term of office shall be renewable.

Except in the case of a general replacement of the Commission, such appointments shall be made after the Commission has been consulted.

In the event of retirement or death, the President and Vice-President shall be replaced for the remainder of their terms of office in accordance with the procedure laid down in the first paragraph of this Article.

E.A.E.C. 131

The Council and the Commission shall consult together and shall settle by mutual agreement their methods of collaboration.

The Commission shall adopt rules of procedure to ensure that both it and its administrative services operate in accordance with the provisions of this Treaty. It shall ensure that its rules of procedure are published.

E.A.E.C. 132

The resolutions of the Commission shall be adopted by a majority of the number of members provided for in Article 126.

A meeting of the Commission shall only be valid if the number of members laid down in its rules of procedure are present.

E.A.E.C. 133

The Council may agree unanimously that a qualified representative be accredited to the Commission by the Government of a Member State to undertake permanent liaison duties.

E.A.E.C. 134

1. There shall be etablished, attached to the Commission, a Scientific and Technical Committee with consultative status.

The Committee must be consulted where required by this Treaty. It may be consulted in all cases where the Commission deems it appropriate.

2. The Committee shall be composed of 20 members, appointed by the Council after consultation with the Commission.

The members of the Committee shall be appointed in a personal capacity for a term of five years. This term shall be renewable. They shall not be bound by any mandatory instructions.

The Scientific and Technical Committee shall appoint annually its Chairman and its officers from among its members.

E.A.E.C. 135

The Commission may undertake any consultations and establish any study groups necessary to the achievement of its tasks.

E. Provisions Common to Several Institutions

E.A.E.C. 161

[*Apart from differences of wording, of no legal consequence, in the opening phrase as far as the word "Treaty", this Article is identical with E.E.C.* 189, ante, *p.* 26.]

E.A.E.C. 162

[*Identical with E.E.C.* 190, ante, *p.* 26.]

E.A.E.C. 163

[*Identical with E.E.C.* 191, ante, *p.* 26.]

E.A.E.C. 164

[*This is substantially identical with paragraphs* 2–4 *of E.E.C.* 192 ante, p. 26. *As to the suspension of enforcement of an administrative act* (*E.A.E.C.* 164, *para.* 3) *see*, post, *p.* 158. *As to the stay of execution of a judgment of the Court itself* (*a judgment is also an act of an Institution of the Community*) *see* post, *p.* 177.]

F. The Personality and Legal Acts of the Community

E.A.E.C. 184

[*Identical with E.E.C.* 210, ante, *p.* 28.]

E.A.E.C. 185

[*Identical with E.E.C.* 211, ante, *p.* 28.]

The comments on E.E.C. 210 and 211 apply *mutatis mutandis* to E.A.E.C. 184 and 185.

G. The Contractual and Tortious Liability of the Community

E.A.E.C. 188

[*Identical with E.E.C.* 215, *the comment on which* (ante, *p.* 28) *applies* mutatis mutandis *to E.A.E.C.* 188.]

H. The Relation of the Community to the Internal Law of Member States

E.A.E.C. 155

[*Identical with E.E.C.* 183. *The comment thereon* (ante, *p.* 29) *substituting E.A.E.C.* 188 *for E.E.C.* 215, *applies* mutatis mutandis *to E.A.E.C.* 155.]

E.A.E.C. 191

[*Identical with E.E.C.* 218. *The comment thereon* (ante, *p.* 29), *substituting identical articles of E.A.E.C. for those of E.E.C. mentioned therein, applies* mutatis mutandis *to E.A.E.C.* 191.]

The twenty Articles of the E.A.E.C. Protocol on Privileges and Immunities are identical (apart from non-material differences of wording in the English translations) with the first twenty Articles of the E.E.C. Protocol. (The one additional Article (Article 21) of the E.E.C. Protocol is concerned with the European Investment Bank and has no counterpart in the E.A.E.C. Protocol).

III. THE EUROPEAN COAL AND STEEL COMMUNITY

A. ESTABLISHMENT

The European Coal and Steel Community is immediately established upon the entry into force of the Treaty.

E.C.S.C. 1

By this Treaty the High Contracting Parties establish among themselves a European Coal and Steel Community, founded upon a common market, common objectives and common institutions.

"... This Treaty ...". E.C.S.C. 84 provides:

"For the purpose of this Treaty, the words "this Treaty" shall include the provisions of the Treaty and its Annexes, the Protocols annexed to it and the Convention containing the Transitional Provisions".

Territorial application. E.C.S.C. 79 provides:

"This Treaty shall apply to the European territories of the High Contracting Parties. It shall also apply to those European territories for whose external relations a signatory State assumes responsibility; an exchange of letters between the Government of the German Federal Republic and the Government of the French Republic concerning the Saar is annexed to this Treaty. Each High Contracting Party binds itself to extend to the other Member States the preferential measures which it enjoys with respect to coal and steel in the non-European territories over which it has authority."

As to "High Contracting Parties" see this heading, *infra*).

Language of the Treaty. The only official and authentic language of the Treaty is French. (in E.E.C. and E.A.E.C. there are four official and authentic language versions (French, German, Italian and Dutch,) see E.E.C. 248, *ante*, p. 14 and E.A.E.C. 225, *ante*, p. 35).

Entry into force. E.C.S.C. 99 provides:

"... The Treaty shall come into force on the date of deposit of its instrument of ratification by the last signatory State to do so [with the Government of the French Republic]".

That date, in the event, was 1952.

Revision of the Treaty. See E.C.S.C. 96 under (b) the Council (*n*), *post*, p. 56.

Duration. E.C.S.C. 97 provides:

"This Treaty is concluded for a period of fifty years from the date when it comes into force".

The date of termination is therefore

"... The High Contracting Parties ...". See under E.E.C. (*ante*, p. 14).

"**... Establish among themselves a ... Community ...**". The comment under this heading to E.E.C. 1 (*ante*, p. 15) applies *mutatis mutandis* to E.C.S.C. The "undertakings" (Fr. *"entreprises"*) which are directly within the nexus of legal relationships that is the Coal and Steel Community are defined by E.C.S.C. 80:

"The term "undertaking" shall, for the purposes of this Treaty, mean any undertaking engaged in production in the field of coal and steel within the territories mentioned in the first paragraph of Article 79; and in addition, as regards Articles 65 and 66, and also as regards the information required for their application and as regards proceedings based upon them, any undertaking or body regularly engaged in distribution other than sale to domestic consumers or to small craft industries".

Provision for the definition of the terms "coal" and "steel" is made by E.C.S.C. 81:

"The terms "coal" and "steel" are defined in Annex I to this Treaty. Additions may be made to the lists set forth in that Annex by unanimous decision of the Council".

"Undertaking" is an economic (not a legal) concept. The question of who owns or operates the undertaking is relevant to the rights of parties to bring an action at the Court (see, *e.g.* E.C.S.C. 33, *post*, p. 89).

"**... Founded upon a common market, common objectives and common institutions ...**". That these words are linked in one sentence to those which provide that "the High Contracting Parties establish among themselves a Community" may be read as indicating that, in law, the Common Market is brought into existence contemporaneously with the Community. In the two later Treaties there is no such linking, in one sentence, of the provision establishing the Community with the more tangible manifestations of the phenomena of which it consists, and the establishment of the Common Market in E.E.C. or the pooling of nuclear resources in E.A.E.C. is made expressly executory. In E.C.S.C. the view that, in law, the Common Market is immediately established is possibly borne out by E.C.S.C. 2, post, p. 49, in which paragraph one contains the wording "through the creation of a Common Market in accordance with the provisions of Article 4". This wording in the authentic French (*"grâce à l'établissement d'un marché commun"*) might seem to indicate an action accomplished rather than one remaining to be carried out, though the opposite reading is also possible. This distinction between E.E.C. E.A.E.C. and E.C.S.C. is limited in its practical effects particularly by the "convention containing the transitional provisions" which was "drawn up in pursuance of Article 85 of the Treaty" in order to make provision for the measures necessary for setting up the Common Market and for adapting production progressively to the new conditions created thereby, while facilitating the disappearance of the unbalanced circumstances resulting from the previous state of affairs. E.C.S.C. 4, however, is to take immediate effect in prohibiting practices imcompatible with the Common Market, and to that extent establishes it immediately. E.C.S.C. 4. provides:

"The following are recognised to be incompatible with the Common Market for Coal and Steel and are accordingly abolished and prohibited, as laid down in this Treaty, within the Community:

(*a*) import and export duties, or charges having equivalent effect, and quantitative restrictions on the movement of products;

(*b*) measures or practices which discriminate between producers, between purchasers and between consumers especially as regards price or delivery terms and transport rates and conditions, as well as measures or practices which hamper the purchaser in the free choice of his supplier;

(*c*) subsidies or assistance granted by States or special burdens imposed by them in any form whatsoever;

(*d*) restrictive practices tending to the allocation or exploitation of markets."

On the other hand, E.C.S.C. 2 and 3 (*infra*) also express provision for executory tasks of the Community and it is a legitimate reading of this Article to consider the establishment of the Common Market in Coal and Steel as one of these tasks.

B. THE GENERAL DUTY OR TASK (FR. "*mission*") OF THE COMMUNITY

E.C.S.C. 2

The European Coal and Steel Community shall have as its task to contribute, in harmony with the general economy of Member States and through the creation of a common market in accordance with the provisions of Article 4, to economic expansion, growth of employment, and a rising standard of living in Member States.

The Community shall progressively bring into being conditions which will by themselves ensure the most rational distribution of production at the highest possible level of productivity, while safeguarding continuity of employment and being careful not to give rise to fundamental and persistent disturbances in the economies of Member States.

C. THE PARTICULAR DUTIES OR TASKS OF THE COMMUNITY

E.C.S.C. 3

The Community's institutions shall within the limits of their respective competence and in the common interest:

(*a*) ensure an orderly supply to the Common Market, taking account of the needs of third countries;

(*b*) ensure that all consumers in comparable positions within the common market have equal access to the sources of production;

(*c*) ensure the establishment of the lowest possible prices under such conditions that these prices do not result in corresponding increases in the prices charged by the same undertaking in other transactions or in the general price level at another time, while allowing for necessary amortisation and providing normal opportunities for a return on invested capital;

(*d*) ensure the maintenance of conditions which will encourage undertakings to expand and improve their productive capacity and to promote a policy of rational exploitation of natural resources so as to avoid their unprepared for exhaustion;

(*e*) promote better conditions of living and of work and employment for workers in each of the industries for which it is responsible so as to lead to their progressive harmonisation and improvement;

(*f*) promote the development of international trade and ensure that equitable limits are observed in prices charged when selling outside the Community;

(*g*) promote the orderly expansion and the modernisation of production as well as the improvement of equality, under conditions which preclude any protection against competing industries unless it is justified by improper action by or in favour of such industries.

The Institutions which carry out the duties enumerated in this Article are set out in E.C.S.C. 7 (see under "D. The Four Institutions of the Community", *infra*). The degree of intervention by the Community (which is, in practice, intervention by the Institutions) is to be limited.

E.C.S.C. 5

The Community shall carry out its task, as laid down in this Treaty, with a limited amount of intervention.

To this end the Community shall:

enlighten and facilitate the action of the parties concerned, by gathering information, organising, consultation, and defining general objectives;

place sources of finance at the disposal of undertakings for their capital investments and participate in the expenses of readaption;

ensure the establishment, maintenance and observance of normal competitive conditions and exert direct influence upon production or upon the market only when circumstances so require;

publish the reasons for its actions and take the necessary measures to ensure the observance of the rules laid down in this Treaty.

The Community's institutions shall carry out these activities with a minimum of administrative machinery and in close cooperation with interested parties.

D. The Four Institutions of the Community

They are: (a) the High Authority (*post*, p. 51); (b) the Common Assembly (*post*, p. 54); (c) the Special Council of Ministers (*post*, p. 54) and (d) the Court of Justice. These are the subject of Title 11 (Articles 7–45) of the Treaty.

E.C.S.C. 7

The Community's Institutions shall be:
A HIGH AUTHORITY, assisted by a Consultative Committee;
A COMMON ASSEMBLY, hereinafter referred to as "the Assembly";
A SPECIAL COUNCIL OF MINISTERS, hereinafter referred to as "the Council";
A COURT OF JUSTICE, hereinafter referred to as "the Court".

The Community's Institutions act "within the limits of their respective competence and in the common interest" (E.C.S.C. 3, *supra*). The first three Institutions named in E.C.S.C. 7 are treated below under (a), (b) and (c), respectively. The fourth Institution, the Court of Justice, is, in its organizational aspects, the concern of Chapter 3 of this book.

(a) The High Authority

E.C.S.C. 8

It shall be the duty of the High Authority to ensure the attainment of the objects set out in this Treaty, as laid down herein.

The High Authority is listed first among the Institutions of E.C.S.C. (E.C.S.C. 7, *supra*) whereas the Commissions of E.E.C. and E.A.E.C. are each listed third among four (see E.E.C. 4, *ante*, p. 17 and E.A.E.C. 3, *ante*, p. 38). No particular significance attaches to this order of listing, as such, but it is a fact that the powers of the High Authority, which is the principal executive Institution in E.C.S.C. are greater and more directly exercisable (that is, with less obligation to seek approval, or await decisions, of the Council (*post*, p. 54) on which Member States are directly represented) in respect of the other parties in relationship with it in the legal nexus which is the Community, than are the powers of the Commissions (the only Institutions comparable to the High Authority) in the later Communities (but see under E.C.S.C. 14 "Decisions, recommendations, opinions", *post*, p. 52). As from January 1st, 1966, a single body to be known as the Commission of the European Communities is to exercise the functions of the E.E.C. Commission, the E.A.E.C. Commission and the E.C.S.C. High Authority (see paragraph beginning "As from January 1st, 1966", *ante*, p. 19).

The independence of an Institution of the Community in relation to the national governments (whose ratification of the Treaty brought it into existence) is one criterion of the "supra-national" character of the Community, or at least of the Institution enjoying that independence. It is for that reason that the word "supra-national", in reference to the nature of the duties of Members of the High Authority, is in fact used in E.C.S.C. 9 (not reprinted in this book). To the extent that in the later Treaties the Commissions are less completely independent of control by Member States collectively or individually the later Communities may be considered less supra-national. But a second criterion of the supra-national character of the Communities, of greatest relevance to the work of the Court of Justice, is the power that resides therein to exercise direct executive (or legislative) control, in the Member States, upon private parties (in E.C.S.C., the "undertakings") that by virtue of each Treaty are brought into the nexus of legal relationships which is the Community, and to exercise that direct control without the legislative or other mediation of such Member States, or in an extreme case, even against their wishes. Such direct control by Community Institutions exists in E.E.C. and E.A.E.C. as in E.C.S.C., and broadly speaking the jurisdiction of the Court of Justice in regard to it is much the same in all three Communities, but its exercise, in E.E.C. and E.A.E.C., is more hedged around with safeguards capable of being used to protect what Member States may consider to be their interests or those of private parties within their jurisdiction. A provision which has no equivalent in E.E.C. or E.A.E.C. is that of E.C.S.C. 90:

> "If an infringement by an undertaking of an obligation under this Treaty also constitutes an infringement of an obligation under the legislation of the State to which the undertaking is subject, and if legal or administrative action is taken against the undertaking in question under such legislation, the State in question shall so inform the High Authority, which may defer coming to a conclusion".

E.C.S.C. 13

Decisions of the High Authority shall be taken by a majority of its members.

The rules of procedure shall determine the quorum. This quorum, however, must be greater than one-half of its total membership.

The word "decision" used in the English translation must not be understood in the technical sense of "decisions" in E.C.S.C. 14 (*infra*) but as embracing also the recommendations or opinions of the High Authority defined in the same Article. That this is so is apparent from the French original of E.C.S.C. 13: "*Les délibérations de la Haute Autorité sont acquises à la majorité des membres qui la composent*", in which neither the word "*décide*" nor "*décision*" is used. "*Les délibérations*" might preferably have been rendered as "resolutions" here, and elsewhere in the Treaty translation in respect of the acts of the Assembly and Council (for example, in E.S.S.C. 38, for text of which see *post*, p. 118.

E.C.S.C. 14

"In order to carry out the tasks assigned to it and in accordance with the provisions of this Treaty, the High Authority shall take decisions, make recommendations and give opinions.

Decisions shall be binding in their entirety.

Recommendations shall be binding with respect to the objectives which they prescribe, while leaving to those to whom they are directed the choice of appropriate methods for attaining those objectives.

Opinions shall have no binding force.

When the High Authority is empowered to take a decision, it may restrict itself to making a recommendation."

Decisions, recommendations and opinions. These are technical forms of the "decisions" (*délibérations*) referred to in E.C.S.C. 13 (*supra*) to be used by the High Authority in carrying out the (executive) duties assigned to it.

In the two later Treaties the equivalent articles defining the administrative acts to be taken in execution of the Treaty (E.E.C. 189 identical with E.A.E.C. 161, *ante*, p. 26) apply to both the Council and the Commission of each Community. This reflects back on the importance of the High Authority relative to the other Institutions of E.C.S.C. But the fact that E.C.S.C. 14 does not apply to the E.C.S.C. Council does not mean that the Council is not required, under the Treaty, to take decisions or give opinions (for list of which see under (c) the Council, *post*, p. 55).

Recommendations in E.C.S.C. are in many respects comparable to "directives" in E.E.C. and E.A.E.C. (see E.E.C. 189, *ante*, p. 26 and E.A.E.C. 161, identical therewith) but whereas the most important function of the latter is to promote and achieve a harmonization of national laws, E.C.S.C. recommendations should be understood principally in contrast to the direct action of E.C.S.C. decisions, and as the means whereby Community intervention in the affairs of Member States can be brought within the limited degree required by E.C.S.C. 5 (which see under "The Particular Duties or Tasks of the Community", E.C.S.C. 3, *ante*, p. 49). Moreover, private parties (*i.e.* "undertakings") may in certain circumstances bring an action before the Court of Justice in respect of an E.C.S.C. recommendation (see *post*, pp. 90, 100) but in E.E.C. and E.A.E.C. cannot do so in respect of directives. A directive is by its very nature addressed to a Member State and it is out of the question that a private party could infringe it as such directly—or even indirectly, except in the unreal sense that in infringing the law of a Member State to which that party is subject, where that law has been modified as a consequence of a directive for harmonization with other national laws, such an infringement could be looked upon as running counter to the directive itself. An E.C.S.C. recommendation, on the other hand, may be addressed to either a Member State or to a private party (for examples of the latter see E.C.S.C. 60, para. 3(a); 66 para. 7; 68 para. 2 and para 3; not printed in this work).

Recommendations are passed by the High Authority by majority vote (E.C.S.C. 13, *ante*, p. 52). Directives of the Commissions of E.E.C. and E.A.E.C. are similarly passed, but where the Council issues a directive it may frequently be required to do so unanimously or by qualified majority vote and on the proposal of the Commission, while in some instances the Assembly must be consulted, or the Economic and Social Committee. Recommendations (and decisions) which are not "individual in character" (E.C.S.C. 15 *post*, p. 54) take effect upon publication (that is in the Journal Officiel). E.E.C. and E.A.E.C. directives are not required to be so published (E.E.C. 191, E.A.E.C. 163) for the purpose of entry into force, but in practice they are published in the Journal Officiel as information.

"Opinions shall not be binding". Exceptionally, E.C.S.C. 54 para. 5 provides:

"If the High Authority finds that the financing of a programme or the operation of the installations which it involves would involve subsidies, aid, protection or discrimination, contrary to this Treaty, its unfavourable opinion based on these grounds shall have the force of a decision, within the meaning of Article 14, and shall have the effect of prohibiting the undertaking concerned from resorting to resources other than its own funds, to carry out that programme".

"When the High Authority is empowered to take a decision, it may restrict itself to making a recommendation". This general right of the High Authority always to choose the weaker form of act has no counterpart in E.E.C. or E.A.E.C. but exists only where a choice is specifically conferred on the Council or Commission, as the case may be.

E.C.S.C. 15

Decisions, recommendations and opinions of the High Authority shall be fully reasoned and shall refer to any opinions required to be obtained by it.

When decisions and recommendations are individual in character, they shall become binding upon being notified to the party concerned.

In all other cases, they shall take effect as a result of mere publication.

The High Authority shall determine the manner in which effect is to be given to this Article.

"Decisions, recommendations and opinions of the High Authority shall be fully reasoned. . . ." See the ruling of the Court as to "sufficiency of reasoning of a decision", in Chapter 2, *post*, p. 100).

"When decisions and recommendations are individual in character. . .". The distinction between individual and general decisions has not been retained in the two later Treaties. That distinction, as it re-appears in E.C.S.C. 33, paragraph 2, has undoubtedly complicated much of the litigation before the Court, based on that article. (See Chapter 2, especially the comment under "general and individual decisions," *post*, p. 106).

". . . as a result of mere publication". See under E.C.S.C. 14, comment on "recommendations" (*ante*, p. 52).

(b) The Assembly

The Assembly exercises supervisory powers.

E.C.S.C. 20

The Assembly, which shall consist of representatives of the peoples of the States who have come together in the Community, shall exercise the supervisory powers which are conferred upon it by this Treaty.

A single Assembly, operating in respect of E.C.S.C., E.E.C. and E.A.E.C., was established as a result of the "Convention Relating to Certain Institutions Common to the European Communities" of 1957 (see *ante*, p. 19).

(c) The Council

The Council consists of representatives of the Member States (E.C.S.C. 47 not printed in this work). As from January 1st, 1966, a single body is to exercise the functions of the E.E.C. Council, the E.A.E.C. Council and the E.C.S.C. Council (see paragraph beginning "As from January 1st, 1966, *ante*, p. 19). The Council of E.C.S.C. has a general duty as set out *infra*.

E.C.S.C. 26

The Council shall exercise its power in the cases provided for and in the manner set out in this Treaty, with a view in particular to harmonising the action of the High Authority with that of the Governments which are responsible for the general economic policy of their countries.

To this end, the Council and the High Authority shall exchange information and consult each other.

The Council may request the High Authority to examine any proposals and measures which the Council may consider appropriate or necessary for the achievement of the common objectives.

In execution of E.C.S.C. 26 the Council may, in the circumstances laid down in the Treaty give a confirmatory opinion (*avis conforme*) or take a decision, though neither of these is within E.C.S.C. 14 (*ante*, p. 52) defining *inter alia*, decisions and opinions of the High Authority. Either of them may be required by the Treaty to be unanimous (see E.C.S.C. 28, not printed here) or may be by qualified or simple majority. Instances where the Treaty requires a decision or confirmatory opinion of the Council are:

(*a*) reduction of number of members of the High Authority (by unanimous decision) (E.C.S.C. 9);

(*b*) salaries of members of the High Authority and of judges (by majority vote) (E.C.S.C. 29);

(*c*) increase in the number of judges (by unanimous decision on a proposal of the Court) (E.C.S.C. 32);

(*d*) authorize a levy by the High Authority at a rate in excess of 1% (by two thirds majority vote) (E.C.S.C. 50, para. 2);

(*e*) authorize the High Authority to facilitate the financing of such programmes as it may approve, in respect of industries not within Community control, of new and economically sound activities (by confirmatory opinion) (E.C.S.C. 56(b));

(*f*) authorize the establishment by the High Authority of a system of production quotas (by confirmatory opinion) (E.C.S.C. 58, para. 1);

(*g*) authorize increases in levies under E.C.S.C. 58 para. 1 (*supra*) (E.C.S.C. para. 3);

(*h*) authorize various measures by the High Authority or take such measures in cases of serious shortage of any or of all of the products over which it has authority (by unanimous decision) (E.C.S.C. 59);

(*i*) request the High Authority to fix maximum or minimum prices (by unanimous decision) (E.C.S.C. 61);

(*j*) fix maximum and minimum rates of customs duties of Member States applicable to third countries, on proposal of the High Authority (by unanimous decision) (E.C.S.C. 72);

(*k*) appoint an Auditor (implicitly by decision, but voting requirements not specified) (E.C.S.C. 78, para. 6);

(*l*) add to the lists set out in Annex 1 (which defines "coal" and "steel") (by unanimous decision) (E.C.S.C. 81, para. 2);

(*m*) either: authorize, after consulting the Consultative Committee, a decision or recommendation of the High Authority to achieve one of the Community's objectives in a case not provided for by the Treaty (by unanimous confirmatory opinion) or: submit to the Court, jointly with the High Authority, amendments of the rules for the exercise of its powers by the High Authority (by five-sixths majority) (E.C.S.C. 95);

(*n*) approve a conference of representatives of governments of Member States to agree Treaty amendments (opinion in favour by two-thirds majority) (E.C.S.C. 96);

(*o*) accession of European State to the Treaty and terms of such accession (by unanimous decision) (E.C.S.C. 98);

(*p*) remove Advocates-General from office (by unanimous decision upon advice of the Court) (Statute of the Court Art. 13).

(*q*) fix further waiting periods in respect of setting up the Common Market (Convention containing Transitional Provisions, Art. 8).

Annulment of the above resolutions ("*délibérations*") of the Council on the ground of lack of jurisdiction or of non-observance of basic procedural rules (but on no other ground) may be ordered by the Court of Justice on the application of a Member State or of the High Authority (see *post*, p. 118).

E. The Personality and Legal Acts of the Community, Internationally and in Relation to Member States

E.C.S.C. 6

The Community shall have legal personality.

In international relations the Community shall enjoy the legal capacity necessary to perform its functions and to achieve its ends.

In each of the Member States, the Community shall enjoy the most extensive legal capacity granted to legal persons constituted in that State and in particular may acquire and transfer immovable and movable property, and may sue and be sued in its own name.

The Community shall be represented by its institutions each within the limits of its competence.

E.C.S.C. 83

The setting up of the Community shall not in any way prejudice the rules pertaining to ownership of the undertakings to which this Treaty applies.

E.C.S.C. 76

The Community shall enjoy in the territories of the Member States the privileges and immunities necessary for the achievement of its tasks, under conditions defined in a Protocol annexed to this Treaty.

The Privileges and Immunities enjoyed by the Community and set out in the Protocol required by this Article are substantially the same as those of E.E.C. and E.A.E.C. Reference should be made to the comment on E.E.C. 218, *ante*, p. 29.

The Jurisdiction of the Court

INTRODUCTORY

The European Court has no exclusive jurisdiction over the Communities. As a general principle none of the Communities is immune from the jurisdiction of national courts and the purport of the Treaties is that the Communities should be subject to that jurisdiction except where it is expressly or impliedly excluded in favour of that of the European Court by the Treaties (annexures thereto and implementing Regulations) themselves. The provision to this effect is more maturely formulated in E.E.C. and E.A.E.C. than in E.C.S.C.

E.E.C. 183

[Printed on p. 29, ante.]

E.A.E.C. 155

[Identical with E.E.C. 183, ante, p. 29.]

E.C.S.C. 40 paragraph 3

Any other disputes arising between the Community and third parties, outside the scope of the provisions of this Treaty and its implementing regulations, shall be brought before the municipal courts or tribunals.

The International Court of Justice has no jurisdiction in respect of the Community Treaties. The effect of the three Treaties is to oust all jurisdiction of that Court over disputes between Member States of the Communities concerning the interpretation or application of the Treaties—to which Court such disputes might otherwise normally have been expected to be submitted— and to oust all other methods of settlement that might normally be followed by States, in favour of those provided for in the Treaties themselves. The commonest method of settlement provided for involves submission of the dispute to the Court of Justice of the European Communities. The following Articles contain the general provision from which these results follow.

E.E.C. 219

Member States undertake not to submit a dispute concerning the interpretation or application of this Treaty to any method of settlement other than those provided for in this Treaty.

E.A.E.C. 193

[Identical with E.E.C. 219.]

E.C.S.C. 87

The High Contracting Parties undertake not to avail themselves of any treaties, conventions or declarations existing among themselves so as to submit any dispute arising out of the interpretation or carrying out of this Treaty to any method of settlement other than those provided for therein.

This article should be read in conjunction with E.C.S.C. 89, paragraph one

"Any dispute between Member States as to the implementation of this Treaty, which cannot be settled by another procedure provided for in this Treaty, may be submitted to the Court on application from one of the States which are parties to the dispute."

A. General Role of the European Court

The general role of the Court is to "ensure that the law is observed in the interpretation and implementation" of the three Community Treaties (and of Regulations made thereunder) (See "The task of the Court", *ante*, p. 13). In some aspects of the fulfilment of that role the Court's jurisdiction is not altogether exclusive, being at some points concurrent with that of the judicial authorities of Member States (notably in respect of interpretation of the Treaty in E.E.C. and E.A.E.C; see *post*, pp. 130 *et seq.*). The passages taken from judgments of the Court and quoted immediately below clarify the general role of the Court under E.C.S.C. 31 (and similarly by inference under E.E.C. 164 and E.A.E.C. 136).

(a) The Court and the Internal Law of Member States of the Communities

In *Friedrich Stork & Cie c. Haute Autorité* (Case 1/58, R. Vol. V p. 63) the Court stated:

". . . by virtue of Article 8 of the (E.C.S.C.) Treaty, the High Authority is only called upon to apply the law of the Community; the Court has no competence to apply the internal law of the Member States; furthermore, in accordance with Article 31 of the (E.C.S.C.) Treaty the task of the Court is only to ensure the observance of law in the interpretation and application of the Treaty and the regulations for its execution; as a general rule, the Court has not to pronounce on the rules of internal law; consequently the Court is not in a position to examine the claim that, in taking its decision, the High Authority allegedly violated the principles of German constitutional law (in particular articles 2 and 12 of the Basic Law) . . .".

In *Firma I. Nold K.G. c. Haute Autorite* (Case 18/57, R. Vol. V. p. 160) the Court stated:

"Article 31 of the E.C.S.C. Treaty provides: 'The Court shall ensure that the law is observed in the interpretation and implementation of this Treaty . . ..' The Court therefore examines whether the Institutions of the Community have respected in their activity the provisions of the Treaty. It is the same with the limitative enumeration of grounds in E.C.S.C. 33. [see Chapter 2, *post*, p. 93]. If a decision of the High Authority can only be challenged on this basis, the organism which takes the decisions is under no duty to respect rules other than those described in the same place . . .".

In *Comptoirs de Vente du Charbon de la Ruhr "President" etc.* c. *Haute Autorité* (Consolidated cases 36, 37, 38, 40/59; R. Vol. VI (ii) at p. 890) the Court stated:

". . . The applicant in support of his claims invokes decisions of German Courts relating to the interpretation of article 14 of the Basic Law of the Federal Republic, guaranteeing private property. It is not the task of the Court, judge of the legality of the decisions taken by the High Authority and hence of those taken in the present case by virtue of article 65 of the Treaty, to ensure observance of the rules of internal law, even of constitutional law, in force in one or other of the Member States. Therefore the Court can neither interpret nor apply article 14 of the German Basic Law in inquiring into the legality of a decision of the High Authority . . .."

(b) Relation of Community Law to the Legislative and Administrative Acts of Member States

In *Jean E. Humblet* c. *Etat Belge* (Case 6/60 R. Vol. VI (ii) at p. 1145) a case concerning the interpretation or application of the Protocol on the Privileges and Immunities of E.C.S.C., the Court stated:

". . . The Court has no jurisdiction to annul legislative or administrative acts of a Member State. Indeed the Treaty is conceived on the principle of a rigorous separation of the competence of the Community Institutions on the one hand and that of the organs of Member States on the other. Community law does not confer on the Institutions of the Community the right to annul the legislative or administrative acts of a Member State. Thus, the High Authority, if it is of the opinion that a State has failed to carry out one of the obligations incumbent on it by virtue of the Treaty, by promulgating or maintaining in force provisions contrary to the Treaty, cannot itself annul or abrogate these provisions, but can only note, in accordance with article 88 of the Treaty, that such failure has occurred and thereupon set in motion the procedure therein laid down to lead the State in question itself to correct the measures it had taken. It is the same with the Court of Justice which, guardian of the observance of community law in the terms of article 31, is competent by virtue of article 16 of the Protocol to rule on any disputes relating to its interpretation or application, but cannot, however, on its own authority, annul or abrogate the national laws of a member State or administrative acts of its authorities.

In *M. Flaminio Costa* c. *E.N.E.L.* (*Ente Nazionale Energia Elettrica impresa già della Edison Volta*) (Case 6/64, R. Vol. X, p. 1141) which was a reference for a preliminary ruling by the Court under E.E.C. 177 as to the interpretation of E.E.C. 102, 93, 53 and 37, the Court found that articles 53 and 37(2) conferred directly on persons, subject as nationals to the jurisdiction of Member States, rights which the courts of these States were bound to safeguard. The Court found that E.E.C. 53 "prohibited any new measure aimed at subjecting the establishment of nationals of the other Member States to stricter requirements than those applied to nationals" (of the Member State contemplating the measure) "whatever the legal regime governing the undertakings." The purpose of the provisions of E.E.C. 37(2) was "to prohibit any new measure aiming at, or resulting in, a fresh discrimination between nationals of Member States in the conditions of supply, or marketing, of goods by means of monopolies or other bodies. These provisions must have as their object dealings in a commercial product open to competition and exchange as between Member States, in which exchanges it was intended the provisions should play an effective role."

(c) Relation of the Court to the National Courts and Tribunals of Member States

In Case 6/60 (*loc. cit., ante*, p. 59 at p. 1150) the Court stated:

"... it is desirable to look into the further question whether the claim is not inadmissible because the applicant should in the first place have exhausted the remedies in administrative law or in the ordinary law which might be available to him in accordance with the law of the State to which he is subject. As far as administrative law is concerned it can be stated as a fact that in the stage now reached in the proceedings the possibilities are exhausted, the director of direct taxation for the province of Liége having rejected, by a decision of the 15th June 1960, the claim presented by the applicant against the charge to tax which is in dispute. As far as the ordinary law is concerned it is apparent from the parties' declarations that the applicant has brought an action before the Liége Court of Appeal, so that a beginning has been made in seeking possible remedies available in Belgian law, but, in the present stage of the proceedings, these have not been exhausted. However, the Treaties setting up the European Communities have not superimposed the Court of Justice of these Communities on to the judicial authorities of the Member States in the sense that the rulings of these authorities would be capable of being challenged before the European Court."

(*Cf.* quotation from *Demande de décision préjudicielle* etc. Case 13/61, *post*, pp. 132–133.)

B. Range of Jurisdiction of the European Court

The subject of this Chapter is that Jurisdiction of the European Court which is (*a*) concerned with cases that are primarily and essentially in matters of substance; (*b*) conferred by the Treaties themselves (irrespective, that is, of the annexed Protocols and of the Rules of Procedure) and (*c*) exercised by means of a judgment (as distinct from an order. As to the difference see "Judgments and Orders" *post*, pp. 253 *et seq.*). The Chapter falls into 23 sections corresponding to the types of matter over which the Court has jurisdiction. All 23 (see list under "Jurisdiction by virtue of the Treaties", *post*, p. 61) have the characteristics (*a*), (*b*) and (*c*) above (with the exception of XIX where jurisdiction is conferred by Protocol, and XXII, where it is implied rather than expressed by the Treaties).

Into a general category distinct from the above falls the jurisdiction, or competence, of the Court which is (*a*) in matters that are primarily procedural; (*b*) conferred by the Statute(s) of the Court or the Rules of Procedure, or these two in interaction; (*c*) related to the Court's continuing competence, after judgment delivered, to make (usually by a further judgment) certain types of adjustment of the judgment so delivered, or (*d*) exercised (usually by order) during the course of procedure leading to, and for the purpose of ensuring a proper, judgment. This general category may be tabulated as follows

Procedural Competence
(as distinct from substantive jurisdiction)

The list is divided into two, corresponding to (*c*) and (*d*) above.

(C) or (S) indicates whether the decision is that of the whole court or of a Section; J or O indicates whether the decision is by judgment or order; O* indicates an order that has the quality of finality of a judgment;

"E.E.C. St." etc. refers to the Court's Statute(s); R.P. to the Rules of Procedure. Where both appear together this indicates that competence is conferred by their inter-action.

(c)   (i) (C). J.—to conduct a retrial when a claim for such is made following judgment by default (E.E.C. St. 38 and equivalents; R.P. 94);

    (ii) (C). J.—to modify its own judgment following retrial on third party application (E.E.C. St. 29 and equivalents; R.P. 97);

   (iii) (C). O*.—to rectify its own judgment (R.P. 66);

   (iv) (C) (presumably). J.—to remedy an omission (in a judgment) to rule on a count in either party's submissions (R.P. 67);

    (v) (C). J.—to reconsider its own judgment (E.E.C. St. 41 and equivalents; R.P. 98 and 100);

   (vi) (C). J.—to interpret its own judgment (E.E.C. St. 40 and equivalents; R.P. 102);

(d) (vii) (C or S). O*.—to bar legal adviser or legal representative from the proceedings (R.P. 35 (1)),

  (viii) (C or S). O.—to determine measures for calling of evidence (R.P. 45, 46 (1));

   (ix) (C). O.—to require proof of certain facts by witnesses (R.P. 47 (1));

    (x) (C). O.—to summon witness(es) (R.P. 47 (2));

   (xi) (C). O.—to effect fresh service of summons on witness (R.P. 48 (2));

  (xii) (C). O.—to require expert's examination and report (R.P. 49);

  (xiii) (C). O.—to require the taking of a "measure of enquiry", (*i.e.* one of the steps in "the procedure of enquiry"), or re-opening and extension of the "procedure of enquiry" (R.P. 60);

  (xiv) (C). O. to re-open the "oral procedure" (R.P. 61);

  (xv) (S). O*.—to determine dispute on recoverable costs (R.P. 76);

  (xvi) (S). O*.—to grant free legal aid (R.P. 76);

  (xvii) (C). O*.—to strike a case from the register (R.P. 77, 78);

 (xviii) (C, or President alone) O*—to give decision in summary procedure in case of urgency (R.P. 86 (1));

  (xix) (C). O*.—to rule on admissibility of intervention (R.P. 93 (3));

  (xx) (C). O.—to order letter of request (for evidence) (Supplementary R.P. 1).

The items in the above list are treated, in the sequence of the Rules of Procedure relating to them, in Chapter 4, (*post*, pp. 209 *et seq.*), Chapter 5, (*post*, pp. 270 *et seq.*) and Chapter 6, (*post*, pp. 299–310).

C. Jurisdiction by Virtue of the Treaties

The matters in respect of which the European Court has jurisdiction by virtue of the Treaties (and which are the subject of the present Chapter) may conveniently be classified under the following heads:

     I. Claim that a Member State of E.E.C. or E.A.E.C. has failed to fulfil any of its obligations under the Treaty.

    II. Review of penalty or fine.

   III. Legality of acts (of an administrative or executive body).

   IV. Failure to act (on the part of an administrative or executive body).

V. Review of the justification of a High Authority decision in a situation susceptible of provoking fundamental and persistent disturbances in a Member State's economy.

VI. Preliminary Ruling (*"Décision à titre préjudiciel"*).

VII. Community liability in tort.

VIII. Disputes concerning relationships between the Community and its servants.

IX. Disputes relating to the European Investment Bank.

X. Reference by virtue of a *clause compromissoire*.

XI. Reference by virtue of a "special agreement" between States.

XII. Claim for suspension of enforcement of administrative act.

XIII. Claim for interim measures.

XIV. "In any other case provided for by the Treaty" or by the law of a Member State.

XV. Preliminary opinion (as to compatibility of agreements and conventions with the Treaty or proposals for Treaty amendments, etc.).

XVI. Application to retire or suspend a Member of the Commission or High Authority, etc.

XVII. Formal legality of decision of E.A.E.C. Arbitration Committee, etc.

XVIII. Fulfilment of conditions for the granting, in E.A.E.C., of non-exclusive licenses by arbitration or official action.

XIX. Authorization of an administrative or legal measure of constraint relating to Community property, etc.

XX. Under E.A.E.C. 81, President of the Court to decide as to warrant for enforcement of supervisory measure or to give subsequent approval of Commission's written order to proceed with a supervisory measure.

XXI. Application to give judgment by default.

XXII. Application to stay the execution of its judgment.

XXIII. Jurisdiction conferred by special provisions.

The above heads (I–XXIII) are treated seriatim below.

I. CLAIM THAT A MEMBER STATE OF E.E.C. OR E.A.E.C. HAS FAILED TO FULFIL ANY OF ITS OBLIGATIONS UNDER THE TREATY

Or by a Member State of E.C.S.C. against a High Authority decision, finding that the State had failed to fulfil a Treaty obligation.

("... *Qu'un Etat membre a manqué à une des obligations qui lui incombent en vertu du présent traité* ...;

... *ein Mitgleidstaat gegen eine Verflichtung aus diesem Vertrag verstoszen.*

"... *dat een kid-Staat een van de krachtens dit Verdrag op hem rustende verplichtingen niet is nagekomen* ...;

... *che uno Stato membre abbia mancato a uno degli obblighi a lui incombenté in virtù del presente trattato.*)

Such a claim may be brought by the Commission (of E.E.C. or E.A.E.C.), the High Authority (of E.C.S.C.), another Member State (of any of the three Communities) or, in regard to obligations under the Statute of the European Investment Bank, by the Board of Directors of the Bank. It is treated below under the following headings:

A. Claim by E.E.C. Commission (E.E.C. 169, 225), *post*, p. 63.

B. Claim by E.A.E.C. Commission (E.A.E.C. 141, 38, 82) *post*, p. 70.

C. Claim by Member State of E.C.S.C. against a decision of the High Authority finding that the State had failed to fulfil a Treaty obligation (E.C.S.C. 88) *post*, p. 71.

A. Claim by E.E.C. Commission

E.E.C. 169

If the Commission considers that a Member State has failed to fulfil any of its obligations under this Treaty, it shall issue a reasoned opinion on the matter after giving the State concerned the opportunity to submit its comments.

If the State concerned does not comply with the terms of such opinion within the period laid down by the Commission, the latter may refer the matter to the Court of Justice.

"Reasoned opinion" (*"avis motivé"*; *"eine mit Gründen versehene on a omkleed advies"*; *"een met redenen "Stellangrahme"*, *parere motivato"*). Opinions, like recommendations, of the E.E.C. Council or Commission have no binding force (see E.E.C. 189 *ante*, p. 26) nor are they, in general, required to be reasoned, as are regulations, directives and decisions of the Council or Commission (under E.E.C. 190 *ante*, p. 26). To this latter general principle the article constitutes an exception: ". . . the Commission . . . shall issue a reasoned opinion". Though such an opinion does not have binding force in the sense of E.E.C. 189 its mere issue may result in some compliance therewith inasmuch as "If the State concerned does not comply with the terms of such opinion within the period laid down by the Commission, the latter may refer the matter to the Court of Justice."

When opinion reasoned sufficiently in law. See the passage from the judgment of the Court in *Commission (C.E.E.* c. *Gouvernement de la République Italienne* (Case 7/61, R. Vol. VII at p. 654) quoted at *post*, p. 64, B(a) para. 2.

The powers conferred upon the Commission by E.E.C. 169 are, by virtue of E.E.C. 180, enjoyed by the Board of Directors of the European Investment Bank in relation to the fulfilment by Member States of the obligations arising under the Statute of the Bank (see *post*, p. 78).

Relation of E.E.C. 169 to E.E.C. 171 (and 226): when a decision is in law sufficiently reasoned

In *Commission de la C.E.E.* c. *Gouvernement de la République Italienne* (Case 7/61 R. Vol. VII at pp. 653—5) the Court stated:

"A. As to the object of the claim—

. . . The correspondence exchanged between the parties following the 1st March 1961, and deposited with the Registry on the 18th November 1961, reveals that the Italian government ultimately conformed with the point of view of the Commission and established, as from the 1st July 1961, a schedule of minimum prices for certain of the products with which the present case is concerned, while, on the other hand, re-establishing complete freedom of import for the others. It is the duty of the Court to examine whether the submissions in the Request have not now lost their purpose, so that there would be no occasion to give judgment.

It follows from the terms of article 171 that the object of the claim is to secure recognition by the Court that a Member State has failed to fulfil one of the obligations incumbent upon it under the Treaty. It is for the Court to say whether the failure has been committed, without having to examine whether, subsequent to the introduction of the claim, the State in question has taken the necessary steps to terminate the infringement.

It is true that article 169 (2) does not confer on the Commission the right to take action before the Court unless the State concerned does not conform with the opinion of the Commission within the time-limit fixed by the latter,—a time-limit which permits the interested State to regularize its position in conformity with the requirements of the Treaty. If, however, the Member State does not conform with this opinion within the time-limit laid down, the Commission cannot be deprived of the right to obtain from the Court a ruling in respect of the failure to fulfil the obligations under the Treaty. In the present case, and although it recognizes that the Italian government has ultimately carried out its obligations, though after the expiry of the above-mentioned time-limit, the Commission retains an interest in having judically determined as a matter of law the question whether the failure to fulfil the obligation has occurred. The claim cannot be declared to be without purpose.

B. As to admissibility—

Three objections of inadmissibility have been raised against the claim:

(a) The first consists in maintaining that the letter of the Commission of the 21st December 1960 did not constitute a "reasoned opinion" within the meaning of article 169, because it did not examine the pertinence of the arguments put forward by the Italian Government as to the existence and gravity of the crisis affecting the pig market and as to the necessity of the provisional measures taken to end it.

The opinion required by article 169 must be considered sufficiently reasoned in law when it contains as in the present case a coherent statement of the reasons that had led the Commission to the conviction that the State concerned has failed to fulfil one of the obligations incumbent on it under the Treaty. The aforesaid letter of 21st December 1960, though not drawn up in due form, fulfils this requirement.

(b) The defendant contends in the second place that there is a contradiction between the attitude of the Commission as at the date of the reasoned opinion (21st November 1960), when it considered itself to be in a position to appreciate the situation and to issue a reasoned opinion, and as at the date of its reply (10th March 1961) to the claim (made to the Commission by the State concerned—*author*) for application of protective measures, when it affirmed it was awaiting the necessary information to rule on the claim.

A claim based on article 226 requires both an enquiry and an appreciation, as part of one certain process, followed by a decision. On the other hand article 169 paragraph one applies each time the Commission considers, rightly or wrongly, that a Member State has failed to fulfil one of the obligations incumbent on it under the treaty. It would not be possible to hold that any contradiction exists between the attitude of the Commission, at the date when it issued the reasoned opinion, and its attitude at the date of its reply to the claim for the application of protective measures.

(c) In the third place the defendant contends that a claim under article 169 paragraph two is not admissible unless the State in question has not conformed with the reasoned opinion, and that it did in fact so conform by sending to the Commission, on the 5th January 1961, before expiry of the time-limit granted, a claim for the application of protective measures based on article 226.

In order to conform with the reasoned opinion the Italian Government ought in good time to set in motion the necessary procedure for putting an end to the measures of suspension (of the import of pig-meats) held to contravene Article 31. The presentation of a claim for the application of protective measures has a quite different purpose and is in reference to quite different circumstances.

For the reasons set forth above the objections of inadmissibility raised by the defendant must be rejected".

Admissibility of claims by the Commission under E.E.C. 169

In *Commission de la Communauté économique européenne* c. (1) *Grand Duché de Luxembourg*, (2) *Royaume de Belgique* (Consolidated Cases 2 and 3/62, R. Vol. VIII at pp. 824–826) the Court ruled on the admissibility of the claims brought by the Commission under E.E.C. 169 and stated:

". . . The defendants, raising the inadmissibility of the claim, charge the Commission with having prevented the regularization of the situation now the subject of litigation, by wrongly demanding the suspension of the measures that it criticized before ruling on the claims advanced by the defendants on the basis of article 226 of the Treaty—and of a Regulation issued by the Council of Ministers, by virtue of article 235, on the 4th April 1962. By 'misusing its powers and by an excess of legalistic formalism' ('*abus de pouvoir et excès de juridisme*'; '*Ermessens Miszbrauch und übertriebenes Rechtsformalismus*'; '*abus de pouvoir en juridische subtiliteiten*'; '*abuso di potere ed eccesso di scrupoli giuridici*') and by failing to rule as a matter of urgency on these requests as it should have done, the Commission is no longer qualified, in the contention of the defendents, to take action against them for infringement of the Treaty. The Commission, which is bound by virtue of article 155, to ensure that the provisions of the Treaty are carried out, cannot be deprived of the right to exercise the power essential thereto, which is conferred on it by article 169. If it were possible to negative the effect of article 169 by a demand for regularization, the article would lose all efficacity.

A claim to make an exception from the general rules of the Treaty, introduced moreover very late in this case, cannot legalize unilateral measures taken in contravention of the said rules and cannot, consequently, legitimate retroactively the original infringement. The procedures for making an exception used in the present case and the result of which was dependent on the appreciation of the Commission of the claim for an exception to be made, are distinct both as to their nature and as to their effects from the procedure under artice 169 by which the Commission may bring pressure to bear. They can in no way immoblize the Commission.

Without having to examine whether what might possibly be an abuse of law on the part of the Commission can deprive it of all the means of action open to it by virtue of article 169, it is sufficient to find that in the present case such an abuse has neither been demonstrated, nor the offer to prove it made. From the oral procedure it is apparent that the defendants neglected to furnish the Commission with the data necessary for it to rule on their claims. Furthermore the possible negligence of the Commission, the existence of which could be judicially determined separately, would not affect in any way the claim for infringement of the Treaty, directed against decisions which are still in force as at today's date and the legality of which the Court is required to examine. The claims must, in consequence, be declared admissible."

Private parties in relation to E.E.C. 169. The question arises as to what, if any, action may be taken before the Community Court by private parties injured by what they allege to be a failure of the Member State of which they are nationals to fulfil its obligations under the Treaty.

In *Société Rhenania, Société Rhenus and Société Westfälische Transport— Aktien-Gesellschaft* c. *Commission C.E.E.* (Case 103/63; judgment 2nd July 1964) the above situation arose in relation to the following facts.

The Council of E.E.C. adopted, on the 4th April 1962, Regulation 19 providing for the gradual setting up of a common organisation of the market in cereals (Official Journal 20. 4. 62, pp. 933 *et seq.*). Article 5 of the Regulation lays down, in the first two paragraphs, that:

"1. Member States shall determine annually, for each of the products covered by article 4, at the phase of wholesale purchase, a basic price, to be valid for a given standard of quality on the business centre of the zone most deficient, taking into account the price obtainable on production within the framework of the Council's decisions in respect of price fixing. This price, determined before the winter sowings, shall come into force at the beginning of the active trading in the product. It shall be communicated to the other Member States and to the Commission.

2. If the discrepancy, due to the natural conditions of price determination on the market, between the market price in the business centre of the most deficient zone, on the one hand, and in the business centre of the zone with the greatest excess on the other, is more than 5%, the Member States shall determine, starting from the basic price referred to in paragraph one, target prices derived therefrom for business centres of importance on a regional scale, related to the differences in price due to the natural conditions of price formation".

The beginning of article 7 of the same regulation provides that:

"1. In order to guarantee to producers that their sales should be at a price as near as possible to the target prices, taking market variations into account, the Member States shall determine, before the beginning of active trading, prices at which they will intervene in respect of the products for which the target prices are determined. These intervention prices shall be equal to the target prices as reduced by a fixed percentage determined by each Member State between a minimum of 5% and a maximum of 10%.

2. Nevertheless, for centres other than the centre of the most deficient zone, the Member States may determine prices for intervention at a level higher than the prices for intervention which should have been fixed taking into account the derived target prices. This increase in intervention prices shall not exceed, in the centre where the target price is lowest, 50% of the difference between the target price and the intervention price determined according to paragraph 1. In the intermediate centres, the difference between target and intervention prices must increase to the extent that the level of derived target prices approaches the price valid in the centre of the zone with the greatest deficiency".

The applicants were of the opinion that the then state of German legislation did not meet the requirements of Regulation 19 and that, in particular, the legislation excluded from the prices the German Government was required to fix, all the purely port installations, which would result, in the centres with purely port installations, in a difference, between the derived target price and the derived intervention price, of a higher percentage then the difference between these same prices in the business centres of the zone with the greatest deficiency.

Through their lawyer, and before the action was brought, the applicant companies wrote to the Commission (31st July 1963) requesting it "in accordance with E.E.C. 155 (for text of which see *ante*, p. 21) to ensure that the Government of the Federal Republic of Germany fulfilled the obligation incumbent on it in consequence of article 7, paragraph 2, of Regulation 19, by removing without delay, in the determining of inter-vention prices, all discrimination with respect to purely port installations." A telegram was sent on the 21st November asking for this letter to be examined and answered. On the 29th November the applicants brought their action, and on the same day received an answer, to the July letter, dated 25th November 1963, which, *inter alia*, stated:

". . . we have pointed out that an undertaking, within the meaning of E.E.C. 175 paragraph three, is not entitled to bring an action before the Court by virtue of E.E.C. 175 paragraphs one and two, unless an In-stitution of the Community has omitted to take, in relation to that undertaking, a measure other than a recommendation or opinion. Your letter and telegram do not enable us to ascertain what measure the Commission has in your opinion failed to take. The measures which the Commission may feel itself called upon to take within the framework of Regulation 19 do not appear to us in any event capable of resulting in the Commission taking a measure in relation to (your clients). Consequently, we do not find ourselves in a position to hold that the conditions for the application of E.E.C. 175, paragraph two are met."

In their Request to the Court the applicants had asked the Court to declare, *inter alia*, that the Commission had

"infringed E.E.C. 155 and article 7, paragraph 2, third sentence of Council Regulation 19 . . . in failing . . . in respect to the Federal Re-public of Germany to make use of the power conferred upon it by E.E.C. 169, in accordance with the obligations incumbent on the Commission as a result of E.E.C. 155 . . ."

In the event the action was not taken to a conclusion because it became known, during the proceedings, that by a letter dated 23rd April 1964 addressed to the Federal Republic of Germany, the Commission had set in motion the procedure laid down in E.E.C. 169.

Exception to E.E.C. 169 (and 170) in connection with Aids granted by Member States

Aids granted by States which distort or threaten to distort competition by favouring certain undertakings or the production of certain goods are, so far as they adversely affect trade between Member States, in general deemed to be incompatible with the Common Market (E.E.C. 92, *post*, p. 68). The Commission may under prescribed conditions, where it finds that aid granted by a State is not compatible with the Common Market "decide that the State concerned shall abolish or modify such aid within a time-limit to be prescribed by the Commission" (E.E.C. 93 (2), *post*, p. 69). "If the State concerned does not comply with this decision within the prescribed time-limit, the Commission or any other interested State may, notwithstanding the provisions of E.E.C. 169 and 170, refer the matter to the Court of Justice direct" (E.E.C. 93 (2), *post*, p. 69). The decision ("that the State concerned shall abolish or modify such aid within a time-limit") is, unlike an opinion, binding in every respect upon those to whom it is directed (E.E.C. 189). Thus a failure of the State concerned to carry out the decision will indubitably be considered by the Commission a "failure to fulfill any of its obligations under this Treaty" in the sense of E.E.C. 169

(*ante*, p. 63) but exceptionally, in the case of the decision by the Commission under E.E.C. 93 it does not ensue as a consequence that the Commission must "issue a reasoned opinion on the matter after giving the State concerned the opportunity to submit its comments" (E.E.C. 169, *ante*, p. 63). Instead, it "may . . . refer the matter to the Court of Justice direct" (E.E.C. 93 (2), *post*, p. 69).

E.E.C. 92

1. Except where otherwise provided for in this Treaty any aid granted by a Member State or through State resources in any form whatsoever which distorts or threatens to distort competition by favoring certain undertakings or the production of certain goods shall, in so far as it adversely affects trade between Member States, be deemed to be incompatible with the Common Market.

2. The following shall be compatible with the Common Market:

   (*a*) aid having a social character, granted to individual consumers, provided that such aid is granted without discrimination on the grounds of the origin of the products concerned;

   (*b*) aid intended to make good the damage caused by natural disasters or other extraordinary events;

   (*c*) aid granted to the economy of certain regions of the Federal Republic of Germany affected by the division of Germany, in so far as such aid is required so as to compensate for the economic disadvantages caused by that division.

3. The following may be deemed to be compatible with the Common Market:

   (*a*) aid intended to promote the economic development of regions where the standard of living is abnormally low or where there is serious under-employment;

   (*b*) aid intended to promote the execution of an important project of common European interest or to remedy serious disturbance in the economy of a Member State;

   (*c*) aid intended to facilitate the development of certain activities or of certain economic regions, provided that such aid does not adversely affect trading conditions to such an extent as would be contrary to the common interest. Any grants of aid to shipbuilding existing as on 1 January, 1957, shall, in so far as they serve only to offset the absence of customs protection, be progressively reduced under the same conditions as apply to the abolition of customs duties, subject to the provisions of this Treaty concerning common commercial policy in regard to third countries;

(*d*) such other types of aid as may be specified by the Council by qualified majority vote on a proposal of the Commission.

E.E.C. 93

1. The Commission shall, in conjunction with Member States submit to constant examination all systems of aids existing in those States. It shall propose to the latter any appropriate measures required by the progressive development or by the functioning of the Common Market.

2. If, after given notice to the parties concerned to submit their comments, the Commission find that aid granted by a State or through State resources is not compatible with the Common Market within the meaning of Article 92, or that such aid is being improperly used, it shall decide that the State concerned shall abolish or modify such aid within a time-limit to be prescribed by the Commission.

If the State concerned does not comply with this decision within the prescribed time-limit, the Commission or any other interested State may, notwithstanding the provisions of Articles 169 and 170, refer the matter to the Court of Justice direct.

The Council may, at the request of a Member State, unanimously decide, if such a decision is justified by exceptional circumstances, that any aid granted or planned by that State shall be deemed to be compatible with the Common Market, notwithstanding the provisions of Article 92 or the regulations provided for in Article 94. If the Commission had, as regards the grant of aid in question, already initiated the procedure provided for in the first sub-paragraph of this paragraph, the request made to the Council by the State concerned shall cause such procedure to be suspended until the Council has made its attitude known.

If, however, the Council has not made its attitude known within three months of the said request being made, the Commission shall give its decision on the case.

3. The Commission shall be informed, in sufficient time to enable it to submit its comments, of any plans to grant or modify grants of aid. If it considers that any such plan is incompatible with the Common Market within the meaning of Article 92 it shall without delay initiate the procedure provided for in the preceding paragraph. The Member State concerned shall not put its proposed measures into effect until this procedure has resulted in a final decision.

E.E.C. 225

If the measures taken under the conditions envisaged in Articles 223 and 224 have the effect of distorting conditions of competition in the Common Market, the Commission shall, jointly with the State concerned, investigate the conditions under which these measures may be adapted to the rules laid down by this Treaty.

Notwithstanding the procedure provided for in Articles 169 and 170, the Commission or any Member State may apply directly to the Court of Justice if it considers that another Member State is making an improper use of the powers provided for under Articles 223 and 224. The Court of Justice shall sit *in camera*.

"...The Commission or any Member State may apply directly ..." "Directly" ("*directement*"; "*unmittelbar*"; "*rechtstreeks*; "*direttamente*") is in point of time and "notwithstanding the procedure provided for" in Article 169 under which the Commission may not refer to the Court unless the Member State against which the claim is brought has not complied with the terms of the Commission's reasoned opinion "within the period laid down by the Commission", the latter not being entitled to issue the reasoned opinion until "after giving the State concerned the opportunity to submit its comments". (See "may refer the matter immediately" *post*, p. 71). The same considerations apply to a claim by a Member State under this article (see *post*, p. 74).

The consequences of a finding by the Court that a Member State has failed to fulfil an obligation under the Treaty. These are as follows:

E.E.C. 171

If the Court of Justice finds that a Member State has failed to fulfil any of its obligations under this Treaty, such State is bound to take the measures required for the implementation of the judgment of the Court.

Limitations on judgment. As to the limitations on the judgment that may be given by the Court where a Member State is a defendant see *post*, p. 78, under "Pleine jurisdiction".

B.   CLAIM BY E.A.E.C. COMMISSION

E.A.E.C. 141

[*Identical with E.E.C. 169, ante, p.* 63]

E.A.E.C. 38

The Commission shall make recommendations to Member States with regard to the level of radioactivity in the air, water or soil.

In urgent cases the Commission shall issue a directive in which it shall require the Member State concerned to take, within a period laid down by the Commission, all necessary measures to prevent the basic standards from being exceeded and to ensure compliance with regulations.

If the State in question does not comply with the Commission's directive within the period laid down, the Commission or any

Member State concerned may refer the matter immediately to the Court of Justice, notwithstanding the provisions of Articles 141 and 142.

"Recommendations". "Recommendations and opinions shall have no binding force" (E.A.E.C. 161).

"In urgent cases the Commission shall issue a directive ...". "Directives shall be binding, as to the result to be achieved, upon each Member State to which they are directed, while leaving to national authorities the choice of form and methods" (E.A.E.C. 161).

"... may refer the matter immediately ...". "Immediately" appears to be synonymous with "directly" in E.E.C. 225, *ante*, p. 69 (*cf.* E.A.E.C. 82, *infra*).

E.A.E.C. 82

Inspectors shall be recruited by the Commission. They shall be responsible for obtaining and verifying the accounting mentioned in Article 79. They shall report any infringement to the Commission.

The Commission may issue a directive in which it calls upon the Member State concerned to take, within a period of time laid down by the Commission, all necessary measures to put an end to the infringement which has been established; it shall inform the Council thereof.

If the Member State does not comply within the specified time with the Commission's directive, the Commission or any Member State concerned may, notwithstanding the provisions of Articles 141 and 142, refer the matter immediately to the Court of Justice.

"... may refer the matter immediately ..." *cf.* under E.A.E.C. 38, *supra*. For the consequences of a finding by the Court that a Member State has failed to fulfil an obligation under the Treaty, see the following

E.A.E.C. 143

[*Identical with E.E.C.* 171, ante, *p.* 70 (*see comment following E.E.C.* 171, ante, *p.* 70)].

C. Claim by Member State of E.C.S.C. Against A Decision of the High Authority that the State has Failed to Fulfil a Treaty Obligation

E.C.S.C. 88

If the High Authority considers that a State has failed to fulfil any of its obligations under this Treaty, it shall record the failure in a reasoned decision, after allowing the State in question an opportunity to present its views. It shall set the State in question a time limit within which to take steps to fulfil its obligation.

Such a State may have recourse to the plenary jurisdiction of the Court within two months of the decision being notified.

If the State has not taken steps to fulfil its obligation within the period set by the High Authority or, in the case of proceedings, if its application has been rejected, the High Authority may, if it receives a concurring opinion from the Council passed by a two-thirds majority:

(*a*) suspend the payment of sums which the High Authority may owe to the State in question under this Treaty;

(*b*) take measures or authorise the other Member States to take measures involving derogation from the provisions of Article 4, so as to correct the effects of the failure in question.

Proceedings may be brought by way of recourse to the Court's plenary jurisdiction against decisions taken under paragraphs (*a*) and (*b*) within two months of their notification.

If the above measures should prove ineffective, the High Authority shall refer the matter to the Council.

"... **Plenary jurisdiction** ...". For comment on this expression see *post*, p. 78 under "Full Jurisdiction" and "Pleine Juridiction".

Full jurisdiction, and claim for annulment. In *Gouvernement de la République Fédérale d'Allemagne* c. *Haute Autorité* (Case 3/59, R. Vol. VI(1) at pp. 145.7) Adv. Gen. Lagrange submitted:

"... Thus (to speak for the moment only of States) article 88 applies both to the creation by a State of a situation contrary to the treaty and to the refusal or failure on its part to carry out a decision of the High Authority, for it goes without saying that to refuse or fail to carry out a decision of the High Authority that is obligatory in nature constitutes for a State a failure 'to fulfil one of the obligations under the Treaty,' to use the language of article 88, that result not only from the principle laid down in article 14 which we have recalled but, in addition, from the terms of article 86 and of the undertaking assumed by the States in accepting this provision.

That said, it is very evident that the *nature of the failure* will be very different according to whether the concern is with the first or second case we have just distinguished: in the first case, in fact, it is the High Authority which must take the initiative in uncovering in the action of a State what it considers to be enfringement of the Treaty. If the State maintains its attitude it is because it considers, for its part, that it is not infringing the Treaty. The legal dispute which arises from this contradiction, if not resolved amicably, will be brought before the Court in accordance with the procedure of article 88, and it is through the recourse made possible by the second paragraph of this article that the Court will find itself called upon to adjudicate on the main issue, that is to say the question whether the action of the State is or is not compatible with the Treaty. Obviously, it was in considering cases of this sort that the authors of the Treaty resolved to institute a procedure giving to States the maximum of safeguards and, in particular, that of recourse to the full jurisdiction.

In the second case, on the other hand, the procedure under article 88 will be purely formal, since its only object will be a finding that the State has not complied with a decision, by hypothesis executory, of the High

Authority. In those circumstances it is evident that the claim under article 88 cannot go to the main issues, because that would imply reopening the question of the legality of the decision the non-observance of which is precisely the reason—and the only reason—of the failure. The recourse to the full jurisdiction can only relate to the *circumstances* of observance or of non-observance, which may very well raise certain difficulties. As to the legality of the decision, that can only be contested by the means afforded by the Treaty for the purpose, which is the claim for annulment under article 33. It was not thought necessary, here (in Article 33) to provide, specially for the benefit of the States, a recourse to the full jurisdiction, because, in that case, a decision of the High Authority has been made subject to all the surrounding safeguards: the common law of the Treaty applies, and you know how numerous, in the instant case, these formalities were—a commission of experts sitting for a number of years, consultations with Governments, local inquiries, etc. You also know to what limits can extend the control of legality that the Court exercises on the basis of article 33, and the safeguards which this control comprises, especially for the States, not restricted as to the grounds of claim in the same way as the undertakings . . .".

The obligation to give reasons, of E.C.S.C. 88. In *Groupement des Industries Sidérurgigues Luxembourgeoises* c. *Haute Autorité* (Consolidated Cases 7 and 9/54, R. Vol. II at p. 102) the Court stated:

". . . the obligation" (of article 88 to give reasons) "concerns the decision which, in the eyes of the applicant, the High Authority was obliged to take in respect of the Government of the Grand Duchy. Nothing in the text of article 88 makes it permissible to think that a similar obligation exists in respect of a refusal to take a decision by virtue of this article. Consequently, the lack of reasoning in the implicit negative decision does not constitute an infringement of the provisions of article 88 of the Treaty".

The High Authority's complete discretion in assessing a failure of a Member State. In *De Gezamenlijke Steenkolenmijnen in Limburg* c. *Haute Autorité* (*Case* 30/59 R. Vol. VII at p. 72) Adv. Gen. Lagrange submitted:

"It must not be forgotten that the finding of a failure [to observe a Treaty obligation] of a State is the object of a special provision of the Treaty, article 88, which presents two particularities. The first is the necessity of a prior formality: the State in question must have been put in a position to present its observations. The second is that the recourse to the Court made available to it against the decision comprising the finding of failure and affording it a given period of time to attend to the carrying out of its obligations, is an appeal to the full jurisdiction, which implies that the High Authority enjoys a complete discretion in assessing the existence of the failure; its powers, like those of the Court, thus extend beyond the sphere reserved to claims of annulment".

The High Authority may not, by virtue of E.C.S.C. 88, take decisions of approbation in respect of Member States. In *De Gezamenlijke Steinholenmijnen in Limburg* c. *Haute Autorité* (Case 17/57, R. Vol. V at p. 25) the Court stated:

". . . article 88 . . . does not make it possible for the High Authority to take decisions of approbation in respect of Member States but only decisions making findings of failures to fulfill obligations imposed by the Treaty . . .".

The High Authority may not exercise, by virtue of E.C.S.C. 88, a rule making competence parallel to the competence conferred by the general law of the Treaty. *In Gouvernement de la République Italienne c. Haute Autorité* (Case 20/59 R. Vol. VI (ii) at pp. 691–2) the Court stated:

"... neither the wording nor the general conception of article 88 permit the High Authority to make use of its provisions to exercise a rule making competence on a par with the competence conferred by the general law of the Treaty, which must be used in the forms in which it is made available by article 14; .... Indeed the terms of article 88 confer upon the High Authority only the power to find that a State has failed to observe an obligation imposed on it by the Treaty. This obligation must be the result, either of an imperative provision, or of a decision or recommendation antecedent to the application of this Article. The "reasoned decision" envisaged by article 88 paragraph 1 can only have as its object the finding of the failure, and can have no rule making effect of its own. To contend the contrary would be equivalent to holding that the High Authority possesses a rule making power extending beyond the general law of the Treaty, exercisable in respect only of the Member States. The reasoning required by article 88 paragraph 1 must justify the finding of a failure, and the time limit laid down in the paragraph is that within which there must be ensured the execution, not of an obligation created by the decision taken on the basis of this article, but of an obligation already in existence before the decision was taken. If it were possible to equiparate the "decision" contemplated by article 88 with a decision within the meaning of article 14, by which the High Authority executes the tasks entrusted to it, it would be difficult to explain why a rule laid down by virtue of article 88 should be a possible object of a recourse to the full jurisdiction permitting all grounds to be invoked, not only those that relate to the question of the legality, but also those that derive from all causes justifying a failure to comply with it, whereas decisions promulgated in the form laid down in article 14 would be subject to the rules and the restricted time-limits governing claims under article 33".

Relationship of E.C.S.C. 88 to other E.C.S.C. articles. See "Relationship of E.C.S.C. 33, 86 and 88," *post*, p. 114 and "Suspension of enforcement of administrative act," under E.C.S.C. 39, *post*, p. 159. An appeal based on article 88 has no suspensory effect (see *post*, p. 161).

D. CLAIM BY MEMBER STATE OF E.E.C.

E.E.C. 170

Any Member State which considers that another Member State has failed to fulfil any of its obligations under this Treaty may refer the matter to the Court of Justice.

Before a Member State institutes, against another Member State, proceedings relating to an alleged infringement of the obligations under this Treaty, it shall refer the matter to the Commission.

The Commission shall deliver a reasoned opinion after the States concerned have been given the opportunity both to submit their own cases and to reply to each other's cases (*de présenter contradictoirement leurs observations*) both orally and in writing.

If the Commission, within a period of three months from the date on which the matter was referred to it, has not given an opinion, the absence of such opinion shall not preclude reference to the Court of Justice.

"**...Any of its obligations...**". It is submitted that this article, though it does not altogether preclude determination of what such obligations may be, is primarily concerned with clear and accepted obligations and the question of fact to what extent a Member State has failed to carry them out. Where there is a dispute between Member States as to the object of the Treaty (hence, it may be, as to the legal obligations to which it gives rise) this may be submitted to the Community Court direct by a "special agreement" between the Member States concerned (see *post*, pp. 156 *et seq*.). That the present article is primarily concerned with the factual question of the effective carrying out of clear and accepted obligations is borne out by the requirement of a prior reference to the Commission for its reasoned opinion, the Commission being the fact finding body par excellence of the Community.

Exception to E.E.C. 170 in connection with Aid granted by Member States. Compliance with a decision of the Commission directed to it is an obligation on a Member State under the Treaty (by virtue of E.E.C. 189). Exceptionally, where such a decision is taken in respect of State Aid under E.E.C. 93, the failure of a State to comply with it does not entail the procedures of E.E.C. 170. "Any other interested State may (under E.E.C. 93) refer the matter to the Court of Justice direct". This means, in other words, that the requirements of E.E.C. 170 that "before a Member State institutes, against another Member State, proceedings relating to an alleged infringement of the obligations under this Treaty, it shall refer the matter to the Commission" which "shall deliver a reasoned opinion after the States concerned have been given the opportunity both to submit their own cases and to reply to each others' cases both orally and in writing" do not apply. (See *ante*, p. 67).

Disputes between Member States, and International Law. In relation to their rights and duties arising from Treaties to which they are parties, Sovereign States would normally be governed by international law, and would normally accept and expect that disputes between them should be determined by the International Court of Justice at The Hague. To the extent that the European Treaties themselves provide a method of settlement, however, recourse to the International Court is not possible in respect of those Treaties. This position is the result of *E.E.C.* 219 *and E.A.E.C.* 193 which are in identical terms: "Member States undertake not to submit a dispute concerning the interpretation or application of this Treaty", and, similarly, E.C.S.C. 87 (see, *ante*, pp. 57, 58).

In the settlement of disputes between Member States the European Court may, nevertheless, fall back upon international law, as a source of Community law. (See "Restrictive Interpretation of a Community Treaty," *infra*.)

Restrictive Interpretation of a Community Treaty.

In *Fédération Charbonniére de Belgique* c. *Haute Autorité* (Case 8/55 R. Vol. II, p. 199 et seq) the Court was confronted with the argument that the E.C.S.C. Treaty being an international Treaty the Court must follow the method of restrictive interpretation that allegedly always prevails where international

treaties are concerned. On that point, Adv. Gen. Lagrange submitted
(*loc. cit.*, at pp. 263–264):

"On this . . . point, we shall not address you at length. No doubt one
might remind you that our Court is not an international court, but that
of a Community created by six States to a pattern approaching much
more that of a federal than an international organisation, and that the
Treaty the application of which it is the Court's mission to ensure, though
it was indeed concluded in the form of international treaties, and is
incontestably such a treaty, none the less constitutes, from the material
point of view, the charter of the Community, the rules of law that derive
from it forming *the internal law of that Community*. As for the *sources* of that
law, there is no reason why they should not be sought, if need be, in
international law, but normally, and most frequently, they will be found
in the internal law of the various Member States. The claimants themselves indeed followed this course in the present action in respect, for
example, of the notion of *détournement de pouvoir*, where it transpired that
the national laws constitute an infinitely richer source than the really
somewhat summary theory of "abuse of power".

But it seems to us pointless to enter upon a doctrinal discussion on this
point, since, whether international treaties or internal laws are concerned,
a commonly accepted principle to which we have already referred is that
there is no place for interpretation and for an inquiry into the presumed
intention of the authors of the text except in case of obscurity or ambiguity,
and that the literal wording, when it is formal, must always prevail.
Though being by no means a specialist in international law—so that it is
with modesty and great reserve that we venture on this field—it is our
impression that there do not exist in fact two different doctrines for the
interpretation of the wording of internal laws and international treaties,
but that *in fact*, international courts tend to be more timid about departing
from the literal interpretation than do the national courts, which is easily
explainable. Indeed, on the one hand, the common will (the common
intention of the parties) which must be the basis for the interpretation of
a contractual act, is usually difficult to establish with certainty for acts
such as international agreements which are usually the result of more or
less laborious compromise, and where the obscurity or the lack of precision
in the drafting often merely conceal basic disagreements. On the other
hand, what are called the general principles of law are necessarily much
vaguer when they must be sought in a universal setting than when recourse
may be had to traditional thinking followed in a single country.

Thus, we are fully in agreement as to the method of interpretation".

"Travaux Préparatoires" *and the interpretation of a Community*
Treaty. In *Fédération Charbonniére de Belgique* c. *Haute Autorité* (Case 8/55,
R. Vol. II at p. 254) Adv. Gen. Lagrange submitted:

"We cannot leave unanswered the remarks made by one of the eminent
advocates of the claimants concerning the passage in the explanatory note
accompanying the Luxembourg law ratifying the treaty. It is quite true
that the explanatory note accompanying a law, or, more exactly, a Bill,
like the other documents it is customary to list under the heading of
"*travaux préparatoires*", has no binding force for the interpretation of the
text and can never, in particular, be set up against the text itself, when
this is clear and unambiguous. But it is universally admitted that judges
may have recourse to it for the purpose of informing themselves, and draw
from it such elements as make it possible, should the need arise, to
illuminate the intendment of the legislator. It is beyond question that to
do this the judges are completely free in their appreciation. No doubt,

when one is concerned with a Treaty, documents emanating from an internal source [that is, originating in a single State, *author*] relating to the ratification procedure can never be strictly relevent to anything other than the intendment or the conception of one of the signatory governments. But nevertheless one must not presume that in presenting the Treaty to its parliament for ratification, a government could allow itself to express an opinion which it knew not to be shared by the governments of the other signatory states, and which was not, at least in the belief of that government, the reflection of their common agreement. As far as the Treaty of 18th April 1951 is concerned, the "*travaux prépara- toires* of the treaty itself are practically inexistent—or secret (which comes to the same thing); the explanatory memoranda emanating from national sources thus have, by virtue of that fact, a greater importance, and this is all the more true because some degree of co-ordination of these explanatory memoranda took place in order to prevent contradictions between them— which would have been most harmful."

In its judgement in the above case, the Court stated:

"In our opinion it is permissible, without fully embracing an extensive interpretation, to apply a rule of interpretation generally accepted both in international and in national (domestic) law and according to which the norms established by an international treaty or by a law imply the norms without which the Treaty or the law would be without meaning and would not permit of a reasonable and useful interpretation."

The judgement from which this passage is taken concerned an E.C.S.C. case, but there is no reason to suppose the Court would think differently in a case concerning E.E.C. or E.A.E.C.

E.E.C. 225

[For text and comment, see ante, *p.* 69.]

E. Claim by Member State of E.A.E.C.

E.A.E.C. 142

[Identical with E.E.C. 170, *printed on* ante, *p.* 74.]

E.A.E.C. 38

[Printed on ante, *p.* 70.]

"...The Member State concerned...". The meaning of "con- cerned" has not been judicially determined. Comparison may be made concerning them, under E.C.S.C. 33, *post*, p. 89.

A Member State concerned may, alternatively to the Commission, refer immediately to the Court the matter in respect of which another Member State has not complied with the Commission's directive within the period laid down by the latter. (For further comment on E.A.E.C. 38, see under "Claim by E.A.E.C. Commission," *ante*, p. 71).

E.A.E.C. 82

[Printed on ante, *p.* 71.]

F. Claim by Member State of E.C.S.C.

E.C.S.C. 89 paragraph 1

Any dispute between Member States as to the implementation of this Treaty, which cannot be settled by another procedure provided for in this Treaty, may be submitted to the Court on application from one of the States which are parties to the dispute.

"As to the implementation of this Treaty". (*"au sujet de l'application du présent Traité"*) is wider than a claim on the basis "that another Member State has failed to fulfil any of its obligations under this Treaty" of E.E.C. 170 and E.A.E.C. 142, and would clearly embrace the latter. Since "application" necessarily depends upon "interpretation" E.C.S.C. 89 paragraph 1 can serve the purpose not only of E.E.C. 170 and E.A.E.C. 142, but of the provisions of the later Treaties for Preliminary Rulings by the Court for the interpretation of the Treaties, for which E.C.S.C. otherwise has no equivalent. (See *post*, pp. 130 *et seq.*).

G. CLAIM BY BOARD OF DIRECTORS OF THE EUROPEAN INVESTMENT BANK

E.E.C. 180

The Court of Justice shall be competent within the limits hereinafter set out to hear disputes concerning:

(*a*) The fulfilment by Member States of the obligations arising under the Statute of the European Investment Bank. The Board of Directors of the Bank shall, in this respect, enjoy the powers conferred upon the Commission by Article 169;

(*b*) [*Printed on* post, *p.* 152.]

(*c*) [*Printed on* post, *p.* 153.]

(For text of E.E.C. 169, see *ante*, p. 63).

II. REVIEW OF PENALTY OR FINE

E.E.C. 172

The regulations enacted by the Council pursuant to the provisions of this Treaty may confer on the Court of Justice full jurisdiction as to the merits (*compétence de pleine juridiction*) in regard to the penalties provided for in these regulations.

"Full jurisdiction". (*"Compétence de pleine juridiction"*; *". . . eine Zuständigkeit . . ., welche die Befugnis zu unbeschränkter Ermessensnachprüfung und zur Änderung oder Verhängung solcher Maßnahmen umfaszt"*, *". . . volledige rechtsmacht . . ."* *"una competénza guirisdizionale anche di merito . . ."*) *"Pleine juridiction"* is a term of art in French administrative law, which provided the main inspiration for the principles of the judicial control, laid down in the Treaty, of the acts of the executive authority which it brought into being. On the question of the inspiration drawn from French law and the interpretative reliance to be placed upon this source see under "Acts of the High Authority, E.C.S.C. 33," *post*, pp. 91, 96, 98; also *ante*, p. 76.

"Pleine juridiction". *"Pleine juridiction"* is distinguished in French administrative law from the more limited "jurisdiction to annul" an administrative act (as to which see under "Acts of the Council or Commission" E.E.C. 173 and E.A.E.C. 146, *post*, pp. 83 *et seq.*). In France, as elsewhere in the original six Member States, all administrative causes must be subject to either one or the other. Similarly, much of the work of the European Court is in respect of one or other of these two general types of jurisdiction, but it exercises others, among which, as far as E.E.C. and E.A.E.C. are concerned, the jurisdiction to interpret the Treaties and other instruments is probably the most important, (see "Preliminary Ruling", E.E.C. 177 and E.A.E.C. 150, *post*, pp. 130 *et seq.*) together with its jurisdiction in E.E.C. or E.A.E.C. to find that a Member State has failed to fulfil a Treaty obligation (see *ante*, p. 62) which finding is by virtue neither of jurisdiction to interpret or annul, nor of "full jurisdiction".

What is implicit in the expression *"pleine juridiction"* in French (or Belgian) law is made clear, in the Italian, by the use of the words *"anche di merito"* (not altogether happily rendered by "as to the merits") and, in the German, by the careful, if somewhat lengthy, paraphrase used in the article (reproduced in the preceding comment). This indicates that an unlimited discretion to review the penalty or fine is conferred on the Court, together with the power to alter or suspend it.

"Full jurisdiction" thus comports a power of adjudicating fully *inter partes*.

Two types of application. "The two types of application, (in) annulment and full jurisdiction, do not stand in clear contrast the one to the other, rather do they present differences of degree. One may apply the well known adage: 'Who can do the greater can do the lesser'. Moreover, it frequently happens that the annulment of an administrative act may be applied for and ordered in a submission to full jurisdiction. We have already mentioned an example which results from the Treaty: a prior administrative decision may be annulled within the framework of an application which puts in issue the liability of the Community. We would refer, in French Law, to de Laubadère, *Traité théorique et pratique des contrats administratifs*, 1956, vol. II p. 196: 'The judge of the contract is free in principle to annul the measures taken by the administration contrary to its contractual undertakings'; he gives other examples from the case-law of the Conseil d'Etat. Lastly, we would refer to the statutes of international administrative tribunals and cite, for example, article 9 of the Statutes of the Administrative Tribunal of the United Nations, in respect of disputes of personnel: 'If it finds the application well-founded, the Tribunal shall order the annulment of the challenged decision or the execution of the obligation which is invoked'."

(*Per* Adv. Gen. Roemer in *M. René Bourgaux* c. *Assemblée Commune de la C.E.C.A.*, Case, 1–56, R. vol. II at p. 451).

The conferment by a Regulation of the E.E.C. Council of full jurisdiction upon the Court. E.E.C. Council Regulation 17, Article 17 provides:

"The Court of Justice shall have full jurisdiction within the meaning of Article 172 of the Treaty to adjudicate on proceedings instituted against the decisions by which the Commission has fixed a fine or a penalty; it may cancel, reduce or increase the fine or the penalty imposed" (unofficial translation).

(See Chapter 1, *ante*, p. 22, the comment on Reg. 17. Art. 9).

Similarly, by Article 25 of E.E.C. Council Regulation No. 11 concerning the removal of price discrimination and discrimination in transport conditions, the Court has "full jurisdiction" in application of E.E.C. 172 regarding any penalty or fine imposed under Articles 17 and 18 of Regulation No. 11.

E.C.S.C. 36

Before imposing a monetary penalty or ordering a periodic penalty payment as provided for in this Treaty, the High Authority must give the party concerned an opportunity to comment.

Against monetary penalties and periodic penalty payments imposed under the provisions of this Treaty, recourse may be had to the plenary jurisdiction of the Court.

In support of such recourse and under the terms of the first paragraph of Article 33 of this Treaty, applicants may contest the legality of the decisions and recommendations which they are alleged to have contravened.

"... **The party concerned ...**". In its applicability to private parties E.C.S.C. 36 is not in terms restricted as is E.C.S.C. 33 (which see under "Legality of Acts," *post*, p. 89) to undertakings (Fr. *"entreprises"*) as defined by E.C.S.C. 80, or association of undertakings, but it would seem probable that "the party concerned" must be a party upon whom the High Authority has the power of directly imposing a sanction. See the comment "Persons subjected to the penalities laid down in E.C.S.C. 66 (6)", *post*, p. 113.

"... **Plenary jurisdiction ...**". See "full jurisdiction", *ante*, p. 78.

"... **Contest the legality of the decisions and recommendations ...**". "Regularity", rather than "legality" would have been a more accurate translation, though the original authentic French in using *"irrégularité"* clearly envisages irregularity as going to illegality. (The German and Italian translations, *"sind fehlerhaft"* and *"irregolarità"*, similarly skirt round direct mention of illegality, but not the Netherlands' which uses *"onrechtmatigheid"*).

In contesting the legality of a decision or recommendation as provided for in E.C.S.C. 36 an applicant is enabled to do so "under the terms of the first paragraph of Article 33" on the basis of any of the four grounds available under E.C.S.C. 33 (see *post*, p. 89) without the time-limit of two months from the making of the decision or recommendation, laid down in E.C.S.C. 33 for the bringing of a claim against them, having any application. This exception from the time-limit rule of E.C.S.C. 33 in the case of E.C.S.C. 36 is known as the "exception of illegality" (for the main treatment of which in respect of E.C.S.C. 33, see *post*, pp. 110 *et seq.*).

The exception of illegality may be invoked only against rule-making decisions, regulations. In *Gouvernement de la République d'Allemagne* c. *Haute Autorité* (Case 3/59). R. Vol. VI (i) at p. 147) Adv. Gen. Lagrange submitted:

"... The applicant wrongly invokes the case law of the Court that relates to the exception of illegality; this exception can in fact only be invoked as against rule making decisions, regulations, adopted by way of application of the Treaty, disregard of which is tantamount to a disregard of the provisions of the Treaty itself and in respect of which it is possible that the legal interest in invoking their illegality does not arise until the moment arrives to put them into application. Now, in the present case, we are confronted with an individual decision concerning one particular Government and applying, to a certain number of concrete cases, rules laid down in the Treaty; this (decision) is a refusal of authorization which has not the slightest rule making character. All your decisions are in this sense . . . ".

In the same case, the court stated (*loc. cit. supra* at p. 134):

". . . if even article 36 does not permit the re-opening of the inquiry into the legality of an individual decision of the High Authority, the time-limit for the bringing of an action having expired, *a fortiori* it is not possible to hold, the text being silent on the matter, that it is allowed by article 88".

"Preliminary character" of the procedure under E.C.S.C. 36. In *Acciaierie Ferriere e Fonderie di Modena* c. *Haute Autorité* (Case 16/61, R. Vol. VIII at p. 575) the Court stated:

". . . It is not desirable to reject this legal argument for the reason that it was not presented when the matter was still being handled in the administrative sphere, as the High Authority proposes. Such an exclusion, incidentally incompatible with the purely preliminary character of the procedure laid down in article 36, would unduly restrict the applicant's rights in the action . . ."

Under E.C.S.C. 36 revision of an (administrative) decision (whether annulled or not) may be made by the Court. In *Acciaierie Laminatori Magliano Alpi (A.L.M.A.)* c. *Haute Autorité* (Case 8/56, R. Vol. III at p. 191) a fine of 800,000 lire had been imposed by the High Authority on the applicant. Though the Court held that this was in breach neither of article 64 nor of article 36 it declared as follows:

"*C. Amount of the fine.* The Court has examined the question whether there is justification for reducing the amount of the fine. The Court realizes that it is exercising its jurisdiction where the appeal is to its 'full jurisdiction' (article 36 second paragraph) so that in consequence it is invested with the power not only to annul but also to recast the decision taken. Although the applicant has made no formal submissions in that sense, the Court takes the view, as does the Advocate General, that the passage in the Request drawing attention to the modest circumstances of the applicant may be interpreted as a submission, made incidentally, that a reduction should be made. Moreover, even in the absence of formal submissions, the Court would be entitled to reduce the amount of an excessive fine, since such would not go beyond the bounds of the petition, but, quite to the contrary, would amount to partial admission of the claim in the Request. . . ."

E.A.E.C. 144

The Court of Justice shall exercise full jurisdiction as to the merits (*compétence de pleine juridiction*) with regard to:

(*a*) proceedings instituted in accordance with Article 12 to determine the appropriate conditions for the granting by the Commission of licences or sub-licences;

(*b*) appeals instituted by persons or undertakings against penalties imposed on them by the Commission in accordance with Article 83.

"Full jurisdiction" see under E.E.C. 172, *ante*, p. 78.
Article 12: The text is as follows:

"On addressing a request to the Commission, Member States, persons or undertakings shall be entitled to obtain non-exclusive licences pertaining to patents, provisionally protected patent rights, petty patents (*modèles d'utilité*) or patent applications owned by the Community, to the extent that they are able to make effective use of the inventions to which they relate.

On the same conditions, the Commission shall grant sub-licences pertaining to patents, provisionally protected patent rights, petty patents or patent applications, where the Community holds contractual licences conferring this power.

The Commission shall grant these licences or sub-licences on conditions to be agreed with the licensees and shall furnish all the information required for their use. These conditions shall be concerned in particular with a suitable payment and, where appropriate, the right of the licensee to grant sub-licenses to third parties as well as the obligation to treat the information as a trade secret (*secret de fabrique*).

If no agreement is reached on the conditions referred to in paragraph 3, the licensees may refer the matter to the Court of Justice so that appropriate conditions may be determined".

Article 83. The text is as follows:

"1. In the event of an infringement on the part of persons or undertakings of the obligations imposed by this Chapter the Commission may impose sanctions upon them.

These sanctions shall be, in order of severity:

(*a*) a warning;

(*b*) the withdrawal of special privileges such as financial or technical assistance;

(*c*) the placing of the undertaking for a maximum period of four months under the administration of a person or board appointed by mutual agreement between the Commission and the State having jurisdiction over the undertakings;

(*d*) the total or partial withdrawal of source material or special fissile material.

2. Decisions of the Commission, requiring the delivery of material, taken in implementation of the provisions of the preceding paragraph, shall have the enforceability of a Court Judgment (*forment titre exécutoire*). They may be enforced in the territories of Member States in accordance with the provisions laid down in Article 164.

Notwithstanding the provisions of Article 157, appeals brought before the Court of Justice against decisions of the Commission which impose any of the sanctions provided for in the preceding paragraph shall suspend operation of the Act in question. The Court of Justice may, however, at the request of the Commission or of any Member State concerned, order the immediate implementation of the decision.

The protection of injured interests shall be ensured by an appropriate legal procedure.

3. The Commission may make any recommendation to Member States concerning laws and orders designed to ensure that obligations arising under this Chapter are observed in their territories.

4. Member States shall be bound to ensure that sanctions are put into effect and, where necessary, that the parties responsible remedy any infringement".

E.A.E.C. 145

If the Commission considers that a person or undertaking has committed an infringement of this Treaty to which the provisions of Article 83 do not apply, it shall call upon the Member State having jurisdiction over that person or undertaking to cause penalties to be imposed in respect of such infringement in accordance with its domestic legislation.

If the State concerned does not comply with such a request within the period laid down by the Commission, the latter may refer the matter to the Court of Justice in order to have the existence of the infringement of which the person or undertaking concerned is accused put on record.

"... **to which the provisions of Article 83 do not apply. ...**". For the text of Article 83 see *ante*, p. 82.

III. LEGALITY OF ACTS (OF AN ADMINISTRATIVE OR EXECUTIVE BODY)

La légalité des actes; Rechtmäszigkeit des Handelns"; "wettigheid"; "legittimità (degli) atti"). Acts, other than recommendations or opinions, of the Council or Commission of either E.E.C. or E.A.E.C. may be challenged as to their legality by a Member State, the Council, the Commission, or by "any natural or legal person". Decisions of the Board of Governors of the European Investment Bank may be challenged in the same way by Member States, by the Commission or by the Board of Directors. Decisions of the Board of Directors may also be challenged in the same way by Member States or the Commission in certain defined cases. (See *post*, p. 153). Acts of the High Authority of E.C.S.C., namely decisions and recommendations, may be challenged by a Member State, the E.C.S.C. Council or by "undertakings" (Fr. "*enterprises*") or associations of undertakings. The Court has "jurisdiction to annul" such acts as it finds illegal. (For the distinction between this jurisdiction and "full jurisdiction" see the comment on E.E.C. 172, *ante*, p. 78). As to the effect of a declaration by the Court that an act is null and void see "consequences of Annulment", *post*, pp. 89 and 116.

Experience of this type of appeal under the E.C.S.C. Treaty, which has been responsible for by far the largest part of its case law, led to some modifications to the relevant principles in the later E.E.C. and E.A.E.C. Treaties (in particular the omission in the later treaties of the limitations in the E.C.S.C. Treaty upon the Court's power to "evaluate the situation resulting from economic facts and circumstances in the light of which the decisions were taken"). But the principles governing the jurisdiction to annul are substantially similar in all three treaties and it is to be expected that the Court will have regard to the case law developed under the E.C.S.C. Treaty in applying the comparable provisions of the E.E.C. and E.A.E.C. Treaties.

Other than as a result of a direct application for annulment, which is the subject of this section, the Court may also rule on the validity of Community acts by way of preliminary ruling, on a reference from a domestic tribunal of a Member State. (See "Preliminary Ruling", *post*, p. 130).

A. ACTS OF THE COUNCIL OR COMMISSION OF E.E.C. OR E.A.E.C.

E.E.C. 173

Supervision of the legality of the acts of the Council and the Commission other than recommendations or opinions shall be a matter for the Court of Justice. The Court shall for this purpose have jurisdiction in proceedings instituted by a Member State, the Council or the Commission on the grounds of lack of jurisdiction, substantial violations of basic procedural rules, infringements of this Treaty or of any rule of law relating to effect being given to it or of misuse of powers (*détournement de pouvoir*).

Any natural or legal person may, under the same conditions, appeal against a decision directed to him or against a decision which, although in the form of a regulation or a decision directed to another person, is of direct and individual concern to him.

E.A.E.C. 146

[*Identical, in the authentic languages of the Communities, with E.E.C. 173, supra.*]

"... acts ... other than recommendations or opinions ...". That is, regulations, directives and decisions, which are the acts which have binding force, whereas recommendations and opinions have not (see E.E.C. 189 and E.A.E.C. 161 which are identical). Decisions of the Board of Governors or the Board of Directors of the European Investment Bank are comprised within the category of acts which have binding force (see this *Chapter, Section IX, post,* pp. 152 *et seq.*).

Grounds for proceedings. "... proceedings instituted ... on the grounds of lack of powers, violations of basic procedural rules, infringement of the Treaty or of any rule of law relating to its implementation, or misuse of powers** (*détournement de pouvoir*)". For comment on these four grounds for the institution of proceedings, see under "Acts of the High Authority, E.C.S.C. 33", *post,* pp. 93 *et seq.*).

"Any natural or legal person may, under the same conditions, appeal ...". The category of persons entitled to apply to the Court by virtue of this provision appears not to be limited to such as are nationals of one of the Member States, nor even to such as in a wider sense (residence, mere presence, etc.) are within the jurisdiction of a Member State. It appears to embrace all persons within the Community nexus as defined in Chapter 1 (*ante,* pp. 15 and 36).

The English translation, of the E.A.E.C. but not of the E.E.C. Treaty, includes after "natural or legal person" the French "*personne physique ou morale*" of which it is the rendering. This wide category of private parties entitled to institute proceedings at the Court is in contrast with the relatively narrow class of undertakings (Fr.–"*enterprises*") or associations of undertakings which are similarly entitled under the E.C.S.C. Treaty (see under "Acts of the High Authority E.C.S.C. 33," *post,* p. 91). The reason for this is the far wider and more generalized economic ambit of the later Treaties, that of E.E.C. in particular.

Comparison of E.E.C. 173 with E.C.S.C. 33 as regards natural and legal persons. In *Confédération nationale des producteurs de fruits et légumes et autres c. Conseil de la C.É.E.* (Consolidated Cases 16 and 17/62 R. Vol. VIII at pp. 917–9) the Court stated:

"1. According to the terms of article 173, paragraph 2, natural or legal persons cannot make a claim to the Court against an act of the Commission or Council unless this act represents either a decision directed to them or a decision which, although in the form of a regulation or a decision directed to another person, is of direct and individual concern to them. It follows that such persons are not qualified to bring an action for annulment of regulations issued by the Council or by the Commission.

The Court agrees that the regime thus instituted by the Treaties of Rome lays down conditions, for the admissibility of actions for annulment by private parties, that are more restrictive than the E.C.S.C. Treaty. It is not, however, for the Court to express an opinion as to the merits of this regime, which regime is clearly apparent from the text under examination. In particular the Court could not adopt the interpretation proposed by one of the applicants in the course of the oral procedure, according to which the expression "decision" employed in paragraph two of article 173 would also cover regulations. This extensive interpretation encounters the difficulty that article 189 draws a clear distinction between the respective notions of "decision" and "regulation". It is inconceivable that the expression "decision" could be employed in article 173 in a meaning different from the technical meaning of article 189.

The result of the preceding considerations is that the claims must be rejected as inadmissable if the act it is sought to upset constitutes a regulation. In examining this question the Court must consider not only the official designation of the act but must take account in the first place of its object and of its content.

2. By virtue of the provisions of E.E.C. 189 the regulation has a general ambit and is directly applicable in every Member State, whereas a decision is only mandatory as regards the persons to whom it is expressly destined and whom it designates. The criterion of the distinction must be whether the act in question has a general "ambit" or not. The essential features of a decision are the result of the limitation of the persons to whom it is directed and addressed, whereas the regulation, essentially rule-making in character, is applicable not to the person or persons designated or identifiable, to whom it is directed, but to categories conceived of in the abstract and taken as a whole. Thus, in order to determine in doubtful cases whether one is confronted by a decision or a regulation it is necessary to examine whether the act in question is of individual concern to specified persons. In these circumstances, if an act described by its author as a regulation contains provisions which are of a nature to concern certain natural or legal persons in a manner that is not only direct but also individual, it must be admitted that in any event, and without prejudice to the question whether this act considered in its entirety may justly be described as a regulation, its provisions do not have a rule—making character and may thus be challenged by such persons by virtue of article 173, paragraph 2.

3. In the present case the act in question was described by its author as a "regulation". However, the applicants contend that the provision sought to be upset has in reality the character of a "decision taken with the appearance of a regulation". No doubt it is possible that a decision can also have a very wide sphere of application. However, one could not regard as a decision an act applicable to situations objectively determined and having immediate legal consequences, in all the Member States, in respect of categories of persons envisaged in a general and abstract manner, unless it is proved that it is of individual conern to certain persons in the meaning of article 173, paragraph 2.

In the present case the provision it is sought to upset involves immediate legal effects, in all the Member States, in respect of categories of persons envisaged in a general and abstract manner. In fact, article 9 of the said provisions—particularly the subject of the present case—annuls, for certain products and within certain periods, the quantitative restrictions on import and measures of equivalent effect. It requires, moreover, the renunciation on the part of Member States of the application of the provisions of E.E.C. 44, that is to say in particular the right to suspend or temporarily reduce imports. Consequently the said article eliminates the restrictions on the freedom of economic operators to export or import within the Community. It remains to examine whether the provision sought to be upset is of individual concern to the applicants.

Though this provision, in requiring the States to bring to an end or to renounce the various measures capable of favouring agricultural producers, by that very fact affects their interests and those of the members of the applicant associations, it must be realised that the said provision is the concern of these members in the same way as it is the concern of all agricultural producers in the Community. Furthermore, it is not possible to accept the principle according to which an association, as representing a category of entrepreneurs, is individually concerned by an act affecting the general interests of that category. This principle, having as a result the concentration upon one person subject to law of the interests pertaining to the members of a category who are affected as such by what are in truth regulations, would injure the system of the Treaty, which does not admit the claim of private parties for annulment except in respect of decisions which affect them because it is to them the decisions are directed, or against acts which affect them in a similar manner. In these circumstances, it cannot be admitted that the provision in dispute is of individual concern to the applicants.

From the foregoing it follows that the defendant was perfectly right in describing the aforesaid provision as a regulation. The objection of inadmissibility is therefore to be allowed . . .''.

Distinction of principle between E.E.C. 173 and E.C.S.C. 33. In *Eva von Lachmüller etc.* c. *Commission C.E.E.* (Consolidated Cases 43, 45 and 48/59, R. Vol. VI (ii) at p. 987) the President of the Court, in his order, stated:

"The defendant has raised the question whether the Court has jurisdiction to rule on disputes between the Community and its servants, inasmuch as the Statute provided for in E.E.C. 179 is not as yet promulgated. This question being one of public policy [*"ordre public"*; the German text of R. here uses the French expression *"ordre public"*; *"openbore orde"*; *"questione di portata generale"*] it is necessary to determine it at the outset. Unlike the provisions of the E.C.S.C. Treaty, article 173 of E.E.C., which is concerned with claims for annulment, is drafted in such a fashion that it also applies to servants (of the Community) and confers on them the right to take action against decisions of concern to them. In these circumstances it is not possible to interpret article 179 in any way other than as empowering the drafters of the Statute to limit or extend the conditions that are in general laid down for recourse to the Court, such as for example, time limits for the various steps in the proceedings, the conferring of the right, in specific circumstances, of recourse to the full jurisdiction, etc. . . .''

Decisions of the E.E.C. Commission under Article 9 or Article 11(5) of Regulation 17 of the Council. These may be challenged as to their legality on the basis of E.E.C. 173.

"Decision . . . in the form of a regulation". The distinction between "individual decision" and "general decision" of E.C.S.C. 33 (see comment under "Acts of the High Authority," *post*, pp. 106 *et seq.*) which had occasioned difficulties of interpretation has been abandoned in the later Treaties.

"...Is of direct and individual concern to him". In *Plaumann &
Co. c. Commission C.E.E.* (Case 25/62, R. Vol. IX p. 196 at p. 223) the Court
stated:

"No person other than those to whom a decision is addressed can
establish that it is of individual concern to him unless the decision touches
him either because of certain characteristics which are special and
particular to him, or because of special circumstances differentiating him
from all other persons, which single him out individually in an analogous
way to the person to whom the decision is in fact addressed."
(Re-iterated verbatim in *S.A. Glucoseries Réunies c. Commission C.E.E.*,
Case 1/64).

"...Within a period of two months...". Notwithstanding the
expiry of this period, where a regulation made by the Council or Commission
(of E.E.C. or E.A.E.C.) is the subject of legal proceedings, any of the parties
concerned may invoke the grounds set out in E.E.C. 173, paragraph 1 (or,
identically, in E.A.E.C. 146, paragraph 1) in order to submit that the
regulation in question does not apply. This exception to the principle of the
limitation of time in which an action to annul an administrative act must be
brought is provided for in identical terms by E.E.C. 184 and E.A.E.C. 156:
"Where a regulation made by the Council or the Commission is the
subject of legal proceedings, any of the parties concerned may, notwithstanding the expiry of the period laid down in E.E.C. 173(3), invoke the
grounds set out in E.E.C. 173(1), in order to submit to the Court of
Justice that the regulation in question does not apply."
This exception is known as the "exception of illegality" (*"exception d'illégalité"*).

The exception of illegality (*"exception d'illégalité"*). The exception
whereby E.E.C. 173, paragraph 1 or E.A.E.C. 146, paragraph 1 may be
invoked outside the time limit occurs in circumstances where proceedings
are brought before the Court to establish that a measure (such as the im-
position of a fine) taken by virtue of a Regulation should not be enforced.
In support of his case the claimant may contest the legality of the Regulation
on the grounds upon which it could have been annulled under E.E.C. 173
(or E.A.E.C. 146) had it been legally permissible to make the attempt
within the time limit of two months. A successful action on this basis does
not have the result of formally annulling the Regulation, but it may well
happen in practice that in order to avoid similar actions being brought
against it the Community Institution may proceed to a new administrative
act free from the taint of illegality.
The "exception of illegality" as embodied in E.E.C. 184 and E.A.E.C. 156
represents the more developed form to which the Court had brought it by
its judgments enlarging the narrower concept of E.C.S.C. 36 (as to which see
ante, pp. 8 and 80. See also *post*, pp. 110 *et seq*. For the text of E.E.C. 184
(and E.A.E.C. 165) see *supra*.

**E.E.C. 184 does not make possible an action similar to that of
E.E.C. 173.** In *Milchwerke Heinz Wöhremann & Sohn KG etc. c. Commission
C.E.E.* (Consolidated Cases 31 and 33/62, R. Vol. VIII at pp. 978–979)
the Court stated:
"The applicants, basing their action on E.E.C. 184, deduce from this
article, as far as jurisdiction is concerned, the right to bring an action
before the Court for a declaration that article 3 of the decision of the
Commission dated 15 March 1961 and the decision of the Commission of
13th December 1961 are null and void or inapplicable.

Before going into the question whether the acts it is sought to upset are, by their nature, decisions or regulations, it is desirable to make certain whether E.E.C. 184 empowers the Court to pronounce on the inapplicability of a regulation when its inapplicability, as in the present case, is relied upon before a tribunal of a Member State.

E.E.C. 184 allows any party, notwithstanding the expiry of the time limit laid down in E.E.C. 173 paragraph 3, for the bringing of a claim for annulment, to set up before the Court the inapplicability of a regulation on the occasion of a lawsuit the result of which depends on its applicability and to avail himself for that purpose of the grounds provided for in article 173, paragraph 1.

From the fact that article 184 does not specify before which judicial authority an action must be brought when the issue depends on the applicability of a regulation, the applicants draw the conclusion that the inapplicability of such regulation may in any event be set up before this Court. Thus there is made possible a means of action parallel to that of E.E.C. 173.

Such is not, however, the ambit and effect of E.E.C. 184. It is clear from its wording and content that it is only concerned with the declaration of inapplicability of a regulation—declaration made incidentally with limited effect—in proceedings before the Court brought on the basis of some other provision of the Treaty. It is apparent, in particular from the reference to and adoption of the time-limits of E.E.C. 173, that it only applies within the framework of proceedings before the Court and that it does not open up the possibility of eluding the time-limits laid down in this provision. The sole purpose of E.E.C. 184 is to protect a party against the application of an illegal regulation, without the regulation itself becoming thereby capable of being upset, since the expiry of the time-limit of E.E.C. 173 has put it beyond the reach of legal action before the Court.

It must be stressed that the respective jurisdiction of the Court and that of the tribunals of Member States are clearly defined by the Treaty. Indeed, both E.E.C. 177 and E.E.C. St. 20 provide that it is the tribunal of a Member State which decides to stay proceedings and refer to the Court. If the parties to an action before a tribunal of a Member State could themselves apply directly to the Court for a preliminary ruling, they would be in a position to compel the judge of the national tribunal to stay proceedings pending the decision of this Court. Neither the Treaty nor the Protocol on the Statute of the Court make provision for such limitation of the powers of the national judge.

Whereas, therefore, E.E.C. 184 does not afford a sufficient basis to enable the Court to determine the dispute in its present state, E.E.C. 177 can, on the other hand, enable it to give a ruling, were a tribunal of a Member State, before which proceedings were being taken, to refer to the Court in accordance with the article.

From the foregoing considerations it is clear that the Court must declare it has no jurisdiction in respect of the present claims, both as far as the submission seeking the annulment of the decisions are concerned, and also the submissions seeking to establish their inapplicability . . .''.

Withdrawal of claims not permitted.   Withdrawal of a claim following agreed settlement by the parties (as provided for by R.P. 77, *post*, p. 265) is not permitted in the case of claims under E.E.C. 173, E.A.E.C. 146 and E.C.S.C. 33 (nor in respect of a claim for failure to act, see *post*, p. 120).

Inter-relation of E.E.C. 173 and E.E.C. 179.   See "Relation of E.E.C. 179 to E.E.C. 173", *post*, p. 150).

Consequences of annulment of an act of a Community Institution

E.E.C. 176

An institution responsible for a measure subsequently declared null and void or an institution whose failure to act has been declared contrary to the provisions of this Treaty shall be required to take the necessary steps to implement the judgment of the Court of Justice.

This obligation shall not affect any obligation arising from the application of the second paragraph of Article 215.

E.A.E.C. 149

[*Identical with E.E.C. 176*]

Compare E.E.C. 176 with E.C.S.C. 34 (*post*, p. 116).

"**Measure ... declared null and void**". "*L'acte annulé*"; *nichtig erklärte Handeln*"; "*de vernietigde handeling*"; "*l'atto annulato*".

"**. . . Any obligation arising under E.E.C. 215, second paragraph**". (E.A.E.C. 188 second paragraph). The effect of this is that measures taken by the Institution responsible for the annulled act are without prejudice to the rights of the successful claimant for annulment, in respect of damages. E.E.C. 215, second paragraph, provides:

> In the case of non-contractual liability, the Community shall, in accordance with the general principles common to the laws (*droits*) of Member States, make good any damage caused by its institutions or by its servants in the performance of their duties.

E.A.E.C. 188, second paragraph

[*Identical with E.E.C. 215, second paragraph, supra.*]

B. ACTS OF THE HIGH AUTHORITY

E.C.S.C. 33

The Court shall be empowered to decide upon applications, from one of the Member States or from the Council, to quash decisions and recommendations of the High Authority on the grounds of lack of powers, violations of basic procedural rules, infringement of the Treaty or of any rule of law relating to its implementation, or misuse of powers. However, the Court's enquiry into the case may not cover the evaluation of the situation, resulting from economic facts and circumstances, in the light of which such decisions or recommendations were taken, except where the High Authority is accused of having misused its powers or of having patently misinterpreted the provisions of the Treaty or any rule of law relating to its implementation.

The undertakings or associations referred to in Article 48 may, subject to the same conditions, make applications against decisions and recommendations concerning them that are individual in character or against general decisions and recommendations which they consider to involve a misuse of powers affecting them.

The proceedings provided for in the first two paragraphs of this Article shall be instituted within one month from the date of notification or publication, as the case may be, of the decision or recommendation.

"... **To quash decisions and recommendations.** ..." These acts have binding force, whereas opinions have not (see E.C.S.C. 14). The E.C.S.C. Treaty distinguishes "general" and "individual" decisions, which the later Treaties do not; as to this distinction see comments "individual decisions and recommendations concerning them" and "General and Individual decisions" (*post*, pp. 100 and 106).

E.C.S.C. 63

1. If the High Authority finds that discrimination is being systematically practised by buyers, in particular as a result of provisions governing contracts entered into by bodies subordinate to a public authority, it shall make appropriate recommendations to the Governments concerned.

2. To the extent that it finds necessary, the High Authority may decide that:

(*a*) undertakings must frame their conditions of sale in such a way that their customers and their agents shall undertake that they will comply with the rules made by the High Authority in accordance with the provisions of this Chapter.

(*b*) undertakings shall be made responsible for breaches of any obligations thus entered into which are committed by their direct agents or by agents acting on behalf of such undertakings but in their own name.

In case of a breach committed by a purchaser of the obligation thus entered into, the High Authority may limit the right of Community undertakings to deal with the said purchaser to a degree which may in case of repetition include a temporary prohibition. If a limitation is imposed, and without prejudice to the provisions of Article 33, the purchaser shall have a right of recourse to the Court.

3. In addition, the High Authority is empowered to make to the Member States concerned any recommendations appropriate to ensure that all undertakings or bodies engaged in distribution in the sphere of coal or steel observe the rules laid down under Article 60 (1).

"... **Decisions** ... **of the High Authority** ...". Such include decisions taken, with its authority, on its behalf. The Court has held:

"... the notifications made by the C.P.F.I. (the Compensation Office for Imported Scrap) in fact constituted the administrative decision without appeal, which the High Authority could have avoided if it had established, against the decisions taken by the bodies in Brussels, a method of recourse in well defined circumstances . . . It is therefore necessary to accept, if the undertakings are not to be deprived of the protection to which they are entitled under E.C.S.C. 33, that decisions taken by the C.P.F.I. by virtue of article 12(2) of decision 2–57 are equivalent in law to a decision of the High Authority, and by that token are capable of being quashed in the circumstances provided for in E.C.S.C. 33."

"Undertakings or associations . . .". Private parties who may have recourse to the Court by virtue of E.C.S.C. 33 must be within the category of undertakings (Fr. *"entreprises"*) as defined by E.C.S.C. 80 (for text, see pp. 92, 93) and associations of such undertakings. It should be noted that undertaking is essentially an economic (not a legal) concept, and that *any* undertaking, by whomsoever owned or operated "engaged in production in the field of coal and steel in the territories" of the Member States is within the category. Parties within the category may have a right of recourse to the Court for damages against the Community under E.C.S.C. 34 (*post*, p. 116). (Comparison may be made with the wider category of "the party concerned" in E.C.S.C. 36, *ante*, p. 80). See "The notion of undertaking in E.C.S.C." *post*, p. 92; "Private parties (undertakings, etc.) entitled to bring an action at the Court," *post*, p. 92.

A purchaser temporarily deprived of access to the market has a right of appeal to the Court "without prejudice to the provisions of E.C.S.C. 33" (see E.C.S.C. 63, *ante*, p. 90).

Conception of administrative law generally, in E.C.S.C. 33. In *Associazione Industrie Siderurgiche Italiane (ASSIDER) c. Haute Autorité* (Case 3/54 R. Vol. I at p. 169) the Advocate General submitted:

"It is only necessary to read Article 33 in order to perceive that it embodies a system between the two extreme conceptions, and which is roughly the system of France-Benelux at the present time, if one may so express oneself, that is, one that admits a broad conception of "infringement of the law" and makes of it the principal but not the only ground for which a claim for annulment may be brought; that does not mean, of course, that the judgment of the Court should follow one or other of the national systems of case law, in particular the French which is very restrictive at the present time. . . ."

Note: the two extreme conceptions to which the Advocate General referred were explained by him in general terms in an earlier passage in the same submission:

". . . the legal principles at the basis of judicial control of the Administration are really common to our six countries. These principles rest on the same conception of administrative action, considered as required to be exercised within the limits of law, and on the same conception of the role of the judge of this administrative action, which is to verify that these limits have been respected. The identity extends as far as the *process* chosen to ensure this control, that is the claim for annulment. As for the differences—which certainly exist—they appear to us to rest in reality on a mere difference of *presentation*. On the one hand, stress is laid primarily on the notion of powers and of limits to these powers: that was the original conception in France of the claim for annulment, which, precisely, was called *"claim for excès de pouvoir" (ultra vires)*; it is the conception to which Germany and Italy have remained attached, while making significant developments in it. On the other hand, there is more particular insistence on the notion of "infringement of the law", understood as disregard for the rule of law as revealed objectively, not only of the written law, but of the general principles which underly it; that is the present conception in France, Belgium, Luxembourg, and as we believe we have shown, in Holland. But it appears that ultimately the two conceptions join, for it is obvious that any disregard by a public authority of the extent of its powers necessarily constitutes an infringement of the rule of law, supposedly defined beforehand. They are two aspects of the same notion. That said, there are obviously certain differences in legal technique, used in one or other system, though both lead to the same results. That is why it is necessary to know, in this respect, what solution is offered by the Treaty" (*loc. cit., supra,* pp. 168–169).

The notion of undertaking in E.C.S.C. In *Klockner-Werke A.G. Hoesch A.G.* c. *Haute Autorité* (Consolidated Cases 17 and 20/61 R. Vol. VIII at pp. 646–7) the Court stated:

"The High Authority in decision 22–54 and subsequent decisions has referred to the criterion of the purchase of scrap by the consumer undertaking. As the Court has recognized in its judgment in Consolidated Cases 42 and 49/59 (R. Vol. VII at p. 155) this criterion must be broadly interpreted . . . to define this criterion it is desirable to examine the notion of undertaking. An undertaking is made up of personal, tangible and intangible elements constituting an organisation connected to a legally autonomous subject, and engaged on a long term basis in a given economic object. According to this notion, the creation of any and every subject of law in the realm of economic organization necessitates the forming of a distinct undertaking. Indeed, an economic activity cannot be considered as constituting a unit in the legal sense when the legal consequences of this activity have to be separately connected to several distinct subjects of law. So, by the very fact of creating a distinct legal person, the law recognizes that it has its own formal autonomy and responsibility, with the consequence that the conferring of legal personality on its different branches has as its aim and as its result the conferring upon each of them, in law, the management and risk of its activity. This change in the legal position is brought about by the sole conferring of legal personality, leaving aside the permanence of the economic situation existing prior to this change. Thus, looked at in this way, it cannot be denied that the conditions for the existence of a legally autonomous undertaking are also fulfilled in the case of a legal person the interests of which are closely linked to those of other subjects of law, and the mind or will of which is determined by directives from outside itself. Thus even in the case of a group of undertakings under the direction of a parent company which have a closely integrated cycle of production, where account is taken of the product of the whole and not of that of the branches considered individually, it has to be recognised that, in law, the activity of the group is carried on between subjects of law who are legally parties to the economic exchanges. . . ."

(This passage of the judgment was re-iterated verbatim by the Court in *Mannesmann A.G.* c. *Haute Autorité,* (Case 19/61 R. Vol. VIII at pp. 705–706)).

Private parties [undertakings] entitled to bring an action at the Court. In *Firma J. Nold K.G.* c. *Haute Autorité* (Case 18/57 (summary procedure) R. Vol. VIII at p. 240) the Court, in its order, stated:

". . . Though, in principle, access to the Court is restricted by the rules laid down in E.C.S.C. 33 and following articles to undertakings "engaged in production in the sphere of coal and steel," E.C.S.C. 80 provides that "any undertaking or body regularly engaged in distribution other than sale to domestic consumers or to small craft industries" is assimilated to producers "as far as E.C.S.C. 65 and 66, and also the information required for their application and the claims presented in respect of them, are concerned".

A mere distributor. A distributor who is not also a producer, may claim on the basis of E.C.S.C. 33 (second paragraph) by virtue of E.C.S.C. 65(4). In *Friedrich Stork et. Cie.* c. *Haute Autorité* (Case 1/58 R. Vol. V. at pp. 61–2) the Court stated:

"In its principal submissions the Request seeks to upset the decision of the High Authority of 27th November 1957, which, having had notice of a decision of the Landgericht of Essen not to deliver judgment, had ruled that the prohibitions set out in article 65(1) of the Treaty did not apply to the decisions of the six sales consortiums taken on the 5th February 1953. In accordance with article 65 (4, para (2)) of the Treaty the Court has jurisdiction in respect of a claim against such a decision of the High Authority and is therefore competent to determine the present dispute. Within the terms of article 65 the applicant is entitled by virtue of article 80 to bring an action before the Court although it is engaged, not in the production, but in the distribution of coal. This right of action of undertakings engaged in distribution is not limited to cases in which the undertakings themselves participate in the agreement which is in question, but extends also to the case where a decision based on article 65, as in the present case, directly concerns the sphere of interest of the undertaking effecting distribution which has applied to the Court by Request.

In the present case the Court does not have to decide whether a claim founded on article 65(4) must also satisfy all the conditions set out in article 33 for the claim for annulment, since there is no doubt that they are in fact satisfied: the case concerns an individual decision affecting the applicant; the decision was notified on the 6th December 1957 and the applicant made a claim against it on the 4th January, that is to say within the time-limit of one month laid down in article 33 (para. 3); the decision which it is sought to upset is an individual decision since it rules on the legal validity of concrete decisions taken by well defined undertakings; it affects the applicant because it was taken in the course of a dispute between another party and the applicant, on the outcome of which dispute the decision can exert an influence".

"Undertakings". The inter-relation of Articles 33, 35, 48 and 80 for determination of what party has a right of action was suggested in *Groupement des Industries Sidérurgiques Luxembourgeoises* c. *Haute Autorité* (Consolidated Cases 7.54 and 9.54 R. Vol. II at p. 114) by Adv. Gen. Roemer:

"Article 80 relates to undertakings which are producers in the field of coal and of steel. Manifestly, this text does not embrace only those undertakings which produce either coal or steel, or both of these, and it is in that sense it must be understood. This definition is valid for the whole of the Treaty and, consequently, for Articles 48, 33 and 35".

The four grounds for quashing decisions and recommendations of the High Authority.

 (i) lack of powers;
 (ii) violations of basic procedural rules;
(iii) infringement of the Treaty or of any rule of law relating to its implementation; or
(iv) misuse of powers.

 (In the original Treaty languages (though in E.C.S.C. only French is authentic) the equivalents are:

 (i) *incompétence; Unzuständigkeit; onbevoegdheid; incompetenza;*

(ii) *violation des formes substantielles; Verletzung wesentlicher Formvorschriften; Schending van wezenlijke vormvoorschriften; violazione delle forme sostanziali;*

(iii) *violation du présent traité ou de toute règle de droit relative à son application; Verletzung dieses Vertages oder einer bei seiner Durchführung angewendeten Rechtsnorm; schending van dit Verdrag of van enige uitvoeringsregling daarvan; violazione del presente Trattato o di qualsiasi norma guiridica relativa alla sua applicazione;*

(iv) *détournement de pouvoir; Ermessensmiszbrauch; misbruik van bevoegdheid; sviamento di potere).*

Infringement of the Treaty, patent disregard of its provisions, misuse of powers (*détournement de pouvoir*) and violations of basic procedural rules, (insufficient reasons for a decision etc.), were all part of the case brought by the Dutch Government against the High Authority (Case 6/54 R. Vol. I p. 201 at pp. 219–227) in respect of its decision (no. 18–54) and two further decisions (19–54 and 20–54) in execution thereof. The Government's contention was that in the circumstances, prices should have been completely freed, because maximum prices were inadmissible in addition to being unnecessary, and because the structure of the market, given its illegal character, could not be taken into consideration; that in reality the High Authority took the decision to avoid action against the sales organisations of the Ruhr and the coalmines of the French departments Nord and Pas de Calais; finally, that the decision was unsupported by reasons or at least was so supported insufficiently in law.

In its judgment the Court dealt at some length with "substantial violations of basic procedural rules", "infringement of the Treaty", "patent disregard of the provisions of the Treaty" and "*détournement de pouvoir*" (in that sequence, and in that part of the judgment headed "in law", following the Court's statement of the facts found, and of the arguments of the parties).

The Court said:

"Violations of basic procedural rules. The claimant contends in the first place that the reasons supporting decision No. 18–54 were formally insufficient, since the High Authority was, as was alleged, content to justify its measures by ascertaining in a purely hypothetical form that the structure of the Common Market might compromise the realisation of the aims of Article 3 of the Treaty. The claimant further contends that by the terms of Article 61, it should have recognised and enunciated a necessity and specified the aim or aims compromised in the event of total abolition of maximum prices. The Court finds that the general provisions of Articles 5 and 15 of the Treaty require the High Authority to give reasons for its decisions and to publicize its reasons, but that no details are laid down either as to the form or as to the extent of this obligation.

It also finds that on a reasonable construction, these requirements oblige the High Authority to mention in the reasons for its decision the essential elements in the assessment of facts upon which the legal justification for the decision depends; that the Treaty does not require the High Authority to reiterate—still less to refute—the opinions expressed in the matter by the consultative organs or any of their members."

The Court next passed to the question of the observance by the High Authority of Article 61[a] and found that the High Authority's decision invoked and affirmed the necessity there indicated, taking care to show that it arose from the existence of certain organisations with a preponderant influence on the market excluding effective competition, and that it referred expressly to a situation prejudicial to the pursuit of the aims of Article 3 insofar as either prices or production, or employment of workers is concerned; and, finally, that though the reasons did not precisely indicate the aim or aims of Article 3 which were specially pursued, the reasons could be considered as meeting the conditions of application of Article 61^a, and concluded this part of the judgment: "the decision is sufficiently supported by reasons in law".

But the Court held that it was also necessary to verify, as submitted by the Advocate General, whether the procedural rules laid down by the Treaty for the decisions challenged had been respected. Article 61 required a decision by the High Authority, fixing maximum prices, to be taken (i) on the basis of studies carried out in conjunction with undertakings and associations of undertakings in conformity with Articles 46 and 48; (ii) after consultation with the Consultative Council and (iii) after consultation with the Council of Ministers. The text of the decision affirmed that (ii) and (iii) had taken place, but the Court held it was not thereby dispensed from conducting its own investigation into the applications of the above-mentioned requirements. Since it appeared to the Court that the consultations envisaged in Article 61 were directed both to the desirability and expediency of the measures contemplated and to the level of prices, it held that "in this respect no procedural rule laid down for the validity of the decision has been disregarded".

Under the head of "Infringement of the Treaty" the Court examined (*a*) "the intrinsic legality of the decision in relation to the terms of Article 61 paragraph 1 of the Treaty, which empowers the High Authority to fix maximum prices for one or more products subject to its jurisdiction", and found first that the requirements of Article 5, which had to be read with Article 61, and prescribed "limited interventions" (by the High Authority), were met, and secondly, that the Treaty, in making possible the establishment of maximum prices within the Common Market, did not go beyond distinguishing this from the external market, but did not aim to prohibit measures directed only at certain sectors of the Common Market, while in any event the decision challenged in the action did indirectly affect the whole of the Market. It then (*b*) went into the claimant's contention, in support of the claim based on infringement of the Treaty, that the High Authority's decision was directed to a structure of the Market illegal in character (which it held unfounded). Next (*c*) it examined the claim that the High Authority had invoked in its decision the general objects of the Treaty and that this general reference was insufficient as a reason to support the decision because of the special provisions of Article 61 (*a*), and found no basis in law for this argument. Lastly, (*d*) it went into the claim that the decision challenged rested on materially erroneous grounds or reasons, and concluded from this part of the examination that it must "inquire into, as to their general import and their actual existence in the instant case, the two conditions alone permitting an appreciation of whether a decision was well founded in terms of economics, that is, a patent disregard of the provisions of the treaty and *détournement de pouvoir*".

Patent disregard of the provisions of the Treaty: The claimant had not argued as a separate ground for annulment that there had been a patent disregard of the provisions but adduced the argument solely with the object of requiring the Court "to examine the situation resulting from the economic facts and circumstances" material to the case. In its judgment under this head, the Court enunciated two important general principles: (*a*) that Article 33 does not require a complete proof in advance before such an examination can be made (which would of itself automatically involve the annulment of the decision as being an infringement of the Treaty); (*b*) that on the other hand the mere assertion of a patent disregard could not suffice to allow the Court to investigate the economic appreciation, since then a claim on this ground would become a clause automatically inserted; but pertinent indications accompanying the claim would suffice.

"Misuse of powers" (*Détournement de pouvoir*). "Misapplication of power" might be more clearly indicative in English of the meaning of the original French, insofar as it directs attention to the end or object for which the power is (allegedly wrongly) used, rather than to the intrinsic nature of the power itself.

"The legal defect of *détournement de pouvoir* consists in the turning away of the power from the object for which it was instituted and its use for ends other than those for which it was destined . . . *Détournement de pouvoir* results from a disregard of the spirit of the rule of law involved. To uncover the *détournement de pouvoir* the judge . . . cannot limit himself to examining the external legality or even only the objective legality of the decision in issue before him, he must seek out the motives ("*mobiles*") which inspired the author of this decision and determine whether these motives were legally in order" (Odent: *Cours de Contentieux Administratif*, last edition Vol. III p. 615).

The definition used in a large number of decisions of the Conseil d'Etat is: "the use (by the administrative authority) of its powers for an object other than that for which they were conferred upon it" (and is given in these same words in Alibert: "*Le Contrôle juridictionel de l'Administration au moyen du recours pour excès de pouvoir*," 1926, p. 236). "There is *détournement de pouvoir* when an administrative authority carries out an act within its powers with all legal regularity but for an *object* other than that for which the act could legally be made" (de Laubadère, *Droit administratif*, p. 389).

In French legal history *détournement de pouvoir* derived directly from *incompétence* expressed in a law of 1790, following a dispute between the executive body of the Department of Haute Sâone and the municipality of Gray, which provided: "Claims of *incompétence* in respect of administrative bodies are not justiciable by the Courts; they shall be referred to the King, head of the general administration". Where a public authority went beyond the limits of its *compétence* there was *excès de pouvoir* (*ultra vires*), but this legal concept was a pretorian (judge made) creation of the Conseil d'Etat, which until 1832 did not need to refer to the law of 1790. As Alibert states (*loc. cit.*):

"On close examination, *détournement de pouvoir* is a species of *incompétence*. A decision embodying a *détournement de pouvoir* is, in some measure, vitiated by *incompétence*, if not by the provisions it lays down, at least by the *end* it seeks to attain. It can thus be readily understood that, relatively early, case law came to disengage the concept of *détournement de pouvoir*, deriving this ground of annulment of administrative acts from the original or primitive ground of *incompétence* properly so called, or usurpation of power: turning a power away from its legal object is indeed, basically, to act without *compétence*".

Pursuing that line of thought it becomes clear that the rule or principle dominating all administrative law is that of the end or object. For, compared with the rights of private persons which (apart from statutory requirements) are bounded in their exercise only by the need to respect the rights of other private persons, the rights of public authorities are in reality powers, which may not be exercised except for the ends or objects for which they were conferred. In a broad sense it is always the public interest that is envisaged as the end or object, but in practice powers are conferred for particular ends within that general whole. It may thus happen that there may be a *détournement de pouvoir* even in the case where the end sought to be attained by the administration is not illegal in itself and is not against the public interest, but where the act of the administrative authority is not directed to the end it was bound to pursue within the limits of its own special function; at that point *détournement de pouvoir* is again very close to *incompétence*.

In French administrative law practice, *détournement de pouvoir* as a ground for annulment encounters the most rigorous examination. For whereas the question of proof is normally handled in respect of claims for annulment on other grounds, by means of a somewhat pragmatic application of an investigatory procedure by the administrative judge, in the case of *détournement de pouvoir* the claimant must either furnish proof himself or it must clearly result from the "documents on the file". The reason of that lies in the necessity of a subjective investigation into the intention of the administration; there must be no existing suspicion regarding that intention and, until the contrary is proven, the administration must be presumed to have acted in the interest of the service for which it bears the responsibility.

It is true that early in its history the Court (in its judgment in *Fédération Charbonnière de Belgique* c. *Haute Autorité*, Case 8/55, R. Vol. II at pp. 309–310) was ready to concede that *détournement de pouvoir* could be established other than by a purely subjective analysis of intention: ". . . Even if the defendant has made mistakes in choosing the date on which it has based its calculations, it does not follow that these mistakes constitute *ipso facto* the proof of a *détournement de pouvoir* if it is not further established that the defendant, the High Authority, through grave lack of foresight or circumspection equivalent to disregard of the legal object, has pursued aims other than those with a view to which the powers . . . were conferred." Since 1945 *violation de la loi*, (the counterpart of which in the Treaty is "infringement of the Treaty etc.") has grown in importance as a ground for annulment as *détournement de pouvoir* has declined, the former being dependent on objective, not subjective, assessment.

A broadly comparable development may occur in the case law of the European Court, quite apart from the fact that the Economic Community and Atomic Energy Community Treaties do not make of *détournement de pouvoir* the particular use of it that is to be found in the Coal and Steel Community Treaty (where it is the sole ground on which a private party may attack a general decision). But it cannot be stressed too strongly that the Court is not bound to any one of the national systems, nor, in any strict sense, to all of them collectively, though it is well recognized that the general principles of law of the Member States are a source of Community law, to which, certainly in case of difficulty, the Court will have regard.

The reason for including the above brief summary of *détournement de pouvoir* in French law (taken essentially from the submissions of the Advocate general in one of the earliest cases before the Court, see Case 3/45 R. Vol. I. p. 149 et seq.) was that it was this law which provided the predominant inspiration for the wording and the legal content of the four grounds of annulment of Article 33. This was recognized to be so by the six countries negotiating the E.C.S.C. Treaty. The Report of the French Delegation stated: "There will be found in the Treaty the classic distinction of French administrative law between the action for annulment (the *"recours pour excès de pouvoir"* or "action for *ultra vires*") and that of "full jurisdiction" . . . .
Three of the four traditional grounds for the action for annulment (lack of jurisdiction, substantial violation of basic procedural rules, *détournement*

de pouvoir) were admitted without difficulty: the notion of *détournement de pouvoir*, in particular, was well understood and readily accepted by our foreign partners" (*Rapport de la Délégation Française sur le Traité instituant la Communauté européenne du charbon et de l'acier et la Convention relative aux dispositions transitoires*, Octobre 1951). The explanatory note to the German law authorising the ratification of the Treaty states: "An action for annulment may be brought by the undertaking and associations of undertakings subject to the jurisdiction of the Community, as well as by Member States and the Council of Ministers. The grounds in support of the action are enumerated in paragraph 1 (of Article 33) which was taken from the French theory of *ultra vires* corresponding in essentials to the basic elements of German legal doctrine concerning defective administrative action".

In *Gouvernement de la République Française* c. *Haute Autorité* (Case 1.54 R. Vol. I at p. 33) the Court stated:

"Even if an injustified reason, that is to say the desire to avoid fines on defaulting undertakings, had been linked with other reasons which, by themselves, justify the action of the High Authority, the decision would not by virtue of that fact be vitiated by *détournement de pouvoir*, inasmuch as they do not injuriously affect the essential object which is the prohibition of practices of unfair competition and of discrimination".

The above passage was re-iterated largely verbatim by the Court in *Gouvernement de la République Italienne* c. *Haute Autorité* (Case 2/54 R. Vol. I at p. 103).

In *Fédération Charbonnière de Belgique* c. *Haute Autorité* (Case 8/55 R. Vol. II at pp. 309–310), the Court stated:

"Even if the defendant (the High Authority) has committed certain errors in the choice of data for the making of its calculations, as is the case here in respect of the base year of reference, and as it might well be the case in respect of the amortizations and the grouping of various categories of coal, it does not follow that these errors *ipso facto* constitute the proof of a *détournement de pouvoir*, if it is not also established that the High Authority has in the instant case objectively pursued, through grave lack of foresight or of circumspection, equivalent to a disregard of the legally permissible object, ends other than those envisaged in the attribution of the powers provided for in paragraph 26, 2^a of the Convention" (on Transitory Provisions).

Misuse of powers (*détournement de pouvoir*) Admissibility of an action by undertaking or association of undertakings (*recevabilité*).
In *La Société des Charbonnages de Beeringen etc.* c. *Haute Autorité* (Case 9–55 R. Vol. II at p. 351) the Court stated:

"For an action to annul a general decision to be admissible it is sufficient for the claimants to contend formally that there has been a *détournement de pouvoir* affecting them, indicating at the same time in a pertinent manner the reasons why, in their opinion, it follows there has been *détournement de pouvoir*".

In *Associazione Industrie Siderurgiche Italiane (ASSIDER)* c. *Haute Autorité* (Case 3–54 R. Vol. I p. 138–139) (Repeated verbatim by the Court in *Industrie Siderurgiche Associate (I.S.A.)* c. *Haute Autorité* (Case 4/54 R. Vol. I at p. 193. *Cf.* also judgment in Case 8/55, *infra*) the Court stated:

"The Court is of the opinion that the Treaty neither provides nor requires any additional condition for an action to lie, such as, in particular, proof that a *détournement de pouvoir* affecting the claimant has in fact been committed. This proof will be necessary to establish that the claim is well founded—but this question is part of the examination of the issues and does not concern the point whether the action lies".

In Case 4/54 (*loc. cit., supra,* at p. 193) the Court added:

"In the case of a claim brought by an association of undertakings, it is sufficient for the action to lie that it is contended that a *détournement de pouvoir* exists with regard to one or more of the undertakings members of the association".

Détournement de pouvoir as introducing for undertakings and associations, the possibility of invoking the other three grounds of annulment. In *La Société des Charbonnages de Beeringen* c. *Haute Autorité* (Case 9/55 R. Vol. II at pp. 353–4) the Court stated:

"The claimants consider not only that they are legally entitled to invoke all the grounds for annulment provided that they claim, with supporting reasons, that there has been a *détournement de pouvoir*, but moreover that to buttress the *détournement de pouvoir* they may prove that (the decision is) legally vitiated on the other grounds; in their opinion the Treaty sets up a legal system in which private undertakings, for their action to lie, have only the ground of *détournement de pouvoir* affecting them; it would be illogical for that reason to give this ground only an exceptional and subsidiary character.

This argument must be rejected; if the Treaty lays down that private undertakings have the right to claim annulment of a general decision for *détournement de pouvoir* affecting them, it follows that a right of action on other grounds is not attributed to them.

If the argument of the claimants were correct, undertakings would have as complete a right of action as that of the Member States and Council, and it would be inexplicable that Article 33, instead of simply assimilating the actions of undertakings to those of Member States or of the Council, should have introduced a very clear distinction between individual decisions and general decisions, and limiting at the same time, in the case of undertakings, the annulment of general decisions to the ground of *détournement de pouvoir* affecting them. The insertion "subject to the same conditions" could not be interpreted as meaning that undertakings, after having established a case of *détournement de pouvoir* affecting them, would be entitled to invoke in addition the other grounds of annulment since, when the *détournement de pouvoir* affecting them is established, the annulment of the contested decision follows as a matter of law without having to be ordered afresh for other reasons.

These considerations run clearly counter to the illogical supposition of the claimants that the interpretation of the Treaty must be subordinated to the desire to give private undertakings a right of action practically identical to that of Member States or the Council. Such a wish is comprehensible, but the Treaty does not contain any indication from which the inference may be drawn that private undertakings have been granted any such right of control of the "constitutionality" of general decisions, that is to say, of their conformity with the Treaty, inasmuch as it is a question of quasi legislative acts emanating from a public authority and having a rule-making effect *erga omnes*.

It is true that Article 33 admits a right of action to annul a general decision on the ground of *détournement de pouvoir* affecting an undertaking, but this is a question of an exception explained by the fact that, in this case, it is still the individual element (in the general decision) which prevails".

In *Associazione Industrie Siderurgiche Italiane (Assider)* c. *Haute Autorité*. (Case 3–54, *loc. cit., ante,* p. 98, at p. 171) Advocate General Lagrange Submitted:

"There can be no question of *détournement de pouvoir* in paragraph 2 having a wider significance than the same phrase in paragraph 1.

. . . The rule laid down by Article 33 paragraph 2 is that undertakings and associations may appeal only against individual "decisions and recommendations concerning them". Why does the text add "or against general decisions and recommendations which they consider to involve a misuse of powers affecting them"? The only justifiable explanation is that the authors of the Treaty imagined the case of a decision, in reality an individual one *affecting* an undertaking, dissimulated under the appearance of a general decision."

Rather than leave it to the Court to construe such a decision as in reality an individual decision, which it would be most likely to do, thus arriving at the same practical result, it was thought preferable to make the addition in the Treaty. That what was aimed at was the individual decision in either form is borne out by the explanatory note accompanying the Luxembourg law ratifying the Treaty, quoted by the Advocate General, which is in the following terms: "Only individual decisions of the High Authority or those which are general, but which the concept of *détournement de pouvoir* makes it possible to assimilate to an individual decision, may be directly challenged by the undertakings or associations against whom they are directed", (see reference to the Luxembourg explanatory note in connection with *travaux préparatoires, ante*, p. 76). (In general, on diminishing role of *détournement de pouvoir*, see *ante*, p. 6).

Sufficiency of reasoning of a decision. In *Koninklijke Nederlandsche Hoogovens en Staalfabrieken N.V.* c. *Haute Autorité* (Case 14/61, R. Vol. VIII at p. 523) the Court stated:

"The applicant contends that the disputed decision is not reasoned or is not reasoned sufficiently, constituting an infringement of basic procedural rules. This contention cannot be accepted by the Court. If the reasons may appear to be insufficiently developed, the enquiry into the issues in the case has demonstrated their pertinence. They thus suffice as reasoning in support of the disputed decision. Reasoning must be adjudged sufficient to satisfy articles 15 and 33 of the Treaty when it permits both the interested parties and the Court to ascertain the essential elements of the reasoning of the High Authority . . .".

Individual "decisions and recommendations concerning them". The Court said in *Groupement des Industries Sidérurgiques Luxembourgeoises* c. *Haute Autorité*, (Consolidated Cases, 7/54 and 9/54 R. Vol. II p. 87):

"For an action by an undertaking or association against a decision or recommendation to lie, it is sufficient that this decision or recommendation should not be general but have the character of an individual decision, *without it being necessary for it to have this character in direct relation to the claimant*" (author's italics).

Distinction between individual decision and general decision. In *la Société des Charbonnages de Beeringen* c. *Haute Autorité* (Case 9/55, R. Vol. II at p. 350) the Court stated:

"The fact that the decision (No. 22–25 of the High Authority) comprises a detailed and concrete set of rules, applicable in different situations, does not deny a general character to the decision. Indeed, the Treaty, in Article 50 paragraph 2, states that the method of assessment and collection of the levies shall be fixed by a general decision of the High Authority, which shows that the detailed and varied concrete consequences of a general decision do nothing to alter its general character.

For an action for annulment of a general decision to lie, it is sufficient for the claimant to contend formally that there has been a *détournement de pouvoir* affecting him, indicating appositely the reasons which, in his opinion, show the existence of this *détournement de pouvoir*".

"Camouflaged" individual decision. In *La Société des Charbonnages de Beeringen etc.* c. *Haute Autorité* (*loc. cit., ante*, p. 100, at p. 352) the Court stated:
"The defendant (the High Authority) maintains that an undertaking cannot invoke the ground of *détournement de pouvoir* affecting itself except where the High Authority has camouflaged a decision that is individual with regard to that undertaking under the appearance of a general and rule making measure. This argument must be rejected; indeed a camouflaged individual decision remains an individual decision, the character of a decision not depending on its form but on its ambit. Besides, such an interpretation of Article 33 and in particular of the words "affecting them" could not be accepted, since the expression "affecting them" has no other meaning than that of the words which express it, namely that relating to an undertaking which is the object or at least the victim of the *détournement de pouvoir* which it claims exists. The Court considers that Article 33 states clearly that associations and undertakings may contest not only individual decisions but also general decisions in the strict meaning of the term".

The interest of the claimant. "Underlying and inherent in the claim for annulment is the concept of interest of the claimant (in the decision challenged). The Treaty does not proceed, however, by explicitly introducing the concept and leaving to the Court the task of defining it by case-law. It has attempted instead to settle the matter by laying down, for each category of decision, *who* may bring an action. In the result, the right of undertakings to bring an action is limited. This feature was the most criticized in the early years following the coming into force of the Treaty.
An explanation would be that the extreme importance of the decisions the High Authority might have to take necessitated that the interest in them required of the claimant seeking an annulment must be of the same order of importance. Only the State (as in Article 33 paragraph 1) representing by definition the general interest, could be considered as meeting that condition. As the advocate of the Italian Government explained in an earlier case (2–54), Article 33 confers in a general way on the governments of Member States the task of guaranteeing the interests of their nationals."
(From the submissions, part paraphrased, of Adv. Gen. Lagrange in Case 3/54, *loc. cit., ante*, p. 100, at pp. 172–174).

Interest, and admissibility. See extract from the judgment in Consolidated Cases 24, 34/58, *post*, p. 226.

An objection to a claim alleging *détournement de pouvoir* does not go to its procedural admissibility. In *Compagnie des Hauts Fourneaux de Chasse* c. *Haute Autorité* (Case 2/57, R. Vol. IV p. 129 at pp. 145–6) the Court stated:
"The defendant considers that the applicant characterizes as *détournement de pouvoir* a series of charges which, for various reasons, are not related to this ground of annulment, but to infringement of the Treaty. For that reason the defendant maintains that article 33 does not permit the applicant to establish a case on the basis of these charges.
The Court rejects this reasoning.
It is true that in the Request the applicant has claimed there has been a *détournement de pouvoir* affecting itself and has developed a number of arguments which it considers capable of supporting this claim.

It is possible that these arguments do not sustain the existence of a *détour-nement de pouvoir*, but in order to know whether that is so, the issues in the case must be examined; in such circumstances, in accordance with the case law of the Court, the objection raised by the defendant is no obstacle to the (procedural) admissibility of the claim."

"The claim of an association of undertakings is (procedurally) admissible when one or more *détournement(s) de pouvoir* affecting its members are formally alleged and when apt reasons why these acts should be considered *détournement(s) de pouvoir*, together with the arguments advanced in support, lead to the view that the High Authority, in making the challenged decisions, used powers conferred on it by the Treaty for ends different from those for which the powers were conferred". (From the headnote to *Groupement des Hauts Fourneaux et Aciéries Belges* c. *Haute Autorité* (Case 8/57, R. Vol. IV at p. 227).

The above words are taken verbatim from the judgment and are reiterated in *Chambre Syndicale de la Sidérurgie Française* c. *Haute Autorité* (Case 10/57, R. Vol. IV at p. 416) and again in *Syndicat de la Sidérurgie du Centre Midi* c. *Haute Autorité* (Case 12/57, R. Vol. IV at p. 490).

But such a claim is not (procedurally) admissible to the extent it is based on other grounds such as infringement of the Treaty (see *Wirtschaftsvereinigung Eisen-und Stahlindustrie etc.* c. *Haute Autorité* (Case 13/57, R. Vol. IV at pp. 286–287).

Action by undertaking to annul individual decision, admissibility. In *De Gezamenlijke Steenkolenmijnen in Limburg* c. *Haute Autorité* (Case 30/59 R. Vol. VII at p. 35) the Court stated:

"For an action brought by an undertaking for annulment of an individual decision to be admissible it is sufficient if the applicant contends that this decision concerns it and supports its contention by demonstrating in a pertinent manner the interest it has in the annulment of the decision . . .".

Meaning of the phrase *détournement de pouvoir* the same in both paragraphs 1 and 2 of article 33. In *Fédération Charbonnière de Belgique* c. *Haute Autorité* (Case 8–53, R. Vol. II at p. 253) Adv. Gen Lagrange submitted:

"Contrary to what the High Authority maintains, it is our opinion that it is not possible to attach a different meaning to the words *détournement de pouvoir* in the first and second paragraphs of Article 33. There is only in the second paragraph an additional requirement; it is necessary for the alleged *détournement de pouvoir* to affect the claimant; no doubt, this view leads to the widening of the field of application of the second paragraph beyond the case of a *détournement de pouvoir* consisting in "camouflaging" an individual decision behind the appearance of a general decision, but, as we pointed out in our previous submissions, this explanation of the camouflaged individual decision, though in our opinion the only justifiable one, cannot be set up in opposition to the text being applied as it stands, the strict interpretation leading to claims by associations against general decisions being deprived in practice of all scope. It is true that if the Court were to follow our suggestions regarding the nature of individual decision concerning associations, this difficulty would be in practice reduced, as a result of the reduction in the number of decisions having a general character in relation to associations. Nevertheless, the objection remains valid."

The theory of "objective *détournement de pouvoir*". In *Fédération Charbonnière de Belgique* c. *Haute Autorité* (Case 8/55, R. Vol. II at pp. 253–6) the parties in the case were in agreement on the definition of *détournement* *de pouvoir* as meaning "the use made by a public authority of its powers for an object other than that for which it was conferred upon it". Adv. Gen. Lagrange submitted:

"How then can one explain that such complete divergence should re-appear when it is a matter of passing from definition to application? How can one explain that the claimants come, in every case, to make the ground of *détournement de pouvoir* co-exist with a ground of illegality?

It is at this point that there intervenes a theory which, for us, is mysterious and which, in spite of persevering efforts, we admit in all humility that we have so far been unsuccessful in penetrating—the theory known as "objective *détournement de pouvoir*" which is placed in contradistinction to the theory said to be based entirely on a criterion of intention.

When we say that we do not understand the so called "objective" theory do not let us be misunderstood: we mean that we do not understand it starting out from the classical definition (as given in the first paragraph hereto).

The classical definition supposes in the first place that the Authority sued has a power which is a discretionary power, at least within certain limits. Indeed, on the one hand, if it has not this power, it obviously cannot turn it away (*détourner*) from its legal object; and if, on the other hand, it has a power, but subject to such conditions that it is legally obliged to employ it in a certain way and not in another, the possibility of *détournement de pouvoir* does not arise either: that is what is called a fettered competence ("*compétence liée*").

As for the criterion of intention we would not wish to adhere to it too firmly if the expression offends or alarms certain minds. It is obviously not a matter of a heart-searching inquisition to determine the thoughts or the secret *arrière-pensées* which the author of the act might have entertained when he took the decision; such an inquiry of a psychological nature would be all the more ridiculous because the decision may emanate, as in the present case, from an authority consisting of several individuals acting together. But it is a matter of discovering *what was the object in fact pursued* by the author of the act, when he took the decision, in order to be able to compare it with the object he ought to have pursued and which, unless the contrary is proved, he is deemed to have pursued. Thus it is not the *results* of the decision, in particular its *illegality*, even less a going beyond the authority's competence, which can constitute a proof in this respect, or else words have lost all meaning.

But then, how can the proof of the object really pursued be made? This proof may result from one or more factual elements (such as correspondence, declarations, etc.) *in consequence strictly objective in character* which will demonstrate that the author of the act has not really had in view the legal object, but some other object which is not legal.

We wish to make two further observations:

1. We admit freely, and have never said the contrary, that *détournement de pouvoir* may exist even in the hypothesis that the object to be pursued by the authority is *defined by the law itself*; such a hypothesis occurs frequently in the Treaty and is the case in paragraph 26, 2ᵃ of the Convention (relative to transitory provisions) which concerns us in this case. Obviously, nothing would be more arbitrary than to exclude *détournement de pouvoir* for *the sole reason* that the object is presented in a law. But it is only to the extent that the power exists and has a discretionary character that it is possible to conceive of a *détournement de pouvoir*: if the discretionary limits are exceeded, there is *excès de pouvoir* and not *détournement* (*ultra vires* and not misapplication) of power (in the Italian wording *eccesso di*

potere not *sviamento di potere*). This in the treaty system is represented by
either a lack of jurisdiction, or an infringement of the law (or by both at
once, the rules of competence being usually determined by law).

2. The argument has often been advanced, in support of a widening of
the classical concept of *détournement de pouvoir* for the purposes of the
application of Article 33, that in practice this concept would never be
made to operate. How is it possible to conceive, the argument runs, that
the High Authority could lower itself to commit what is called a "sordid"
détournement de pouvoir? It would be tantamount to thinking of it as on a
level with a mayor of a very small country town.

In our opinion, this objection is completely erroneous. First of all,
it overlooks that the greatest have often great weaknesses. . . . But above
all, it overlooks two things: first that the classical conception of *détournement
de pouvoir* is by no means restricted to "sordid" cases, or let us say rather, to
avoid this undoubtedly exaggerated word, the cases where a particular or
personal interest has taken the place of general interest. In its traditional
form *détournement de pouvoir* is also found in cases where the object pursued is
perfectly honest, even perfectly legitimate, but is not the one it should
be. . . .

Second, if *détournement de pouvoir* is considered in this light, it can be
realised that the High Authority is particularly likely to commit it. Is it
not likely, for example, to use its powers (or to refuse to use them) ne-
glecting the interests with which it is entrusted, to the profit of the economy
of a single Member State? Is it not that, precisely, with which it is charged
in the present case . . . . To use powers against the interest of coal
producers in order to meet the policy, perfectly honest in itself and
inspired by the best considerations of general interest, of some dynamic
Minister of Economics, whether he were Belgian or German, would that
not be, if we may use the expression, a *détournement de pouvoir* "measuring
up to" the High Authority?

Whether it could be established is another matter. But what we wanted
to show was that it is not correct to maintain that the classical concept of
détournement de pouvoir is almost inconceivable in the Treaty. It seems to us
the opposite is true.

. . . if one admits a too extensive notion of *détournement de pouvoir*, it
merges for all practical purposes into "infringement of the law", in "lack
of jurisdiction", so that undertakings and their associations, by virtue of
such an interpretation, would find themselves recognized to possess the
same rights against general decisions as the Member States and the
Council. Such a consequence, so obviously, so directly, contrary to
Article 33, is enough in our opinion to condemn the extensive system (of
interpretation)".

In the case from which the above quotations are taken the Court ruled
(p. 224):

"The Treaty contains no indication from which the conclusion can be
drawn that there is conferred on private undertakings . . . a right to the
control of the "constitutionality" of general decisions, that is to say of
their conformity with the Treaty, inasmuch as these are quasi-legislative
acts originating with a public authority and having a rule making effect
"*erga omnes*"—a right which would be identical from the practical point
of view with that of States and the Council".

What is a decision? In *De Gezamenlijke Steenkolemijnen in Limburg* c.
Haute Autorité (Case 17/57, R. Vol. V at p. 36) **Adv. Gen. Legrange** submitted:

"... a mere taking up of a position, whether manifested by a letter, a declaration to the Common Assembly, or in any way at all, which involves an explanation by the High Authority of the reasons why it considers that a given situation, in given circumstances, is not to use the phrase of Steindorff 'a measure bringing about legal effects in respect of other parties ("*a l'extérieur*") and implying the exercise of a prerogative of public authority'. It is not a decision in the sense of articles 14 and 33."

In *Phoenix-Rheinrohr A.G. c. Haute Autorité* (Case 20/58, R. Vol. V at p. 181) the Court stated:

"... a letter ... which may have given rise to immediate obligations, affecting the body to which it was addressed and not the undertakings which are consumers of scrap, this situation being confirmed, moreover, by the fact that this letter, dated the 18th December 1957, was not published in the Journal Officiel of the Community until the 1st February 1958, is [for these and other reasons] not a decision in the sense of the Treaty ...".

The Advocate General (Lagrange) in his submissions had taken the contrary view: "For me, there is no doubt, the letter in question is certainly a decision" against which an application for annulment may be brought (*loc. cit.*, at p. 191). The headnote to the judgment reads: "(*a*) The appreciation of the legal nature of a measure of the High Authority depends above all on its object and content. (*b*) When the High Authority addresses a letter to an auxiliary body which it has charged with the carrying out of certain specific tasks, advising it of certain practices followed until then, this letter may constitute a mere internal administrative instruction, even if it has been published in the Journal Officiel and refers to the measures which the body must take with regard to undertakings of the Community. That is the case in any event if it appears from the letter of the High Authority that it did not contemplate that it was taking a decision, but merely confirming principles that rightly or wrongly it considered it could logically declare from its previous decisions. The fact that with regard to third parties an agent of the High Authority should have qualified this letter as a "decision" does not deprive the above affirmation of value."

In *Felton and Guillaume Carlswerk Eisen-und Stahl A.G. Walzwerke A.G. c. Haute Autorité* (Case 21/58, R. Vol. V, pp. 211 *et seq.* see esp. 226–227) and in *Bochumer Verein fur Gussstahlfabrikation A.G. Niedertheinische Hütte A.G. Stahlwerke Südwestfalen A.G. c. Haute Autorité* (Case 22/58, R. Vol. V, pp. 231 *et seq.*) the same letter as in Case 20/58 (*supra*) was again in question, with the same result, as also in *Mannesmann A.G. Hoeschwerke A.G. (and others) c. Haute Autorité* (Case 23/58, R. Vol. V, pp. 253 *et seq.*; see esp. pp. 270–271), and in *Société des Aciers Fins de l'Est (S.A.F.E.) c. Haute Autorité* (Case 42/58 R. Vol. V, pp. 381 *et seq.*, at p. 402).

In *Société Nouvelle des Usines de Pontlieue-Aciéries du Temple (S.N.U.P.A.T) c. Haute Autorité* (Consolidated Cases 32/58 and 33/58 R. Vol. V. p. 273 *et seq.*) the Court held a letter of the C.P.F.I. (*Caisse de Péréquation des ferrailes importées*—Compensation Fund for Imported Scrap) of 12th May 1958, a "notification" by the C.P.F.I. within the requirements of the High Authority decision 2/57 inviting the applicant to pay a given sum by way of duty on purchased scrap and to draw up its declarations in accordance with the letter of the High Authority of 18th December 1957 (which letter had been held by the Court not to be a "decision"—see immediately preceding cases, *supra*, and was again so held in this case, *loc. cit.*, p. 302). It further held that a decision by the C.P.F.I. was equivalent in law to a decision of the High Authority itself and the application for annulment of the letter of 12th May 1958 was therefore admissible.

General decisions. In *Firma I. Nold K.G. c. Haute Autorité* (Case 18/57 R. Vol. V. at p. 113) the Court stated:

"... general decisions are quasi-legislative acts, made by a public authority and having a rule-making effect *erga omnes* ...".

General and individual decisions. In *Phoenix-Rheinrohr A.G. c. Haute Autorité* (Case 20/58, R. Vol. V. at pp. 192–3). Adv. Gen. Lagrange submitted:

"... does the case concern a "general" decision in the sense of article 33 as the High Authority maintains, or an "individual decision concerning" each of the applicants, as the latter maintain?

The applicants rely mainly on the judgment in consolidated cases 7 and 9/54 (*Groupement des Industries Sidérurgeques Luxembourgeoises c. Haute Autorité* R. Vol. II at p. 55) where it was held that a decision aimed solely at a particular activity of a public organism designated by name is an individual decision, without it being necessary for it to present this characteristic "in respect of the applicant", given that it concerns him.

It appears difficult, as the legal representative of the defendant has emphasized in his oral pleading, to apply this criterion precisely to the present case, since it is evident that a decision taken by the High Authority as authorised by article 15 of the decision 2–57 cannot be individual in character *by virtue of the mere fact* that it is in the form of a letter addressed to the Common Office for Scrap Consumers (O.C.C.F.): the activity of the Common office is not a "particular activity", to adopt the expression used in the judgment in Cases 7 and 9/54, since the Common Office has competence in respect of every matter which concerns the mechanism of compensation: in respect of this mechanism the Office's operations are not particular but general. But it is necessary to have regard to the *object* of the decision. Now, in the present case, the decision sought to be upset has as its object to determine a certain number of disputed matters concerning the calculations of the contribution towards compensation due from certain undertakings; without doubt, as often occurs in such cases, examination of the problem may lead the competent authority necessarily to take sides on questions of principle, but the object of its intervention is none the less to determine such concrete cases as are submitted to it. We are therefore of the opinion that this is an individual decision, that it concerns each of the applicants and that, consequently, reliance by the latter on all the grounds of article 33 is admissible".

In *Firma I. Nold K.G. c. Haute Autorité* (Case 18/57, R. Vol. V at p. 241) the Court stated:

"... at the present stage of the action, there is no necessity at all to examine whether in the present case the decisions in issue are individual or general, inasmuch as the applicant has formally alleged a misapplication of power affecting him and has indicated the reasons by virtue of which in his opinion the misapplication of power must be held to exist; every application based on this ground is admissible. ..."

Earlier in the same judgment (*loc. cit., supra.* at p. 112) the Court had stated:

"... the Treaty being silent on the point, it cannot be held that a decision which is individual in respect of the undertakings to which it is addressed could at the same time be considered as a general decision in respect of third parties".

In *Società Metallurgica di Napoli (S.I.M.E.T.) etc. c. Haute Autorité* (R. Vol. V. at pp. 352–3) the Court stated:

"Is decision 13–58 (of the High Authority) general or individual? ... decision 13–58 has as its principal object the correction of the irregularities in decision 14–55 of 26th March 1955, drawn attention to in judgment 9 and 10/56; as the Court held in *Meroni et Cie* (case 9/56), decision 14–55 is a general decision; to the extent it permits modifications to be made in decision 14–55, decision 12–58 partakes of the characteristic of generality of the former; the general character of decision 13–58 is the direct consequence of its contents which establish a number of ruling principles, lay down in an abstract manner the conditions of their application and formulates the legal consequences which derive therefrom; decision 13–58 lays down a number of rules of general organization which, like the earlier general decisions on the mechanism of compensation which they are to modify, may reveal themselves of importance in an identical manner in any number of cases; the rules are or will be applicable to any matter or person which is or finds itself at any time in the circumstances where their application is intended; consequently, the argument of the applicants to the effect that insofar as decision 13–58 authorises the High Authority to review, in order either to confirm them or to refer them back, the decisions taken by the Compensation Office and the Common Office, it "is aimed individually and directly at a small number of iron and steel undertakings in the Community that are very readily identifiable", cannot be upheld; for these reasons decision 13–58 is, in the meaning of article 33 of the Treaty, a general decision".

In *De Gezamenlijke Steenkolenmijnen in Limburg* c. *Haute Autorité* (Case 30/59 R. Vol. VII at p. 68) the Advocate General, in his submissions, stated:

". . . the Court has rejected the suggestions made by the Advocates-General, some favourable to associations of undertakings, some unfavourable to undertakings, regarding the possibility of recognizing that a decision may be of a mixed character, either by adopting a criterion of relativity (a single decision being capable, for example, of presenting an individual character with respect to an association and a general character with respect to an undertaking), or else by disengaging different elements in the decision (for example, a decision of authorization and the commercial rule-making which it authorizes)—the judgment in *Fédération Charbonnière de Belgique* c. *Haute Autorité* (Case 8/55 R. Vol. II at p. 206) exemplifying the former case, the judgment in *Firma I. Nold K.G.* c. *Haute Autorité* (Case 18/57 R. Vol. III p. 235 and R. Vol. V. p. 91) exemplifying the latter . . .".

In *Société des Charbonnages de Beeringen etc.* c. *Haute Autorité* (Case 9/55 R. Vol. II at p. 350) the Court stated:

"The fact that the decision No. 22–25 (of the High Authority) comprises a detailed and concrete set of rules, applicable in different situations, is not in contradiction with the general character of the decision. Indeed, the Treaty in Article 50 paragraph 2 states that the method of assessment and collection of the levies shall be fixed by a general decision of the High Authority, which shows that the detailed and varied concrete consequences of a general decision do nothing to alter its general character".

In *Le Groupement des Industries Sidérurgiques Luxembourgeoises* c. *Haute Autorité* (Consolidated Cases 7 and 9/54, R. Vol. II at pp. 86–7) the Court stated:

"In requiring that decisions capable of being annulled as a result of a claim by undertakings and associations must be individual in character, when they are not vitiated by *détournement de pouvoir* affecting them, the Treaty has withheld from private persons, in all cases where no *détournement de pouvoir* affecting them is claimed, all (judicial) appreciation of decisions and recommendations of general purport. In these circumstances it is sufficient to enable a claim to be brought by an undertaking or association against a decision or recommendation, that this decision or recommendation is not of a general nature, but has the character of an individual decision without it being necessary for it to have this character relatively to the claimant".

In *Fédération Charbonnière de Belgique* c. *Haute Autorité* (Case 8/55 R. Vol. II at pp. 247 *et seq.*) Advocate General Lagrange submitted:

"What is relatively clear is the distinction between the *regulation*, on the one hand, that is, the administrative act designed to take effect with respect to a general and impersonal situation by virtue of rule-making provisions, and which, from the material point of view at any rate, partakes of the nature of the law, which it is normally destined to complete, and on the other hand, the opposite extreme, the act which is individual, of which the object is to apply the rule to a given person (for example, a fine, or the grant or refusal of a permit). But the difficulty results from the existence, between the two extremes, of a whole series of intermediary cases. For some of these the choice is easy: for example, collective decisions are in reality no more than the juxtaposition of individual decisions as in an employees' grading schedule). But in other cases, the difficulty is greater. That is true where the decision applies to a concrete situation, which it regulates directly, without, however, the persons aimed at being designated by name, or even without it being possible to know what persons it concerns, other than by a special examination of each individual case. In support of a restrictive interpretation of the notion of individual decision recourse might be had to Article 15 of the Treaty: 'When decisions and recommendations are individual in character, they shall become binding upon being notified to the party concerned', whereas 'In all other cases they shall take effect as a result of mere publication'. But our opinion, and that of M. Roemer (the other Advocate General) is that the essential object of this provisions is to make ascertainable when there is sufficient publication of the decision to have obligatory effect: this is relevant primarily to the time limits for the claim for annulment.

In our view, to resolve the difficulty of what we have called the intermediary cases it would be desirable to refer for assistance to a subjective criterion of relativity. By that we mean that a decision which, by hypothesis, has no rule-making character and is intended to govern directly a concrete situation, can be considered as an individual decision *in respect of those persons* (undertakings or associations) which are immediately and directly aimed at by this decision *taken in its entirety*. The character of being an individual decision, on the other hand, must be withheld from the same decision with respect to those persons it does not concern directly or concerns only partially. The idea is that some correlation, not mathematical, of course, but fairly strict, should be established between the field of application of the decision and the field of the interests represented by the person who brings an action against this decision.

This appears to us justified on two grounds. First, it makes it possible to give an interpretation of Article 33 based essentially on the notion of interest, which underlies, as we have said, the whole article . . . . Second . . . it opens wide the possibility of access to the Court to the producers' associations of Article 48, which we also consider necessary. Indeed, the associations represent collective interests and too great a restriction of the concept of individual decision would result in the majority of cases in making it impossible for them to avail themselves of the right of action which Article 33 grants them: they could not challenge general decisions except in case of "*détournement de pouvoir* affecting them" and they could not challenge individual decisions in the narrow sense (for example, a fine or a permit) because it is, we believe, a generally admitted principle that a legal person such as an association or a syndicate cannot substitute itself for one of its members for the purposes of bringing an action properly belonging to that member. The Conseil d'Etat of France has a consistent case law (*jurisprudence constante*) to that effect (see Odent, *op. cit., ante*; p. 96 at pp. 542–3).

Now the associations of undertakings envisaged in Article 48 have an important role in the Treaty, which Article 48 itself defines. It seems to us indispensable that this role should be exercised also in the defence before the Court of the collective interests with which they are entrusted, all the more so because as experience has shown, some decisions of the High Authority can injure these interests without any Member State considering it useful to bring proceedings at the Court. One might even say that in the case of coal this is virtually the normal situation, because usually, and particularly when price is in question, the interests of coal undertakings conflict at one and the same time with the High Authority, whose mission is to "seek the establishment of the lowest possible prices" (Article 3c), with all the consumers and in particular the steel makers, and with the governments whose general economic policy attempts also, for the most part, to restrain the prices of this basic material".

". . . the Court's enquiry into the case may not cover the evaluation of the situation. The object of a decision." Extent to which the Court may enquire into this. In *Société Métallurgique de Knutange* c. *Haute Autorité*, a case concerning an individual decision relating to duties payable in respect of scrap (Consolidated cases 15 and 29/59 R. Vol. VI(i) at pp. 27–8) the Court stated:

". . . the Court's inquiry cannot go into the question of the expediency or desirability of the mechanism (for equalizing the burden of cost of scrap—author) established by the High Authority, in order to arrive at the object of this decision, because such an inquiry would overstep the limits of the control of legality which the Court may exercise by virtue of the Treaty. Indeed, such an inquiry would necessarily entail an appreciation of the complex situation of the market in respect of which the general decision 2–57 was taken. Such an appreciation, according to article 33 of the Treaty, the Court has no jurisdiction to make unless the High Authority is charged, with pertinent indications in support of the charge, with having committed a *détournment de pouvoir* or with "having patently misinterpreted the provisions of the Treaty." The applicant has not charged the High Authority with *détournement de pouvoir* or patently misinterpreting the Treaty provisions. . . ." (see also *ante*, pp. 5–6).

In *Hamborner Bergbau A.G. Friedrich Thyssen Bergbau A.G.* c. *Haute Autorité* (Consolidated Cases 41 and 50/59 R. Vol. VII (ii) at p. 1061–2) Adv. Gen. Roemer submitted:

"*The Total of the Guarantee Fund.* The applicants have admitted that the High Authority clearly had a certain discretion and freedom of appreciation in regard to determining the amount of the guarantee fund. As we have said, this point of view is correct . . . . That leads us to examine the question whether in principle the Court can exercise its power of legal control at this point [having regard to article 33 paragraph 1, second sentence]. It cannot be denied that the fixing of the total required for the guarantee fund depends also on the appreciation or assessment of the situation resulting from the economic facts and circumstances, nevertheless, in its consideration of the extent to which loans may be necessary or of the likely amount to which recourse may be made to the High Authority to ensure the service of the loan, the High Authority is obliged to take into account the future trend of production and the trend of the capital markets, that is to say the general economic situation. In fact, referring to article 33, paragraph one, second sentence, the applicants expressly charge the High Authority with *détournement de pouvoir* and patent misinterpretation of the provisions of the Treaty. If we understand article 33 aright that fact alone [*i.e.* the allegation of the applicants] does not suffice to open the way to control by the Court. Admittedly, the proof of a *détournement de pouvoir* or of a patent misinterpretation of the provisions of the Treaty cannot be insisted upon because, in that case, the claim could be upheld without further inquiry. Nevertheless, the existence of the legal faults just referred to must, in some degree, be rendered credible, that is to say the applicants must demonstrate a high degree of probability that the decision is vitiated by *détournement de pouvoir* or patent misinterpretation of the provisions of the Treaty".

The Advocate General then briefly summarized the arguments put forward by the parties in the course of the written procedure, before continuing as follows:

"This examination permits us to reach the following conclusions. In our opinion the applicants have not succeeded in demonstrating the probability of the existence of patent misinterpretation of the provisions of the Treaty and have not shown sufficiently clearly that a *détournement de pouvoir* must be suspected. In accordance with the principles of article 33 regulating the jurisdiction of the Court, this finding has as a consequence that the Court cannot inquire into the sphere of appreciation in which the High Authority acts in this part of the matters in litigation . . .".

The "exception of illegality": Claims brought "under the terms of the first paragraph" of E.C.S.C. 33 by virtue of E.C.S.C. 36. (*"Exception d'illégalité"; "Einrede der Rechtswidrigkeit"; "exceptie van onwettigheid"; "eccezione d'illegitimità"*). First see "Exception of Illegality", *ante*, p. 87. In *Compagnie des Hauts Fourneaux de Chasse c. Haute Autorité* (Case 15/57 R. Vol. IV at pp. 203–205). Adv. Gen. Lagrange submitted:

"In three of the Member States, France, Belgium and Italy, this exception is freely admitted, being considered as forming part of the normal sphere of application of the claim for annulment. This is due to the fact that in these three countries, rules made by the executive power are considered, *as far as the right to appeal against them is concerned*, from the formal point of view, that is to say as being administrative acts liable to be annulled if they are contrary to the law [*administrative acts* is a term of art which embraces those acts of the Administration which have effect in and are governed by administrative law, as distinct from the ordinary or civil, law. Acts of the Administration which are not subject to administrative law are not administrative acts in the strict sense (*cf. post*, p. 134) —*author*]. Given that the direct claim for annulment is possible with regard to them, there is no objection in principle to the (judicial) control of their legality being also exercised when individual claims are made of which they are the object. The advantage is that the exception of illegality may be set up at any time, even when the time-limit for a claim against the regulation or the general decision has expired. On the other hand, if the claim is successful only the individual decision [based on the regulation in general decision] is annulled, which avoids the grave consequences of the annulment of the regulation itself, declared with retroactive effect *erga omnes*.

As far as France is concerned we will cite, amongst many, two judgments of the Conseil d'Etat: *Abbé Barthélémy*, 9 July 1926, Recueil p. 713;

Marcin-Kowsky, 28 November 1957, Recueil p. 548. These decisions are interesting because they begin by rejecting as presented out of time the submissions that the rule should be annulled, and, immediately following, pass judgment on the legality of the very same rule in respect of submissions directed against an individual decision applying the rule. Case law shows, however, that the legality of the rule can only be contested in respect of those of its provisions which provided the basis for the individual decision taken in application of the rule (*Dame Denayer* 18 February 1949, Recueil p. 80).

In the three other countries of the Community, Germany, Holland and Luxemburg, there is a strong tendency to remain attached to the material criterion, by virtue of which a regulation is a piece of secondary ["dele-gated"]—legislation no different in its legal nature from the law itself. Nevertheless the subordination of the rule to the (general) law remains an established legal principle and, if the former conception causes some hesitation with regard to *direct* claims for annulment of regulations, the second conception, on the other hand, more readily permits the setting up of the exception of illegality. In criminal law, this exception is very freely admitted. In administrative law it is also admitted. The principal difficulties in the latter field lie mainly in determining which judge is competent to rule on the question of legality: that happens, particularly, in France, a country in which the principle of the separation of powers is very strictly applied and where, in consequence, a reference to the administrative Court for a preliminary ruling on legality is often made in defiance of the principle according to which the judge in the action is also judge in respect of the exception; but such considerations do not arise where, as in the instant case, the same judge has competence.

Are there any special reasons for adopting a different solution for the application of the Treaty? We do not think so. On the contrary, article 41, which confers jurisdiction on the Court—without any restriction as to the nature of the grounds which may be put forward, nor as to the nature of the decision against which the claim is made—to give a preliminary ruling as to the validity of resolutions of the High Authority when the question arises in a dispute the subject of litigation before a national court, is an added argument in favour of there being no restrictions, for there is no reason which could justify a more restrictive solution in respect of undertakings having direct access to the Court, than in respect of third parties who may on occasion need the Court's judgment with regard to a decision of the High Authority."

In a later case, *Compagnie des Hauts Fourneaux de Chasse* c. *Haute Autorité* (Case 15/57 R. Vol. IV at p. 205) Adv. Gen. Lagrange submitted:

"We call attention to the fact that if article 36 has considered it necessary to provide *in terminis* for the exception of illegality in the case of an appeal against fines and other measures of constraint, it is no doubt in order to avoid all hesitation. For, if it is correct, as we have recalled, that the exception of illegality is generally admitted in criminal matters, because criminal law is in essence legislative, one might have harboured a doubt because of the fact that the fines and other measures of sanction provided for by the Treaty are administrative sanctions, not criminal sanctions, and that article 36 which is their *lex specialis*, creates in this respect a means of recourse known as of full jurisdiction. It has seemed preferable to define the limits of this full jurisdiction by indicating in an explicit manner that the judge exercising such jurisdiction could remain, without restriction, *in this matter also*, judge of the legality. In contra-distinction to this, in article 33 we are dealing with the jurisdiction to annul, and it was not necessary, in that article, to say more."

In *Meroni & Co.* c. *Haute Autorité* (Case 10/56, R. Vol. IV at pp. 101–2) Adv. Gen. Roemer submitted:

"Does the rule in article 36 paragraph 3 constitute a special rule for matters of fines and other measures of constraint or is it simply an important example of the application of a general notion of law, particularly emphasized by the Treaty for that reason? We consider there is no valid reason to think that the rule is concerned with an exception which must be subject to restrictive interpretation. On the contrary, the sphere of application of the exception of illegality must be extended beyond the case of fines or measures of constraint, to make complete the protection in law of undertakings. Whereas they cannot seek to upset general decisions by means of a claim for annulment except in narrow limits, undertakings must be entitled, when obligations, injunctions and prohibitions are the direct result for themselves that flows from general decisions, to claim against the irregularity of the general decision that is applied. It is in this light that article 41 must also be viewed: the general decision is the basis of the claims made before national courts and the party to the action can attack the validity of the decision of the High Authority which is of concern for the judgment which the national Court has to render. It is only in exceptional circumstances that undertakings may be held to have a sufficient interest to make a direct claim for annulment of general decisions; often the interest of the undertakings cannot be recognized until an individual decision is taken applying the general decision to them. On the other hand it cannot be denied that there is every reason not to allow that an irregular general decision should be specifically applied to an undertaking or that obligations thought to follow from the general decision should be made to fall upon that undertaking."

The three grounds other than misuse of powers (*détournement de pouvoir*) are exceptionally available to an [applicant] undertaking by virtue of E.C.S.C. 36. In *Meroni & Co.* c. *Haute Autorité* (Case 9/56 R. Vol. IV at p, 26), the Court stated:

"E.C.S.C. 36 provides that in respect of a claim against a decision of the High Authority imposing a fine (or other measure of sanction) 'in support of such recourse and under the terms of E.C.S.C. 33 paragraph 1, applicants may contest the legality of the decisions and recommendations which they are alleged to have contravened'.

There is no reason for considering this provision of Article 36 as a special rule, applicable only in the case of fines and other measures of sanction, but it must be seen as the application of a general principle, which Article 36 provides shall be made to apply to the particular case of a claim to the "full jurisdiction". The explicit mention in Article 36 does not found an argument excluding *a contrario* the application of the rule in cases where it has not been explicitly mentioned, the Court having held, in its judgment 8/55, that an argument *a contrario* is not admissible unless no other interpretation appears adequate and compatible with the text, the context, and their intendment".

(re-iterated verbatim in *Compagnie des Hauts Fourneaux de Chasse* c. *Haute Autorité* (Case 15/57, R. Vol. IV at p. 184).

". . . the E.E.C. and E.A.E.C. Treaties expressly adopt a similar point of view, which they set out respectively in their Articles 184 and 156 . . . this factor, although not constituting a determining argument, confirms the above reasoning by showing that it appealed similarly to the authors of the new Treaties".

(*Idem* at p. 27. Re-iterated verbatim by the Court in *Meroni & Co.* c. *Haute Autorité*, Case 10/56 R. Vol. IV at p. 66.)

"Persons subjected to the penalties" [fines] "laid down in" E.C.S.C. 66 (6) (penalties imposed by the High Authority in respect of concentrations) "may have recourse to the Court" (by virtue of E.C.S.C. 66 (6)) under the conditions provided for in E.C.S.C. 36". (See under E.C.S.C. 36, *ante*, p. 80).

"Exception of illegality" not raised where it might have been. Attitude of Court. In *Société des Fonderies de Pont-a-Mousson* c. *Haute Autorité* (Case 14/59 R. Vol. V at p. 474) the Court stated:

"The applicant has not explicitly raised an exception of illegality against decision 2.57 and it would be difficult to argue that such a charge had been formulated implicitly; nevertheless, it appears undesirable to allow doubts to remain as to the regularity of decision 2.57 so far as their removal affects the present dispute; for that reason the Court considers it necessary in any event to examine to what extent the second ground of the applicant is well-founded".

Individual decision and the "exception of illegality". In *Société Nouvelle des Usines de Pontlieu Aciéries du Temple* c. *Haute Autorité* (Consolidated cases 32 and 32/58, R. Vol. V. at p. 300) the Court stated:

"According to the consistent case law ["*jurisprudence constante*", see *ante*, p. 9,] the undertaking which seeks to upset an individual decision is entitled to raise the exception of illegality against the general decision on which it is based".

(Re-iterated verbatim by the Court in *Société des Aciers fins de l'Est* (S.A.F.E.) Case 42/58 R. Vol. V, at p. 400).

The "exception of illegality" in relation to a general decision". In *Meroni & Co.* c. *Haute Autorité* (Case 9/56. R. Vol. IV at p. 27) the Court stated:

". . . the possibility that is open to an applicant to avail himself [by virtue of E.C.S.C. 36—author] after the time limit laid down in the last paragraph of article 33 has expired, in support of a claim against an individual decision, of the irregularity of the general decisions and recommendations on which the individual decision is based cannot result in the annulment of the general decision but only of the individual decision founded on it".

(Re-iterated by the Court in the same words in *Meroni & Co.* c. *Haute Autorité* (Case 10/56 R. Vol. IV at p. 67.) Also in the same sense, see *Compagnie des Hauts Fourneaux de Chasse* c. *Haute Autorité* (Case 15/57 R. Vol. IV p. 155 at p. 185)).

Relationship of E.C.S.C. 33 and E.C.S.C. 35. In *Groupement des Industries Sidérurgiques Luxembourgeoises* c. *Haute Autorité* (Consolidated cases 7/54 and 9/54 R. Vol. 11 at 9.85) the Court stated:

"The conditions of Article 33 govern a claim brought under Article 35 paragraph 3, for it is in fact a claim for annulment on the grounds of infringement of the Treaty and violation of a basic procedural rule."

See under E.C.S.C. 35. "Annulment E.C.S.C. 33. It is not permissible, by the device of using the procedure directed against a failure to act, for an applicant to seek the annulment of a decision" after the time-limit of E.C.S.C. 33 has expired (*post*, p. 124).

Relationship of E.C.S.C. 33 and E.C.S.C. 37. See under E.C.S.C. 37 "The ambit of the Article", *post*, pp. 127 *et seq.*, especially p. 129.

Relationship of E.C.S.C. 33, 86 and 88. In *Gouvernement de la Ré-publique Fédérale d'Allemagne c. Haute Autorité* (Case 3/59, R. Vol. VI (i) at pp. 131–3) the Court stated:

". . . [the applicant maintains] that article 58 gives Member States a special means of appeal, distinct from that provided in article 33, enabling them to benefit by recourse to the full jurisdiction of the Court extending even to an inquiry into the legality of the (general) decisions on which (the individual decision of the High Authority addressed to the applicant—author) was based. This argument cannot be accepted. It cannot be maintained that Member States are entitled to seek to upset by recourse to the full jurisdiction not only the decisions taken by the High Authority in accordance with article 88, but also the decisions it takes in the exercise of the general powers conferred on it by the Treaty. Indeed, article 33 which makes available, to Member States as to undertakings, a claim for annulment and not an appeal to the full jurisdiction, stands in the way of the interpretation put forward by the applicant. If a Member State without having obtained the annulment of a decision of the High Authority, or the suspension of the enforcement of this decision, does not abide by the decision, it makes itself responsible by that very fact, by virtue of article 86 paragraph 1, for a failure to carry out its obligations, a failure which the High Authority is obliged to take note of in accordance with article 88, paragraph 1. In the instant case, by the decision which it is sought to upset, the High Authority has fulfilled this obligation; consequently the said decision must be interpreted in the sense that it is confined to taking note of the formal failure [of the Member State] without re-opening the factual questions settled by its earlier [general] decisions of February 1958. The applicant maintains that such an interpretation deprives of its meaning the appeal to the full jurisdiction provided for in article 88, but this argument cannot be accepted. For the object of the appeal provided for in article 88 paragraph 2 is to subject to legal review by the Court the finding which the High Authority has made of a failure of a Member State, and the measures of the High Authority consequent upon that finding. On the other hand, the decisions taken by the High Authority in the exercise of its powers and in cases where article 88 has no application may—generally speaking—constitute the object of an appeal by virtue of article 33. The High Authority can find to be a failure of a Member State to carry out an obligation a failure in relation either to some provision of the Treaty or to some decision taken by the High Authority itself. Thus the distinction must be kept clear between the possible appeal—by virtue of Article 33—against a decision of the non-observance of which the High Authority has subsequently complained, and the appeal—by virtue of article 88 paragraph 2— against the finding of non-observance of the decision.

Indeed the object of the two appeals is quite distinct. The object of the first is a declaration by the Court of the illegality of a decision taken in a case to which Article 88 does not apply. The second can only have as its object:

(a) to secure the annulment of the finding of failure to observe, by showing that the Member State did conform to the obligations flowing from the decision the non-observance of which is held against it, which excludes the possibility of putting in issue at the same time the legality of the decision itself;

(b) to secure the annulment or the modification of the measures taken by the High Authority following the finding of the failure.

It may be well to note that if the interpretation of the applicant were adopted, it would follow that Member States might disregard decisions taken in respect of themselves by the High Authority and wait until there is set in motion against them the procedure of article 88, to set in motion themselves a procedure directed against the decisions whenever they deem it useful to do so."

Relationship of E.C.S.C. 33 and E.C.S.C. 80, 65 and 66. Undertakings engaged in distribution may, by virtue of Article 80, appeal to the Court in respect of an application of article 65 and 66 affecting their interests (but the general requirements of admissibility of article 33 (2), which vary according to the nature of the decisions it is sought to upset, must be complied with).

". . . The terms of article 80 in respect of "appeals based upon articles 65 and 66" relate not only to those based on the direct application of articles 65 and 66 to distributors under the head of agreements and concentrations, but they also refer to those cases in which, like the present one, the application of these articles affects the interests of distributors. The appeal must fulfil the general requirements of admissibility of article 33 paragraph 2, according to the nature of the decisions thus sought to be upset . . ." (*per* the Court in *Firma I. Nold K.G. c. Haute Autorité*, Case 18/57 (summary procedure) R. Vol. III at p. 241).

". . . The Request seeks to upset the decision of 27th November 1957 of the High Authority, which, notified of the decision of the Provincial Court (Landgericht) of Essen not to render judgment, had affirmed that the prohibitions set out in article 65(1) of the Treaty did not apply to the decisions of the six Sales Organizations for Ruhr Coal taken on the 5th February 1953. In accordance with article 65(4) paragraph two, the Court can admit an appeal against such a decision of the High Authority and therefore has jurisdiction to determine the present dispute . . ." (*per* the Court in *Friedrich Stork et Cie c. Haute Autorité*, Case 1/58 R. Vol. v at p. 61).

The legality of a decision depends solely on its conformity with the Treaty. In *Compagnie des Hauts Fourneaux de Chasse c. Haute Autorité* (Case 2/57, R. Vol. IV at p. 148) the Court stated:

"The present claim must be rejected, since the legality of the decision against which the action is brought cannot be made to depend on its conformity with the memoranda published by the High Authority, but solely on its conformity with the Treaty. . . ."

These words were repeated by the Court in a later case between the same parties (Case 15/57, R. Vol. IV at p. 194):

"The present claim must be rejected since the legality of basic decisions cannot be made to depend on their conformity with the memorandum which the High Authority has published, but solely on their conformity with the Treaty. Indeed, the memorandum does not by any means contain the only possible definition of the legitimate object which the High Authority is entitled to pursue. To establish the misapplication of power, the applicant should have shown that the decisions themselves were in reality pursuing an object other than the one with regard to which the High Authority was entitled to act; the difference to which the applicant has drawn attention, between the wording of the memorandum and that of the basic decisions, is not significant as a proof of this . . .".

Relationship of E.C.S.C. 33 to E.C.S.C. 66(5). Where the High Authority issues a reasoned decision declaring a concentration unlawful, E.C.S.C. 65(5) (for text, see under "Suspension of enforcement of administrative act", *post*, p. 160) provides that "Any person directly concerned may make an application against such decisions under the conditions provided for in Article 33." In so doing, E.C.S.C. 66(5) also provides for derogation from E.C.S.C. 33, by conferring full jurisdiction on the Court "to decide whether the course of action taken is a concentration within the meaning of paragraph 1 of this Article. "As to what party may make an application under E.C.S.C. 66(5) it has been suggested by Paul Reuter in "*La Communanté Europeenne du Charbon et de l'acier* p. 221" that "*ces recours sont ouverts à tous intéressés, donc au besoin à des étrangers.*" As to suspensive effect of such an application see *loc. cit. supra.*

Consequences of annulment of an act of the High Authority

E.C.S.C. 34

If the Court quashes a decision or recommendation it shall refer the matter back to the High Authority. The latter shall be required to take the necessary steps to comply with the decision to quash. If direct and special injury is suffered by an undertaking or a group of undertakings by reason of a decision or recommendation, held by the Court to involve a wrongful act or default of such a nature as to render the Community liable, the High Authority shall, using the powers which are conferred upon it by the provisions of the present Treaty, take suitable measures to ensure equitable redress for the injury resulting directly from the decision or recommendation which has been quashed and, as far as may be necessary, to grant fair damages.

If the High Authority fails to take within a reasonable time the necessary steps to comply with a decision to quash, proceedings for damages may be instituted in the Court.

Compare E.E.C. 176 (and E.A.E.C. 148) *ante*, p. 89 and see under E.C.S.C. 40, *post*, p. 144.

The Court's judgment annulling an act cannot anticipate or prejudice the measures which the High Authority is required by E.C.S.C. 34 to take. In *Sociétés Minières du bassin de la Ruhr . . . Geitling* c. *Haute Autorité* (Case 2/56, R. Vol. III at p. 35) the Court stated:

". . . In the course of the oral procedure the argument was advanced that a claim could not be admissible if it seeks the annulment of an isolated provison of a multiple decision, inasmuch as a partial annulment would transform the rest of the decision, making it a new decision, which would be contrary to article 34 of the Treaty. This provides, in the case of annulment of a decision, for it to be remitted to the High Authority.

This objection is not well-founded since by the terms of the said article 34, the judgment could not anticipate or prejudice the measures which the High Authority is required to take to modify the decision, taking account of the annulment".

In *Gouvernement de la Republique Italienne* c. *Haute Autorité* (Case 2/54 R. Vol. I at p. 104) the Court stated:

"According to Article 34 of the Treaty, in the event of annulment, the matter must be remitted to the High Authority which is under an obligation to take the measures which are involved in the execution of the order of annulment.

To the extent the claim for annulment is held well founded and by reason of the interest a decision on the grounds advanced has for the claimant, this treaty provison remains applicable notwithstanding the fact that the annulment of the first Article of the High Authority's decision

No. 2–54 can not be formally pronounced by the Court, since this Article was annulled prior to the present judgment, although on the same date". In *M. Antoine Kergall* c. *Haute Autorité* (Case 1/55; R. Vol. II at p. 48) the Court Stated:

"It follows from Article 34 of the treaty that any illegal measure, even if it were to be annulled as a result of a claim for annulment, does not *ipso facto* import an obligation to pay damages with interest. In the same way, in French law, the illegal character of a measure is certainly a necessary condition of liability (in tort, *"responsabilité"*) but this condition does not suffice by itself. In particular an infringement of formal requirements is of no importance unless it has exerted an influence on the contents of the administrative decision itself. The indemnity has no penal quality, is not a fine imposed on the administration for the non-respect of legal rules, but the making good of damages resulting from a measure *in essence* unjustified".

Duty of High Authority under Article 34 where there is annulment of a failure to act. In *Groupement des Industries Sidérurgiques Luxembourgeoises* c. *Haute Autorité* (Consolidated Cases 7/54 and 9/54 R. Vol. II) where an action against the High Authority was under Article 35 paragraph 3 of the treaty and on the basis of its failure to act, and the claimant in addition to annulment of this failure to act sought the prohibition "in consequence" of certain activities of the "Office" and of the *"Caisse de Compensation"*, these submissions were held inadmissible. Adv. Gen. Roemer (at pp. 114–5) submitted:

"Indeed, in the treaty system, in the case of claims in respect of failure to act, the Court cannot oblige the High Authority to carry out a given administrative act. Quite the contrary, in the event of annulment, the case must be remitted to the High Authority, in accordance with Article 34 of the treaty, and it is then for the High Authority to act as required by this article. The claimant admitted this during the oral procedure.

The claim mentioned in Article 35 paragraph 3 and not defined— cannot be other than a claim for annulment. This claim is directed against an (administrative) decision. At the basis of it one finds the grounds of action of Article 33 together with the special characteristics resulting from a failure to act. Any other consequences there may be can be determined only by virtue of Article 34, the matter being remitted to the High Authority in the event of annulment of the decision of refusal to act; the High Authority from that point onwards must act within the framework of the Court's judgement. [*idem* at p. 120].

According to Article 34, in the event of annulment, the Court remits the matter to the High Authority. For its part, the High Authority is bound to take the measures that necessarily follow from the execution of the judgement of annulment. It is not for the Court to decide what these measures are. It is for the High Authority, on the basis of the judgment, to re-examine the matter" [*idem* at p. 133].

Restriction, in E.C.S.C. 34, of categories of persons entitled to claim damages. In *Société Commerciale Antoine Vloeberghs S.A.* c. *Haute Autorité* (Consolidated Cases 9, 12/60, R. Vol. VII at p. 447) Adv. Gen. Roemer submitted:

". . . Some authors consider, justifiably, that the fact that E.C.S.C. 34 restricts the categories of persons entitled to claim damages is unsatisfactory. Only undertakings and associations of undertakings are mentioned, which is far from comprising all the applicants who, by virtue of article 33, are entitled to originate an action for annulment. The attempt has therefore been made to proceed to a reasonable extension. It is considered that it should be held legally possible, by virtue of article 34, for undertakings and individuals foreign to E.C.S.C. ["foreign" in what sense is not here defined, but it appears to mean "outside the field covered by the treaty" and not to be concerned with nationality—*author*] to whom the Treaty exceptionally grants the right to originate actions for annulment, to bring claims to impose limitations on dealing of undertakings within the Community (*viz*, purchasers, according to article 63(2) paragraph 2; participants in concentrations of undertakings, foreign to the Community, according to article 66(5)) or, alternatively, it is proposed, by way of analogy, that there should be given to undertakings foreign to the Community the right to originate an action for annulment [under article 33] and consequently the action for "*faute de service*" of article 34. . . ."

E.C.S.C. 34 contains no provision for the annulment of an act.   In *Società Metallurgica di Napoli etc.* (SIMET) c. *Haute Autorité* (Consolidated Cases 36, 37, 38, 40 and 41/58, R. Vol. V. at p. 372) Adv. Gen. Roemer submitted:

"What the applicants are seeking, on the contrary, is the annulment of a decision taken by the High Authority in order to put into effect the judgment of the Court quashing a decision. But article 34 contains no provision with respect to the procedure for annulment of a decision. The result of this legal position is that the annulment which the applicants seek can only be obtained by means of the procedure in article 33."

C. Resolutions of the E.C.S.C. Assembly or Council

E.C.S.C. 38

The Court may, on the application of a member State or of the High Authority, quash decisions of the Assembly or of the Council.

The application shall be made within one month from the publication of a decision of the Assembly or the notification of a decision of the Council to the member States or to the High Authority.

The sole grounds for such recourse shall be lack of powers or violation of basic procedural rules.

"Décisions".   (Fr. *délibérations*) is a general expression which must be taken to embrace the decisions and opinions of the Council (listed in Chapter I *ante*, p. 55) and certain acts of the Assembly (for which provision is made in E.C.S.C. 21–25, not printed in this work) of which potentially the most important is a vote of censure on the general report of the High Authority, which, if carried by a two-thirds majority of the votes cast and representing a majority of the members of the Assembly, makes obligatory the collective resignations from office of the members of the High Authority. Whether "Regulations" come within the provision of E.C.S.C. 38 is not clear.

"The grounds".   The grounds of annulment of resolutions are identical with two of the four grounds upon which, under E.C.S.C. 33 (see *ante*, p. 93) the recommendations and decisions of the High Authority may be quashed. That the annulment of resolutions of the Assembly and Council is thus limited to the successful proof of lack of jurisdiction or violation of basic procedural rules has been explained by the essentially political rather than administrative character and function of the Assembly and Council.

Restricted jurisdictional control provided by E.C.S.C. 38. In *M. René Bourgaux* c. *Assemblée Commune, C.E.C.A.* (Case 1/56, R. Vol. II at p. 435) the Court stated:

". . . claims in administrative matters, common to all employees of the four Institutions, are organically distinct from the restricted jurisdictional control provided for by E.C.S.C. 38 and related to the activity of the Assembly as an Institution. . . ."

But see the Court's interpretation of E.C.S.C. 42 in relation to E.C.S.C. 38, in the same case, under E.C.S.C. 42, *post*, p. 156).

(IV) FAILURE TO ACT

(On the part of certain Community Institutions other than the Court of Justice).

Not only may a positive act be annulled for illegality (see "Legality of Acts," *ante*, p. 83), but failure of certain Community Institutions to act may equally constitute an illegality which is a ground for action before the Court. Under E.E.C. and E.A.E.C. the failure to act may be that of the Council or Commission; under E.C.S.C. that of the High Authority.

A. FAILURE TO ACT, OF COUNCIL OR COMMISSION OF E.E.C. OR E.A.E.C.

((*Le Conseil ou la Commission*) *s'abstient de statuer;* (*der Rat oder die Kommission*) *unterläszt . . . einen Beschlusz zu fassen;* (*de Raad of de Commissie*) *nalaat een besluit te nemen;* (*il Consiglio o la Commissione*) *si astengano dal pronunciarsi*)

E.E.C. 175

Should the Council or the Commission in violation of this Treaty fail to act, the Member States and the other institutions of the Community may refer the matter to the Court of Justice in order to have the said violation placed on record.

No proceedings arising out of the said reference shall be heard unless the institution concerned has been called upon to act. If within two months of being so called upon, the institution concerned has not made its attitude clear, the said proceedings may be brought within a further period of two months.

Any natural or legal person may bring proceedings before the Court of Justice, under the conditions laid down in the preceding paragraphs, on the ground that one of the institutions of the Community has failed to send him a formal document, such document not being a recommendation or an opinion.

E.A.E.C. 148

[*Identical with E.E.C.* 175)]

". . . In violation of this Treaty fail to act . . ." "The Council and the Commission shall, in the discharge of their duties and in accordance with the provisions of this Treaty issue regulations and directives, take decisions and formulate recommendations or opinions" (E.E.C. 189, E.A.E.C. 161, Chapter 1, *ante*, p. 26).

"**. . . The Member States and the other Institutions of the Community may refer the matter . . .**". There are four Institutions in each of the two Communities, namely Assembly, Council, Commission and Court of Justice (see under "Acts of the Institutions of the Community" *post*, p. 134). It should be noted that any one of them may refer a failure to act to the Court, whereas the legality of a positive act may be challenged before the Court, only, among the Institutions, by the Council or the Commission (see "Legality of Acts," *ante*, p. 83).

"**. . . In order to have the said infringement placed on record . . .**". The effect of this, by virtue of E.E.C. 176 (and E.A.E.C. 148) (see under "Legality of Acts," *ante*, p. 89) is that the "Institution whose failure to act has been declared contrary to the provisions of this Treaty shall be required to take the measures necessary for the implementation of the judgment of the Court of Justice".

"**Any natural or legal person . . .**". As to the persons included within this expression see "any natural or legal person . . ." under E.E.C. 173 (*ante*, p. 84).

"**. . . On the ground that one of the Institutions has failed to send him . . .**". This wording includes, literally, all four Institutions (Assembly, Council, Commission, Court of Justice) whereas the failure to act, in infringement of the Treaty, referred to in paragraph one, is that of the Council or Commission only.

"**. . . Not being a recommendation or opinion**" (as to the administrative purpose and legal force of these see in Chapter I E.E.C. 189 and E.A.E.C. 161, *ante*, pp. 26 and 46). The Council and Commission may formulate recommendations and opinions. Their failure to do so, in infringement of the Treaty, may be referred by the Member States and the other Institutions of the Community to the Court of Justice by virtue of E.E.C. 175 (and E.A.E.C. 148) paragraph one. (See also generally *ante*, pp. 18–20.)

See the reference to E.E.C. 175 in the extract from *Société Rhenania etc.* c. *Commission C.E.E.* under E.E.C. 169 (*ante*, p. 67).

Withdrawal of an appeal. Following agreed settlement between the parties (as provided for by R. P. 77 (*post*, p. 265) this is not permitted in respect of an appeal under E.E.C. 175, E.A.E.C. 148 and E.C.S.C. 35 (as to E.C.S.C. 35 see immediately *infra*, and as to impossibility of withdrawal of claim for annulment of an act see *ante*, p. 88).

B. Failure to Act, of High Authority of E.C.S.C.

E.C.S.C. 35

Whenever the High Authority is required by a provision of this Treaty, or of regulations in implementation thereof, to take a decision or make a recommendation and fails to fulfil this obligation, the States, the Council or the undertakings and associations, as the case may be, shall have the right to bring the matter before it.

The same shall apply if the High Authority, when empowered by a provision of this Treaty or regulations in implementation thereof to take a decision or make a recommendation, abstains from doing so and such abstention constitutes a misuse of powers.

If at the end of two months the High Authority has not taken any decision or made any recommendation, an appeal may be made to the Court within one month against the High Authority's implied refusal to take action which is to be inferred from its silence on the matter.

Conditions precedent to right of appeal. "Whenever the High Authority is required . . . to take a decision to make a recommendation and fails to fulfil this obligation . . ." or ". . . when empowered . . . to take a decision or make a recommendation abstains from doing so and such abstention constitutes a misuse of powers". Neither of these occurrences, of itself, gives a right of appeal to the Court. But one or the other occurrence must have been present in order that such a right of appeal may come into existence. Either constitutes the necessary "matter" which "the States, the Council or the undertakings and associations, as the case may be, shall have the right to bring . . . before it" (the High Authority). It is the failure of the High Authority, "at the end of two months" from the matter having been brought before it, to have "taken any decision or made any recommendation" in regard to it, that constitutes "the implied refusal to take action which is to be inferred from its silence on the matter", and against which "an appeal may be made to the Court, within one month".

In *Chambre Syndicale de la Sidérurgie de l'Est de la France etc. c. Haute Autorité* (Consolidated Cases 24, 34/58, R. Vol. VI (ii) at p. 609) the Court stated:

". . . article 35 of the Treaty provides that recourse against the High Authority for failure to act is not made possible unless the High Authority has first had the failure brought before it, and that recourse for failure to act can have no other subject than the refusal of the High Authority to take the decision the demand for which has been expressly made. Since no such demand was made, the High Authority, in accordance with article 35 paragraph one of the Treaty, cannot be held to have taken the implicit negative decision provided for in paragraph three of the same article . . .".

In *Hamborner Bergbau A.G. Friedrich Thyssen Bergbau A.G. c. Haute Autorité* (Consolidated cases 41, 50/59, R. Vol. VI (ii) at p. 1016) the Court stated:

". . . by having the failure brought before it in accordance with article 35, the High Authority is invited to define its attitude with regard to what the applicant maintains in respect of a specific factual and legal situation; the implicit negative decision relates both to the demand made by virtue of the failure being brought to the High Authority's attention and to the factual and legal situation invoked in making the demand. It would not be feasible to admit, against the implicit negative decision, a claim supported with reference to a *different* demand and a *different factual and legal situation* . . .".

What constitutes bringing the matter before it (the High Authority). In *Società Industriale Acciaieria San Michele etc. c. Haute Autorité* (Consolidated cases 5 to 11 and 13 to 15/62, R. Vol. VII at p. 881 the Court stated:

". . . The letter which the applicants state to constitute "a bringing of the matter before" the High Authority within the meaning of article 35, is dated 27th November 1961 and was received on the 29th December 1961 by the High Authority. The High Authority took a decision on the 23rd February 1962 which reached the applicants on 12th March, according to their allegation which is not contested by the defendant.

This decision of 23rd February 1962, whether or not considered by the High Authority as being in response to the demands of the applicants, does in fact meet the desire they expressed, that is to say, "to take a prior decision, in accordance with article 14, in which the High Authority will rule on all the points in dispute defined in the present letter". Without giving an explicit ruling on all the points contained in this letter of the 27th December 1961, some of which might appear to be of doubtful pertinence, the decision now in issue did settle, at least indirectly, the questions raised by the applicants, thus rendering it possible for them to appeal to the Court by virtue of article 33 of the Treaty. The fact that this indirect reply was different from what the applicants had solicited can not open up the possibility of a claim based on article 35, because this provision is not applicable unless the High Authority has taken no decision in the matter to which the demands made to it by the said applicants referred . . .".

"As the case may be" (*selon le cas*). In *Groupement des Industries Sidérurgiques Luxembourgeoises* c. *Haute Autorité* (Consolidated Cases 7/54 and 9/54 R. Vol. II at p. 83) the Court stated:
". . . in Article 35 the expression 'as the case may be' (*selon le cas*) must be looked upon as conferring the right to sue the High Authority on such of the bodies enumerated by the article as have an interest in the decision which it is claimed the High Authority has an obligation to take or in the recommendation it is claimed it is obliged to formulate".

"Undertakings and associations". In Consolidated cases 7 and 9/54 (*loc. cit. supra*, at p. 86) the Court stated:
". . . the associations envisaged can only be the associations of undertakings in the sense given to the word "undertaking" by Article 80 for the whole of the Treaty; if, indeed, it were not so, an association might find that the right of bringing an action was conferred upon it which no one of the members constituting the association would in isolation and of itself be entitled to; and in the absence of a contrary indication, the Treaty does not establish such a disparity of treatment between an association and the members which constitute it . . .".
(For text of E.C.S.C. 80 see under "Establish . . . among themselves a . . . Community . . .", *ante*, p. 48).
"No provision in the Treaty, as the Advocate General has submitted, requires that the special nature of the producers' activity must be strictly linked to the special nature of the activity with which the action is concerned".
(Compare comment "Any natural or legal person" *ante*, p. 120 and p. 84).
The above passage was re-iterated verbatim by the Court in *Association des Utilisateurs de Charbon du Grand Duché de Luxembourg* c. *Haute Autorité* (Consolidated Cases 8 and 10/54, R. Vol. II at p. 186).

When the cause of action arises. In *Groupement des Industries Sidérurgiques Luxembourgeoises* c. *Haute Autorité* (*loc. cit.*, *supra*, at pp. 88–90) concerning the "consequences of a letter from the High Authority of 27th November 1954 giving reasons, after "the end of a period of two months" (para. 3, article 35) for its refusal to take (in respect of the Luxemburg "Caisse de Compensation") the decision requested by the claimant," the Court stated:
"In its defence, the High Authority affirms that the letter of 27th November 1954 transformed its silence into an explicit refusal containing the broad reasons for the same, so that, in these circumstances the action brought on the basis of Article 35 would be deprived of all legal foundation and the claim would be without object. The letter setting out the High

Authority's reasons was written following the expiration of the period of two months provided for in paragraph 3 of Article 35. At the end of that period the "implicit negative decision" envisaged in this paragraph was presumed to exist and the right to bring an action was definitely open for the claimant. Moreover, the object of the claim is not the silence of the High Authority, but its refusal to take the decision (in the sense of Article 14) which in the eyes of the claimant it was obliged to take; the letter indicating the reasons for the High Authority's refusal does not affect the existence of this refusal, definitely established at the end of the period of two months provided for in the third paragraph of Article 35 of the Treaty; the implicit negative decision presumed to result at the end of this period, from the silence of the High Authority, does not substantially modify the situation resulting from (that silence), but merely gives it a positive expression, making it thus a possible object of a claim under the third paragraph of Article 35; the letter containing reasons of 27th November 1954 has also not modified this position, so that, as the Advocate General submitted, it neither removed the object of the claim nor prevented the claimant from proceeding with his action based on Article 35 of the Treaty".

The Court may inquire of its own volition into the question whether a decision has been made within the two months stipulated in article 35 paragraph three. In *Société Nouvelle des Usines de Pontlieue Aciéries du Temple (S.N.U.P.A.T.)* c. *Haute Autorité* (Consolidated Cases 32/33/58 R. Vol. V. at p. 299) the Court stated:

". . . the defendant raises no objections with regard to the admissibility of the claim for failure to act, inasmuch as it admits that no decision was made within the period of two months provided for in article 35 paragraph 3. However, this question must be examined *ex officio* by the Court".

It proceeded to trace the steps that had been taken, found that no decision had been taken within the two months and concluded: "the claim directed against the implicit negative decision is therefore admissible".

Misuse of powers must be present where the High Authority abstains (paragraph two) in order for there to be "the right to bring the matter before it". In *Société Nouvelle des Usines de Pontlieue Aciéries du Temple (S.N.U.P.A.T.)* c. *Haute Autorité* (Consolidated Cases 42, 49/59 R. Vol. VII at p. 148) the Court stated:

". . . the contested decision being an individual decision, the applicant is in principle entitled to avail itself of all the grounds laid down in article 33 paragraph one, and not only the misuse of powers (*détournement de pouvoir*). Consequently, there is no necessity to decide the question whether a misuse of powers (*détournement de pouvoir*) is conceivable in the case of power conferred [on the High Authority] for a particular purpose ("*compétence liée*"; "*Gebundene Kompetenz*"; "*(adozione) d'un atto vincolato*"). Nevertheless it is necessary to inquire into the contention of the intervener Hoogovens that the rule does not apply in the present case since a claim for failure to act based on the second paragraph of Article 35, as is expressly stated in that article, can only be a claim for misuse of powers (*détournement de pouvoir*). The intervener overlooks that the claim is in fact based on the first paragraph of article 35; indeed the applicant has clearly expressed the opinion that the High Authority *is required* to act in the sense of the prior demand that the applicant had addressed to it . . .".

Annulment (of a decision) based on E.C.S.C. 35.   In *De Gezamenlijke Steenkolenmijnen in Limbourg* c. *Haute Autorité* (Case 17/57 R. Vol. V at pp. 26–7) the Court stated:

"B. As concerns the claim for annulment based on article 35. In the absence of a decision by the High Authority confirming the failure [of a member State to fulfil its obligations under the Treaty] provided for in article 88 (paragraph 1) of the Treaty, the applicant could have no complaint against the High Authority other than the abstention provided for in article 35 of the Treaty. In its reply the applicant declares that 'if, contrary to all expectation, the Court were to rule that the High Authority, as the Authority maintains, has taken no decision . . . it would be necessary to suppose that the claim is based on article 35'. In any event the head of claim under which a Request is framed cannot be altered, even in a minor way in the Reply. Moreover, a claim may not be brought by virtue of article 35 except to the extent that the applicant has first complained to the High Authority in accordance with the provisions of the first paragraph of the said article. This initial formality is essential not only because the demand addressed to the High Authority forms the starting point for the time-limits with respect to which the interested party must act, but also because of the importance of a notification which, protesting against the inaction of the High Authority, constrains it to make up its mind within a given time regarding the lawfulness of its inaction. The letter of 11th July 1957 addressed by the applicant to the High Authority asking to be informed of the decision which the High Authority might have taken in the matter now in dispute, cannot be considered as constituting the formality provided for in the first paragraph of article 35. Nor does the letter of the 22nd August, in which the applicant confined itself to announcing that it contemplated appealing against the decision which it presumed to have been taken by the High Authority, constitute the required formality. In consequence the claim of the 'Association des Charbonnages réunis de Limburg' is not admissible, either under the head of article 33 or under the head of article 35".

Annulment—E.C.S.C. 33.   It is not permissible by the device of using the procedure directed against a failure to act of the High Authority, for an applicant to seek the annulment of a decision the possible nullity of which is remedied by the expiry of the time-limit laid down in the third paragraph of article 33. In *Meroni & Co. etc.* c. *Haute Autorité* (Consolidated Cases 21, 26/61 R. Vol. VIII at pp. 153–6) a case concerning an objection brought under R.P. 91 (*post*, p. 275) and not involving inquiry by the Court into the issues in the main action ("*sans engager le débat au fond*", "*im Wege der Vorabentscheidung*"; "*zonderen te gaanop de zaakten grunde*"; "*senza impegnare la discussione sul merito*") the Court stated:

". . . The second count of the applicants' submissions reads as follows: 'to quash for lack of powers, violations of basic procedural rules, infringement of the Treaty and misuse of powers affecting them, with all legal consequences, the implicit negative decision said to result from the silence of the High Authority, having regard to the claim made by the applicant for the elimination, as from the day when they were implicitly granted (or merely tolerated), of the exemptions from the compulsory payment of contributions for compensation for scrap granted to other undertakings to which article 80 applies, which are consumers of purchased scrap placed in a comparable position'.

First of all the Court must of its own initiative inquire into the question whether there has been failure to act on the part of the High Authority, that is to say an implicit negative decision. A letter signed by M. Rollman, director general for steel of the High Authority and M. Peco, director, is annexed to the Request and must be taken into consideration. This letter constitutes a reply to the first series of occasions on which the applicant brought the matter to the attention of the High Authority between the 4th and 9th September 1961. This letter is dated 27th October 1961. It appears *prima facie* therefore to interrupt the running of time of the two months at the end of which an implicit negative decision is presumed to result from the silence of the High Authority. On further examination of the letter it appears that it is not making an explicit refusal to act but is reciting and explaining the previous legal position of the High Authority. In particular the third paragraph of this letter states:

'in any event, before the High Authority may be called upon to state its position in the matter in question, it seems desirable that the fullest details should be furnished concerning the complaints that have been made . . .'

There is therefore no explicit refusal to act of the High Authority.

It is desirable to examine whether the procedure of Article 35 is applicable. To that end it is important to ascertain whether, in accordance with the contention of the defendant the implicit negative decision, relied upon by the applicant, is not merely a confirmation of the rules already in force. In that connection there must be taken into consideration the decision which in the opinion of the applicants the High Authority ought to have taken. The letters bringing the matter to the attention of the High Authority, as well as the Requests themselves, permit the content of that decision to be presumed with sufficient certainty. The description of the object of the appeal with which the applicants opened their Requests is as follows:

'the applicant asks the Court to declare that the High Authority must confirm by a decision the fact that in exempting from the compensation charges on the consumption of purchased scrap the steel producers which are the subject of annex III of the Treaty and the foundries, in respect of the proportion of consumption of scrap corresponding to the proportion of production of unfinished steel of the foundry, it has disregarded the obligations incumbent on it by virtue of the Treaty and must in consequence cancel the provisions which appear discriminatory'.

The applicants in their communication of 8th September 1961 drawing attention to the matter asked in the penultimate paragraph that:

'the discrimination in question . . . should be removed by the adoption by the High Authority of a decision making all scrap purchases without exception liable to the payment of the compensation charge, including those purchases destined for the production of the steels which are the subject of Annex III of the Treaty and for the production of steel castings'.

The paragraph preceding the submissions in the Requests reads as follows:

'Finally, taking into account that the applicant relies on the wise discretion of the Court in respect of the question whether the implicit negative decision of the High Authority, refusing to remove the illegal and discriminatory exemptions contained in points (b) and (d) (of article 10) of decision 2–57, is of individual or general effect'.

These texts establish sufficiently for legal purposes that, in any event, the decision which in the opinion of the applicants the High Authority was required to take, should cancel the disputed decisions permitting exemptions and in particular sub-paragraphs (b) and (d) of article 10 of decision 2–57, repeated in the same sub-paragraphs of decision 16–58, as

well as the practice of the High Authority having the same result, prior
to decision 2–57.

As far as decision 2–57 is concerned the Request must be rejected
because it is not permissible, by the device of using the procedure directed
against a failure to act of the High Authority, for an applicant to seek the
annulment of decisions the possible nullity of which is remedied by the
expiry of the time-limit laid down in the third paragraph of article 33.
. . . the objection of inadmissibility raised by the defendant is upheld".

V. REVIEW OF THE JUSTIFICATION OF A HIGH AUTHORITY DECISION IN A SITUATION SUS-CEPTIBLE OF PROVOKING FUNDAMENTAL AND PERSISTENT DISTURBANCES IN A MEMBER STATE'S ECONOMY

E.C.S.C. 37

If a Member State considers that in a given case an action
of the High Authority or a failure to act is of such a nature
as to provoke fundamental and persistent disturbances in its
economy it may bring the matter before the High Authority.

The High Authority, after consulting the Council, shall
recognise where appropriate the existence of such a situation
and decide on the measures to be taken under the terms of
this Treaty to end it, while at the same time safeguarding the
Community's essential interests.

When application is made to the Court under the provisions
of this Article against such a decision or against an explicit
decision or a decision to be implied refusing to recognise the
existence of the situation referred to above the Court shall
consider whether the decision is justified.

If the Court quashes the decision, it shall be the duty of the
High Authority within the terms of the Court's judgment
to decide on the measures to be taken for the purposes indicated
in the second paragraph of this Article.

In *Groupement des Industries Sidérurgiques Luxembourgeoises* c. *Haute Autorité*
(Consolidated Cases 7 and 9/54, R. Vol. II at p. 120) Adv. Gen. Roemer
submitted:

"According to this article, the Court has power to annul explicit or
implicit decisions of refusal and, in case of annulment, the High Authority
is required to take measures to be determined upon (by it) within the
framework of the judgment (to correct the position or to put matters
right).

It is beyond dispute that the technical structure of the application for
annulment has been borrowed from the contentious procedure of French
administrative law. But, in French law the '*recours en carence*' (application
to annul a failure to act) is only a simple case of the '*recours pour excès de
pouvoir*' (application for *ultra vires*). Neither the writings of jurists, nor
case law, have ever considered it a special case of the application for
annulment. This latter requires a decision to have been taken. With
regard to this condition for the exercise of the '*recours pour excès de pouvoir*',

jurists draw attention to the fact that the decision required to have been taken may also be 'an implicit decision of refusal' constituting the object of a '*recours*' (application) in accordance with the above rules."

The ambit of the article. In *Niederrheinische Bergwerks-Aktiengesellschaft etc. c. Haute Autorité* (Consolidated Cases 2 and 3/60, R. Vol. VII at pp. 286–291) the Court stated:

". . . To decide the questions of admissibility raised in the present case it is necessary first of all to define the ambit of article 37. Article 37 is in direct relationship with article 2 paragraph 2. [The Court quoted the article; for text see *ante*, p. 49]. The authors of the Treaty observed, however, that in certain situations 'an action of the High Authority or a failure to act' (article 37 paragraph one) might be 'of a nature . . . to provoke fundamental and persistent disturbances' in the economy of a Member State. They therefore considered it necessary to confer on the High Authority, subject to the control of the Court, an exceptional power enabling the High Authority to ward off the consequences which would be brought about by the application of the clauses of the Treaty not directed especially at the existence or the threat of fundamental and persistent disturbances. It is perfectly clear from the words of the first paragraph of article 37 that the right to 'bring the matter before the High Authority' is given exclusively to the State in which the disturbances have appeared or threatened to appear. Only the member State concerned is in a position to appreciate whether its economic situation requires the application of article 37. The second paragraph of article 37 confers on the High Authority the competence to recognize the existence of disturbances and, should it do so, to take the appropriate measures. By the provisions of the third paragraph of article 37, both the decision taken by the High Authority under the second paragraph after it has had the matter brought to its attention by the member State concerned, and also the explicit or implicit decision refusing to recognize the existence of disturbances, may form the object of an action before the Court, on which are conferred the most extensive powers of control. The third paragraph of article 37 does not define who may originate the action. The text being silent on the point it is necessary to examine, in order to determine the admissibility of the present claim, whether considerations of logic require the restriction of the access to the Court in this matter. It is certain that a claim against the explicit or implicit refusal to recognize disturbances can only be made by the member State concerned, since this State alone has the right to bring the matter before the High Authority, and thus can be the only party able to put forward an interest justifying the making of the claim. For the same reasons, the right of appealing against a decision by which the High Authority has adopted measures which the member State concerned considers insufficient can appertain only to that State. However, a decision by the High Authority taken by virtue of the second paragraph of article 37, which did not injure the interested member State, might harm the interests of the other member States, or the undertakings within the jurisdiction of the Community. In order to determine whether, by its very nature, an appeal on the basis of the third paragraph of article 37 by the other member States or by the undertakings of the Community is to be considered admissible, or whether the right to present such an appeal must be reserved solely to the other member States, it is desirable to conduct a thorough examination into the powers conferred on the High Authority by the second paragraph of article 37 on the one hand, and of the jurisdiction conferred on the Court by the third and fourth paragraphs of the same article, on the other. The essential object of article 37 is to facilitate the reconciliation of the interests of a member State affected by the existence of fundamental and persistent disturbances or the threat of the same (and that, in application of the fundamental provision laid down in article 2 paragraph 2) with the general interests of the Community. The second requirement is underlined by the words of paragraph two of article 37: 'while at the same time safeguarding the Community's essential interests'. The exceptional power conferred on the High Authority by article 37 is not unrestricted. The limits of it are to be inferred from the exceptional nature of the powers conferred and are moreover defined by the phrase 'while at the same time safeguarding the Community's essential interests'. It follows that the measures adopted by the High Authority must be *necessary* and *opportune* (expedient) and must therefore, on the one hand, constitute a *remedy calculated* to meet the disturbances provoked by its action or failure to act, and, on the other hand, safeguard the *essential interests* of the Community.

Whether these conditions taken together are met is a question subject to the control of the Court, on which the widest jurisdiction is conferred for the purpose. A finding by the Court that the conditions are met suffices to determine the admissibility of the appeal, without it being possible at this stage to examine whether, in the given case, the High Authority has or has not overstepped the limits in question. Consequently, when a member State believes that it finds itself in a state of fundamental and persistent disturbance, the responsibility of arbitrating between the special interests of this State and the general interests of the Community and to seek the appropriate remedies, is conferred, subject to control by the Court, upon the High Authority, and carries with it the conferment of an exceptional power. An appeal against a decision of the High Authority taken by virtue of article 37 and accepting the claim made by a member State, holding that its economy is affected by a fundamental and persistent disturbance, requires an assessment to be made of the economic situation of the member States and also makes it obligatory to examine whether, taking this situation into account, the measures taken can be considered necessary and appropriate. The appeal thus puts in issue the political responsibilities of the governments of member States and of the High Authority, and that, particularly with regard to the reconciliation between the general interest of a member State and the general interest of the Community. In these circumstances it is not conceivable that undertakings or associations of undertakings should be recognized as having the quality necessary to permit them to avail themselves of article 37 paragraph 3. Yet, for the reasons set out above it must be recognized that not only the member State which has brought (the disturbance) to the attention of the High Authority, but also the other member States, must be recognized as capable of bringing the appeal provided for in article 37 paragraph 3. This interpretation is confirmed by the second paragraph of article 37, which obliges the High Authority, before deciding in respect of a claim made by the interested member State, to consult simply the Council of Ministers, without being bound by its opinion. Given the importance of the interests which may be concerned, this fact can only be explained if it is admitted that any member State finding itself unable to share the opinion of the High Authority has the right to bring an action at the Court to obtain its decision on the question whether the measures taken were justified and opportune (expedient). This interpretation is completely reconciliable with the refusal to recognize that undertakings have a right of appeal, seeing that member States who, by their nature, are in a position that enables them to furnish all data useful for an exhaustive examination by the Court, and who, being members of the Council, are also responsible for safeguarding the essential interests of the Community, have the necessary quality to intervene with a view to the protection of public interests of the same kind as those of the applicant State. This interpretation is confirmed by the discussions which took place in the Parliament of the Netherlands at the time of the ratification of the Treaty (Année Parlementaire 1950–51, No. 2228, p. 86).

Given that, for the reasons stated above, an appeal by undertakings or associations on the basis of article 37 is not admissible, it remains to examine whether the undertakings or associations of undertakings have the necessary quality to seek, either on the basis of article 33 taken in isolation or taken together with article 37, to upset a decision of the High Authority, taken by virtue of article 37 paragraph two. The conditions of application of article 37 are closely bound up together and cannot therefore be the object of separate examination which makes any judgment impossible unless rendered in exercise of the special jurisdiction conferred on the Court by article 37. Thus an appeal by virtue of article 33 jointly with article 37 is not conceivable, because it necessarily leads to an assessment both of the existence of a disturbance as recognized by the High Authority and of the necessity and expediency of the decision it took. In consequence, the Court must use the exceptional powers which the third paragraph of article 37 has conferred upon it, not as part of a general competence or jurisdiction, but only to the end of exercising legal control over the power, also exceptional, conferred on the High Authority by the second paragraph of the same article. Finally, an appeal on the basis of article 33 taken in isolation is also not conceivable. Such an appeal could not be limited to maintaining that a decision taken by the High Authority in application of the second paragraph of article 37 is not in conformity with the other provisions of the Treaty, because it would also lead the Court to examine whether this decision is in any event justified by article 37. In those circumstances it would be necessary to examine whether the measures adopted by this decision are actually necessary and opportune (expedient) in order to remedy a disturbance affecting the economy of a member State and whether, moreover, they safeguard the essential interests of the Community. Consequently the judgment could no longer be based on the provisions of article 33, but would have to be based on article 37. In other words, a claim which might result in a judgment of annulment on the basis of article 33 might not have that effect if the decision sought to be upset had been taken by virtue of article 37, since the special power conferred on the High Authority permits it to act outside the normal scope of its authority. (The appeal of the applicants must therefore be declared inadmissible)".

The contention that fundamental and persistent disturbances in the economy are probable can be made on the basis of no other article than E.C.S.C. 37. In *Compagnie des Hauts Fourneaux et Fonderies de Givors etc. c. Haute Autorité* (Consolidated Cases 27, 28, 29/58, R. Vol. VI (i) at p. 53) the Court stated:

". . . the applicants contend . . . that the contested decision is of a nature to provoke fundamental and persistent disturbances in the French economy and because of that the decision infringes article 2 paragraph 2 of the Treaty. This argument must be rejected because the existence of such disturbances can, in view of their general effect with regard to the national economy, only be invoked by the interested State and in

6

accordance with the procedure established by article 37. The Government of the French Republic has not intervened in the present dispute and has not used the procedure available to it under the said article".

Applicability of E.C.S.C. 37 when matter brought before the High Authority before it made the contested decision(s). In *Gouvernement de la République Fédérale d'Allemagne* c. *Haute Autorité* (Case 19/58 R. Vol. VI (i) at pp. 487–8) the Court stated:

"... As far as the applicability of article 37 is concerned, the applicant has alleged and offered to prove that, both before as well as after the contested decisions were made, it drew the attention of the High Authority to the fact that, in its opinion, the regulation which the decisions contemplated establishing, was capable of provoking fundamental and persistent disturbances in the German economy. It does not, however, follow that the conditions of admissibility of a claim based on article 37 are to be found in the present case. Indeed, as far as concerns the observations which the applicant may have made to the High Authority *before* the contested decisions were made, these did not relate to an 'action' of the High Authority in the sense of the first paragraph of article 37. This expression has to be construed as comprising only an action already taken and not a decision which the High Authority proposes to take if there were a case for taking it. On the other hand, as far as concerns the observations which the applicant may have made after the decisions were taken, it requires to be observed that, according to the first three paragraphs of article 37, a claim based on this article cannot be directed against the decision which the State maintains has provoked the said disturbances but only against such later decision as there may be which refuses to recognize the existence of these disturbances. The claim is therefore to be looked upon as a claim for annulment according to article 33 which, having been brought within the time period, is admissible".

Earlier decisions of the High Authority may be inquired into by the Court, by virtue of E.C.S.C. 37. In *Gouvernement de la République Fédérale d'Allemagne* c. *Haute Autorité* (Case 3/59 R. Vol. VI (i) at p. 133) the Court stated:

"Though article 88 does not afford the possibility of subjecting earlier decisions of the High Authority to the review of the Court, article 37 does however afford this possibility to member States in the special circumstances there provided for".

VI. PRELIMINARY RULING (*"DÉCISION À TITRE PRÉJUDICIEL"*)

(*"Entscheidung im Wege der Vorabentscheidüng: een uitspraak te doen, bij wijze van prejudiciele beslissing"; "prounnciarsi in via pregiudiziale"*).

The provision in the Treaties for preliminary ruling by the Community Court has as its object the ensuring of uniformity in the interpretation and application of Community law by judicial authorities in the member States.

The general position and importance of the "mechanism for reference for preliminary ruling", as he described it, was thus outlined by Advocate General Lagrange in case 7/61 *Bosch* v. *de Geus* (see *post*, p. 135):

[This mechanism] "is obviously called upon to play an essential role in the application of the (E.E.C.) Treaty. The progressive implementation of this Treaty in the juridical, social and economic life of the member countries must increasingly involve the necessity of its application—and therefore, as the need arises, its interpretation—in domestic litigation under private or public law, and this will be true not only of the provisions of the Treaty itself, but of those of the Regulations made in execution of it, which also may give rise to difficulties of interpretation, even of legality. The provisions (for preliminary rulings) should, if they are aptly applied—one is tempted to say loyally applied—permit the establishment of a genuine and fruitful collaboration between the national courts and the Court of the European Communities, in mutual regard of their respective competences. This is the spirit in which it will be proper to resolve, on both sides, the sometimes delicate problems which are occasioned by any mechanism for preliminary ruling and which in the present context are inevitably aggravated because of the differences that exist in respect of such mechanisms in the legal systems of the Member States".

(On these differences see comment on E.E.C. Statute 20, *post*, pp. 293 *et seq.*).

It is only in respect of the giving of preliminary rulings (on the specific matters enumerated in the Treaties) that the European Court is brought into direct relationship with the courts and tribunals of Member States of the Communities. But this relationship is at no point that of a Court of Appeal, final or other. It is limited to this particular jurisdiction of the European Court to give preliminary rulings, conclusive and binding on the courts and tribunals of Member States, in respect of certain matters arising from the Treaties when such matters are in issue before such courts and tribunals. The jurisdiction of the European Court to give such preliminary rulings is not exclusive of that of the courts and tribunals of Member States, except that in E.E.C. and E.A.E.C. national courts and tribunals of last instance (but not lower courts and tribunals) are obliged to refer to the European Court for a preliminary ruling in respect of all matters specified in the Treaties.

The conclusive and binding nature of such a ruling is more clearly manifest in the French expression "*à titre préjudiciel*" (which is used in all three Treaties) than in the English rendering "preliminary ruling". "*A titre préjudiciel*" means "by way of a pre-judgment", the word "*préjudiciel*" carrying no implication of "prejudice" in the ordinary meaning of that word in English. (It may also be helpful at this point to distinguish "*à titre préjudiciel*" from "*au préalable*", rendered in the English translation as "as a preliminary" (see "Preliminary Opinion" and E.E.C. 228 and equivalents, *post*, p. 163). The French wording assists more than the English in clarifying the legal difference between a ruling of the European Court that pre-judges a matter in issue before a national court or tribunal and on which it is binding (which is the concern of this section) from an opinion of the Court rendered as a preliminary in point of time, but addressed at their request to the Council, the Commission, or a Member State (of E.E.C. and somewhat similarly under E.A.E.C.) and not binding in the same sense.

It appears to be the prevailing opinion in Continental Europe that a preliminary ruling ("*préjudiciel*") is binding, as a matter of law, only in respect of the case before a domestic court in which the need for it arose. As a matter of practice, however, it is considered likely that such a ruling will be followed in other cases before national courts of the same or any other member State where the same question at issue in the preliminary ruling arises again (see "Precedent in Community Law" *post*, p. 138).

The range of matters specified in E.E.C. and E.A.E.C. in respect of which a preliminary ruling (*préjudiciel*) may be requested is considerably wider than was the case under E.C.S.C. This aspect is clarified in the detailed comment on E.E.C. 177, E.A.E.C. 150 and E.C.S.C. 41, *post*. But at this point it may be noted that the reason for this is twofold. In the first place the E.C.S.C. has a narrower economic ambit, being concerned with only three commodities (coal, steel and scrap). In the second place it was contemplated that the putting into effect of the later Treaties (particularly E.E.C.) would devolve to a larger extent upon the Member States than in the case of E.C.S.C. (where the greater pre-dominance of the executive power in the Community, namely the High Authority, in relation to the other Community Institutions, as compared with the position under the later Treaties, laid more stress on the supra-national principle).

E.E.C. 177

The Court of Justice shall be competent to give preliminary rulings (*à titre préjudiciel*) concerning:—

(*a*) the interpretation of this Treaty;
(*b*) the validity and interpretation of acts of the institutions of the Community;
(*c*) the interpretation of the status of any bodies set up by a formal measure of the Council, where the said statutes so provide.

Where any such question is raised before any court of law of one of the Member States, the said court may, if it considers that a decision on the question is essential to enable it to render judgment, request the Court of Justice to give a ruling thereon.

Where any such question is raised in a case pending before a domestic court of a Member State, from whose decisions there is no possibility of appeal under domestic law, the said court is bound to refer the matter to the Court of Justice.

E.A.E.C. 150

[*Identical with E.A.E.C. 177 in the English translations except that (1) the word "décisions" is retained in line 1 in E.A.E.C. 150; (2) in sub-paragraph* (c) *"formal measure" in E.E.C. 177 is "act" in E.A.E.C. 150; (3) in sub-paragraph* (c) *"where the said statutes so provide" in E.E.C. 177 is "except where these statutes provide otherwise" in E.A.E.C. 150—this might operate as a fundamental difference; (4) in paragraph two, additional words ("in a case pending before") after "raised" in line 1, appear in E.A.E.C. 150; (5) in the last paragraph the words "of a Member State" after "domestic court" in line 1, appear only in E.E.C. 177.*]

The jurisdiction and competence of the Court under this article. In *Demande de décision préjudicielle . . . Société Kledingverkoopbedrijf de Geus en Vitdenbogerd* c. 1. *Société de droit allemand Robert Bosch G.M.B.H.* 2. *Société Anonyme Maatschappij tot voortzetting van de zaken der Firma Willem van Rijn* (Case 13/61 R. Vol. VIII at pp. 161–3) the Court stated:

"The parties Bosch and van Rijn and the Government of the French Republic [*in accordance with E.E.C. St. 20 paragraph two, statements were delivered not only by the French Government, but also by the E.E.C. Commission, and the German, Dutch and Belgian Governments. The parties also delivered observations in accordance with E.E.C. St. 20 paragraph two—author*] have expressed doubt whether the request of the Hague Court of Appeal is susceptible of preliminary ruling, inasmuch as an appeal to the Court of Cassation (of Holland) has been lodged against the judgment making the request to this Court. This doubt arises from an interpretation of E.E.C. 177 according to which such a request could only be the subject of a ruling if the judgment which formulates it has acquired the force of *res judicata*. This interpretation of E.E.C. 177 is not confirmed by the letter (wording) of the Article. Besides, it disregards the fact that the national law of the forum which requests a preliminary ruling ['national law' is, in the originals, respectively *'le droit national'*; *'das innerstaatliche Recht'*; *'het nationale recht'*, *'il diritto interno'*—author] and community law constitute two distinct and different legal order s[*c.f. cases quoted under comment "general role of the European Court" ante*, pp. 58 *et seq.*—author]. Indeed, just as the Treaty does not prevent the national Court of Last Appeal (Cassation) from ruling on the appeal, but leaves the inquiry into its admissibility to internal law and to the appreciation of the national judge, the Treaty subordinates the competence of the Community Court to adjudicate to no more than the mere existence of a request in the meaning of E.E.C. 177, without there being need for the Community judge to inquire into the question whether the decision of the national judge has acquired the force of *res judicata* according to the provisions of the national law.

The parties Bosch and van Rijn as well as the French Government further contend that the request of the Hague Court of Appeal is not susceptible of a preliminary ruling, inasmuch as it is not confined to a simple question of interpretation within the meaning of E.E.C. 177, but that in reality it aims, as its tenor indicates, at securing determination by the Court of a question of application of the Treaty to a particular case. However, the Treaty makes no explicit or implicit provision as to the form in which the national court or tribunal is required to present the request for a preliminary ruling. The meaning of the expression "the interpretation of the Treaty" in E.E.C. 177 can itself be the object of an interpretation, and it is therefore permissible for the national court or tribunal to formulate its request in a direct and simple form which leaves the (Community) Court the task of ruling on the request only within the limits of its jurisdictional competence, that is to say only to the extent that it comprises questions of interpretation of the Treaty. The direct terms in which the present request has been formulated allow the questions of interpretation that are included in the request to be clearly disengaged . . . accordingly the Court is competent to rule on the present request for a preliminary ruling in the meaning of E.E.C. 177 . . ."

First paragraph of E.E.C. 177 and E.A.E.C. 150. Under this, the Court may be concerned with questions of interpretation (of the Treaty; of acts of Community Institutions; of the statutes of bodies set up by the Council) or with questions of the validity (of acts of Community Institutions). The giving of a preliminary ruling on such questions is a particular exercise of the Court's general duty under E.E.C. 164 and E.A.E.C. 136: "The Court of Justice shall ensure the observance of law in the interpretation and application ("implementation" in English translation of E.A.E.C. 136) of this Treaty".

Sub-paragraph (a) "the interpretation of this Treaty". The competence of the Community Court (of E.E.C. or E.A.E.C.) under this sub-paragraph is limited to questions of interpretation and must not be extended to a determination of the issue pending before the national court. This does not have the effect, however, of imposing on the national court any particular form in which its question must be addressed to the Community Court. In the case of *Bosch* c. *de Geus* (see under Bosch v. de

Geus" for the wording of the reference by the Dutch Court, *post*, p. 136)
the point was taken, both by the party who had been the appellant in the
action before the Dutch Court, and by the French Government, which had
presented its comments to the Community Court (on presentation of
comments, see *post*, p. 295), that the request from the Court of Appeal of the
Hague was not capable of being the subject of a preliminary ruling, inasmuch
as it was not limited to a mere question of interpretation in the sense of
E.E.C. 177, but, as its formulation indicated, was likely to cause the Community Court to determine a question concerning the application of the
Treaty to a particular case. In respect of this contention the Court stated:
> ". . . the Treaty does not lay down either explicitly or implicitly the
> form in which the national court must present its request for a preliminary
> ruling; since the meaning of the words 'the interpretation of the Treaty'
> in Article 177 can itself constitute the object of an interpretation [*pre-
> sumably the Court had in mind the combined effect of E.E.C. 177(a) and E.E.C.
> 164 quoted ante under comment on the first paragraph of E.E.C. 177—author*] it is
> permissible for the national judge to formulate his request in a direct and
> simple form which leaves the (Community) Court the task of passing
> judgment upon this request only within the limits of its competence, that
> is to say only to the extent that it comprises questions of interpretation
> of the Treaty; the direct terms in which the present request is formulated
> make it possible to disengage with precision the questions of interpretation
> comprised in the request . . . ."

Sub-paragraph (b) ". . . acts of the Institutions of the Community".
As to Institutions see Chapter 1 under European Economic Community,
European Atomic Energy Community and European Coal and Steel
Community respectively, the Assembly, Council, Commission and Court of
Justice of the two later Communities, and the High Authority, Assembly,
Council and Court of Justice of the European Coal and Steel Community
(*ante*, pp. 18 *et seq.*).

The acts comprised within this wording are of a considerably wider
category than the "acts of the Council and the Commission other than
recommendations or opinions", the supervision of the legality of which is a
matter for the Court (under E.E.C. 173 and E.A.E.C. 146, *ante*, p. 83) in
proceedings instituted by a Member State, the Council, the Commission, or a
natural or legal person, on the specific grounds laid down in the Treaties.
This latter category consists of administrative acts in the strict legal sense
(see under "Acts of the High Authority", E.C.S.C. 33, *ante*, pp. 89 *et seq.*), the
former extends to "acts" not strictly "administrative". (See "administrative
act is a term of art", *ante*, p. 4).

Thus, in the first place, acts of the Institutions of E.E.C. and E.A.E.C.
which have no binding force (recommendations and opinions) are within
the category. So are resolutions ("*délibérations*"). So, presumably, are
Regulations (though this has been doubted). But beyond these there is a
wide variety of actions (*i.e.* not 'acts' in the technical sense) that the
Assembly, the Council or the Commission may be called upon, or consider
themselves called upon, to take. They would appear to be within the category of acts in respect of the validity or interpretation of which the Court has
jurisdiction under the Article to give a preliminary ruling.

A comparison with the position under E.C.S.C. is of value at this point.
There the Court has no competence to give a preliminary ruling except as to
the validity of resolutions ("*délibérations*") of the High Authority and Council
where such validity is in issue in a case pending before a national court.
It may give no preliminary ruling as to interpretation whatsoever and has no

competence in respect of a resolution of the Assembly (see E.C.S.C. 41, *post*, p. 140).

The Court of E.E.C. or E.A.E.C. could presumably give a preliminary ruling (under E.E.C. 177 or E.A.E.C. 150) interpreting one of its own judgments, since such are "acts" of "one of" the institutions of the Community", without recourse being made to the Special Procedure for Interpretation of Judgments under R.P. 102 (See *post*, pp. 291–292).

A formal measure of the Council setting up any body referred to in (*c*) of E.E.C. 177 paragraph 1, is itself an act of an institution the validity of which might be the subject of a preliminary ruling under (*b*), by virtue of which, of course, a preliminary ruling as to its interpretation could also be given. Both matters would presumably be included in one reference.

Paragraph 2 of E.E.C. 177 and E.A.E.C. 150. "Where any such question is raised before any court of law ("before a court" in E.A.E.C. 150) of one of the Member States . . . the said Court . . . may request the Court of Justice . . .". Reference by the national court to the Community Court of E.E.C. and E.A.E.C. is at the discretion of the former (unless it be a court "from whose decisions there is no possibility of appeal under domestic law," see comment on E.E.C. 177, paragraph 3 and E.A.E.C. 150, *post*, p. 137) if it considers that a decision on the question is essential to render judgment.

Reference by virtue of E.E.C. 177 made use of indirectly by private party to seek a decision equivalent in effect to an annulment by virtue of E.E.C. 173 (which the private party was not entitled to implement, because it had not the necessary "quality" and the time limit had in any case expired).

In *N.V. Internationale Crediet en Handelsvereniging "Rotterdam" et De Cooperative Suiderfabriek en Raffinaderie G.A. "Puttershoek"* c. *Le Ministère de l'Agriculture et de la Pêche à La Haye* (Consolidated cases 73–74/63) two requests for a preliminary ruling were presented to the Court under E.E.C. 177, by a Netherlands tribunal exercising administrative jurisdiction in economic matters, known as the College van Beroep voor het bedrijfsleven. The facts in case 74/63 were as follows: On the 27th July 1960, on the application of the Federal Republic of Germany, the E.E.C. Commission made a decision (notified to the interested Governments but not published in the Official Gazette) on the basis of E.E.C. 226, provisionally authorizing, until 31st December 1960, this Member State to levy a compensatory duty (amongst other things) on *pâte à fondant* (the position of the tariff ex 1704 C) on the import of this product coming from the Netherlands, being a duty of 18.25 florins per 100 kilograms, its levy being authorized except in the case of the Netherlands levying it on the export of the said product. This decision was prorogated on the 21st December 1960 (unpublished); renewed by decision of the Commission on the 28th June 1961 (Official Gazette 1230/61); prorogated a second time on 22nd December 1961 (J.O. 192 and 193/62) and was modified on the 27th February 1962 (J.O. 861 and 862/62).

In execution of these decisions of the Commission, the Netherlands Ministry of Agriculture and Fisheries, by decision of the 3rd August 1960 (S.T.C. rt. No. 150) imposed a duty on the export of *pâte à fondant en vrac* on the joint basis of article 42 of the Dutch agricultural law and the order 1958 relative to the import and export of agricultural products (this decision was designated "de Heffingsbeschickking fondantmasse 1960").

On the 27th April 1962 the "Hoofdproductschap voor Akkerbouwproducten", a body invested with attributions of public law in connection with the marketing of agricultural products, sent the first applicant (in the name of the defendant) a bill for duty payable in the amount of 4,000 florins for having exported, on the 27th February 1962, to the Federal Republic of Germany, 20 tons of *pâte à fondant en vrac* produced by the second applicant. This bill was based on "Heffingsbeschickking fondantmasse 1960". The applicants brought an action before the "College van Beroep voor het bedrijsleven" seeking the annulment of the bill for duty. In their application to that tribunal the applicants raised, amongst others, a number of objections based on the E.E.C. Treaty (in particular E.E.C. 12, 16, 38 (paragraph three), 226).

The "College van Beroep voor het bedrigfsleven" (a tribunal of final appeal) submitted, by virtue of E.E.C. 177, the following questions to the European Court:

1. Does the decision of the E.E.C. Commission of 27th July 1960 (as later prorogated and modified) establishing safety measures in respect of the import into the Federal Republic of Germany of bread and *pâte à fondant* coming from other Member States, confer competence on the Netherlands to impose a duty on the export of *pâte à fondant* to the Federal Republic of Germany?

2. If the answer to question 1. is in the affirmative, (*a*) was the E.E.C. Commission competent, by virtue of E.E.C. 226 to confer such a competence on the Netherlands inasmuch as they had not asked to have it? And if not, (*b*) is the decision of the E.E.C. Commission not therefore void, insofar as it deals with the conferring of this competence on the Netherlands?

3. In the event of the answers to questions 2(*a*) and (*b*) not establishing that the decision of the E.E.C. Commission is void, (*a*) must there be included in the difficulties envisaged in E.E.C. 226 (paragraph one) those that result exclusively from the application of the imperative rules of the Treaty, in particular the application of the rules concerning the removal of internal tariffs? And if this question is answered in the negative, (*b*) can the conclusion be drawn that the decision of the E.E.C. Commission is not valid insofar as it confers on the Netherlands the competence mentioned above? Or must it be held that the decision is invalid because it infringes Community law, as is suggested by the applicant's argument, according to which the Commission, when it took its decision, had recourse to the procedure of E.E.C. 226 in order to avoid the procedure of E.E.C. 235? (Though the Court in the event held the Commission's decision valid, the private applicant, it will be noted, had been successful in bringing before it, by the mechanism of E.E.C. 177, a question of validity of no material difference in principle from a question that is normally brought before it under E.E.C. 173).

Bosch v. de Geus. This case (13/61 quoted also *ante*. pp. 132 *et seq.*) was the first example of a request to the E.E.C. Court under paragraph 2 of E.E.C. 177. It was made by the Court of Appeal of the Hague by letter of 10 July 1961, following its judgment of 30 June 1961 (101 R/60), for a preliminary ruling "on the question whether a prohibition on exports imposed by Robert Bosch (GmbH) of Stuttgart on its clients and accepted by contract is null and void by virtue of Article 85, paragraph 2, of E.E.C., in so far as concerns export to Holland". In the Dutch domestic judicial system a judgment of the Court of Appeal is subject to appeal to the Court of Cassation (the "*Hoge Raad*"). The appellant before the Dutch court in fact took the matter to the Court of Cassation on 21st September 1961 claiming inter alia that the Appeal Court was in error in referring the question to the Community Court and submitting that the latter should have awaited the decision of the Court of Cassation before giving its ruling, since, by virtue of Article 398, last paragraph, of the Dutch Code of Civil Procedure, the reference to the Court of Cassation suspends the execution of the judgment on appeal. The respondent contended that the reference to the Court of Cassation had no effect on the matter pending before the European Court because of the supervisory result of Article 20 of the Protocol on the Statute of the Court of E.E.C. (see comment on E.E.C. Statute 20, *post*, p. 293). By letter of 19th October 1961 the Registrar of the European Court informed the parties that, in the opinion of the Court, the reference to the Court of Cassation did not suspend *de plein droit* the proceedings before the European Court. (See in Chapter 5, comment under "... the decision of the domestic court which suspends its proceedings" *post*, p. 294).

"... Court of a Member State". The wording appears to preclude a reference by a Court of a State not a member State. But compare "the wording of E.C.S.C. 41" (*post*, p. 140).

Paragraph 3, E.E.C. 177 E.A.E.C. 150. The national court of last instance has no option but is bound to refer to the Community Court for a preliminary ruling any question of Treaty interpretation which is relevant to the issue before it and is not clear. Any national court of last instance, not merely those forming part of the ordinary judicial system in the narrower sense, are within this obligation. Thus the Tariefcommissie of Amsterdam, an administrative tribunal of final appeal in taxation questions, in respect of the case pending before it of *N.V. Algemene Transport en Expeditie Onderneming Van Gend en Loos* v. *The Customs Administration of Holland*, referred to the Community Court the question (*a*) whether E.E.C. 12 takes direct effect internally (in a Member State) in the sense submitted by the applicant, in other words, whether citizens (of a Member State) can by virtue of the Article base themselves on rights which the judge must respect; (*b*) if the answer to (*a*) is in the affirmative whether the import duty has been illegally increased in the instant case or whether what has been done is no more than a logical differentiation from what was valid up to 1st March 1960, so that although this differentiation, looked at in the mathematical sense, constitutes an increase, it has not the character of an increase such as is prohibited in Article 12 (J.O. 27.9.62; 2312/62; Communications, Case 26/62). The Court gave its decision on 5th February 1963 (answering (*a*) in the affirmative and holding (*b*) to extend beyond its jurisdiction).

Reference of a question substantially identical with one already the subject of a preliminary ruling. The Tariefcommissie case (26/26 R. Vol. IX, at pp. 1 *et seq.*) referred to in the preceding paragraph was followed by further references by the same Tribunal for a preliminary ruling in the three similar cases before it of *Da Costa en Schaake N.V.*, *N.V. Schuitenvoerderij en Expeditiekantoor v/h Jacob Meijer, en Hoechst Holland N.V.* v. *the Netherlands Revenue Department.* These cases were consolidated (28, 29 and 30/62 R. Vol. IX, pp. 59 *et seq.*) by the Community Court, which, in respect of the reference for a preliminary ruling on a question substantially identical with one already ruled upon, stated:

"The Commission, which is a party to the proceedings on the basis of Article 20 of the Statute of the Court of Justice of E.E.C., argues that the request for a preliminary ruling should be refused because it no longer has any purpose, the questions of interpretation referred to the Court of Justice in the present cases having already been decided by the ruling of 5 February in the analogous Case 26/62."

This argument is not well-founded. A distinction must be made in the first place between the obligation laid on national courts of last instance in article 177 (3) and the power conferred on all national courts by paragraph 2 of the same Article to refer a question of interpretation of the Treaty to the Court of Justice of the Communities. Even if the last paragraph of Article 177 binds, without any restrictions, national courts, such as the Tariefcommissie, from whose decisions no appeal lies under national law, to refer to the Court of Justice any question of interpretation of the Treaty arising in cases pending before them, the authority of an interpretation already given by the Court of Justice under Article 177 can in a given case remove the grounds for this obligation.

This is particularly true when the question put is substantially identical to a question already the subject of a preliminary ruling in an analogous case.

When the Court of Justice, in the context of a case pending before a national jurisdiction, gives an interpretation of the Treaty, it confines itself to deducing from the spirit and letter of the Treaty the meaning of the rules of Community law, leaving it to the national courts to apply the rules thus interpreted to the case in point. This conception corresponds to the function of the Court of Justice under Article 177, *i.e.* that of ensuring the uniform interpretation of Community law in the six Member States. That this is the intention of Article 177 follows moreover from the fact that the procedural provisions of Article 20 of the Statute of the Court of Justice, which provide that the Member States and the Community Authorities may be parties to the proceedings, and Article 165(3), according to which the Court of Justice must sit in plenary session, would otherwise have no *raison d'être*. This understanding of the way in which the Court of Justice acts in proceedings under Article 177 is borne out by the fact that there are here no parties in the real sense of the word.

On the other hand Article 177 allows the national jurisdiction at any time to re-submit questions of interpretation to the Court of Justice if they think fit. This follows from Article 20 of the Statute of the Court of Justice according to which the procedure of the preliminary question is initiated *ex officio* as soon as a national court submits such a question.

Having regard to all these considerations the Court of Justice is obliged to render a decision on the present requests.

As to the substance of the questions put it must be observed that the interpretation of Article 12 of the E.E.C. Treaty now asked for was already given by the judgment of the Court of 5 February 1963 in Case 26/62, when the Court ruled as follows:

"1. Article 12 of the Treaty establishing the European Economic Community has direct effects and creates individual rights for those affected that must be upheld by the domestic courts.

2. In deciding whether customs or charges with equivalent effect have been increased, contrary to Article 12 of the Treaty, the factor to be considered is the duties and charges actually applied by the Member State concerned at the date of entry into force of the Treaty.

   Such an increase may equally well arise from a new arrangement of the customs tariff, placing a product under another heading subject to a higher rate of duty, as it may from an actual increase in the rate of duty applied".

The questions of interpretation submitted in the present cases are identical with those already decided; no new circumstances have emerged. The Tariefcommissie must therefore be referred to the earlier ruling".

Precedent in Community Law. Two passages in the judgment just quoted (Consolidated Cases 28, 29 and 30, *supra*) provide a firm basis for principles of precedent in Community Law. In the first place the sentence "The questions of interpretation submitted in the present cases are identical with those already decided, no new circumstances have emerged. The Tariefcommissie must therefore be referred to the earlier ruling" indicates that normally the European Court will follow its own previous decision, though there is (not surprisingly) no statement that it will be bound by its earlier decision. In the second place (referring to the obligation upon national courts of last instance to refer to the European Court any question of interpretation of the Treaty arising in a case pending before them) the sentence ". . . the authority of an interpretation already given by the Court of Justice under Article 177 can in a given case remove the grounds for this obligation. This is particularly true when the question put is substantially identical to a question already the subject of a preliminary ruling in an analogous case" indicates that decisions of the European Court under E.E.C. 117 are precedents which it is not only safe for national courts to follow but which they should in fact follow. Such decisions of the European Court are however not precedents in the sense of being binding, in the way that expression is understood by English lawyers.

There is a certain body of opinion in Continental Europe which holds that in respect of preliminary rulings thereon the validity of community acts should have been treated differently in the Treaties from questions of interpretation, being made subject to the exclusive jurisdiction of the Community Court so that domestic courts at lower level than that of last instance would have no discretion but to refer to the Community Court (as is the principle in E.C.S.C. 41, *post*, p. 140). Part of that argument for differential treatment of validity of acts and questions of interpretation is rested on the circumstance that really only the Courts of last instance of the original Member States determine case law, so that questions of interpretation can safely be left to reference to the Community Court at that level. It seems doubtful whether such an argument could be sustained in respect of the United Kingdom were it to become a member of the Community.

Concurrent jurisdiction of the E.E.C. Commission (or, on appeal therefrom, the Community Court) and courts and tribunals of Member States, resulting from Regulation 17(9)(3). In case 13/61 (*loc. cit., supra*) Adv. Gen Lagrange submitted:

"As far as the power of ruling that there has been an infringement is concerned, this is truly a matter of concurrent jurisdiction which runs the risk of a court or tribunal of a Member State and the Commission (or, it may be, the Community Court, on an appeal from a decision of the Commission) making contradictory decisions. The Regulation, it is true has attempted to avoid such consequences by the provision in its article 9 paragraph 3".

[The Advocate General quoted the paragraph (for text, see Chapter 1, *ante*, p. 24) emphasising in the first line the words in italics "So long as the Commission *has not* initiated any proceedings . . ."].

"Can one construe this text, by reasoning *a contrario* that once the Commission has initiated proceedings in applications of articles 2, 3 or 6 of the Regulation 'the authorities of Member States', *including their* judicial authorities, no longer have jurisdiction? That is certainly the case with article 6, which deals with the exclusive jurisdiction to apply E.E.C. 85(3). It is not true in my opinion of article 2, dealing with 'negative clearance'. It is very desirable it should be true—though very doubtful—of article 3, dealing with deciding whether there has been an infringement. What can in any event be agreed is that the court or tribunal of a Member

State, which has before it a question bearing on the application of E.E.C. 85(1) or 86, should stay proceedings on learning that the Commission, perhaps aroused precisely because of the action, has decided for its part to initiate one of the procedures provided for in article 9(3) of the Regulation. The grant, or the refusal of a grant, of the negative clearance will be an important element in the assessment made by the court or tribunal of the Member State. As for a ruling on the infringement, especially if it has been the object of a judgment of the Community Court, this should be binding on the court or tribunal of the Member State, legally, if in such a situation one admits the authority of *res judicata*, or at least, morally. I do not think, however, that it is necessary to determine this question as a matter of law in the present case . . .".

E.C.S.C. 41

The Court shall have sole jurisdiction to give preliminary rulings on the validity of decisions of the High Authority and of the Council, where such validity is in issue in proceedings brought before a municipal court or tribunal.

"... the validity of resolutions of the High Authority and of the Council". The resolutions of only two of the four institutions of the Community (unlike the E.E.C. and E.A.E.C., *ante*, p. 132) may be the subject of a preliminary ruling as to validity. Resolutions (French "*délibérations*") of the High Authority are not defined in the Treaty, as are decisions, recommendations and opinions of the High Authority. On these latter Article 14 is specific. (See E.C.S.C. 14 in Chapter 1,; *ante*, p. 52). Is "resolution" a generic expression for these three types of specified act or is it distinct therefrom. (As far as the Council is concerned, note use of "*délibéré*" or "*délibérations*" translated "discussion" and "proceedings". Note that the discussion need not necessarily lead to a vote, and other matters in E.C.S.C. 28).

Preliminary Rulings in questions of Treaty interpretation are not provided for in E.C.S.C. as they are in E.E.C. and E.A.E.C.

E.C.S.C. 41 has been analysed by the Advocate General in two cases primarily concerned with E.C.S.C. 36 (see under "exception of illegality", *ante*, pp. 111-112).

VII. COMMUNITY LIABILITY IN TORT

Each of the three Treaties confers directly upon the European Court jurisdiction to adjudicate in respect of compensation by the Community for damage caused by its wrongful acts other than in contract. (In respect of the latter, jurisdiction may be conferred on the European Court indirectly. See "Reference by virtue of a 'clause compromissoire'," *post*, p. 153).

The jurisdiction thus directly conferred upon the European Court is not expressed by the Treaties to be exclusive of that of the national courts of Member States of the Communities, and the general principle laid down in E.E.C. 183 and E.A.E.C. 155 (for text of which see *ante*, pp. 29 and 46) is that "cases to which the Community is a party shall not for that reason alone be excluded from the jurisdiction of national courts". But the principal reason for wishing so to exclude cases of community liability in tort would be promotion of clarity and uniformity in the principles for determining and assessing that liability, through the concentration of the judicial work upon one tribunal rather than its diffusion over several. A trend towards such concentration, in practice, is to be expected.

The Treaty Articles directly conferring jurisdiction upon the European Court are E.E.C. 178 (together with E.E.C. 215, paragraph 2), E.A.E.C. 151 (together with E.A.E.C. 188, paragraph 2), and E.C.S.C. 40, which are treated in that order below. At this point, the provisions of the Court's Statutes for limitation of actions in tort against the Communities should first be noted.

E.E.C. St. 43

Proceedings against the Community in matters arising from non-contractual responsibility shall be statute-barred after a period of five years from the occurrence of the circumstance giving rise thereto. The running of time shall be interrupted by the institution of proceedings before the Court or by a prior formal demand directed to the relevant institution of the Community by the aggrieved party. In this event proceedings must be instituted within the two months provided for in Article 173; the provisions of Article 175, second paragraph, shall apply, where appropriate.

E.A.E.C. St. 44

[*Identical in substance with E.E.C.St.* 43]

E.C.S.C. St. 40

Proceedings provided for in the first two paragraphs of Article 40 of the Treaty shall be statute-barred after a period of five years from the occurrence of the circumstance giving rise thereto. Any time already run within that period shall be disregarded if proceedings are instituted before the Court or if a prior formal demand is made to the relevant institution of the Community by the aggrieved party. In this latter event proceedings must be instituted within the period of one month provided for in the last paragraph of Article 33; the provisions of the last paragraph of Article 35 shall apply where appropriate.

E.E.C. 178

The Court of Justice shall be competent to hear cases relating to compensation for any damage caused as provided for in Article 215, second paragraph.

E.A.E.C. 151

[*Identical with E.E.C.* 178]

E.E.C. 215 paragraph 2

In the case of non-contractual liability, the Community shall, in accordance with general principles common to the laws (*droits*) of Member States, made good any damage caused by its institutions or by its servants in the performance of their duties.

E.A.E.C. 188 paragraph 2
[Identical with E.E.C. 215 paragraph 2]

Limitation of actions. (Prescription). In *Société Nouvelle des Usines de Pontliene Aciéries du Temple (S.N.U.P.A.T.)* c. *Haute Autorité* (Consolidated Cases 42 and 49/59 R. Vol. VII at pp. 167–170) Adv. Gen. Lagrange submitted:

"The purely protective reasons for which the Request was presented have been explained at the bar. The applicant feared that prescription might later be set up against it, if it did not take action within the lawful time-limit against the decision of rejection taken by the High Authority. In reality, the applicant further explains, it had no intention of introducing before the Court at the present time a claim for compensation, and it merely asks the Court to acknowledge judicially its reservation of the right to introduce 'a *fresh* claim for damages' against the High Authority,—'an appeal to the full jurisdiction for compensation for a wrongful act or default in the performance of the Community's functions' ["*faute de service*"—*author*]—states the Reply, thus modifying in some degree the original submissions.

I understand the applicant's scruples but the remedy it considers it has found is, in our opinion, ineffectual. The mistake of the applicant, given that it did not intend to bring an action for compensation immediately, was to address a claim in that sense to the High Authority. Indeed it is not necessary, as for example before the French Conseil d'Etat, to show the existence of a prior decision, explicit or implicit, to originate an action before the Court for indemnity for injury. E.C.S.C. 40 makes no mention of it and E.C.S.C. St. 40 merely fixes a time-limit for *prescription* which is five years from the occurrence of the event giving rise to the action, so that the introduction of a claim for annulment based on the illegality of this or that decision of the High Authority . . . would in no way have prejudiced the rights of the applicant in respect of a subsequent action for indemnity . . .".

Prescription not a matter of public policy. In *Meroni & Cie. et autres* c. *Haute Autorité* (Consolidated Cases 14.16, 17, 20, 24, 26 27/60 and 1/61, R. Vol. VII at p. 346) Adv. Gen. Lagrange, in respect of a contention on behalf of the defendant that the applicant's claim was barred by the rule of prescription in E.C.S.C. St. 40, submitted:

"I do not think it (prescription) is a matter of public policy: In France, article 2223 of the Civil Code provides: '*les juges ne peuvent pas suppléer d'office le moyen résultant de la prescription*'. This rule, it is true, is not, as consistent case law shows, applicable in criminal cases. But it is applicable, as shown by a no less consistent case law, in administrative cases, a field in which, however, the notion of public policy is more frequently met than in civil law: only the competent authority, for example for debts due by the State, the Minister or the official delegated for the purpose, is qualified to set up what is called the 'four-year expiry', which at the present time constitutes the law of prescription for State debts. It has even been judicially held that an observation made in a procedural document was not sufficient: a special decision of the competent authority setting up prescription is necessary (Conseil d'Etat, 21 July 1934, *Gouvernement Général de l'Indochine*, Rec. p. 852).

I do not know exactly what is the state of the law in the other countries of the Community. But I think that in civil law, prescription is not considered as being of public policy; it must be set up by the debtor. I also think that since the liability of public authority, in all countries of the Community other than France, is a matter for the jurisdiction of the (ordinary) courts (of '*droit commun*') it must be the rules of civil law that are applicable in these countries.

I see no special reason for ensuring the protection of the public finances of the European Community (E.C.S.C.) by means of an unusual privilege which is not conferred for the protection of national public finances."

In *Société Nouvelle des Usines de Pontlieue Aciéries du Temple (S.N.U.P.A.T.)* c. *Haute Autorité* (Consolidated Cases 42, 49/59; R. Vol. VIII at p. 142) the Court stated:

". . . The real aim of the present claim is to establish the liability of the High Authority for 'a wrongful act or default in carrying out the Treaty'. Such a finding cannot be the result of an action for *ultra vires* as provided for in article 33 of the Treaty, under which the present action is brought and which envisages the annulment of the decisions of the High Authority, but could only be based on article 40 or conceivably article 34. No argument to the contrary can be drawn from the third sentence of E.C.S.C.St. 40; indeed, though this provision is concerned with the case of a person who considers himself to have suffered damages as the result of a '*faute de service*' of the Community and has first made a prior demand on the competent institution of the Community, the provision does no more than fix a time-limit for prescription without thereby altering the nature of the recourse to the court which is laid down for such matters . . .".

". . . In accordance with the general principles common to the laws (*droits*) of Member States . . .". (E.E.C. 215 paragraph 2). The French word "*droit*" has been retained in the English translation to make it clear that in the original authentic texts the reference is to a wider source than to the general principles common to the "*lois*" of Member States, there being no English word other than "laws" to translate both "*droits*" and "*lois*". The word "*loi*", however, embraces only codified and statute law. "*Droit*" includes "*loi*" and also two other elements making up the general body of law, namely customary law and case law.

The writings of legal publicists of recognized competence (referred to as "*la doctrine*," "*la dottrina*," etc) exercise a very considerable influence on both legislative and judicial law-making in the original Member States. But until the views of such writers have been consciously adopted by the national law-making authorities care must be taken to distinguish them from a source of law in the strict sense. Nothing in the Treaties confers upon the European Court the duty or the right to apply, as part of the laws (*droits*) of Member States, the teachings of legal writers in the way that, in the realm of international law, the Statute of the International Court of Justice (in Article 38, 1d) charges that court to "apply" as one of the sources of international law, . . . "the teachings of the most highly qualified publicists of the various nations, as subsidiary means for the determination of rules of law".

The writings of leading legal publicists are of course frequently adduced before the European Court for purposes of explanation or description of what the national law(s) on a given point or trend may be.

The "general principles common to laws (*droits*) of Member States", as the case-law of the European Court has repeatedly confirmed, is recognised as a source of Community law, indeed probably its principal source other than the Treaties and the valid administrative acts of a law-making nature taken by virtue of them. The express reference to such principles is limited, however, to the single instance in E.E.C. and E.A.E.C. with which this section is concerned, for there was no such express reference in E.C.S.C. It may be that even were it not required by this express reference so to do the European Court would wish to determine questions of Community non-contractual liability in accordance with the general principles common to the laws (*droits*) of Member States, for the difficulties that are so prone to arise in the ascertainment of tortious liability upon the basis of the principles of private international law are thereby avoided. It is convenient that the inclusion of this express reference in the second paragraph of E.E.C. 215 and E.A.E.C. 188 respectively should result in the allocation, by these articles taken as a whole, of the various aspects of liability to defined governing laws, the other aspects being: Community contractual liability to the proper law of the contract, (see comment on E.E.C. 215 and E.A.E.C.188, paragraph 1 in each case, *post*, p. 155) and personal liability of Community servants towards the Community by paragraph 3 of the same articles (see conslusion of next paragraph, *infra*).

"... **The Community shall ... make good any damage caused ... by its servants in the performance of their duties.**" (E.E.C. 215, paragraph 2). The Community's liability arises without distinction as to whether the acts of its servants which caused the damage were, with respect to what they had authority to do, *intra vires* or *ultra vires*. (This distinction had been the basis underlying E.C.S.C. 40; see *infra*). The omission of this distinction in E.E.C. and E.A.E.C., which appears to be in line with the most recent trend concerning non-contractual liability of the State and public authorities in the national laws of the original Member States, gives rise to the inclusion of paragraph three of E.E.C. 215 and E.A.E.C. 188 providing the legal basis upon which the Community may recoup itself from its servants. Paragraph three provides: "The personal liability of its servants towards the Community shall be defined in the provisions establishing their statute of service or their conditions of employment."

E.C.S.C. 40

Without prejudice to the provisions of the first paragraph of Article 34, the Court shall be empowered to award pecuniary damages against the Community, on the application of the injured party, in cases where injury is caused in carrying out this Treaty by a wrongful act or default in the performance of the Community's functions.

It may also award damages against a servant of the Community in cases where injury results from a wrong for which that servant is personally liable, committed in the course of his duties. If the injured party is unable to recover such damages from the servant the Court may award equitable compensation against the Community.

Any other disputes arising between the Community and third parties, outside the scope of the provisions of this Treaty and its implementing regulations, shall be brought before the municipal courts or tribunals.

Paragraph 1. "Subject to the provisions of the first paragraph of Article 34 ...". Article 34 makes the High Authority responsible for consequential action following the reference back to it of a matter by the Court when the latter has annulled a decision or recommendation made by the High Authority in that matter. Such consequential action may include the taking of "suitable measures to ensure equitable redress for the injury resulting from the decision or recommendation which has been annulled, and, as far as may be necessary", the granting of "fair damages". (For details, see comment on E.C.S.C. 34 under "Legality of Acts" *ante*, pp. 116 *et seq.*).

It is subject to these provisions, which are for "equitable redress" or "fair damages" to be made directly by the High Authority, and only indirectly by virtue of a judgment of the Court, that Article 40 lays down the principle upon which the Court may itself, directly, make an order for damages against the Community.

Paragraph 1 ... "on the application of the injured party ...". Such an application is a condition precedent for the making by the Court of an order for damages against the Community.

"... The injured party ...". Though in practice such may be the case, the category of private parties who may bring an action for damages for tort against the Community is not in principle restricted to undertakings and associations of undertakings as defined by E.C.S.C. 80 (*ante*, p. 48). Compare E.C.S.C. 33 (*ante*, pp. 91–93 and E.C.S.C. 36 (*ante*, p. 80) and see "Restriction in E.C.S.C. 34" *ante*, p. 117.

That the Court has full jurisdiction (for "full jurisdiction" see comment under "Review of Penalty or Fine", *ante*, pp. 78–79) as a result of an application as referred to in the previous paragraph appears without doubt. "The Treaty does not ... expressly define the nature [effect] of the claim putting in issue the liability of the administration for fault in the execution of its duties ["*faute de service*", see next paragraph of this comment] [which is the hypothesis contemplated in Article 40 paragraph 1 of the Treaty]—though this is a typical example of an action in full jurisdiction in French law—no doubt because it necessarily follows from the object of such an action that there can be no question of anything other than "full jurisdiction" (*per* Adv. Gen. Roemer in *M. René Bourgaux* c. *Assemblée Commune de la C.E.C.A.* Case 1/56 R. Vol. II at p. 449).

Wrongful act or default in the performance of the Community's functions (*"Faute de service de la Communauté"*). *"Faute de service"* is distinguished, in French administrative case law, from *"faute personelle"*. The latter expression is used in paragraph 2 of Article 40 (*infra*) and has been translated as "wrongful act of that servant in the performance of his duties". It is doubtful whether the English translation makes clear that paragraph 1 and paragraph 2 are in fact concerned with completely distinct legal situations. The former, with *"faute de service"*, is concerned with acts of the Community *intra vires* its servants. The latter, in *"faute personnelle"*, is concerned with *ultra vires* acts of a Community servant, though committed "in the performance of his duties". This distinction is omitted from the comparable provisions of E.E.C. and E.A.E.C.

E.C.S.C. 65 provides that the High Authority may obtain information needed for the purposes of the Article "in accordance with Article 47".

"Faute de service" is nowhere defined in the Treaties, and the only example of it given in E.C.S.C. is the breach of professional secrecy in Article 47. This Article specifically confers jurisdiction on the Court to award damages to an undertaking for breach of professional secrecy by the High Authority, according to the provisions of E.C.S.C. 40. For text see *ante*, p. 144.

In one case concerning E.C.S.C. 47 (Appendix, *post*) (*Meroni & Cie.* c. *Haute Autorité*, Case 9/56 R. Vol. IV at pp. 32–33; re-iterated verbatim in Case 10/56 R. Vol. IV at pp. 71–72) the Court stated:

"... In numerous communications addressed to the applicant the Compensation Fund for Imported Scrap never gave any details beyond the tonnage liable to the levy and the amount payable by way of the levy. No information was published either by the High Authority or by the Brussels organizations to inform those subject to the levy of the methods by which their liability was determined or of the factual elements on which the calculations had been based. It was only by 'an additional answer by the High Authority to the questions asked by the Court' that the Court, and apparently, the applicant, were informed of the successive formulas for assessing the levy payable. Article 5 of the Treaty requires the High Authority to 'publish the reasons for its action' and Article 47 provides [*the Court quoted the article and continued*]. In its Further Reply the High Authority set up by way of defence 'the necessity for an elementary respect of professional secrecy'. In the instant case, information collected by the co-operative organizations grouping together at different times, in particular on the 4th July 1955, as many as 136 undertakings taken from the 240 undertakings liable to the compensation levy, cannot be considered secret within the meaning of article 47 of the Treaty. By not publishing, at least in outline, the reasons for its action and in not publishing the data, likely to be useful to Governments or others interested, not covered by professional secrecy, or in not obliging the Brussels organisations to publish them, the High Authority has infringed articles 5 and 47 of the Treaty. For this further reason, in application of article 33 of the Treaty, the decision of 24th October 1956 must be quashed".

In *Acciaieria e Tubificio di Brescia* c. *Haute Autorité* (Case 31/59. R. Vol. VI (i) at p. 213). The President of the Court ruled in his Order:

"... The applicant contends that there is a risk of irreparable material injury because of the fact that if the Court, in its judgment in the main action, were to find that the control imposed was illegal, the data thus collected would no longer benefit from the professional secrecy imposed by article 47 of the Treaty. This thesis is unacceptable because the obligation imposed by article 47 paragraph two of the Treaty which is valid for information legally acquired, applies *a fortiori* to information obtained illegally ...".

An unsuccessful attempt before the Court to establish that a demand by the High Authority to be furnished with bills for electricity consumption was a breach of professional secrecy was made in *Società Industriale Accaierie San Michele et autres* c. *Haute Autorité* (Consolidated Cases 5–11 and 13–15/62. R. Vol. VIII at p. 859, see especially pp. 882–885). The case law of the Court seems to have favoured the absolute and objective responsibility as known to international law, rather than a conception of "*Faute*" requiring the assessment of the degree of culpability involved (as characterizes the determination of, for example, "*faute*" or alternatively "*dol*" in France; "*colpa*" and "*dolo*" in Italy; and comparable concepts in the other member countries). Thus where in a case concerning the non-renewal of a contract of employment by the Community, the circumstances of the non-renewal ... appear irregular and the Bureau ... has committed a "*faute*" in the exercise of its functions ... this "*faute*" involves the responsibility of the Assembly, stated the Court (in *Kergall* c. *Assemblée Commune*, Case 1/55 R. Vol. II p. 25). The only factual considerations the Court required to take into account were breach of the duties incumbent on the Assembly by virtue of the contract of employment, of the principles of good administration, or of a subjective right of the appellant. The "*faute*" that it held to exist seemed thus to be dependent only on certain illegal acts. In a later judgment, however, the Court appeared to indicate that the assessment of the degree of negligence might sometimes be necessary: ". . . it is not necessary in the present case to determine the question whether *"faute de service"* in the meaning of Article 40 of the Treaty, presupposes *"dol"* or at least culpable negligence, or whether any illegal attitude—even unconscious—on the part of an institution may constitute such a *"faute"* (*per* the Court in *Algeri etc.* c. *Assemblée Commune* (Consolidated cases 7/56 and 3–7/57 R. Vol. II p. 25)). The matter is thus not wholly free from doubt.

An action for pecuniary damages based on article 40. This action, brought incidentally to a claim for annulment, is only admissible if it is independent of the claim for annulment with regard to the factual and legal situation on which it is rested. In *Société Fives Lille Caille etc.* c. *Haute Autorité* (Consolidated cases 19, 21/60 and 2, 3/61, R. Vol. VII at pp. 589–90) the Court stated:

"The four applicants seek pecuniary damages from the High Authority for the injury they allege has been caused them by a wrongful act or default in the performance of the Community's function. This act or default is said by them to have three aspects. Firstly, they allege that the High Authority failed in good time to notify its new position in respect of Transport parity and thus caused the undertaking to enter into obligations which, duly informed, they would have abstained from doing. Secondly, they allege that the High Authority did not, by adequate supervision, prevent the organisms operating under its control or direction from taking initiatives or entering into engagements that were illegal. Thirdly, they contend that the High Authority bears the responsibility for the illegal and defective functioning of the mechanism of compensation.

The actions for pecuniary damages of the applicants are therefore not based on the ground that the High Authority illegally withdrew from them the benefit of the rights and advantages which the Common Office for Scrap Consumers (O.C.C.F.) granted them. The actions thus relate to a factual and legal situation quite independent of that to which the claims for annulment relate, and are therefore admissible . . .".

Cases on E.C.S.C. 40

In *A. Kergall* c. *Assemblée Commune* (Case 1/55 R. Vol. II, pp. 11 *et seq.*) the issue of the liability of the Community arose in respect of a decision, taken in irregular circumstances, not to renew a contract of employment. The Court held that the Administration had acted wrongfully in the exercise of its functions (*"faute de service"*). This resulted in its liability to repair the damage caused.

C. Algera etc. c. *Assemblée Commune* (Consolidated cases 7/56 and 3/57 to 7/57 R. Vol. III, pp. 81 *et seq.*) The Court held unlawful in the sense of E.C.S.C. 40 (*"faute de service"*) the illegal revocation of a provision for placing an employee on the roll in accordance with the Statute of Community Personnel. It is noteworthy that the judgment, though holding that no material damage was suffered by the applicants as a result of illegal acts of the Administration, accepted the Request for annulment of the provisions in question and awarded compensation under the head of "moral harm" (*"préjudice moral"*) on the basis of E.C.S.C. 40.

In *F.E.R.A.M.* c. *Haute Autorité* (Case 23/59 R. Vol. V, pp. 486 *et seq.*) E.C.S.C. 40 was invoked to found a Request for compensation for damage caused by the defective functioning of the financial mechanism for compensation in respect of imported scrap. (This was a mechanism, set up in application of E.C.S.C. 53 (b), operated by a consortium the membership of which was compulsory for all Community undertakings using scrap, with the specific task of eliminating the difference in price between scrap originating in the six Member States and scrap originating abroad. A levy was made payable, on scrap originating within the Community, out of which to compensate importers of scrap originating outside the Community. To the latter was equiparated scrap from the salvage of naval vessels because of its greater cost. The consortium operated from 1st April 1954 to November 1958. Important administrative tasks—such as the control of documents of origin—were delegated to two subsidiary bodies, the Fund for Compensation of Imported Scrap (*Caisse de Péréquation de Ferraille Importée*) and the Joint Bureau of Scrap Consumers (B.C.C.F.), both with their seats in Brussels. As from August, 1959, in application of the judgment in the present case, the High Authority reassumed the powers delegated to these two bodies). The defective functioning for which, in the present case, the applicants claimed the High Authority was liable, was the increased contribution to the Fund they had paid as a result of the fraudulent admission to compensation ("*péréquation*"), on the basis of false certificates of origin, of very considerable amounts of scrap. During the years 1956 and 1957 large quantities of scrap from the internal market in Holland were represented as salvage from naval vessels in order that they might benefit from the "*péréquation*". From this was derived an unlawful gain for the authors of the frauds and corresponding collective loss to the undertakings using scrap and obliged to make the payments provided for by the system. These frauds were made possible as the result of the issue for financial gain by an official of the Ministry of Economic Affairs of the Netherlands with responsibility in such matters, of false certificates of origin of the scrap. These misled the officials of the Fund for Compensation.

Compagnie des Hauts Fourneaux de Chasse c. *Haute Autorité* (Case 33/59) R. Vol. VIII p. 719); *Meroni (Erba) et Meroni (Settino Torinesa)* c. *Haute Autorité* (Cases 46/59 and 47/59 R. Vol. VIII p. 783): these three cases are substantially identical with *F.E.R.A.M.* c. *Haute Autorité* (*supra*).

In *Worms* c. *Haute Autorité* (Case 18/60, R. Vol. VII, pp. 369 *et seq.*) the judgment contained no element developing the law beyond the point reached in the four cases referred to immediately above. The facts and allegations on which the applicant had sought to rest "*faute de service*" of the High Authority are of interest, however, being very different from those in the above four cases. The applicant alleged that unlawful activity of the Fund and Bureau had rendered them responsible for an action for boycotting him, making it impossible to carry out his normal activity and causing him very considerable damage, professional and material. The Community was called upon to reply on the basis that these bodies must be considered its organs. The applicant further alleged that the High Authority had itself failed to carry out certain precise obligations, in a series of defined circumstances, thus failing in the duties inherent in the function of a Public Authority—the applicant was successful.

See also *Société Fives Lille Cail etc.* c. *Haute Autorité* (Consolidated cases 19/60 21/60 2/61 and 3/61, R. Vol. VII pp. 545 *et seq.*)

In *A Vloeberghs* c. *Haute Autorité* (Consolidated cases 9/60 and 12/60 R. Vol. VII p. 379 at pp. 424–425) the Court stated:

". . . article 40 paragraph one is concerned with an action against the Community for liability in respect of '*faute de service*'. The action for damages provided for in article 40 differs from a claim for annulment both by its object and by the grounds on which it may be rested. As far as its object is concerned the action for damages arises, not as the elimination of a given measure, but only as the making good of damage caused by an action, or a failure to take action, constituting a '*faute de service*'. As far as the grounds are concerned on which an action for damages may be rested, a finding by the Court against the High Authority can only be founded on a *'faute de service'*, whereas the claim for annulment permits the four grounds set out in article 33 to be relied upon. Thus article 40 confers on the Court a jurisdiction which is clearly distinguished from the jurisdiction it exercises where the action conerns the legality of a decision. In the present case the Court is not called upon to pronounce on the question whether the alleged illegality of an act which has not been annulled can be put forward as in itself constituting a *'faute'* capable of creating a right to damages on the basis of article 50. Not only that, but in the present case no decision of the High Authority creating rights and having legal effects as a consequence had been made. In these circumstances, without it being necessary, in inquiring into the present dispute, to decide the question of the admissibility of an action based on the illegality of a positive act of which the annulment has not been claimed, it is certain that the infringement of the Treaty with which the High Authority is charged as inherent in its inaction can be put forward in support of an action founded on article 40.

The difference between the jurisdiction conferred on the Court by articles 33 and 35 and the jurisdiction conferred by article 40 is confirmed by the saving clause contained in the first paragraph of article 40: 'Without prejudice to the provisions of the first paragraph of Article 34 . . .'. This formula exludes all possibility of invoking article 34 and envisages on the contrary situations in which article 34 has no application, as in the instant case . . .".

Third paragraph of E.C.S.C. 40. In *Firma I. Nold KG c. Haute Autorité* (Case 18/57. R. Vol. V at p. 89) part of the applicant's claim was that the High Authority had acted contrary to German constitutional law. The Advocate General (Roemer), after setting out articles 3, 5, 8, 33, 35, 36 and 37 to demonstrate that an institution or organism of the Community was under no obligation to respect rules other than those laid down in the Treaty, concluded his submissions with the following:

"In this respect one can also invoke the third paragraph of E.C.S.C. 40. It is possible to make a deduction *a contrario* from this paragraph that the Court has no competence to examine legal acts except in the light of the law of the Community, and is not obliged to take note of infringements of the internal law of Member States. That does not exlcude the possibility arising, as part of the inquiry into alleged *détournement de pouvoir*, that it may also be necessary to respect the elementary principles of law which also find expression in the provisions of national constitutions. Strictly speaking, from this point of view, the Court may examine the constitutional provisions which the applicant invokes in his support. But the result is assuredly no different . . .".

VIII. DISPUTES CONCERNING RELATIONSHIPS BETWEEN THE COMMUNITY AND ITS SERVANTS

E.E.C. 179

The Court of Justice shall have jurisdiction to adjudicate in any dispute between the Community and its subordinates within the limits of and under the conditions laid down by their statute or terms of employment.

E.A.E.C. 152

[*Identical with E.E.C.* 179]

E.E.C. 179 was the basis of the Court's jurisdiction in *Mme. Leda de Bruyn* c. *Assemblée Parlementaire Européenne* (Case 25/60, R. Vol. VIII, at pp. 39 *et seq.*). No difficulty of interpretation of the article arose in that case, so that no quotation from it is given here.

Relation of E.E.C. 179 to E.E.C. 173 (E.E.C. 246). In *Eva von Lach-müller etc.* c. *Commission de la C.E.E.* (Consolidated cases 43, 45 and 48/59, R. Vol. VI (ii) at pp. 955–6) the Court quoted E.E.C. 179 and continued:

". . . At the present time, in the absence and pending the promulgation of the Statute (of Community personnel) the servants, in the obvious sense, of the Community, are subject to a special and provisional regime. This regime . . . not having been determined and expressly defined by the competent authorities, is the regime resulting from the express or tacit conditions governing the contracts of service of these servants with the Community. Therefore the Court has jurisdiction to rule on the disputes that arise, in the circumstances and conditions of the present, between the Community and its servants because there is in existence between them a regime which necessarily regulates, even though only provisionally, these relationships. Moreover article 173 lays down the general principle that supervision of the legality of the acts of the Council and of the Commission other than recommendations or opinions shall be a matter for the Court of Justice. To invoke this principle, far from contra-dicting or impeding the application of article 179 in the present case, re-inforces if that were necessary a finding that this application is well-founded. It is therefore necessary to reject as ill-founded the objection that article 179 could not be applied in the instant case because the Community has not drawn up the statute of its servants and, in its absence, has not expressly defined the regime that is provisionally applicable pend-ing the working out of the statute, (not only because of Article 173 but) since also there is necessarily a regime applicable to the legal relations existing between the Community and its servants, as has been stated above . . ."

(The passage referring to E.E.C. 173 and its relationship to E.E.C. 179 was re-iterated verbatim by the Court in *Rudolf Pieter Marie Fiddelaar* c. *Commission C.E.E*, Case 44/59 R. Vol. VI (ii), at p. 1092).

E.C.S.C. 42

The Court shall be competent to give a decision pursuant to any clause conferring jurisdiction on it contained in a contract concluded by or on behalf of the Community, by whatever branch of law such contract is governed.

This article, operating in conjunction with a clause in the contract between the Community and its servants (a "*clause compromissoire*", as to which see *post*, p. 153) conferring jurisdiction on the Court in respect of any dispute arising out of the contract, is the basis of the Court's jurisdiction in E.C.S.C. In *M. Antoine Kergall* c. *Assemblée Commune* (Case 1/55, R. Vol. II at pp. 21–22) the Court stated:

"The jurisdiction of the Court derives from E.C.S.C. 42, invoked by the applicant in her Request, together with article 17 of the contract of service and with article 27 of the Internal Regulation for Staff of the Common Assembly of 12th January 1953. Article 17 of the contract of service provides that all the clauses of the Internal Regulation in force shall apply to the relations between the servant and the Common Assembly to the extent they are not contrary to the provisions of the contract of service. Article 27 of the Internal Regulation lays down that disputes of an individual character which may arise from the application of the Internal Regulation or the execution of the contracts of service, shall be referred to the Court. Article 50 of the provisional Internal Regulation contains a similar provision".

(Further examples of the same principle are given *post*, p. 156).

Contracts between the Communities and their servants. These are contracts of public law in the Continental European sense. The existence of a distinction between public and private law is drawn attention to in E.E.C. 181 and equivalents (which see in "Reference by virtue of a *'clause compromissoire'* ", *post*, p. 153). The importance of the distinction is thrown into sharp relief in respect of contracts of the Communities with their servants, the subject of the present section. The importance lies in the fact that the Community servant is better protected by a contract of public law inasmuch as a decision to terminate his services is, in law, an "administrative act" (for the meaning of this term of art see *ante*, p. 4) the reasons for which the law requires to be set out clearly and fully as part of the act itself. The insufficiency of such reasons is a ground for annulment of the administrative act in question (on the principle of E.E.C. 173 and equivalents; which see under "Legality of Acts", *ante*, pp. 83 *et seq.*).

The logical steps by which this position is reached, and the consequent importance of the distinction between public and private law, may be well followed in, for example, *Eva von Lachmüller, Bernard Peuvrier, Roger Ehrhardt c. Commission C.E.E* (Consolidated cases 43, 45 and 48/59 R. Vol. VI/2 p. 933, especially at pp. 953 *et seq.*) The argument is developed in the Court's judgment as follows (p. 953):

"It is important to know whether these contracts pertain to public law or private law; one of the contracting parties, the E.E.C. Commission acting within the limits of the authority conferred upon it by the treaty, enjoys, in accordance with Article 210 thereof, legal personality; this personality is of public law by virtue of the powers and functions appertaining to the Commission; it follows that the contracts in dispute were concluded by a person of public law; these contracts, moreover, were concluded with a view to the functioning of the linguistic department of the Commission; the activity of this department, the duty of which is to ensure the identity of the contents of the acts of the Commission in the four official languages of the Community, constitutes an important element in the procedure which, for each of the languages in question, is tantamount to elaboration of the acts themselves; the activity thus shares in the public character of the Commission itself; consequently the contracts in dispute pertain to public law and are subject to the general rules of administrative law; [p. 956] they are thus subject to the principle that the action of the (public) authority in the administrative as in the contractual field is always subject to the principle of good faith, and whether the contracts are provisional or permanent in character is immaterial; consequently, the decisions to end the servants' employment must, in order to terminate the contract, be supported by justifying reasons founded on the interest of the department and excluding all arbitrary considerations . . .; the setting out of the reasons of public interest justifying an administrative act must be precise and capable of being contested, otherwise the servant in question would not be able to assure himself whether his legitimate interests had been respected or violated, and, moreover, control of the legality of the decision would be impeded; in the present case the letters bringing the employment to an end were restricted to the notification to the applicants of the desire of the administrator to terminate the contract without any indication of reasons; . . . and must therefore be declared unsatisfactory, constituting a contractual fault for which the Commission is liable . . .''

Actions brought by Community servants in respect of their contracts have been relatively frequent since 1954. Actions by the Communities against their servants are likely to remain rare.

Procedure. Cases the subject of this section are normally dealt with by a section of the Court and not the whole Court (see Chapter 5, "Proceedings by servants of the Communities" *post*, pp. 283–284).

IX. DISPUTES RELATING TO THE EUROPEAN INVESTMENT BANK

Title IV of Part Three (Policy of the Community) of the E.E.C. Treaty is concerned, in its two Articles, with The European Investment Bank.

A European Investment Bank having legal personality, and of which the Member States are automatically members, is established by E.E.C. 129. The Statute of the Bank, as required by E.E.C. 129, is the subject of the first Protocol to the Treaty. The task of the Bank is defined in E.E.C. 130.

It should be noted that in the technical and legal sense the Bank is not an "Institution of the Community" as provided for in E.E.C. 4 (as to which see Chapter 1, *ante*, pp. 17–18) though in the pre-amble to the Rules of Procedure of the Court it is stated: "For the purposes of these Rules the term 'Institutions' refers to the Institutions of the European Communities as well as to the European Investment Bank". Certain matters relating to the Bank are referred by E.E.C. 180 (*infra*) to the jurisdiction of the Community Court, though as regards its banking operations in particular it is provided by Article 29 of its Statute that "Disputes between the Bank on the one hand, and those who have lent funds to it or borrowed from it or third parties on the other hand, shall, subject to the jurisdiction conferred upon the Court of Justice, be decided by the competent national courts". The comment that follows E.E.C. 180 (*infra*) is concerned only with the jurisdiction of the Community Court in respect of the Bank; for further details concerning the Bank's legal position before the national courts, etc. reference should be made to the Protocol.

E.E.C. 180

The Court of Justice shall be competent within the limits hereinafter set out to hear disputes concerning:—

(*a*) The fulfilment by Member States of the obligations arising under the Statute of the European Investment Bank. The Board of Directors of the Bank shall, in this respect, enjoy the powers conferred upon the Commission by Article 169;

(*b*) decisions of the Board of Governors of the Bank. In this matter, any Member State, the Commission or the Board of Directors of the Bank may institute proceedings under the conditions laid down in Article 173;

(*c*) decisions of the Board of Directors of the Bank. Appeals against such decisions, brought in accordance with Article 173, may only be brought by Member States or by the Commission, and solely upon the grounds of non-compliance with the procedure prescribed by Articles 21 (2) and (5) to (7) inclusive of the Statute of the Bank.

Sub-paragraph (a). For the purposes of control by the Community Court of "the fulfilment by Member States of the obligations arising under the Statute of the European Investment Bank" the Board of Directors of the Bank is placed in the same position *vis à vis* the Member States as is the Commission, for the purposes of the fulfilment of Member States' obligations under the Treaty generally, by virtue of E.E.C. 169 (as to which see this Chapter, "Claim that a Member State has failed to fulfil any of its obligations under the Treaty.—(i) Claim by E.E.C. Commission" *ante*, pp. 63 *et seq.* and p. 78).

Decisions of the Board of Governors, or of the Board of Directors, of the Bank. Though the Bank as explained above is not an "Institution" of the Community, these decisions are, by sub-paragraphs (*b*) and (*c*), put on the same legal footing as decisions of the Council and Commission, which are "Institutions". Decisions of the Bank's Board of Governors or Board of Directors are made capable of being the subject of a claim for annulment in accordance with E.E.C. 173 (as to which see this chapter, under "Legality of Acts", *ante*, pp. 83 *et seq.*). E.E.C. 180 (*b*) and (*c*) restrict, however, the categories of legal persons who may institute proceedings, and, in the case of an appeal against a decision of the Board of Directors, the grounds upon which it may be brought.

X. REFERENCE BY VIRTUE OF A *"CLAUSE COMPROMISSOIRE"*

(*"Clause compromissoire"*; *"Schiedsklausel"*; *"arbitragebeding"*; *"clausola compromissoria"*). All three Treaties provide that the European Court may be designated, by a *"clause compromissoire"* (clause conferring jurisdiction) contained in a contract made by or on behalf of the Community, as the forum to which certain matters shall be referred for adjudication when in dispute.

E.E.C. 181

The Court of Justice shall have jurisdiction to give a decision pursuant to any arbitration clause (*compromis d'arbritrage*) contained in a contract concluded, by or on behalf of the Community, whether such contract be governed by public law (*droit public*), or private law (*droit privé*).

"... Public law or private law ..." As to the practical importance of the distinction see under "Contracts between the Communities and their servants", *ante*, p. 151).

E.A.E.C. 153

The Court of Justice shall be competent to make a decision pursuant to any clause referring matters to it contained in a contract concluded, under public or private law (*droit public, droit privé*), by or on behalf of the Community.

E.C.S.C. 42

[Printed on p. 150, *ante.]*

The substantial identity of the provisions in the comparable Articles of the three Treaties (*supra*). This is perhaps veiled to some extent by variations in wording in the original authentic texts. It is unfortunate, moreover, that the (first) unofficial English translations of the three Articles show variations as between each other in addition to those to be found in the originals. What is important is that the expression "*clause compromissoire*" (howsoever rendered in English) is contained in each of the three Articles in the original (French). (See next comment).

The respective jurisdiction of the European Court and the national courts of Member States. The effect of the "*clause compromissoire*" is to oust, in favour of the European Court, the jurisdiction of any other tribunal that might otherwise be competent to determine the matter.

Though, at first impression, there may be thus a certain similarity in its operation with that of an "arbitration clause" in a contract made under English law it is unwise to pursue this analogy. In the first place an English arbitration clause, though it may in practice normally result in the final settlement by the designated arbitral tribunal of the dispute submitted to it, does not have the effect of completely ousting the jurisdiction of the Courts. In the second place the effect of the "*clause compromissoire*" in the Articles of the Treaties under consideration in this section is not a submission to arbitration (at least in the sense in which that expression is commonly understood in Continental Europe, as involving the application of less than strictly legal criteria), but to its adjudication on strictly legal principles. It is therefore unfortunate that the word "arbitration" has found its way into the (first) English translation of E.E.C. 181 and that the phrase "*compromis d'arbitrage*", which does not appear in the original French, should have been included. (An example in the Treaties of a reference of a dispute for settlement by an Arbitration Committee, over which settlement the European Court has jurisdiction, is that of the "*compromis d'arbitrage à l'effet de saisir le Comité d'Arbitrage*" in E.A.E.C. 20, see "Formal legality of decision of E.A.E.C. Arbitration Committee" (*post*, p. 171), and Chapter 5, "Special Forms of Procedure", *post*, pp. 289–291).

A "*compromis*" and a "*clause compromissoire*" are not identical. The former, adequately translated in the Treaties as "special agreement", is the "reference" itself, in the sense of an agreed submission of the points or matter in dispute and therein defined. As a specific reference the "*compromis*" may therefore (but need not) result from a "*clause compromissoire*", which is a general agreement to refer. A good example of a "*compromis*" is that provided for in E.E.C. and E.A.E.C. to permit Member States to submit a dispute under a "special agreement" to the European Court (see E.E.C. 182 and E.A.E.C. 154 under section XI "By virtue of 'special agreement' between States" *post*, pp. 156 *et seq*.). The conferring of jurisdiction on the European Court by a "*clause compromissoire*" is one instance of an exception, therein provided for, to the general principle laid down in E.E.C. 183 and E.A.E.C. 155, which are in identical terms and read as follows:

"Subject to the powers conferred on the Court of Justice by this Treaty, cases to which the Community is a party shall not for that reason alone be excluded from the jurisdiction of national courts".

(See *ante*, p. 29). (There is no similar provision in E.C.S.C. but certainly as far as Community contracts are concerned the same principle there operates in practice). Thus, it is not because the Community is party to a contract that the European Court has jurisdiction. It has jurisdiction by virtue of a *"clause compromissoire"*, and in the absence of such a clause the national courts (probably) have jurisdiction. (In *Bourgaux* c. *Assemblée Commune*, R. Vol. II at p. 447, the Advocate General drew attention to the fact that the defendant, not in fact desirous of contesting the Court's competence, had "merely indicated that *in the absence of* the *"clause compromissoire"* envisaged in Article 42 of the E.C.S.C. Treaty, it might have been possible that the national courts would have been called upon to pronounce upon the dispute". This situation is in line with E.E.C. 211, E.A.E.C. 185 and E.C.S.C. 6).

E.E.C. 211

[For text and comment see ante *p. 28.]*

E.A.E.C. 185

[Identical with E.E.C. 211.]

E.C.S.C. 6

[Printed on p. 56. ante.]

The "proper law" of a Community contract. The law to be applied by the European Court on a reference to it by virtue of a *"clause compromissoire"* contained in a Community contract, may or may not be Community law. This is the inevitable inference from E.E.C. 215, paragraph 1 (identical with E.A.E.C. 188, paragraph 1).

E.E.C. 215 paragraph 1 and E.A.E.C. 188 paragraph 1 provide: "The contractual liability of the Community shall be governed by the law applying to the contract in question". (See *ante*, p. 28, there is no similar provision in E.C.S.C. though the same principle is there implicit). That Community law may not be the applicable law also follows from the express mention, in the Articles under consideration in this section (*i.e.* E.E.C. 181, E.A.E.C. 153 and E.C.S.C. 42), of the possibility of the contract being "governed by public law or private law". This would seem to include in its contemplation the public law or private law of Member States.

To provide, however, that the contractual liability of the Community shall be governed by the proper law of its contract leaves open the question of how the identity of the proper law is to be determined. The Court has so far been asked to decide Community contractual liability in respect only of contracts with its own individual servants, where the "Staff Regulations" (*"Règlement du Personnel"*) upon the terms of which they were employed comprised both the "clause compromissoire" conferring jurisdiction on the Court and also the provisions governing their contract of employment. (Examples are given in the immediately following paragraphs.) In these cases the parties in effect agreed that the proper law of their contract was that particular manifestation of Community law constituted by the "Staff Regulations". In other cases the application of the principles of private international law for the purpose of identifying the proper law of the contract may lead the Court to apply the law of a Member State (or indeed a non Member State). (Such was the view, for example, in respect of E.C.S.C. 42, of a study group of the Belgian Institut des Relations Internationales, in *"La Communauté Européenne du Charbon et de l'Acier"*. Brussels 1953 at p. 233: *"(la Cour) sera tenue d'appliquer le droit de l'Etat qui régit le contrat conformément aux principes du droit international privé"*).

In *Kergall* c. *Assemblée Commune* (Case 1/55 R. Vol. II at p. 20) the Court stated, with regard to its competence:

"The competence of the Court derives from Article 42 of the (E.C.S.C.) Treaty, invoked by the claimant, together with Article 17 of the contract of employment and Article 27 of the "*Règlement intérieur du Personnel de l'Assemblée Commune*" of the 12th January 1953. Article 17 of the contract of employment provides that all the clauses of the "*Règlement intérieur*" in force are applicable to the relations between the employee ("*agent*") and the Common Assembly to the extent that they are not in conflict with the provisions of the contract of employment. Article 27 of the "*Réglement Intérieur du Personnel*" stipulates that disputes of an individual nature to which the application of the "*Règlement*" or the execution of the contract might give rise, are to be referred to the Court of Justice. Article 50 of the provisional "*Règlement du Personnel*" of the 1st July 1953 contains a similar stipulation".

The Court held that it had competence. The terms of Article 50 of the provisional "*Règlement*" of 1st July 1953 were as follows:

"After exhaustion of the administrative channels for settlement of the difference appertaining to each Institution, disputes to which the application of the present "*règlement*" may give rise shall be taken to the Court of Justice".

They were referred to by the Advocate General in his submissions (R. Vol. II at p. 35) as being the "clause compromissoire".

In *Mirossevich c. Haute Autorité* (case 10/55 R. Vol. II at p. 383, similar to the above) the Court held, on the question of competence, that:

"The Court has competence in the present case, its competence deriving from Article 42 of the Treaty together with Article 12 paragraph 2 of the letter of appointment of 12th October 1953 which provides that disputes of an individual nature to which the application of the provisions of the letter of appointment or of the "Règlements" and decisions concerning the personnel shall be referred to the Court of Justice, and also together with Article 50 of the provisional 'Règlement' of personnel which contains an analogous provision."

In *Bourgaux c. Assemblée Commune* (case 1/56 R. Vol. II at p. 435) the Court made a similar finding and also dealt with the argument put forward by the defence "that, since the claimant was seeking the annulment of a decision taken in respect of herself, the Court's competence would be governed and limited by the provisions of Article 38 of the E.C.S.C. Treaty, making the claim inadmissible". On this point it held that "the generality of the terms of Article 42 makes it impossible to conclude that there exists a binding limitation in law in a '*clause compromissoire*' which exludes annulment as a point of claim." On the wider question of its competence it held, similarly to the decisions quoted in the two previous paragraphs, that the competence of the Court derives in the instant case from Article 42 of the E.C.S.C. Treaty together with Article 17 of the contract of employment of the claimant which refers to "the clauses of the '*Règlement*' in force"; that all the internal "*règlements*" sucessively in force in the Common Assembly contained a clause conferring competence on the Court.

XI. REFERENCE BY VIRTUE OF A "SPECIAL AGREEMENT" ("*COMPROMIS*") BETWEEN STATES

("*Compromis*"; "*Schiedsvertrag*"; "*compromis*"; "*compromesso*").

All three Treaties make provision for a "*compromis*" by Member States to refer disputes concerning the object of the respective Treaty to the Community Court. "Special agreement" adequately translates "*compromis*" (as to which see under "The respective jurisdiction of the European Court and the national courts of Member States", *ante*, p. 154). The relevant Articles are:

E.E.C. 182

The Court of Justice shall be competent to decide any dispute between Member States connected with the subject of this Treaty, where the said States submit the said dispute to the Court under a special agreement between them.

E.A.E.C. 154

[*Identical with E.E.C.* 182.]

E.C.S.C. 89, paragraph 2

[*Identical with E.E.C.* 182 *except for addition of "equally"—see comment* infra.]

In the original (French) the wording of the above three Articles is completely identical, (with the sole exception that E.C.S.C. 89 has the word "*également*" ("equally", "also") added in order to link paragraph 2 with paragraph 1, which is concerned with a different method by which a dispute between Member States may be brought before the Court). "*Compromis*" (as to which see "The respective jurisdiction of the European Court and the national courts of Member States", *ante*, p. 154) is better rendered by "special agreement" than by "arbitration clause" as it was in early translations. No arbitration is involved and a "*compromis*" is not, like a "*clause compromissoire*", a clause in a legal document such as an "arbitration clause" might be, requiring future disputes to be settled by reference to a specified method of adjudication. It is an agreement specially made ad hoc as to the method of adjudication on a dispute that has already come into existence. The word "*objet*" (*du présent Traité*) has been variously translated as "subject" (in E.E.C. 182 and E.A.E.C. 154) and "purpose" in E.C.S.C. 89 (2). It is submitted that the latter is a preferable rendering (see "connected with the subject of the Treaty" *infra*).

"Any dispute between Member States..." On the relevance of international law to such a dispute see "Disputes between Member States, and International Law", *ante*, p. 75).

"Connected with the subject of this Treaty". This is the unofficial rendering of "*en connexité avec l'objet du présent Traité*" in the original French. There appears to be no justification for translating "*objet*" as "subject" rather than "object" which is clearly the meaning of the original. (The revised H.M.S.O. translation of "*en connexité avec l'objet du présent Traité* in E.C.S.C. 43 is "related to the aims of this treaty"). That this is so is borne out, in addition to what is shown by a purely philological approach, by the interrelation of these Articles with others, in each Treaty. Thus, it will be noted that E.C.S.C. 89 (2), concerning disputes in connection with the *object* of the Treaty, is juxtaposed to (and linked by "*également*", with) E.C.S.C. 89 (1), where the concern is with disputes relating to the *application* of the Treaty (see "Claim by Member State of E.C.S.C." *ante*, pp. 71 *et seq.*). It would seem to be obvious that an inquiry into the "object" of the Treaty necessarily involves an interpretation of the Treaty. The E.C.S.C. Treaty makes no provision in terms for "interpretation" of the Treaty by the Court, but it is accepted that Article 89 taken as a whole makes provision in fact for the two ways in which alone the Treaty may be basically related to a dispute between Member States; that is to say the dispute must be as to either its application or its interpretation. In the later Treaties it was thought desirable to do two things: first, to provide that where no questions of interpretation arose, at least *prima facie*, and the dispute was as to application, that is the carrying out by a Member State of its clear obligations under the Treaty, this might be taken to the Court by another Member State after the Commission had been asked to find the facts and give its reasoned opinion thereon. Under E.C.S.C. 89 (1) the High Authority had not been interposed in this way between a Member State and the Court (see "Claim that a Member State has failed to fulfil any of its obligations under the Treaty", *ante*, pp. 74 *et seq.*). Second, while retaining (in identical terms) the provision under which disputes between Member States as to the object of the Treaties could be referred to the Court by a "*compromis*", to add a new type of provision, namely that for a Preliminary Ruling, binding on national courts, to be given by the Community Court on questions of Treaty interpretation.

Compare "connected with the subject of this Treaty" with comments following: (1) under "In any other case provided for by the Treaty" . . . "Related to the aims of the . . . Treaty" (*post*, p. 162); (2) "Compatible with the provisions of this Treaty" (*post*, p. 163); (3) "Interpretation of provisions of the Treaty by E.A.E.C. Arbitration Committee" *post*, pp. 171 *et seq.*; (4) "Compatible with the provisions of this Treaty" (*post*, p. 163).

XII. CLAIM FOR SUSPENSION OF ENFORCEMENT (OPERATION) OF ADMINISTRATIVE ACT

All three Treaties contain the substantially identical provision that the bringing of a claim before the European Court has, of itself, no suspensory effect on the enforcement (operation) of an act of a Community Institution (other than the Court). This general principle is subject to a very small number of exceptions specifically provided for in the Treaties, and to the discretion of the Court itself to order a suspension of enforcement where it considers that circumstances require it. (See comment on the relevant Articles, this section, *infra*). The acts covered by the general principle are those that have binding force, that is, regulations, directives and decisions of the Council or Commission of either E.E.C. or E.A.E.C., and decisions or recommendations of the High Autority of E.C.S.C. (see E.E.C. 189, *ante*, p. 26, E.A.E.C. 161, *ante*, p. 46 and E.C.S.C. 14, *ante*, pp. 52 *et seq.*).

The rule that the bringing of a claim against an act of the administration does not of itself suspend its enforcement is well settled in the administrative law of the original Member States, and it was natural that it should be adopted in the European Treaties. The reason for its existence there, as in the administrative law of the Member States, is of course that in providing for judicial control of the legality of administrative acts the way had to be found to avoid unduly impeding the course of administrative activity.

E.E.C. 185

Proceedings instituted before the Court of Justice shall not suspend the operation of the act in question. The Court of Justice may, however, if it considers that circumstances so require, order that the operation of the act in question be suspended.

E.A.E.C. 157

[Identical with E.E.C. 185.]

E.C.S.C. 39, paragraphs one and two

Proceedings instituted before the Court shall not have suspensory effect.

The Court may, however, if it considers that circumstances so require, order that the operation of the contested decision or recommendation be suspended.

Exceptions to the rule that the bringing of a claim has no suspensory effect on the execution of an act. These are contained in: (a) E.A.E.C. 83, under which the effect of an appeal to the Court against a decision of the Commission imposing any of the sactions provided for in the event of an infringement of obligations relating to security, is suspensory, though the Court may order the immediate implementation of the decision at the request of the Commission or any Member State concerned. The full text of E.A.E.C. 83 is:

"1. In the event of any infringement of the obligations imposed on persons or enterprises under the provisions of this Chapter, penalties may be imposed on them by the Commission.

These penalties, in order of gravity, shall be as follows:

(*a*) a warning;

(*b*) the withdrawal of special advantages, such as financial or technical assistance;

(*c*) the placing of the enterprise, for a maximum period of four months, under the administration of a person or board appointed jointly by the Commission and the State having jurisdiction over such enterprise; or

(*d*) the complete or partial withdrawal of source materials or special fissionable materials.

2. Decisions of the Commission which require delivery in implementation of the proceeding paragraph shall be enforceable. They may be enforced in the territories of Member States in accordance with the provisions laid down in Article 164.

Notwithstanding the provisions of Article 157, appeals brought before the Court of Justice against decisions of the Commission which impose any of the penalties provided for in the preceding paragraph shall have a staying effect. The Court of Justice may, however, at the request of the Commission or of any interested Member State, order that the decision be enforced immediately.

The protection of injured interests shall be guaranteed by an appropriate legal procedure.

3. The Commission may make any recommendations to Member States concerning legislative provisions designed to ensure the observance in their territories of the obligations resulting from the provisions of this Chapter.

4. Member States shall ensure the enforcement of penalties and, where applicable, the making of reparation by those responsible for any infringement."

(b) E.C.S.C. 66 (5), paragraph 2 provides that an application brought to annul a decision of the High Authority ordering the separation of undertakings forming an unlawful concentration has suspensory effect on the enforcement of that decision. (As to such an application, see Relationship of E.C.S.C. 33 and E.C.S.C. 66 (5) in III "Legality of Acts," *ante*, p. 115). The full text of E.C.S.C. 66 (5), paragraph 2 reads:

"If a concentration should occur which the High Authority finds cannot satisfy the general or special conditions to which an authorisation under paragraph 2 would be subject, it shall declare this concentration to be unlawful by means of a reasoned decision; after allowing the parties concerned an opportunity to put forward their views, the High Authority shall order separation of the undertakings or assets improperly concentrated or cessation of common control as well as any other action which it considers appropriate to re-establish the independent operation of the undertakings or assets in question and to restore normal conditions of competition. Any person directly concerned may make an application against such decisions under the conditions provided for in Article 33. Notwithstanding the provisions of the said Article, the Court shall have plenary jurisdiction to decide whether the course of action taken is a concentration within the meaning of paragraph 1 of this Article and of the regulations issued in implementation thereof. This application shall have suspensory effect. It may not be made until the measures provided for above have been ordered, unless the High Authority agrees to the lodging of a separate appeal against the decision holding the course of action to be unlawful."

Interim measures. It will be noted that E.C.S.C. 39 empowers the Court to order any other necessary interim measures besides the suspension of enforcement of the decision or recommendation against which the claim was brought. In the later Treaties interim measures form the subject of a separate Article and the last paragraph of E.C.S.C. 39 is treated together with those under "Claim for Interim Measures", *post*, p. 161.

Suspension may be ordered without inquiry into all the issues of the main action. In *Firma I. Nold K.G.* c. *Haute Autorité* (Case 18/57 (Summary Procedure) R. Vol. III at p. 255) Adv. Gen. Roemer submitted:

". . . we consider that at this stage it is not a question of pronouncing on the admissibility of the principal claim, leaving aside the existence of a right to make the claim. On the contrary what we need to do is to inquire solely into the question whether the circumstances exist in which a claim for suspension should be upheld. We shall therefore not have to examine either whether the grounds of violation of basic procedural rules and misuse of powers invoked in the course of the oral procedure in support of the claim for suspension are admissible as well founded. On the other hand, to inquire as we are going to do into the question whether the suspension claimed is necessary, we must take account of the fact that the claim is in respect of a general measure."

In the above case the Request by way of summary procedure (*"référé"*) was for the suspension of enforcement of the provision of decisions Nos. 16–18/57 of the 26th July 1957. The Court by order (*"ordonnance"*) declared the Request admissible and granted the suspension sought pending judgment in the main action. The application, by decision of the President of the Court taken by virtue of E.C.S.C. St. 33 (as to which see *post*, p. 271) and Rule 66 of the former Rules of Procedure, was heard by the Court.

Procedure. Application to the Court to suspend the enforcement of an administrative act or take other interim measures involves urgency and is therefore by way of summary procedure (*"référé"*). This is one of the "special forms of procedure" dealt with in R.P. Title III. (These are the subject of Chapter 5, in which see especially R.P. 83–89, *post*, pp. 270 *et seq.*).

It may here be noted that though the stay of execution of a judgment or order (see "Judgments, Orders" *post*, p. 253) of the Court differs substantively from the suspension of enforcement of an administrative act (the subject of the present section) R.P. 89 (*post*, p. 273) makes applicable to a judgment or order of the Court the rules laid down for administrative acts, as regards the suspension of enforcement. (As to stay of execution of a judgment or order see *post*, p. 177).

No derogation from E.C.S.C. 39 by virtue of E.C.S.C. 88 paragraph three. In *Gouvernement de la République Fédérale d'Allemagne* c. *Haute Autorité* (Case 3/59, R. Vol. VI (i) at p. 130) the Court stated:
". . . contrary to the opinion of the applicant, article 88 paragraph three merely stipulates that measures under (a) and (b) thereof cannot be taken so long as the appeal is pending. It cannot be held that the authors of the Treaty could have intended to confer a suspensory effect on the appeals provided for in article 88; the text being silent–such derogation from the general principle of article 39 cannot be presumed . . ."

XIII. CLAIM FOR INTERIM MEASURES

In identical terms, E.E.C. and E.A.E.C. enable the Court to order any necessary interim measures in any case referred to it. In E.C.S.C. the prescription by the Court of any "other" necessary interim measures is made possible by way of addition to (or instead of?) an order suspending the enforcement of a decision or recommendation the subject of a claim for annulment (as to which see "Claim for suspension of enforcement of administrative act" E.C.S.C. 39, *ante*, p. 159). The later Treaties thus provide for a wider range of contingencies in which interim measures may be ordered, than does E.C.S.C.

E.E.C. 186

The Court of Justice may, in any cases referred to it, prescribe any necessary interim measures.

E.A.E.C. 158

[*Identical with E.E.C. 186.*]

E.C.S.C. 39, paragraph three

The Court may prescribe any other necessary interim measures.

"In any cases referred to it". Under E.E.C. 186 and E.A.E.C. 158 interim measures may be ordered by the Court in respect of any action before it, and not only, as under E.C.S.C. 39 (*supra*), where the action is for the annulment of an administrative act.

"Any other". In E.C.S.C. 39 this means any other than the ordering by the Court "that the operation of the decision or recommendation contested be suspended" (as to which see "Claim for suspension of execution of administrative act", E.C.S.C. 39, *ante*, p. 159).

Procedure. See Chapter 5, Special Forms of Procedure, R.P. 83 *et seq.* (*post*, pp. 270 *et seq.*).

XIV. JURISDICTION "IN ANY OTHER CASE PROVIDED FOR BY THE TREATY" OR BY THE LAW OF A MEMBER STATE

In E.C.S.C. the Articles conferring jurisdiction on the Court in respect of specific types of issue are grouped primarily in Chapter IV of the Treaty—"The Court" (Articles 31–45). One of these provides that jurisdiction may also be conferred on the Court either by a "supplementary provision" of the Treaty (which may be read as meaning one to be found elsewhere than in Chapter IV) or where the law of a Member State confers such jurisdiction in respect of "the object of the present Treaty". This two-fold covering provision is the subject of E.C.S.C. 43 (text, *infra*). The Articles of E.E.C. and E.A.E.C. relating to the Court's jurisdiction are compactly grouped and no provision is made in the same way for supplementary provisions. The determination of "the object of the present Treaty" for the purposes of its application by, and within the jurisdiction of, the Member States is, in the later Treaties, provided for by making possible, or requiring, as the case may be, the giving of Preliminary Rulings by the European Court.

E.C.S.C. 43

The Court shall be competent to decide in any other case provided for by a provision supplementing this Treaty.

It may also decide on all matters related to the aims of this Treaty where jurisdiction is conferred upon it by the law of a Member State.

"**. . . Related to the aims of this Treaty . . . .**" This is the rendering of "*en connexité avec l'objet du présent Traité*" as to which see "Connected with the subject of this treaty", *ante*, p. 157).

Scope of the Article. In *Bourgaux* c. *Assemblée Commune* (Case 1/56, R. Vol. II at p. 450) Advocate General Roemer submitted:

"In contrast to articles 33 and 38 of the Treaty, for example, which limit the power of appreciation of the Court or which canalize it within certain grounds of annulment, Articles 42 and 43 of the Treaty . . . provide simply that the Court is competent to give judgment ("*est compétente pour statuer*") on the issues in question in the cases indicated. The Court is thus not in principle restricted in its inquiry and it may prescribe in its judgment all measures necessary to the determination of the issue with which it is seized."

In *Jean E. Humblet* c. *État Belge* (Case 6/60, R. Vol. VI (ii) at p. 1146) a case concerning the E.C.S.C. Protocol on Privileges and Immunities, the Court stated:

". . . the applicant bases his argument on the text of article 16 of the Protocol on privileges and immunities, jointly with article 43 of the Treaty. Article 16 of the protocol makes provision not only for the 'interpretation' but also for the 'application' of the said protocol. However, it is erroneous to hold that this provision enables the Court to interfere directly in the legislation or administration of Member States. Indeed if the Court in giving judgment draws attention to the fact that a legislative or administrative act promulgated by the authorities of a Member State is contrary to Community law, the said State is obliged, by virtue of article 86 of the Treaty, both to correct the act in question and also to repair the unlawful effects it may have had. This obligation is the result of the Treaty and of the protocol which have the force of law in the Member States following their ratification and which prevail over the internal law of the Member States . . ."

XV. PRELIMINARY OPINION (AS TO COMPATIBILITY OF AGREEMENTS AND CONVENTIONS WITH THE TREATY OR PROPOSALS FOR TREATY AMENDMENTS, ETC.)

The preliminary opinions treated in this section must be distinguished from the preliminary rulings dealt with in section VI (*ante*, p. 130). The latter are directly related to, and in a sense integrated with, since they are binding on, the judicial function exercised by the authorities administering justice in the Member States. Those that are the subject of this section are directed not to the judicial system of Member States but to Community Institutions, Member States or other persons, as circumstances may require. They are concerned with appreciation of the respective Treaty—and in that sense with the interpretation of it—from the point of view of the compatibility with it of agreements for action in the politico-economic field (in the case of E.E.C. and E.A.E.C.) or with proposals for the modification of the Treaty itself as therein envisaged (in the case of E.C.S.C.). The distinction in kind between such preliminary opinions and the preliminary ruling dealt with in section VI is veiled by the use in English of the same adjective ("preliminary") for both. In the original authentic languages differing adverbs or adverbial expressions are used which retain the distinction ("*à titre préjudiciel*"; "*im Wege der Vorabentscheidung*"; "*bij wijze van prejudiciele beslissing*"; "*in via pregiudiziale*", in relation with the "ruling" the subject of section VI, *ante*, p. 130; and "*au préalable*"; "*zuvor*"; "*tevoren*"; "*preventivamente*", in relation with the "opinion" the subject of this present section).

The circumstances in which opinions of the Court may or must be requested before certain steps are taken, and the manner and extent to which parties are bound by them, vary as between the three Treaties. Opinions of the Court fall outside the provisions of E.E.C. 189 and E.A.E.C. 161 under which "opinions shall have no binding force". Though these Articles form part of the Chapter in the Treaties entitled "Provisions common to several institutions" they are concerned with the administrative acts of the Council and Commission, and not the judicial acts of the Court (see "acts other than recommendations or opinions . . .", *ante*, p. 84). Such opinions are provided for in E.E.C. 228, E.A.E.C. 103, 104 and 105, and E.C.S.C. 95, treated seriatim below.

E.E.C. 228

[*Printed at* ante, *pp.* 33 and 34.]

"The Council, the Commission or a Member State may, as a preliminary, obtain the opinion of the Court." The obtaining of an opinion is permissive, not mandatory upon the Council, the Commission, or a Member State. On the force of the words "as a preliminary" see the introductory comment to this section, *supra*.

". . . Compatible with the provisions of this Treaty. . ." ("*la compatibilité . . . avec les dispositions du présent Traité*"). The Court's appreciation is general, not being, as elsewhere in the Treaty, directed to determining "the object (*l'objet*) of the present Treaty" (as it is in E.E.C. 182 which see under "Reference by virtue of a 'special agreement' between States," *ante*, p. 157). It is doubtful, however, in view of the nature of treaty interpretation as exemplified by the International Court of Justice, which the original Member States anticipate to be the method of the European Court, any great weight should be attributed to the omission of any such direction, or any argument constructed on the basis that such omission was deliberate. (As to Treaty interpretation see "Restrictive Interpretation of a Community treaty" *ante*, p. 75).

"An agreement . . . the subject of an adverse opinion. . . shall only come into force under the conditions laid down in Article 236". Article 236 is concerned with amendments to the Treaty, proposed by the Government of any Member State or the Commission. It requires the ratification, by all Member States in accordance with their respective constitutional requirements and following a conference of their Governments convened by the President of the Council, of the Treaty amendments determined upon by common agreement thereat. Though the effect of the reference to E.E.C. 236 in E.E.C. 228 might have been more clearly defined, it would seem that the Council may not finally conclude an agreement which is the subject of an adverse preliminary opinion of the Court. Treaty amendments will be necessary and to secure the implementation of the contemplated agreement the Council may seek agreement on the Treaty amendments at a conference of Governments of Member States and their ratification in accordance with their respective constitutional requirements. Ratification would seem to have to be of the agreement as contemplated. Its actual conclusion would follow on such ratification.

E.A.E.C. 103

Member States shall communicate to the Commission their draft agreements or conventions with a third country, international organisation or national of a third country, in so far as such agreement or convention concerns matters covered by this Treaty.

If a draft agreement or convention contains clauses which impede the giving of effect to this Treaty, the Commission shall, within a period of one month from the date of receipt of the communication addressed to it, make known its observations to the State concerned.

Such state may not conclude the intended agreement or convention until it has removed the Commission's objections or complied with any ruling which the Court of Justice, adjudicating urgently upon a formal request (*requête*) from such State, shall give concerning the compatibility of the proposed clauses with the provisions of this Treaty. Such request may be submitted to the Court of Justice at any time after the State has received the Commission's observation.

E.A.E.C. 104

No person or undertaking concluding or renewing, after the date of the entry into force of this Treaty, agreements or conventions with a third country, international organisation or national of a third country, may invoke such agreements or conventions in order to evade the obligations imposed by this Treaty.

Each Member State shall take all measures it considers necessary to communicate to the Commission at the latter's request, all information relating to agreements or conventions concluded, after the date of entry into force of this Treaty and within its ambit, by any person or undertaking with a third country, international organisation or national of a third country. The Commission may require this communication only for the purpose of verifying that such agreements or conventions do not contain clauses which impede implementation of this Treaty.

At the request of the Commission, the Court of Justice shall give a ruling as to the compatibility of such agreements or conventions with the provisions of this Treaty.

E.A.E.C. 105

The provisions of this Treaty may not be invoked as an obstacle to the implementation of agreements or conventions concluded before the date of the entry into force of this Treaty by a Member State, person or undertaking with a third country, international organisation or national of a third country, where such agreements or conventions have been communicated to the Commission not later than thirty days after the date of the entry into force of this Treaty.

Agreements or conventions concluded in the period between the date of signature and the date of the entry into force of this Treaty by a person or undertaking with a third country, international organisation or national of a third country may not, however, be invoked as an obstacle to this Treaty if, in the opinion of the Court of Justice ruling at the request of the Commission, the intention of evading the provisions of this Treaty was one of the decisive motives of either of the parties in concluding such agreement or convention.

In general the above three Articles of E.A.E.C. have closely inter-related purposes and are concerned with the compatibility with the Treaty of agreements or conventions with persons not directly subject to Community jurisdiction, that is to say, a third country, international organization, or national of a third country, and actually entered into or contemplated, by Member States, persons or undertakings. Exchanges with other countries figure prominently in the general definition of the task of the Community in E.A.E.C.1.: "It shall be the task of the Community to contribute to the raising of the standard of living in Member States and to the development of exchanges with other countries by creating the conditions necessary for the speedy establishment and growth of nuclear industries". In order to fulfil its task the Community is specifically charged by E.A.E.C. 2 (h) to "establish with other countries and international organisations any relationships likely to promote progress in the peaceful uses of nuclear energy".

Seen against these basic provisions the general purpose of E.A.E.C. 103, 104 and 105 is clarified. The purpose is to ensure that agreements and conventions with persons not directly subject to Community jurisdiction contribute primarily to the development of the Community *qua* Community, and, subject to that, to the advancement of the interests of Member States or undertakings or other persons. This matter is approached from three directions.

E.A.E.C. 103. In this article it is the draft agreements of Member States that are dealt with (those of persons or undertakings are the subject of E.A.E.C. 104). These must be communicated to the Commission, and, within one month of receipt of the communication, the Commission must, if the agreement or convention "contains clauses which impede the giving of effect" to the Treaty, make known its observations to the State concerned. Two courses are then open to that State. It may remove the Commission's objections and then conclude the intended agreement or convention. Alternatively it may submit a Request (as to Request see Chapter 4, *post*, pp. 218, 221) to the Court to adjudicate concerning the compatibility of the proposed clauses with the provisions of the Treaty, and having complied with any ruling the Court may give, may then conclude the intended agreement or convention (as to compatibility with the Treaty see under E.E.C. 228 ". . . compatible with the provisions of this Treaty. . .", this section, *ante*, p. 163).

Procedure in respect of such a petition is a "Special Procedure" provided for in the Rules of Procedure, of which the outstanding features are provisions as to time for matters of urgency, and for the Court's decision to be taken in the Judges' Council Chamber. (See Chapter 5, *post*, pp. 296 *et seq.*).

E.A.E.C. 104. In this article it is the agreements or conventions to be concluded or renewed by persons or undertakings after the date of entry into force of the Treaty which are dealt with. At the request of the Commission, which may be made "only for the purpose of verifying that such agreements or conventions do not contain clauses which impede implementation of the Treaty", Member States must communicate all information relating to the agreements or conventions to the Commission. The Commission may then make application to the Court (by Request, see Chapter 5, *post*, pp. 296–297) to give a ruling as to their compatibility with the provisions of the Treaty. (As to compatibility with the Treaty see under E.E.C. 228 ". . . compatible with the provisions of this Treaty. . ." this section *ante*, p. 163).

Procedure. This Article (and E.A.E.C. 105) provide the only examples in the Treaty where the Commission may apply to the Court in respect of the operations of persons other than States. Service of the application is, however (by virtue of the "Special Procedure" contained in the Rules of Procedure) upon the State to the jurisdiction of which the person or undertaking is subject. Procedure thereafter follows the normal course. (See Chapter 5, *post*, pp. 296 *et seq.*).

E.A.E.C. 105. In this article agreements and conventions concluded before the date of entry into force of the Treaty are dealt with, in respect of the situation where the Community does not wish them not to be carried out, even though they might be incompatible with the Treaty. The intention is that the Treaty shall not successfully "be invoked as an obstacle" to their implementation. Such agreements or conventions may be those of Member

States, persons or undertakings. Where such agreements or conventions have been communicated to the Commission and within 30 days after the entry into force of the Treaty (impliedly, in the Article) the latter has taken no action, no question of an application to the Court arises. Where such an agreement or convention is concluded by a person or undertaking in the period between the date of signature and the date of entry into force of the Treaty, the Court may be requested by the Commission to give an opinion as to whether the intention of evading the provisions of the Treaty was one of the decisive motives of either of the parties in concluding it.

Procedure. This is the same as under E.A.E.C. 104, *supra*.

E.C.S.C. 95

In all cases not provided for in this Treaty in which a decision or recommendation of the High Authority appears necessary to achieve, in the operation of the common market for coal and steel and in accordance with the provisions of Article 5, one of the Community's objectives as defined in Articles 2, 3 and 4, such decision may be taken or such recommendation may be made, upon receiving a concurring opinion from the Council acting unanimously, and after the Consultative Committee has been consulted.

Any such decision or recommendation, taken or made in such manner, shall lay down what, if any penalties should be applied.

If, after the transitional period provided for in the Convention containing Transitional Provisions has ended, unforeseen difficulties, becoming apparent in the light of experience, in the methods of application of this Treaty, or a profound change in economic or technical conditions directly affecting the common market for coal and steel, make it necessary to adapt the rules for the exercise by the High Authority of the powers conferred upon it, appropriate amendments may be made provided that they do not affect the provisions of Articles 2, 3 and 4, or the relationship between the powers of the High Authority and those of the other institutions of the Community respectively.

These amendments shall be jointly proposed by the High Authority and the Council, acting by vote of a five-sixths majority of its members, and shall be submitted to the Court for its opinion. When considering the matter, the Court shall be fully competent to review all matters of fact and of law. If, as a result of such consideration, the Court should find that the proposals are in accord with the provisions of the preceding paragraph they shall be forwarded to the Assembly and shall come into force if they are approved by a majority of three-quarters of the votes cast and two-thirds of the total membership of the Assembly.

In "*Demande d'avis introduite par la Haute Autorité et le Conseil spécial de Ministres de la C.E.C.A.*" (R. Vol. V, at p. 562) the Court delivered the following opinion:

"The project of amendment of article 56 of the E.C.S.C. Treaty, as submitted to the Court by the High Authority and the Special Council of Ministers by letter of the 4th December 1959, is not in accordance with the provisions of article 95 paragraphs 3 and 4 of the Treaty, in that:

    (a) its field of application is limited to the coal industry;

    (b) the duration of its validity is limited to 10th February 1963;

    (c) The conditions of application of the proposed text have too broad an ambit."

In "*Demande d'avis en vertu des dispositions de l'article 95 paragraphes 3 et 4 du traité C.E.C.A. presentée par la Haute Autorité et le Conseil spécial de ministres de la C.E.C.A.*" (R. Vol. VIII at pp. 520–521), the Court delivered the following opinion:

"The project of amendment of article 65 of the E.C.S.C. Treaty, as submitted to the Court by the High Authority and the Special Council of Ministers by letter of 20th July 1961, is not in accordance with the provisions of article 95, paragraphs 3 and 4 of the Treaty, in that:

    (a) the proposal to make the agreements relating to the new conditions of expiry liable to authorization in the sense of article 65 paragraph 2, goes beyond an adaptation of the rules relating to the exercise by the High Authority of the powers conferred on it by this provision;

    (b) the proposal providing for a total or partial derogation from the conditions of article 65 (2) paragraph one, (C), goes beyond an adaptation of the rules relating to the exercise by the High Authority of the powers conferred on it by article 65 (2) and moreover offends article 4 (d) of the Treaty"

Procedure.   As to procedure see Chapter 5, Opinions (*post*, pp. 297–298).

XVI. APPLICATION TO RETIRE OR SUSPEND A MEMBER OF THE COMMISSION OR HIGH AUTHORITY (AND TO ANNUL VETO OF APPOINTMENT TO HIGH AUTHORITY)

E.E.C. and E.A.E.C., in identical terms, prohibit members of the respective Commission from engaging in any other paid or unpaid occupation during their term of office. The members of the Commission are also required to give a solemn undertaking to respect the conditions of their office, during and after their term of service, and in particular to exercise honesty and discretion as regards the acceptance, after their term of office, of particular appointments or benefits. Failure to comply with these conditions may lead to the compulsory retirement of the member by the Court or to an order by the Court for forfeiture of pension or other benefits. In E.C.S.C. certain uses of a government's power of veto in respect of the appointment of members of the High Authority may be declared null and void by the Court on the application of another government.

All three Treaties include a virtually identical provision that where a member of the executive authority in the Community (that is, the Commission of E.E.C. or E.A.E.C. and the High Authority of E.C.S.C.) no longer fulfils the conditions required for the performance of his duties or has been guilty of gross misconduct the Court may compulsorily retire him, on the application of the executive authority or of the Council of the Community in question. E.E.C. and E.A.E.C. make provision, in addition, for provisional suspension of a member of the Commission. Provisional suspension of a member of the High Authority is not provided for in E.C.S.C.

These matters are treated *infra* under the four heads: A. Conditions of office, E.E.C., E.A.E.C.; B. Annulment of government veto in respect of High Authority appointments; C. Compulsory retirement from office; D. Provisional suspension from office, E.E.C. and E.A.E.C. (The "Treaty for the Merger of the European Executives", signed in Brussels on the 8th April, 1965, which has some bearing on these matters, was published too late for detailed treatment in the present work.)

A. CONDITIONS OF OFFICE (E.E.C. AND E.A.E.C.)

E.E.C. 157

1. The Commission shall consist of nine members, who shall be chosen on the grounds of their general competence and whose independence can be fully guaranteed.

The Council may by a unanimous decision amend the number of the members of the Commission.

Only nationals of Member States may be members of the Commission.

The Commission shall not include more than two members having the nationality of the same State.

2. The members of the Commission shall act completely independently in the performance of their duties, in the general interest of the Community.

In the performance of their duties, they shall neither seek nor take instructions from any Government or other body. They shall refrain from any action incompatible with the nature of their duties. Each Member State undertakes to respect this principle and not to seek to influence the members of the Commission in the performance of their duties.

The members of the Commission may not, during their term of office, engage in any other paid or unpaid occupation. When entering upon their duties they shall give a solemn undertaking that, both during and after their term of office, they will respect the obligations arising therefrom and in particular their duty to exercise honesty and discretion as regards the acceptance, after their term of office, of particular appointments or benefits. In the event of any breach of these obligations, the Court of Justice, on the application of the Council or of the Commission, may, according to the circumstances, order that the member concerned either be compulsorily retired in accordance with the provisions of Article 160 or forfeit his right to a pension or other benefits in lieu thereof.

E.A.E.C. 126

[*Identical with E.E.C. 157*].

B. Annulment of Government Veto in Respect of High Authority

E.C.S.C. 10, paragraphs 10 and 11

In all cases provided for in this Article in which an appointment is made by a decision of the Governments by five-sixths majority or by means of co-option, each Government shall have a right of veto subject to the following conditions:

If a Government has used its right of veto with respect to two persons in the case of an individual replacement, and to four persons in the case of a general or biennial replacement of members, any further exercise of that right on the occasion of the same replacement may be referred to the Court by another Government; the Court may declare the veto null and void if it considers that the right of veto has been abused.

C. Compulsory Retirement from Office (E.E.C., E.A.E.C. and E.C.S.C.)

E.E.C. 160, first paragraph

If any member of the Commission no longer fulfils the conditions required for the performance of his duties or if he has been guilty of serious misconduct, the Court of Justice, on the application of the Council or of the Commission, may compulsorily retire him from office.

E.A.E.C. 129, first paragraph

[*Identical with E.E.C. 160 first paragraph*]

E.C.S.C. 12, second paragraph

Members who no longer fulfil the conditions required for the performance of their duties or who are guilty of serious misconduct may be compulsorily retired by the Court, on application by the High Authority or the Council.

(Paragraphs one and three of this Article are not here material. They deal with retirement in rotation, termination of appointment by death or resignation, and the filling of vacancies).

D. Provisional Suspension from Office, E.E.C. and E.A.E.C.

E.E.C. 160, paragraphs 2 and 3

In such a case the Council may, by a unanimous decision, provisionally suspend the member from his duties and make provision for his replacement pending the ruling of the Court of Justice.

The Court of Justice may on the application of the Council or of the Commission provisionally suspend the member from his duties.

E.A.E.C. 129, paragraphs 2 and 3
[*Identical with E.E.C. 160 paragraphs 2 and 3, supra.*]

XVII. FORMAL LEGALITY OF DECISION OF E.A.E.C. ARBITRATION COMMITTEE (AND ITS INTERPRETATION OF THE TREATY)

Introductory. ("Formal legality" renders *"régularité formelle"*; *"förmliche Rechtsmässigkeit"*; *formele regelmatigheid"*; *regolarità formale"*). E.A.E.C. establishes an Arbitration Committee (as to which generally see Chapter I, European Atomic Energy Community under E.A.E.C. 2) to which application may be made for the grant of non-exclusive licences. Reference to it by special agreement (*"compromis d'arbitrage"*—see under "By virtue of a *clause compromissoire*", *ante*, p. 154) may occur "when, in the absence of agreement" with the patent owner "the Commission intends" nevertheless "to obtain the granting of licences" (E.A.E.C. 19, *post*, p. 173) "to the Community or to Joint Undertakings accorded the right under Article 48 . . ." or "to persons or undertakings which have applied to the Commission for them" (E.A.E.C. 17, *infra*). The commission must notify the owner of the patent, provisionally protected patent right, petty patent or patent application (E.A.E.C. 19, *post*, p. 173) who may, within one month from receiving the notice, propose a special agreement to refer the question to the Arbitration Committee. Its decision may be the subject of an appeal by the parties to the Community Court under E.A.E.C. 18 (*post*, p. 172).

E.A.E.C. 17

1. In the absence of an amicable agreement non exclusive licences may be granted either by arbitration or official action on the conditions laid down in Articles 8–23 inclusive:

(*a*) to the Community or to Joint Undertakings accorded this right under Article 48 in respect of patents, provisionally protected patent rights (*titre de protection prousoire*) or petty patents (*modèles d'utilité*) relating to inventions directly concerned with nuclear research, to the extent that the granting of these licences is necessary for the continuation of their own research or indispensable to the functioning of their facilities.

If the Commission so requests, these licences shall include the right to authorise third parties to make use of the invention, insofar as they are carrying out work or commissions on behalf of the Community or Joint Undertakings,

(*b*) to persons or undertakings which have applied to the Commission for them in respect of patents, provisionally protected patent rights, or petty patents relating to inventions directly concerned with and essential to the development of nuclear energy in the Community, provided that all the following conditions are fulfilled:—

(i) at least four years shall have passed from the filing of the patent application, except in the case of an invention relating to a specifically nuclear subject;

(ii) the requirements implied by the development of nuclear energy, as envisaged by the Commission, in the territory of a Member State where an invention is protected, are not being met with regard to that invention;

(iii) the owner has been called upon to meet these requirements either himself or through his licencees and has not complied with this request;

(iv) the persons or undertakings applying for the licences are in a position to meet these requirements effectively by making use of the invention.

Member States may not, in order to meet these requirements, take any coercive measures permitted by their national legislation which will limit the protection accorded to the invention unless the Commission first requests them to do so.

2. A non-exclusive licence may not be granted on the conditions laid down in the preceding paragraph if the owner can establish the existence of legitimate reasons, in particular, that he has not had an adequate period of time at his disposal.

3. The granting of a licence under paragraph 1 confers a right to full compensation, the amount of which shall be agreed between the owner of the patent, provisionally protected patent right or petty patent and the licensee.

4. The provisions of the Paris Convention on the protection of industrial property are not affected by this article.

E.A.E.C. 18

An Arbitration Committee shall be established for the purposes defined in this Section. The Council shall appoint the members and determine the rules of procedure of such Committee on a proposal of the Court of Justice.

Within a period of one month from their notification the decisions of the Arbitration Committee may be the subject of an appeal by the parties to the Court of Justice involving suspension of their operation. The Court of Justice shall only examine the formal legality of the decision and the Arbitration Committee's interpretation of the provisions of this Treaty.

The final decisions of the Arbitration Committee shall have the force of *res judicata* between the parties. They shall be enforceable on the conditions laid down in Article 164.

"The Court of Justice shall only examine the formal legality of the decision and the Arbitration Committee's interpretation of the provisions of the Treaty". The question of the formal legality of the decision may most frequently turn upon whether it is made in compliance with the rules of procedure governing the Arbitration Committee. These constitute Regulation 7/63 of the Council of E.A.E.C., of 3rd December 1963 (Official Journal, year 6, 2849/63).

"... **Appeal suspending enforcement** ..." of the decision (*"recours suspensif"*). This, contrary to the usual principle of Continental European administrative law followed generally in the Treaties (as in E.A.E.C., see section III, *ante*, p. 47, also "Claim for suspension of enforcement of administrative acts, *ante*, p. 158), whereby an application to annul an administrative decision does not suspend its enforcement or operation.

Procedure. Appeals from the Arbitration Committee are the subject of a Special Form of Procedure (as to this see *post*, pp. 289 *et seq.*).

Effect of annulment of a decision of the Arbitration Committee. Where the Court annuls the Committee's decision it remits the matter back, if need be, to the Committee. This is the general principle followed in relation to the annulment of administrative acts in the legal system of the original Member States and adopted in the Treaties (as to this see "Consequences of annulment of an act of a Community Institution", E.E.C. 176 and E.A.E.C. 148, *ante*, p. 89 and "Consequences of annulment of an act of the High Authority", *ante*, p. 116).

E.A.E.C. 19

When, in the absence of an amicable agreement, the Commission intends to obtain the granting of licences in one of the cases provided for in Article 17, it shall notify the owner of the patent, provisionally protected patent right, petty patent or patent application, and shall at the same time specify the name of the applicant and the scope of the licence.

E.A.E.C. 20

The owner may, within a period of one month from receiving the notice referred to in Article 19, propose to the Commission and, where necessary, to the applicant that they should conclude a special agreement to refer the question to the Arbitration Committee (*compris d'arbitrage à l'effet de saisir le Comité d'Arbitrage*).

If the Commission or the applicant refuses to enter into an arbitration agreement, the Commission cannot require the Member State or its competent authorities to grant the licence or to cause it to be granted.

If the Arbitration Committee, on the question being referred to it under the special agreement, finds that the Commission's request is in conformity with the provisions of Article 17, it shall give a reasoned decision, containing a grant of the licence to the applicant and laying down the conditions of the licence and the appropiate remuneration, to the extent that the parties have not reached agreement on these points.

XVIII. FULFILMENT OF CONDITIONS FOR THE GRANTING, IN E.A.E.C., OF NON-EXCLUSIVE LICENCES BY ARBITRATION OR OFFICIAL ACTION

Where a patent owner has received notice from the Commission that it intends to obtain the granting of a non-exclusive licence and he does not propose that the matter be referred to the Arbitration Committee (as to which see "Formal legality of decision of E.A.E.C. Arbitration Comittee" *ante*, p. 171) "the Commission may require the Member State or its competent authorities to grant the licence or to cause it to be granted" (E.A.E.C. 21, *infra*.) If met with refusal, or, within four months, given no explanation with regard to the granting of the licence, the Commission may refer the question to the Court. If the judgment of the Court establishes that the conditions laid down in E.A.E.C. 17 (for text see *ante*, p. 171) have been fulfilled "the Member State concerned or its competent authorities shall be bound to take the necessary measures to comply with that judgment" (E.A.E.C. 21, *infra*).

E.A.E.C. 21

If the owner does not propose that the matter be referred to the Arbitration Committee, the Commission may require the Member State concerned or its competent authorities to grant the licence or to cause it to be granted.

If, having heard the owner's case, the Member State or its competent authorities consider that the conditions laid down in Article 17 have not been fulfilled, they shall notify the Commission of their refusal to arrange the granting of the licence.

If they refuse to grant the licence or to cause it to be granted or if, within a period of four months from the date of the request, they do not give any explanation with regard to the granting of the licence, the Commission shall have two months in which to refer the question to the Court of Justice.

The owner must be heard in the proceedings before the Court of Justice.

If the judgment of the Court of Justice establishes that the conditions laid down in Article 17 have been fulfilled, the Member State concerned or its competent authorities shall be bound to take the necessary measures to comply with that judgment.

"...**The Member State concerned**". That is, the Member State having jurisdiction over the patent owner (or the owner of a provisionally protected patent right, petty patent, or patent application) from whom the Commission intents to obtain the granting of a non-exclusive licence.

"...**The conditions laid down in Article 17 ...**". For text see E.A.E.C. 17, *ante*, p. 171).

Procedure. "The owner must be heard in the proceedings before the Court of Justice."

XIX. TO AUTHORIZE AN ADMINISTRATIVE OR LEGAL MEASURE OF CONSTRAINT RELATING TO COMMUNITY PROPERTY ETC.

Each of the three Protocols on the Privileges and Immunities of the three Communities, annexed to the respective Treaties, provides in the following terms:

E.E.C. Protocol on the Privileges and Immunities of the E.E.C., Chapter I Article 1

[*Printed on* ante, *p.* 29.]

E.A.E.C. Protocol on the Privileges and Immunities of the Community, Chapter I Article 1

[*Identical with E.E.C. Protocol,* ante *p.* 29.]

E.C.S.C. Protocol on the Privileges and Immunities of the Community, Chapter I Article 1

[*Identical with E.E.C. Protocol,* ante, *p.* 29.]

"The premises and buildings of the Community shall be invio-lable." The effect of this provision is to assimilate the premises and buildings of the Community in Member States to those of foreign (diplo-matic) Legations and Embassies in their relationship, under international law, to the governmental authority of the State in which they are. The exemption from "search, requisition, confiscation or expropriation" is the result.

"The property and assets of the Community . . ." This includes the premises and buildings. The provision that the property and assets "shall not be the subject of any administrative or legal measure of constraint without the authorization of the Court of Justice" needs to be understood against the background of the general relationship, provided for in the Treaties, of the Communities to the national laws of Member States. In particular it needs to be understood in the light of the principles that: "The Community shall have legal personality."; it "shall in each of the Member States enjoy the most extensive legal capacity accorded to legal persons under their domestic law; it may, in particular, acquire or dispose of movable and immovable property and may sue and be sued in its own name. For this purpose the Community shall be represented by the Com-mission"; and "Subject to the powers conferred on the Court of Justice by this Treaty, cases to which the Community is a party shall not for that reason alone be excluded from the jurisdiction of national courts" (E.E.C. 210, 211 and 183, with which E.A.E.C. 184, 185 and 155 are identical. The same principles are established by E.C.S.C. 6. For comment on them and on the relationship of the Communities to the national laws of Member States generally, see "The Court and the internal law of Member States of the Communities" *ante*, p. 58 and comment on E.E.C. 211 etc. *ante*, pp. 28, 29). The requirement in the Protocol(s) for "authorisation of the Court of Justice" thus establishes a measure of concurrent jurisdiction between the European Court and the national tribunals of Member States. It also establishes a mechanism bringing the European Court into a relationship with the administrative authorities of Member States.

In *Demande d'Autorisation de pratiquer saisie-arrêt entre les mains de la Haute*

Autorité de la C.E.C.A. (Case 4/62 R. Vol. VIII p. 83) the Order of the Court was summarized in the Headnote as follows:

"1. When an authority other than one of its Institutions imposes on the Community the execution of a decision modifying its legal situation, it is the duty of the Court, in its capacity of guardian of the major interests of the Community, to examine whether the application of legal provisions of a Member State which are the foundation of the decision in question constitutes the constraint provided for by Article 1 of the Protocol on Privileges and Immunities.

2. An order of attachment made by a Luxembourg court and having repercussions on assets of the Community must be considered a constraint in the meaning of Article 1 of the Protocol on Privileges and Immunities, the procedure of attachment constituting a single means of execution, while comprising in Luxembourg law two phases each of which, however, alter the legal position of the third party whose assets are attached. An authorisation is therefore necessary in this case."

XX. UNDER E.A.E.C. 81, PRESIDENT OF THE COURT TO DECIDE AS TO WARRANT FOR ENFORCEMENT OF SUPERVISORY MEASURE OR TO GIVE SUBSEQUENT APPROVAL OF COMMISSION'S WRITTEN ORDER TO PROCEED WITH A SUPERVISORY MEASURE

E.A.E.C. 81

The Commission may send inspectors into the territories of Member States. Before entrusting an inspector with his first mission in the territories of a Member State, the Commission shall consult the State concerned: such consultation shall cover all future missions of this inspector.

Upon presentation of a document establishing their credentials, inspectors shall at all times have access to all places, data and to all persons who, by reason of their occupation, deal with material, equipment or facilities subject to the supervision provided for in this Chapter, to the extent necessary to exercise supervision over ores, source material and special fissile material, and to ensure that the provisions of Article 77 are observed. Should the State concerned so request, inspectors appointed by the Commission shall be accompanied by representatives of the authorities of such State, provided that the inspectors shall not thereby be delayed or otherwise impeded in the exercise of their functions.

Should there be opposition to the carrying out of a supervisory measure the Commission shall be bound to ask the President of the Court of Justice for a warrant to enforce the carrying out of such supervisory measure. The President of the Court of Justice shall give a decision within three days.

If there is danger in delay, the Commission may itself issue a written order, in the form of a decision, to proceed with the supervisory measure. This order shall be submitted without delay to the President of the Court of Justice for subsequent approval. After the issue of the warrant or decision, the authorities of the State concerned shall ensure that the inspectors have access to the places specified in the warrant or decision.

("Warrant" renders *"mandat"*; *"Gerichtsbefehl"*; *"bevelschrift"*; *"mandato"*).

Procedure. In respect of E.A.E.C. 81 this is a "special form of procedure". See Chapter 5, "Suspension of Enforcement," *post*, pp. 270 *et seq.*

XXI. APPLICATION FOR JUDGMENT BY DEFAULT

The existence of jurisdiction to give judgment by default may perhaps be inferred from the Treaties, but is not there expressly provided for. Jurisdiction to give judgment by default is expressly conferred by the Statutes.

E.E.C. St. 38

Where the defendant, after having been duly notified, fails to file a written defence, judgment shall be given on his case by default. A retrial (*opposition*) may be claimed within one month of the judgment being notified. Unless the Court decides otherwise the enforcement of the judgment by default shall not be suspended by a demand for retrial.

E.A.E.C. St. 39

[*Identical with E.E.C. St.* 38].

E.C.S.C. St. 35

Where recourse is had to the plenary jurisdiction of the Court and the defending party, after having been duly notified, fails to file written submissions, judgment shall be given on his case by default. A retrial may be claimed within one month of the judgment being notified. Unless the Court decides otherwise, enforcement of the judgment by default shall not be suspended by a claim for retrial.

The wording appears to exclude the possibility of judgment by default where the application does not invoke the full jurisdiction (as to which see under "Review of penalty or fine", *ante*, p. 78).

The Rules of Procedure duplicate and implement the above articles of the Statutes (see "Judgment by Default and Retrial, R.P. 94", *post*, pp. 280–281).

Judgment by default is essentially a procedural matter. For comment on the procedural provisions see *loc. cit.*, *supra*).

XXII. APPLICATION TO STAY THE EXECUTION OF ITS JUDGMENT (OR ORDER)

Provision for the stay of execution of its own judgment by the Court is made in the Treaties themselves.

E.E.C. 192, paragraph 4

[*Printed on p.* 27 ante.]

E.A.E.C. 164 paragraph 3

[*Identical with E.E.C.* 192, *printed on p.* 27 *ante.*]

E.C.S.C. 92 paragraph 3

Enforcement may be suspended only by a decision of the Court

The above paragraphs follow provisions (substantially identical in the three Treaties) in the earlier paragraphs of the same articles for the enforcement of the Court's decisions in accordance with the rules of civil procedure in force in the State in the territory of which it takes place. (As to "Execution, enforcement", see Chapter 4, *post*, p. 255). The provision of the necessary legal mechanism for the provisional or final arresting of enforcement procedure and for the relation of that mechanism to Community law, and in particular to a given judgment of the European Court, must be the responsibility of Member States individually.

Procedure.   An application to stay execution involves urgency and is by way of summary procedure ("*référé*") for which particular provision is made as one of the "Special Forms of Procedure" forming the subject-matter of Title III of the Rules of Procedure (see Chapter 5, *post*, pp. 270 *et seq.*).

XXIII. JURISDICTION CONFERRED BY SPECIAL PROVISIONS

 (i) To determine a dispute regarding the application or interpretation of the Agreement establishing an association between E.E.C. and Greece, submitted to the Court by virtue of Article 67 (2) of the Agreement;

 (ii) to determine disputes between the Community and a legal person (not an individual) in receipt of a subsidy from the Development Fund for Overseas Countries and Territories, submitted to the Court by virtue of Article 25 of E.E.C. Council Regulation No. 5;

 (iii) the President of the Court to appoint an arbitrator, by virtue of paragraph two of Article 3 of the Protocol concerning certain provisions affecting France (annexed to the E.E.C. Treaty), when the E.E.C. Commission and the French government cannot agree on the appointment of an arbitrator to decide a question, in regard to which they disagree, concerning the level of monetary reserves of the franc zone;

 (iv) concerning the interpretation or implementation of E.E.C. Council Regulation No. 3 which relates to the social security of migrant workers, when two or more Member States dispute that interpretation or implementation, and the dispute has not been settled by the required direct negotiations between them or by the required reference to the administrative committee;

 (v) to interpret the Statutes of the E.E.C. administrative committee for the social security of migrant workers, by virtue of Article 15 of those Statutes (which require interpretation by the Court in accordance with E.E.C. 177, as to which see, "Preliminary Ruling (*à titre préjudiciel*", *ante*, p. 130);

 (vi) to remove from office or temporarily suspend a Financial Inspector ("*commissaire aux comptes*") of the E.E.C. Control Commission, by virtue of Article 7 of its Statute, on the Request of the Council or

Commission of Control. (Article 7 of the corresponding E.A.E.C. Statute confers jurisdiction in identical terms);

(vii) to rule on a claim brought, under Article 25 of the E.E.C. Council Regulation (pursuant to E.E.C. 209 (a) and (c)) respecting the establishing and implementing of the E.E.C. budget and the responsibility of the statisticians and accountants, by an agent of any community Institution whose duties are to control expenditure, against a reasoned decision of such Institution as to his appointment, promotion, discipline, etc. (Articles 24 and 25 of the corresponding E.A.E.C. Statute confer jurisdiction in identical terms);

(viii) to decide, by the exercise of full jurisdiction, disputes, arising from Article 22 E.E.C. Council Regulation No. 31 determining the status of Community servants and the regime applicable to other agents of the Community. (Article 22 of the Regulation requires the Community servant "to make good, wholly or in part, the damage suffered by the Communities due to serious torts which he committed in the carrying out, or while carrying out, his duties"). See Community liability in tort (*ante*, p. 140) (Article 22 of the corresponding E.A.E.C. and E.C.S.C. Regulations confer jurisdiction in identical terms);

(ix) to exercise supervisory jurisdiction over decisions of the Commission taken pursuant to E.E.C. Council Regulation No. 26 made in application of certain rules of competition governing agricultural products and their marketing (by virtue of Article 2 of the Regulations);

(x) to determine a dispute between Member States concerning the interpretation or implementation of the decision of E.C.S.C. Special Council of Ministers concerning the implementation of E.C.S.C. 69 (dealing with wages and movement of manual workers).

Organisation of the Court
(R.P. 2–36)

I. INTRODUCTORY

The organisation of the Court requires in the first place to be understood in respect of the Court's position relative to the three Communities. That position is as follows. The treaties establishing respectively the three European Communities provide each Community with a Court of Justice as one of its four "Institutions", in E.E.C. 4, E.A.E.C. 3 and E.C.S.C. 7 (for the texts of which see Chapter 1, *ante*, pp. 17, 38 and 51, respectively). A Protocol annexed to each treaty lays down the Statute (that is, the Articles) governing the Court that is to function as an Institution of the Community it establishes. (As required by E.E.C. 188 (and E.A.E.C. 160) identical therewith): "The Statute of the Court of Justice shall be determined in a separate Protocol", and by E.C.S.C. 45: "The Statute of the Court shall be determined in a Protocol annexed to the present Treaty". E.E.C. St. 1 provides: "The Court established by Article 4 of this Treaty shall be constituted and shall perform its duties in accordance with the provisions of this Treaty and of this Statute"; and E.A.E.C. St. 1 and E.C.S.C. St. 1. are, as to their substance, in identical terms). There would, as a result, be three distinct Courts, were it not for the fact that the "Convention relating to certain Institutions common to the European Communities" of 27th March 1957 (annexed to the E.E.C. and E.A.E.C. Treaties, and effecting amendments to the E.C.S.C. Treaty) provides that a single Court shall do the work of all three. As is therefore to be expected, the parts of the three Statutes concerned with organisational matters (Title I, Statutes of Judges and Advocate General; Title II, Organisation), though showing some variations in the order of the provisions and unimportant differences of wording, produce the same result.

The fact that there is a single Court is, however, strictly relevant only to organisational matters, for the single Court serves all three Communities individually and separately. As regards the jurisdiction it exercises there are differences (as well as much in common) between the three Communities respectively (see Chapter 2, *ante* pp. 60–61) and these differences (greatest between E.C.S.C. and the two other Communities) are reflected in those parts of the three Statutes concerned with Procedure (as to which see Chapters 4 and 5, *post*, pp. 209 and 270).

Though the three Statutes (together with the relevant Treaty articles) referred to in the two preceding paragraphs lay down some of the general principles of the Court's organisation, the details of that organisation are completed by the Rules of Procedure (in particular Title I, "Organisation") adopted by the Court itself on 3rd. March 1959 following the unanimous approval by the Council (which approval was required by E.E.C. 188 (and E.A.E.C. 160 identical therewith): "The Court of Justice shall lay down its rules of procedure. These shall require the unanimous approval of the Council". (Approval by the Council had not been required in the earlier E.C.S.C.). By Article 110 of these Rules of Procedure, the Rules of Procedure of the original Court of Justice of the European Coal and Steel Community were abrogated, save for actions already pending (see Chapter 6, *post*, p. 299). Following the Rules of Procedure, the Court (by virtue of Rules 14, 15(5) and 72 of these Rules) laid down its Instructions to the Registrar on 23rd June, 1960. These also have a bearing on the organisational aspects of the Court.

Plan of this Chapter

In the present Chapter of this book the material is treated in the sequence followed by Title 1 ("Organisation of the Court") of the Rules of Procedure in nine sections corresponding to, and with the same headings as, the Chapters in that title. In each section the respective Rule(s) of the Rules of Procedure are set in relation to the antecedent Statute or Treaty, and to the Instructions to the Registrar.

II. PROCEDURE
A. JUDGES (R.P. 2–5)

("*Des juges*"; "*Die Richter*"; "*van de rechters*"; "*Dei guidici*")

The original authority for R.P. 2–5 the subject of this section is provided by the three Treaties, as follows:

E.E.C. 165

The Court of Justice shall consist of seven judges.

The Court of Justice shall sit in plenary session (*séance plénière*). It may, however, set up sections (*chambres*), each consisting of three or five judges, either to take certain steps of investigation (*instruction*) or to judge particular categories of cases in accordance with the provisions of a regulation made for this purpose.

The Court of Justice shall, however, always sit in plenary session to hear cases submitted to it by a Member State or by one of the institutions of the Community or to deal with the preliminary questions submitted to it pursuant to Article 177.

Should the Court of Justice so request, the Council may, by a unanimous decision, increase the number of judges, and make the consequential amendments to the second and third paragraphs of this Article and Article 167, second paragraph.

E.A.E.C. 137

[*Identical with E.E.C. 165.*]

E.C.S.C. 32(1)

[*As amended by the Convention of March* 1957 *referred to*, ante, *p.* 180, *this article is identical with E.E.C.* 165]

"... **Plenary Session**". As to sittings of the Court (and "Sections") see comment so headed under R.P. 18 (*post*, p. 196) and comment on "If... there is an even number" under E.E.C. St. 15 (*post*, p. 202). By E.E.C. St. 13 and equivalents the judges, advocates general and Registrar are required to reside at the seat of the Court. See also E.E.C. St. 14 (*post*, p. 200).

"...**Sections**..." ("*Chambres*"; "*Kammern*"; "*Kamers*"; "*Sezioni*"). There are two of these, see R.P. 24 (*post*, p. 200). As to their Presidency see R.P. 6 (2) and (3) (*post*, p. 188). As to sittings, see references under "... plenary session ..." (*ante*, p. 181). See also E.E.C. St. 15 (*post*, p. 201) as to number of judges of a section.

"...**Certain measures of procedure of enquiry**..." "Procedure of enquiry" and "calling of evidence" constitute a phase of procedure following the written and preceding the oral procedure (see Chapter 4, *post*, p. 233).

"...**Pursuant to Article 177**..." E.E.C. 177 (and E.A.E.C. 150 identical therewith) enables or requires the Courts of Member States to refer for a preliminary decision by the European Court any question of interpretation of the Treaty, (or of the validity and interpretation of acts of the Institutions of the community or of the interpretation of the Statutes of any bodies set up by a formal measure of the Council where the said Statutes so provide) in issue in a case before such Courts. E.C.S.C. 41 provides, but with much more limited scope, for a preliminary ruling. (see "Preliminary Ruling", *ante*, p. 130).

E.E.C. 167

The judges and the advocates-general shall be chosen from persons whose independence can be fully guaranteed and who fulfil the conditions required for the exercise of the highest judicial functions (*fonctions juridictionnelles*) in their respective countries or who are legal experts of universally recognised and outstanding ability; they shall be appointed by mutual agreement between the Governments of Member States for a term of six years.

A partial replacement of the judges of the Court of Justice shall take place every three years. Three and four judges shall be replaced alternately. The three judges whose terms of office are to expire at the end of the first period of three years shall be chosen by lot.

A partial replacement of the advocates-general shall take place every three years. The advocate-general whose term of office is to expire at the end of the first period of three years shall be chosen by lot.

The retiring judges and advocates-general shall be eligible for reappointment.

The judges shall appoint from among their members the President of the Court of Justice for a term of three years. Such appointment shall be renewable.

E.A.E.C. 139

[*Identical with E.E.C. 167.*]

E.C.S.C. 32(b)

[*As amended by the Convention of 1957 referred to on* ante, *p.* 180, *is identical with E.E.C.* 167.]

...**Partial replacement every three years ...**" This is effected "by mutual agreement between the Governments of Member States"—E.E.C. 167, paragraph 1 and equivalents. As to the choice by lot of those whose term of office was to expire at the end of the first three years E.E.C. St. 46 (and the identical E.A.E.C. St. 47 and E.C.S.C. St. 45) provides for this to be done by the President of the Council immediately after taking office.

...**Appoint ... the President ...** See R.P. 6 (1) (3) and (4), *post*, p. 188; also R.P. 7 (1) and (2) *post*, p. 189.

The Status of Judges (and of the Advocates General) is governed by the Statutes (E.E.C. St. 2–7 and equivalents) as follows:

E.E.C. St. 2

Before entering upon his duties each judge shall in open court take an oath to perform his duties impartially and conscientiously and to preserve the secrecy of the Court's deliberations.

E.A.E.C. St. 2

[*Identical with E.E.C. St. 2.*]

E.C.S.C. St. 2

[*Identical with E.E.C. St. 2*]

The Advocates General are also subject to the provisions of the three articles above (see section c, *post*, pp. 190–191, under E.E.C. St. 8 and equivalent).

Immunity of judges. This is governed by the Statutes as follows:

E.E.C. St. 3

The judges shall be immune from suit and legal process. They shall continue to benefit from such immunity after their functions have ceased in respect of all acts done by them in the course of the performance of their official duties, including words spoken or written.

The Court sitting in plenary session, may suspend this immunity.

Only a Court competent to judge the members of the highest national judiciary in each Member State shall have jurisdiction in criminal proceedings against judges whose immunity has been suspended.

E.A.E.C. St. 3

[*Identical with E.E.C. St. 3.*]

E.C.S.C. St. 3

[*First three paragraphs, identical with E.E.C. St. 3, supra.*]

E.C.S.C. St. 3 has a fourth paragraph which provides:
"Judges, whatever their nationality, shall also enjoy in the territory of each of the Member States the privileges set out in paragraphs (*b*) (*c*) and (*d*) of Article 11 of the Protocol on the Privileges and Immunities of the Community".

The same result is arrived at in E.E.C. and E.A.E.C. by a provision in Article 20 of the Protocol on Privileges and Immunities (Chapter 1, *ante*, p. 32) placing the Judges, Advocates General and assistant rapporteurs of the Court of Justice on the same footing as the officials and other servants of the Community, upon whom, by Articles 11–14 and 17 of the same Protocols, privileges, immunities and facilities are conferred irrespective of nationality. These are, in kind, the same as those conferred by Article 11 of the E.C.S.C. Protocol on Privileges and Immunities (which is incorporated by reference in E.C.S.C. St. 3) but are set out in greater detail.

The oath taken by a judge is formulated in R.P. 3 (1), post, p. 18. The Advocates General are also subject to the provisions of the above three articles (see section C, *post*, pp. 190–191, under E.E.C. St. 8 and equivalent).

Judges may occupy no political or administrative post. They are otherwise restricted by the Statutes, as follows:

E.E.C. St. 4

The judges may not hold any political or administrative office.

They may not engage in any paid or unpaid occupation or profession, except by exceptional exemption granted by the Council.

When entering upon their duties, they shall give a solemn undertaking that, both during and after their term of office, they will respect the obligations resulting therefrom, in particular the duty to exercise honesty and discretion as regards accepting certain positions or benefits after they have ceased to hold office.

In case of doubt a decision shall be made by the Court.

E.A.E.C. St. 4
[*Identical with E.E.C. St.* 4]

E.C.S.C. St. 4

[*Identical as to the first two paragraphs with E.E.C. St.* 4, *supra, except that a majority of two thirds of the Council is specifically provided for in E.C.S.C. St.* 4 *in respect of the exceptional exemption from the prohibition on engaging in an occupation or profession.*]

The remaining paragraph of E.C.S.C. St. 4 provides:
"They may not acquire or hold, directly or indirectly, any interest in any business related to coal or steel during their term of office and during a period of three years thereafter".

The Advocates General are also subject to the provisions of the above three articles (see section C, *post*, pp. 190–191, under E.E.C. St. 8 and equivalents).

"...**Solemn undertaking**..." This requirement is re-iterated by R.P. 3 (3), *post*, p. 187. As to the decision by the Court whether a judge "no longer satisfies the obligations inherent in his position" see R.P. 5, *post*, p. 188.

Resignation of judges. This is governed by the Statutes as follows:

E.E.C. St. 5

Apart from retirements in regular rotation and in the case of death the duties of a judge shall be terminated in individual cases by resignation.

Where a judge resigns, his letter of resignation shall be addressed to the President of the Court for transmission to the President of the Council. This notification shall produce a vacancy on the bench.

Save where Article 6 applies, a judge shall continue to hold office until his successor enters upon his duties.

E.A.E.C. St. 5

[*Identical with E.E.C. St. 5.*]

E.C.S.C. St. 6

[*Identical with E.E.C. St. 5.*]

The Advocates General are also subject to the provisions of the above three articles (see section, C *post*, pp. 190–191 under E.E.C. St. 8 and equivalents).

Removal from office of judges. This is governed by the Statutes as follows:

E.E.C. St. 6

The judges may be deprived of office or of their right to a pension or alternative advantages only if, in the unanimous opinion of the judges and advocates-general of the Court, they no longer fulfil the required conditions or meet the obligations resulting from their office. The judges concerned shall not take part in these deliberations.

The Registrar of the Court shall communicate the Court's decision to the President of the Assembly and to the President of the Commission and shall notify it to the President of the Council.

In the case of a decision removing a judge from office, such notification shall produce a vacancy on the bench.

E.A.E.C. St. 6

[*Identical with E.E.C. St. 6.*]

E.C.S.C. St. 7

Judges may be deprived of office only if, in the unanimous opinion of the other Judges, they on longer fulfil the required conditions.

The President of the Council, the President of the High Authority and the President of the Assembly shall be notified of this by the Resigtrar.

Such notification shall produce a vacancy on the bench.

The Advocates General are also subject to the provisions of E.E.C. St. 6 and E.A.E.C. St. 6 above (see section C, *post*, pp. 190–191). As to the Registrar's duty when the Court's decision is adverse to a judge, see *post*, p. 193.

Replacement of a judge whose period of office has not expired. This is governed by the Statutes as follows:

E.E.C. St. 7

A judge appointed to replace a member of the Court whose term of office has not expired shall be appointed for the remainder of that member's term of office.

E.A.E.C. St. 7

[*Identical with E.E.C. St. 7.*]

E.C.S.C. St. 8

A judge appointed to replace a member of the Court whose period of appointment has not expired, shall be appointed for the remainder of the period his predecessor would have served.

The Advocates General are also subject to the provisions of E.E.C. St. 7 and E.A.E.C. St. 7. Where the period of appointment of the President of the Court or a section occurs before the normal end of his term of office the Court appoints a replacement (R.P. 6 (3), *post*, p. 188).

Where judge is required not to sit in respect of a particular case, because previously concerned, or for other reasons. See the following:

E.E.C. St. 16

The judges and advocates-general may not participate in the hearing of cases in which they have previously participated as agent of, legal adviser to, or a counsel for one of the parties, or on which they have been called upon to decide as a member of a Court (*tribunal*), of a commission of inquiry or in any other capacity.

If, for some special reason, any judge or advocate-general considers that he should not take part in the judgment or examination of a particular case, he shall so inform the President. If the President considers that any judge or advocate-general should not, for some special reason, sit or make submissions in a particular case, he shall give notice thereof to the person concerned.

The Court shall decide in case of any difficulties arising as to the effect of this Article.

A party may not invoke either the nationality of a judge or the absence from the Court or from a Section of a judge of his own nationality, in order to ask for a change in the composition of the Court or of one of its sections.

E.A.E.C. St. 16

[*Identical with E.E.C. St. 16.*]

E.C.S.C. St. 19
[Identical with E.E.C. St. 16]

It should be noted that these requirements also apply to the Advocates General (see generally *post*, pp. 190 *et seq.*).

Period of office of a judge. This is provided for in Article 2 of the Rules of Procedure (*infra*).

R.P. 2

The period of office of a Judge shall commence from the date fixed in his appointment. If the formal document of appointment does not fix a date, then the period shall commence from the date of the document.

The oath of the judge and the solemn undertaking. This is provided for in Article 3 of the Rules of Procedure (*infra*).

R.P. 3

Paragraph 1

Before taking up their office, Judges shall swear the following oath at the first public sitting of the Court which they attend after their appointment:

"I swear to perform my duties conscientiously and with complete impartiality: I swear to divulge nothing of the Court's deliberations."

Paragraph 2

The oath may be taken in the manner laid down by the law of the country of the Judge concerned.

Paragraph 3

Immediately after having taken the oath, Judges shall sign a declaration by which they solemnly undertake to respect, both during their term of office and after its termination, the obligations inherent in their position, and in particular the duty of exercising honesty and discretion as regards accepting certain positions or certain benefits after they have ceased to hold office.

These provisions re-iterate E.E.C. St. 4 and equivalents (*ante*, p. 184). As to the decision by the Court whether a judge "no longer fulfils the required conditions or no longer satisfies the obligations inherent in his position" see R.P. 5 (*post*, p. 188).

Order of precedence of judges. This is provided for as follows:

R.P. 4

The order of precedence of Judges shall be governed by their seniority of office.

The precedence of Judges having the same seniority of office shall be governed by their seniority of age.

Retiring Judges who are re-appointed shall retain their original precedence.

If the President of the Court is absent or unable to attend one of the Presidents of Section or if need be one of the other judges shall discharge his functions (by virtue of R.P. 7 (2) *post*, p. 189).

The court ... to decide whether a judge no longer fulfils the required conditions. See article 5 of the Rules of Procedure (*infra*).

R.P. 5

When the Court is called upon to decide whether a Judge no longer fulfils the required conditions or no longer satisfies the obligations inherent in his position, the President shall invite the person concerned to appear in the Judges' Council Chamber and present his comments, without the Resistrar being present.

As to the solemn undertaking by the judge to respect the obligations inherent in his position see R.P. 3 (*ante*, p. 187) and E.E.C. St. 4 (*ante*, p. 184).

Residence at the seat of the Court is required of the judges (and of the Advocates General and the Registrar, by E.E.C. St. 13 and equivalents: "The Judges, the Advocates General and the Registrar shall reside at the Seat of the Court".

B. Presidency of the Court and of its Sections (R.P. 6 and 7)

("*De la présidence de la Cour et des chambres*"; "*Der Präsident des Gerichtshofes und die Kammerpräsidenten*"; "*van het voorzitterschap van het Hof en van de kamern*"; "*Della presidenza della Corte e delle sezioni*").

The Treaties provide that the President of the Court shall be appointed for a three year term, renewable (see E.E.C. 167 and equivalents *ante*, p. 182). Appointment is by election of the judges themselves (R.P. 6, *infra*) and occurs every three years.

R.P. 6

Paragraph 1

The judges shall elect one of their number as President of the Court for a period of three years, immediately after the partial replacement provided for in Articles 32(c) of the E.C.S.C. Treaty, 167 of the E.E.C. Treaty and 139 of the E.A.E.C. Treaty.

Paragraph 2

The Court shall elect for a period of one year Presidents of the Sections referred to in Article 24 of these Rules.

Paragraph 3

In the event of the termination of the period of appointment of the President of the Court or of a President of a Section before the normal end of his term of office, the Court shall appoint a replacement for the remainder of the current period.

Paragraph 4

Voting at the elections mentioned in this Article shall be by secret ballot, the Judge obtaining an absolute majority being elected. Should none of the Judges obtain an absolute majority, a new ballot shall be taken and the Judge obtaining the most votes shall be elected. Where voting is equal, the elder shall be elected.

"**Paragraph 2 ... presidents of the sections ...**". Unlike the President of the Court who is elected for three years (see R.P. 6, *supra*), the presidents of the sections are elected for one year (as to sections see section F, *post*, p. 199 and E.E.C. 165 and equivalents *ante*, pp. 180–181).

R.P. 7

Paragraph 1

The President shall direct the work and the running of the Court; he shall preside at its sittings and at its deliberations in the Judges' Council Chamber.

Paragraph 2

In the event of absence or inability to attend of the President of the Court, or of the post being vacant, his functions shall be discharged by one of the Presidents of Sections according to the order of precedence laid down in Article 4 of these Rules.

In the event of inability to attend of both the President of the Court and the Presidents of Sections, or of all their posts being vacant at the same time, the functions of President shall be taken over by one of the other Judges according to the order of precedence laid down in Article 4 of these Rules.

"... **Paragraph 1 ... he shall preside at its sittings**". As to what this involves see Chapter 4, "Procedure" especially under R.P. 56 and R.P. 57 (*post*, p. 250). See also "... Sittings of the Court ..." (*post*, p. 196).

"**And its deliberations in the Judges Chamber**". "*Délibérations*" means "consideration of (judicial) decisions" and it would have been preferable if the original had been so translated (as in R.P. 27 which see *post*, p. 202. *Cp* also E.E.C. St. 15 and equivalents, *post*, p. 201).

C. Advocates General (R.P. 8–10)

("*Des avocats généraux*"; "*Die Generalanwälte*"; "*van de advocaten generaal*"; "*Degli avvocati generali*")

The treaties provide that there shall be two Advocates General, as follows:

E.E.C. 166

The Court of Justice shall be assisted by two advocates-general.

It shall be the duty of the advocate-general to make reasoned submissions (*conclusions*) in open Court to the Court of Justice on matters referred to it. He shall do so with complete impartiality and independence, with a view to helping the Court to achieve the task assigned to it in Article 164.

Should the Court of Justice so request, the Council may, by a unanimous decision increase the number of advocates-general, and make the necessary amendments to Article 167, third paragraph.

E.A.E.C. 138

[*Identical with E.E.C.* 166.]

E.C.S.C. 32(2)

[*As amended by the Convention of* 1957 *referred to,* ante, *p.* 180 *is identical with E.E.C.* 166.]

Function of the Advocate General. There is no precise equivalent to the office of Advocate General in the English legal system. He is much more than an *amicus curiae*, to whom, however, in his "impartiality and independence" he is akin. His role is of the greatest importance (see "reasoned submissions" *infra*).

"... reasoned submissions" ... (*"conclusions"; "gegründete Schlusz anträge"; "met redenen omklede conclusies"; "conclusioni motivate"*). These constitute an impartial, independent and in essence judicial review, from the factual and legal point of view, of the whole case in issue before the Court, the Advocate General, by virtue of his office, having participated in all stages of the written and oral procedure.

"In order to assist the Court in the accomplishment of the task assigned to it" in E.E.C. 164 (and in E.A.E.C. 136 and E.C.S.C. 31). This task is "to ensure the observance of law in the interpretation and application of this Treaty".

"... Publicly ..." That is, in open Court. But, exceptionally, a sitting may be "ordered to be in camera", in which case the oral proceedings may not be disclosed (R.P. 56 (1), *post*, p. 250).

"Submissions". In point of time the submissions of the Advocate General are made at the end of the oral procedure (as to which see Chapter 4, *post*, p. 252). When they have been presented, the President of the Court closes the oral procedure (R.P. 59 (2) *post*, p. 252) and the Court next delivers judgment. During the oral procedure preceding the presentation of his submissions the Advocate General has the same right (by virtue of R.P. 57, *post*, p. 250) to question the agents, legal advisers or legal representatives of the parties as have the President and the Judges of the Court. His submissions are made orally (R.P. 59 (1), *post*, p. 252; see comment "publicly" *supra*). It is customary for the reasoned submissions to be printed and published with the Court's judgment, in the Official Reports. They constitute a very valuable source of information and enlightment concerning the legal thinking of the Court.

"Appointment". Appointment, partial replacement every three years and re-appointment of the Advocates General is provided for in the same terms as those for judges (by E.E.C. 167 and equivalents, *ante*, p. 182).

The status of the Advocates General. This is regulated by the Statutes. The Advocates General are placed in the same position, as to status, as the judges, by E.E.C. St. 8 and E.A.E.C. St. 8 as follows:

E.E.C. St. 8

The provisions of Articles 2 to 7 inclusive shall apply to the advocates-general (*avocats-généraux*).

E.A.E.C. St. 8
[Identical with E.E.C. St. 8.]

The effect of the above provision is that Advocates General are on the same footing as judges as regards status (*ante*, p. 183), immunity (*ante*, p. 183), resignation (*ante*, p. 185), removal from office (*ante*, p. 185), replacement when their period of office has not expired (*ante*, p. 186).

Residence at the seat of the Court. This is required of the Advocates General, as of the judges and the Registrar, by E.E.C. St. 13 and equivalents (*ante*, p. 181).

Precedence. The Advocates General take precedence after the judges (R.P., 9, *infra*).

Debarred. An Advocate General is debarred from sitting in respect of a particular case for identically the same reasons as debar a judge (see E.E.C. St. 16 and equivalents, *ante*, p. 186).

R.P. 8

The provisions of Articles 2, 3 and 5 of these Rules are applicable to Advocates General.

The effect of this Rule is to make applicable to the Advocates General the provisions concerning judges as regards (a) period of office (see R.P. 2, *ante*, p. 187); (b) oath and solemn undertaking (see R.P. 3, *ante*, p. 187) and decision by the Court on whether continuing to fulfil the required conditions of office (see R.P. 5 *ante*, p. 188).

Precedence of Advocates General. For order, see R.P. 9 (*infra*).

R.P. 9

The Advocates General follow the Judges in order of precedence, according to the rules laid down in Article 4 of these Rules.

The text of R.P. 4 here referred to is at *ante*, p. 187.

R.P. 10

Paragraph 1
When the Sections are set up the Court shall decide on the assignment of an Advocate General to each Section.
The President may, on the Joint proposal of the Advocates General, appoint for a particular case the Advocate General assigned to the other Section.
Paragraph 2
In the event of one of the Advocates General being absent or unable to attend, and where there is a question of urgency, the President may call on the other Advocate General.

D. REGISTRAR's OFFICE (R.P. 11–22)

("Du Greffe"; "Die Kanzlei";
"van de griffie"; "Della cancelleria")

The Rules concerning the Registrar derive their ultimate authority from the Treaties as follows:

E.E.C. 168

The Court of Justice shall appoint its Registrar and determine his status and terms of service.

E.A.E.C. 140

[Identical with E.E.C. 168.]

E.C.S.C. 32(d)

[As amended by the Convention of March 1957, referred to at ante, p. 180, is identical with E.E.C. 168.]

"The Court of Justice shall appoint its Registrar . . .". This takes place after the views of the Advocates General have been heard (R.P. 11, *post*, p. 193).

The above Treaty provisions are implemented and amplified in a sequence of articles in Title II of the Statutes, "Organisation", as follows:

Oath of the Registrar

E.E.C. St. 9

The Registrar shall take an oath before the Court to perform his duties impartially and conscientiously and to preserve the secrecy of the Court's consideration of its judgments (*délibérations*).

E.A.E.C. St. 9

[Identical with E.E.C. St. 9.]

E.C.S.C. St. 14 paragraph 1

[Identical with E.E.C. St. 9.]

". . . Impartially and conscientiously and to preserve the secrecy of the Court's deliberations . . .". These requirements are in identical terms with those applicable to the judges and Advocates General (see E.E.C. St. 2 and equivalents, *ante*, p. 183) and the oath taken by the Registrar is (by virtue of R.P. 11(5) *post*, p. 194) identical with that taken by the judges (and the Advocates General) and formulated in R.P. 3 (*ante*, p. 187), by which Rule it is also required to be taken before assuming office.

Alternate for the Registrar when absent.

E.E.C. St. 10

The Court shall arrange for the Registrar to be represented by an alternate if he is unable to carry out his duties.

E.A.E.C. St. 10

[Identical with E.E.C. St. 10]

E.C.S.C. St. 16, paragraph 1, last sentence

One of them (officials or employees attached to the Court) shall be assigned by the Court to represent the Registrar if he is unable to carry out his duties.

Deputy Registrars may be appointed by the Court (by virtue of R.P. 12, *post*, p. 194). Where they as well as the Registrar are simultaneously absent, "the President shall select an official to carry out the duties of Registrar for the time being" (R.P. 13, *post*, p. 195).

Responsibility of the Registrar for officials and other servants of the Court.

E.E.C. St. 11

Officials and other employees shall be attached to the Court to enable it to carry out its tasks. They shall be responsible to the Registrar under the authority of the President.

E.A.E.C. St. 11

[*Identical with E.E.C. St.* 11]

E.C.S.C. St. 16 paragraph 1, first two sentences

[*Identical with E.E.C. St.* 11]

See "Court administrative services", *post*, p. 199.

The Registrar must reside at the seat of the Court. This is also necessary for the Judges and Advocates General, by virtue of E.E.C. St. 13 and equivalents (*ante*, p. 181).

The Registrar's duty when the Court decides unanimously that a judge no longer fulfils the conditions of office. This duty is to inform the presidents of the Assembly and Commission (of E.E.C. and E.A.E.C.), of the Council, High Authority and Assembly (of E.C.S.C.) and to notify the president of the Council (of E.E.C. and E.A.E.C.) of the Court's decision (as provided by E.E.C. St. 6 and equivalents, *ante*, p. 185). As to "inform" and "notify" compare "communication" and "notification" (*post*, p. 214). The provisions of the Treaties and the Statutes dealt with so far in this section (*i.e.* pp. 192 to 193) are implemented and amplified by the Rules of Procedure in two parts as follows:

Part I. Registrar and Deputy Registrars (R.P. 11–18)

(*"Du greffier et des greffiers adjoints"; "Kanzler und Hilfskanzler"; "van de griffier on de adjunct griffiers"; "Del cancelliere e dei cancellieri agguinti"*)

R.P. 11

Paragraph 1

The Registrar is appointed by the Court, after hearing the Advocates General.

The President shall inform the Judges and Advocates General of the candidates whose names have been submitted for the post, fourteen days before the date fixed for the appointment.

Paragraph 2

Applications shall be accompanied by full details of age, nationality, university degrees, knowledge of languages, present and past occupations and of any experience of candidates in the judicial and international fields.

Paragraph 3

The procedure for appointment shall be that laid down in Article 6, Paragraph 4 of these Rules.

Paragraph 4

The Registrar shall be appointed for a period of six years, and shall be eligible for re-appointment.

Paragraph 5

The provisions of Article 3 of these Rules shall be applicable to the Registrar.

Paragraph 6

The Registrar may be relieved of his office only if he no longer fulfils the required conditions or if he no longer discharges the obligations inherent in his position; the Court shall reach its decision in the Judges' Council Chamber after hearing the Advocates General and the Registrar has been given facilities to submit his comments.

Paragraph 7

Should the Registrar cease to hold office before the end of his period of appointment, the Court shall appoint a new Registrar for a period of six years.

Paragraph 1.—**"The Registrar is appointed by the Court after hearing the Advocates General".** This re-iterates and implements E.E.C. 168 and equivalents (*ante*, p. 192).

Paragraph 3.—**"The procedure for appointment".** This is the same as that provided for the election of the President of the Court and the Presidents of the Sections (*i.e.* by R.P. 6(4), *ante*, p. 188).

Paragraph 5. This implements E.E.C. St. 9 and equivalents (under which see especially ". . . impartially and conscientiously and to preserve the secrecy of the Court's deliberations . . .", *ante*, p. 192). The terms of the Registrar's oath are formulated in R.P. 3 (*ante*, p. 187) to which this paragraph refers.

Paragraph 6. Compare the provisions whereby a judge or advocate general may be relieved of his office (E.E.C. St. 6 and equivalents *ante*, p. 185). By virtue of this paragraph the Registrar is "given facilities to submit his comments". Such facilities are also required to be accorded a judge or an advocate general, by R.P. 5, *ante*, p. 188).

R.P. 12

The Court may, following the procedure laid down for the Registrar, appoint one or more Deputy Registrars to assist the Registrar and to take his place within the limitations specified in the instructions to the Registrar referred to in Article 14 of these Rules.

This Rule, together with R.P. 13 (*infra*) implements E.E.C. St. 10 and equivalents (*ante*, p. 192).

R.P. 13

In the event of the absence or inability to attend of the Registrar and his Deputies, or in the event of their posts being vacant at the same time, the President shall select an official to carry out the duties of Registrar for the time being.

This Rule, together with R.P. 12 (*ante*, p. 194) implements E.E.C. St. 10 and equivalents (*ante*, p. 192).

R.P. 14

The instructions to the Registrar shall be drawn up by the Court on proposals put forward by the President.

The Instructions to the Registrar are set out in Chapter 6 (*post*, pp. 302 *et seq.*).

R.P. 15

Paragraph 1

A register, initialled by the President, shall be kept in the office of the Registrar and under the Registrar's responsibility, recording one after another and in the order of their occurrence or submission all procedural documents and exhibits submitted in support.

Paragraph 2

A note recording entry in the register shall be made by the Registrar on original documents and, if the parties so request, on copies they submit for this purpose.

Paragraph 3

The recording in the register and the noting specified in the foregoing paragraph shall constitute an official record.

Paragraph 4

The way in which the register is kept shall be determined by the instructions to the Registrar specified in Article 14 of these Rules.

Paragraph 5

Any person having an interest in the matter may consult the register in the office of the Registrar and may obtain copies or extracts according to the scale of charges laid down by the Court on proposals put forward by the Registrar.

All parties to a case may furthermore obtain, at the appropriate charge, copies of procedural documents and office copies of orders and decisions.

Paragraph 6

A notice shall be published in the Official Journal of the European Communities indicating the date of the Request instituting proceedings, the names and permanent address of the parties, the matter in dispute and the submissions made in the Request.

"Paragraph 1.—A Register . . .". By virtue of Paragraph 4 of R.P. 15. "the way in which the Register shall be kept" is determined in the Instructions to the Registrar, section 2, "Keeping the Register" (arts. 11–16) for the text of which see *post*, pp. 306–307.

"Paragraph 1 . . . procedural documents . . .". See ". . . Requests, statements of case, defences, comments . . . replies", *post*, p. 216.

"Paragraph 3 . . . an official record". Compare R.P. 53 (*post*, p. 247) and R.P. 62 (*post*, pp. 252–253) and note comment on technical rules as to the evidential value of documents (probative force of instruments) (also under R.P. 37 (4) *post*, p. 220).

"Paragraph 5 . . . scale of charges . . .". The scale is set out in Instructions to the Registrar 20 (see *post*, p. 308).

R.P. 16
Paragraph 1
Subject to the directions of the President, it shall be for the Registrar to receive, send, and preserve all documents, and to effect service when required by these Rules.
Paragraph 2
The Registrar shall assist the Court, the Sections, the President and the Judges in the carrying-out of all their duties and functions.

"Paragraph 1 . . . to effect service . . .". See "Service", Chapter 4, viii (R.P. 79) (*post*, p. 267).

R.P. 17
The Registrar shall have custody of the seals. He shall be responsible for the Court Archives, and be in charge of Court publications.

". . . Court publications . . .". See Instructions to the Registrar (23–26) section 4, "Court publications", *post*, pp. 309–310.

R.P. 18
Subject to the provisions of Articles 5 and 27 of these Rules, the Registrar shall attend the sittings of the Court and the Sections.

". . . Subject to the provisions of R.P. 5 and 27 . . .". The Registrar is not present at sittings of the court when called to decide whether a Judge or Advocate General ought no longer to hold office (R.P. 5, *ante*, p. 188) or at which the court or section is considering a (judicial) decision (R.P. 27, *post*, pp. 202 and 203).

". . . Sittings of the Court and the Sections". "Sitting" ("*séance*"; "*Sitzung*"; "*zitting*"; "*riunione*") (and where the verb "sits" is used; "*siège*"; "*tagt*"; "*vergadert*"; "*è riunita*"; R.P. 27(8)) is a general term embracing all occasions in which the Court (or a section) is called together for the formal conduct of judicial business. It is similarly used in R.P. 25 (*post*, p. 200). There are different types of sitting: a private sitting to consider the preliminary report of the reporting judge (*post*, p. 232); a sitting at which witnesses (or experts) are summoned to attend (R.P. 48, *post*, p. 244), and R.P. 53 (*post*, p. 247); a sitting for the purposes of the oral procedure (without witnesses R.P. 57 (*post*, p. 250) R.P. 62 (*post*, p. 252) and which normally will be public, though it may be in camera (R.P. 56(2) *post*, p. 250); a sitting to consider a (judicial) decision which takes place in private and without the Advocate General, the parties, or their agents, legal advisers, or legal representatives, in the Judges' Council Chamber; or if to consider an administrative decision takes place similarly but with the attendance of both Advocates General; a sitting at which a judgment is delivered in "open court" (R.P. 64). (Note E.E.C. 165 and equivalents (*ante*, p. 181): ". . . The Court sits in plenary session", and, as to the number of judges and as to a quorum, see R.P. 26, *post*, p. 201.) The expressions used in the original languages in the Rules of Procedure referred to in this comment are revealing when tabulated:

R.P. 52 ("sitting")	*"séance"*;	*"Sitzung"*;	*"zitting"*;	*"riunione"*.
R.P. 48 ("attend the proceedings", of a witness)	*"Audience"*;	(no equivalent noun) *"haben der Ladung Folge zu leisten"*:	*"terechtzitting"*;	*"udienza"*
R.P. 53 ("sitting")	*"audience"*;	*"Sitzung"*;	*"Terechtzitting"*;	*"udienza"*
R.P. 56 ("hearing", used for both the interchange of spoken argument and the proceedings where it occurs)	*"les débats"* and *"audience"*;	*"Verhandlung"*; and *"Sitzung"*;	*"mondelinge behandeling"* and *"terechtzitting"*	*"dibattimento"* and *"udienza"*
R.P. 57 ("course" of the hearing)	*"débats"*;	*"Verhandlung"*	*"mondelinge behandeling"*;	*"dibattimento"*
R.P. 62 ("sitting")	*"audience"*;	*"mündliche" Verhandlung* (used elsewhere to denote the more generic "oral procedure")	*"terechtzitting"*	*"udienza"*
R.P. 64 ("open Court")	*"audience publique"*	*"offentliche Sitzung"*;	*"terechtzitting"*	*"udienza"*

Part II. Court Administrative Services (R.P. 19–22)

(*"Des services de la Cour"*; *"Sonstige Dienststellen"*; *"van de diensten van het Hof"*; *"Dei servizi della Corte"*)

R.P. 19
Paragraph 1
The officials and other servants of the Court shall be appointed in manner laid down in the regulations setting out the terms of service of personnel.
Paragraph 2
Before taking up their posts, officials shall take the following oath before the President and in the presence of the Registrar:
"I swear to carry out the duties assigned to me by the Court of Justice of the European Communities with complete loyality, discretion and conscientiousness."
Paragraph 3
The oath may be taken in the manner provided by the law of the country of the official concerned.

R.P. 20

On proposals put forward by the Registrar, the Court shall decide or amend the organisation of the Court administrative services.

R.P. 21

The Court shall set up a language department composed of experts who show that they have appropriate legal knowledge and extensive knowledge of several of the official languages of the court.

R.P. 22

The administration of the Court, the financial management and the keeping of the Court's accounts shall, under the authority of the President, be undertaken by the Registrar with the help of an administrative officer.

E. Assistant Rapporteurs

("Des rapporteurs adjoints"; "Die Hilfsberichterstatter"; "van de toegevoegde rapporteurs"; "Dei relatori aggiunti")

Introduction. The Statutes empower the Court to arrange for the appointment of assistant rapporteurs. The rapporteurs (who are judges appointed so to act in respect of individual cases) are mentioned for the first time in the sequence of the Rules of Procedure at a later point than their assistants (and are accordingly dealt with in this same sequence in this book; see under "F, The Sections" R.P. 24 *post*, p. 200). The enabling provisions (in respect of assistant rapporteurs) in the Statutes are as follows:

E.E.C. St. 12

The Council may, by a unanimous decision, on a proposal of the Court, provide for the appointment of assistant Rapporteurs and lay down their terms of service. The assistant Rapporteurs may be required, under conditions to be laid down by the rules of procedure, to participate in the examination of cases pending before the Court and to collaborate with the judge who acts as rapporteur *(juge rapporteur)*.

The assistant Rapporteurs shall be chosen from among persons whose independence can be fully guaranteed and who possess the necessary legal qualifications; they shall be appointed by the Council. They shall take an oath before the Court to perform their duties impartially and conscientiously and to preserve the secrecy of the Court's deliberations.

E.A.E.C. St. 12

[*Identical with E.E.C. St.* 12.]

E.C.S.C. St. 16, second paragraph

[*Substantially identical with E.E.C. St.* 12, *first paragraph*]

"**... To participate in the examination of cases ...**". "Procedure of enquiry and calling of evidence" (which in the 1964 finally revised

English translation of "examination") is a phase of procedure which, if determined upon, follows written procedure and precedes oral procedure (see Chapter 4, sections 1 and 2) *post*, pp. 234 and 237). It will not be determined upon unless the Court, having considered the report of the rapporteur on this aspect, holds it to be necessary. (See under R.P. 24(1) comment ". . . procedure of enquiry into cases . . ." *post*, p. 200).

"**. . . Impartially and conscientiously and to preserve the secrecy of the Court's deliberations**". These words are identical with those applicable to judges and advocates general (see E.E.C. St. 2 and equivalents, *ante*, p. 183) and the Registrar (see E.E.C. St. 9 and equivalents *ante*, p. 192). The assistant rapporteurs are required to take the same oath as these (see R.P. 23(4) *infra*). As to "secret deliberations" see "consideration by the judges of their decision" (*post*, p. 201). The above enabling provisions of the Statutes are amplified in the Rules of Procedure:

R.P. 23

Paragraph 1

Where the Court feels that it is necessary for the study of and procedure of inquiry into the cases placed before it, it shall, pursuant to Article 16 of the E.C.S.C. Statute and Article 12 of the E.E.C. and E.A.E.C. Statutes, propose the appointment of assistant Rapporteurs.

Paragraph 2

The duties of assistant Rapporteurs are in particular:

to assist the President in the summary procedure in case of urgency;

to assist Judges acting as Rapporteurs in their work.

Paragraph 3

In the carrying-out of their functions the assistant Rapporteurs shall be responsible to the President of the Court, the President of a Section, or the Judge acting as Rapporteur, as the case may be.

Paragraph 4

Before taking up their duties, the assistant Rapporteurs shall take before the Court the oath laid down in Article 3 of these Rules of Procedure.

"**Paragraph 2 . . . summary procedure . . .**". Summary procedure is the subject of a "special form of procedure" (see Chapter 5, *post*, pp. 270 *et seq.*).

"**Paragraph 2 . . . rapporteur judges . . .**". As to these, see section F, R.P. 24(2), *post*, p. 200 also, introduction to this section (*ante*. p. 198).

F. THE SECTIONS

(*"Des Chambres"; "Die Kammern"; "van de Kamers"; "Delle sezioni"*).

The Treaties (E.E.C. 165 and equivalents; for text see *ante*, p. 181) empower the Court to constitute Sections, each of three or five judges, either for the purpose of the "procedure of enquiry and calling of evidence" (see Chapter 4, *post*, p. 233) or to judge certain categories of case (such as claims by Community servants, see 5 "Proceedings by servants of the Communities, *post*, p. 283). The Rules of Procedure have implemented the above

Treaty provisions by exercising the choice of sections composed of three judges, as follows:

R.P. 24

Paragraph 1

The Court shall set up within itself two Sections each of three Judges, which shall undertake the procedure of inquiry into the cases assigned to them.

Paragraph 2

As soon as a Request has been filed, the President shall assign the case to one of the Sections and appoint from within that Section a Judge to act as Rapporteur.

Unless the President decides otherwise, the Judge acting as Rapporteur shall continue to exercise that function, even though he may be appointed to the other Section in the course of the proceedings.

"**Paragraph 1 ... procedure of enquiry into cases...**". The procedure of enquiry begins with the initiation of the written procedure. It may be continued and amplified by the calling of evidence by order of the Court following the close of the written procedure (see Chapter 4, "Calling of Evidence" *post*, p. 233).

"**Paragraph 2.—As soon as a Request has been filed...**". A request by an applicant if in due form, originates an action upon its delivery to the Registrar (see Chapter 4, "Request" *post*, pp. 218 *et seq.*).

"**...A Judge to act as Rapporteur...**". The duties of this judge during the written procedure culminate in the presentation of a "preliminary report" on the question whether (further) procedure of enquiry on the case is required. This report is considered in secret by the other judges concerned. (See Chapter 4, R.P. 44(1), *post*, p. 232, and "Sittings of the Court," *ante*, p. 196).

Paragraph 2 second sentence. If as a result of this provision there is an even number of judges, the junior judge takes no part in the judges' consideration of their decision (by virtue of R.P. 26(1), *post*, p. 201).

G. Functioning of the Court (R.P. 25–28)

("Du fonctionnement de la Cour"; "Geschäftsgang des Gerichtshofes"; "van de werkwijze van het Hof"; "Del funzionamento della Corte")

The Court is required, by E.E.C. St. 14 and equivalents to function permanently, arranging judicial vacations accordingly.

R.P. 25

Paragraph 1

The dates and times of the sittings of the Court shall be fixed by the President.

Paragraph 2

The dates and times of the sitings of the Sections shall be fixed by the President of each of them.

Paragraph 3

The Court and the Sections may, for one or more given sittings, choose a place other than that where the Court has its seat.

As to the Cause List relating to oral procedure see Chapter 4, "Publicity of Hearing", "Cause List" (*post*, p. 248) and R.P. 55 (*post*, pp. 249–250). *Consideration by the judges of their decisions.* The giving of judgment by a single judge sitting alone is in Continental Europe far from being the common phenomenon that it is in England or elsewhere in the common law world. At the European Court it exists only in the exceptional cases where the President may give a decision as sole judge (*e.g.* in summary procedure (R.P. 85 *post*, p. 273) or in respect of a warrant for enforcement of a supervisory measure etc. under E.A.E.C. 8. (See Chapter 2, *ante*, p. 176) See generally the tables of "Jurisdiction by virtue of the Treaties" (*ante*, p. 61) and of "Procedural Competence" (*ante*, p. 60). That being so, rules are necessary to regulate how the judges are to arrive at their collective decisions. The general provision regulating this matter is contained in the Statutes as follows:

E.E.C. St. 15

The Court shall be competent to sit only when sitting with an uneven number of members. The decisions of the Court, meeting in plenary session, shall be valid if five members are sitting. The decisions of the Sections are valid only if three judges sit; in the event of one of the judges of a Section being unable to carry out his duties, a judge of another Section may be asked to sit in accordance with conditions which shall be laid down by the rules of procedure.

E.A.E.C. St. 15

[*Identical with E.E.C. St.* 15.]

E.C.S.C. St. 18

[*Save for very minor differences of wording of no material significance, identical with E.E.C. St.* 15.]

A further general requirement in respect of the judges' consideration of their decision is imposed by the Statutes as follows:

E.E.C. St. 32

The court's consideration of cases shall be and shall remain secret.

E.A.E.C. St. 33

[*Identical with E.E.C. St.* 32.]

E.C.S.C. St. 29

[*Identical with E.E.C. St.* 32.]

The secrecy of the judges' consideration of their decision. This is required to be sworn by each judge to be maintained (see E.E.C. St. 2 and equivalents, *ante*, p. 183).

The general provisions of the Statutes above is implemented in two rules of the Rules of Procedure (R.P. 26 and 27) as follows:

R.P. 26

Paragraph 1

If, by reason of absence or inability to attend or in consequence of Article 24, Paragraph 2, second Sub-paragraph, of these Rules, there is an even number of Judges, then the junior Judge as ascertained under Article 4 of these Rules shall abstain from taking part in the Judges' consideration of their decision.

Paragraph 2

If, when the Court has been convened, it is found that the quorum of five Judges is not present, then the President shall adjourn the sitting until the quorum is present.

"Paragraph 1. If . . . there is an even number of judges . . .". An uneven number is required by E.E.C. St. 15 and equivalents (*ante*, p. 201).

"Paragraph 1 . . . the judges' consideration of their decision" (*"délibéré"; "Beratungen"; "beraadslaging"; "deliberazione"*). *"Délibérations"* is used in general in French to describe either discussions themselves or the conclusions drawn or formulated from discussions (and is rendered into English elsewhere in the Treaties as "Resolutions"—*e.g.* in E.C.S.C. 38 (see Chapter 2, "Resolutions of the E.C.S.C. Assembly or Council," *ante*, p. 118)). In E.C.S.C. French is the only official Treaty language, but the renderings of *"délibérations"* in E.C.S.C. 38 in the three other community languages is of interest; they are—*"Beschlüsse"; "besluiten"; "deliberazione"*. The detailed rules governing the judges' consideration of the decision are set out in R.P. 27 (*infra*).

"Paragraph 2 . . . sitting . . .". See under R.P. 18 ". . . sittings of the Court and the Sections", *ante*, p. 196.

R.P. 27

Paragraph 1

Both the Court and its Sections shall consider their decisions in the Judges' Council Chamber.

Paragraph 2

Only those Judges who took part in the oral procedure and, if required, the assistant Rapporteur entrusted with the study of the case, shall take part in the consideration of the decision to be given.

Paragraph 3

Each of the Judges taking part in the consideration of the decision shall express his opinion giving his grounds therefor.

Paragraph 4

At the request of a Judge, any question shall be phrased in the official languages of his choice and communicated in writing to the Court or Section before being put to the vote.

Paragraph 5

The findings reached by the majority of the judges after final discussion shall constitute the decision of the Court. Votes shall be cast in reverse order of precedence to that laid down in Article 4 of these Rules.

Paragraph 6

In the event of a difference of opinion on the purpose, purport and order of questions, or on the interpretation of the voting, the Court or Section shall decide.

Paragraph 7

When the Court has to decide on internal matters of administration, the Advocates General shall take part in the judgment. The Registrar shall be present, unless the Court decides otherwise.

Paragraph 8

When the Court sits without the Registrar being present it shall instruct the junior Judge within the meaning of Article 4 of these Rules of Procedure to draw up a record of the proceedings if required. This record shall be signed by this Judge and by the President.

"Paragraph 1 . . . consider their decisions." In view of the rules governing this matter set out in R.P. 27, this is in effect a term of art and the expressions representing it in the original official languages, as set out in the comment to R.P. 26 (*supra*) may therefore be noted.

". . . In the Judges' Council Chamber". See under R.P. 18 ". . . sitting of the Court and the sections", *ante*, p. 196.

"Paragraph 2 . . . the assistant rapporteur". See Section E, "Assistant Rapporteurs" (*ante*, p. 198).

"Paragraph 2 . . . opinion giving his grounds therefor". (*"opinion en la motivant"; "trägt seine Auffassung vor und begründet sie"; "gevoelen met redenen omkleed"; "il suo parere motivandolo"*). "Reasons" might have been a preferable translation to "grounds". See in Chapter 4, under R.P. 38 comment on ". . . grounds of fact and law . . ." (*post*, p. 224) and, under R.P. 40 ". . . the arguments of fact and law which are relied upon", and the comparative linguistic table therein contained (*post*, p. 227).

"Paragraph 4 . . . the official languages of his choice . . .". See under "Official Languages", *post*, p. 204.

"Paragraph 7 . . . the advocates general . . .". See under "Advocates General", R.P. 8–10, *ante*, p. 191.

"Paragraph 8 . . . a record of the proceedings". Being for the use of the judges this is not an "official record" within the meaning of R.P. 53(1) (*post*, p. 247) and R.P. 62(1) (*post*, p. 252).

R.P. 28

Paragraph 1

Unless there be a special decision by the Court, the Court vacations shall be as follows:

from 18th December to 10th January;

from the Sunday preceding Easter Sunday to the second Sunday after Easter Sunday;

from 15th July to 15th September.

During the Court vacations, the functions of President shall be exercised in the place where the Court has its seat, either by the President himself, who shall keep in touch with the Registrar, or by a President of a Section or another Judge whom he asks to take his place.

Paragraph 2

During the vacations the President may, in case of urgency, convene the Judges and the Advocates General.

Paragraph 3

The Court shall observe the official public holidays of the place where it has its seat.

Paragraph 4

The Court may, where there are good reasons, grant leave of absence to Judges and Advocates General.

"Paragraph 3 official public holidays . . .".   As to the incidence of these in relation to time limits in respect of procedure see R.P. 80(2) (*post*, p. 268).

H. OFFICIAL LANGUAGES (R.P. 29–31)

("Du régime linguistique"; "Sprachenregelung"; "van het taalgebruik"; "Del regime linguistico").

R.P. 29

Paragraph 1

The official languages of the Court shall be French, German Italian and Netherlands.

Only one of the official languages may be used as the procedural language.

Paragraph 2

The choice of procedural language shall be made by the Applicant with the following reservations:

(*a*) if the Defendant is a Member State or natural person or legal person being a national of or constituted under the laws of a Member State, then the procedural language shall be the official language of that State; in the event of there being more than one official language, the applicant in the case shall be allowed to choose whichever suits him.

(*b*) upon joint request by the parties concerned, the Court may authorise the use of another official language as the procedural language.

(*c*) at the request of one of the parties, after the other party and the Advocate General have been heard, the Court or the Section may, notwithstanding sub-paragraphs (*a*) and (*b*) above, authorise the total or partial use of another official language as the procedural language; this request may not be submitted by one of the institutions of the European Communities.

In the case provided for in Article 103 of these Rules of Procedure, the procedural language shall be that of the court which lays the matter before the court.

Paragraph 3

The procedural language shall be used in particular in the parties' written statements of case and in their addresses to the Court, including such documents and exhibits as are annexed, and in the written record of the proceedings and decision of the Court.

Each exhibit and each document which is produced or annexed and is drawn up in a language other than the procedural language shall be accompanied by a translation in the procedural language.

However, in the case of bulky exhibits and documents, translations of extracts may be submitted. The Court or the Section may, at any time, require a more complete or verbatim translation, either of its own volition or at the request of one of the parties.

Paragraph 4

When witnesses or experts state that they are unable to express themselves properly in one of the official languages, the Court or Section shall authorise them to make their statements in another language. The Registrar shall ensure its translation into the procedural language.

Paragraph 5

An official language other than the procedural language may be used by the President of the Court and Presidents of Sections in directing the proceedings, by the Judge acting as Rapporteur for his preliminary report and his report at the hearing, by Judges and Adovcates General when putting questions and by Advocates General when making their submissions. The Registrar shall ensure translation into the procedural language.

"Paragraph 1 ... Netherlands". (*"le néerlandais"*; *"Niederländisch"*; *"Nederlands"*; *"l'Olandese"*). "Dutch", used to designate the language of Holland, is not synonymous with "the Netherlands language", which is also spoken in Belgium. A result of the Netherlands language being an official language is to give Belgian parties the choice of two languages that are official, French and Netherlands. (The distinction between Netherlands and Dutch cannot readily be drawn in Italian which designates the Netherlands language as *"l'Olandese"*—and the country, Holland, as *"l'Olanda"*.)

"Paragraph 1 ... the language of procedure ...". As to practical features concerning the language of procedure during the "procedure of enquiry and calling of evidence", note paragraph 4 and see in general, "The conduct of the hearing of witnesses" (*post*, pp. 242–243), and similarly, in respect of the oral procedure, see "Some practical features of the hearing" under R.P. 58 (*post*, p. 251). See the judgment in *Acciaieria di Roma* c. *Haute Autorité* in Chapter 5, under R.P. 100 (*post*, pp. 288–289).

Intervention, and the language of procedure. See reference to *De Gezamenlijke Steenkolenmijnen in Limburg* c. *Haute Autorité* (*post*, p. 278).

R.P. 30

Paragraph 1

The Registrar shall ensure that at the request of one of the Judges, of the Advocate General or of one of the parties, a translation into the official languages of his choice is made of what is said or written during the proceedings before the Court or Section.

Paragraph 2

Court publications shall be in the official languages.

R.P. 31

Texts of documents drawn up in the procedural language or, as the case may be, in another language authorised by the Court under Article 29, Paragraph 4 of these Rules, shall be authentic.

"Texts ... shall be authentic". (*"font foi"*; *"sind verbindlich"*; *"heeft rechtskracht"*; *"fa fede"*). Such texts are binding on the Court only in the sense that they may not be challenged on linguistic grounds. They are not by that token in the same category as the "official record" so designated elsewhere in the Rules of Procedure (R.P. 15(3), *ante*, p. 195; R.P. 47(6) *post*, p. 240; R.P. 53(1) *post*, p. 247; R.P. 62, *post*, p. 252); though what is there characterized in English as "official" is in three of the original languages characterized by words meaning "authentic" (*"authentique"*; *"authentieke"*; *"autentico"*) and in German by the equivalent of "public" (*"öffentlich"*).

I. Rights and Obligations of Agents, Legal Advisers and Legal Representatives (R.P. 32–36)

(*"Des droits et obligations des agents, conseils et avocats"*; *"Rechte und Pflichten der Bevollmächtigten, Beistände und Anwälte"*; *"Van de Rechten en Verplichtingen der Gemachtigen, Raadslieden en Advocaten"*; *"Dei Diritti e Doveri degli Agenti, Consulenti ed avvocati"*)

The rights and obligations of the parties' lawyers, in relation to the organizational aspects of the Court are the subject of this section. The procedural aspects of the work of such lawyers before the Court and as representatives of the parties to proceedings before the Court are treated in Chapter 4 (*post*, pp. 213–214 *et seq.*).

R.P. 32

Paragraph 1

Agents representing a State or institution together with legal advisers and legal representatives appearing before the Court, or before a judicial authority empowered by the Court by virtue of letters of request, shall enjoy immunity in respect of spoken words and written documents relating to the case or parties in question.

Paragraph 2

Agents, legal advisers and legal representatives shall also enjoy the following privileges and facilities:

(*a*) all papers and documents relating to the proceedings shall be exempt from search and confiscation. If a right to exemption is contested, the Customs officials or police may seal the papers and documents in question, which shall then be forwarded immediately to the Court for examination in the presence of the Registrar and of the person concerned.

(*b*) agents, legal advisers and legal representatives shall be entitled to such allocation of currency as may be necessary for the carrying out of their tasks.

(*c*) agents, legal advisers and legal representatives shall enjoy such liberty of movement as may be necessary for the carrying out of their tasks.

R.P. 33

In order that the privileges, immunities and facilities specified in the preceding Article may be enjoyed, proof of status shall first be furnished as follows:

(*a*) for agents, by an official document issued by the State or institution which they represent; a copy of this document shall be at once forwarded to the Registrar by the State or institution concerned;

(*b*) for legal advisers and legal representatives, by credentials signed by the Registrar. The validity of these credentials shall be limited to a fixed period, which may be extended or shortened according to the length of the proceedings.

R.P. 34

The privileges, immunities and facilities specified in Article 32 of these Rules are granted solely in the interest of the proceedings.

The Court may waive immunity when it considers that such waiver of immunity is not against the interests of the proceedings.

R.P. 35

Paragraph 1

Any legal adviser or legal representative whose conduct before the Court, a Section or a member of the Court is incompatible with the dignity of the Court, or who makes use of the rights which he enjoys by reason of his position to ends other than those for which they have been granted may at any time be barred from the proceedings by an order of the Court or Section, after the Advocate General has been heard and due provision has been made for the person concerned to reply to the complaint against him.

This order shall be enforceable immediately.

Paragraph 2

Where a legal adviser or legal representative is barred from the proceedings, the proceedings shall be adjourned for a period to be fixed by the President, in order to allow the party concerned to appoint another legal adviser or legal representative.

Paragraph 3

Decisions taken pursuant to the provisions of this Article may be rescinded.

R.P. 36

The provisions of this Chapter shall be applicable to university teachers who have the right to appear before the Court in accordance with Article 20 of the E.C.S.C. Statute and Article 17 of the E.E.C. and E.A.E.C. Statutes.

Procedure before the Court (R.P. 37–82)

(Règlement de Procédure. Titre Deuxième. De la Procédure;
Verfahrensordnung Zweiter Teil. Allgemeine Verfahrensvorschriften;
Reglement voorde procesvoering. Tweede titel. Van de procedure;
Regolamento di Procedura. Titolo secondo–Del procedimento)

I. INTRODUCTION

Plan of this chapter. This chapter is concerned with the normal pattern of procedure before the Court (Title Two of the Rules of Procedure). There exist "special forms of procedure", deviating from the normal pattern, which are the subject of Title Three of the Rules of Procedure (R.P. 83–108) and are dealt with in Chapter 5 of this book (*post*, p. 270).

In the present chapter the rules relating to the normal pattern of procedure (R.P. 37–82) are treated in the same sequence in nine sections (1–9, *post*, pp. 217 *et seq.*) corresponding to the nine chapters into which they are divided in Title Two of the Rules of Procedure and bearing the same headings as those chapters.

Since procedure is also the subject of Title Three of the Statutes of the Court and the articles of this title constitute in many cases the basic provision implemented by a Rule or group of Rules of Procedure, such Articles of the Statutes are treated first in the relevant section on the Rules of Procedure, followed by treatment of the Rules relating thereto. Such articles of Title Three of the Statutes as are not amplified in the Rules of Procedure (or, similarly, Treaty articles) are dealt with at appropriate points in the sequence followed by the Rules of Procedure. Two such unimplemented articles of the Statutes (E.E.C. St. 17, 18 and equivalents), which deal with underlying aspects of all procedure, thus come to be dealt with by way of prelude to section I of this Chapter, in the course of the introductory comments which now follow (see *post*, pp. 211 and 214).

Basic characteristics of procedure. The procedural requirements of the Rules, Statutes (and Treaties) form a loose-knit amalgam or symposium of procedural requirements familiar in the internal legal systems of the original six Member States of the Communities. The lawyer not familiar with these systems may be assisted by a perusal of these introductory comments.

1. The Procedure throughout is by way of "contradiction" ("*procédure contradictoire*") in the following sense. An action is begun by a claim by one party against another. (By the making in due form of a claim there is brought

into existence what may be described as the "judicial contract" (*"contrat judiciaire"*) or, alternatively, as the "relationship of lawsuit" (*"rapport d'instance"*). A defence may be presented by the party against whom the claim is made. This defence may be met by further argument by the original applicant and so in turn may that be met by yet further argument. (E.E.C. St. 18 *post*, p. 214).)

2. The Procedure in all its stages has features commonly described by Continental European lawyers as "accusatorial" (*"accusatoire"*) and "inquisitorial" (*"inquisitoriale"*) for the following reasons: it is accusatorial because the Court is only seized of a dispute by the initiative of the party making a claim before the Court; the prosecution of the action is left, by the Court, to the diligence of the parties (but see 5, *post*, p. 211); either party may discontinue the action (*"désistement"*; *"Klagerücknahme"*) (*"Afstand van instantie"*; *"rinuncia agli atti"*) (R.P. 77–78, *post*, p. 265).

But it is also "inquisitorial" in the sense, for example, that the Court itself has certain powers of investigation and control designed to elucidate the point or points for decision, to further the establishment of proof, or to expedite the action. The Court may of its own volition order the proof of facts by witnesses (R.P. 47(1), *post*, p. 239) and these may be called by the Court itself (or by the parties, or the Advocate General (R.P. 47(1) *post*, p. 239). The President of the Court, may during the oral procedure, put questions to the agents, legal advisers and legal representatives of the parties (R.P. 57, *post*, p. 250) or to the witnesses (R.P. 47(4), *post*, p. 239). The Court itself determines what measures by way of procedure of enquiry or calling of evidence seem necessary (see section II, *post*, p. 133) and either proceeds to take them or entrusts the reporting judge (*"juge rapporteur"*—see Chapter 3, "Rapporteur" *ante*, pp. 200 and 198) with so doing (R.P. 45, *post*, pp. 234 *et seq.*). If an expert's examination and report is ordered by the Court, the expert is placed under the control of the reporting judge and the Court may itself decide that the expert shall be heard orally (R.P. 49, *post*, p. 244).

3. The oral procedure is public unless for grave reasons, either on its own motion or at the request of the parties, the Court otherwise decides (E.E.C. St. 28, *post*, p. 248) or the Treaty requires the Court to sit *in camera* for a specific purpose (*e.g.* E.E.C. 225 paragraph two, *ante*, p. 70). It follows that where the hearings are public, they may be published.

4. There is a widespread impression among common law practitioners that, in Continental Europe, written procedure plays a much more important part in an action than it does, say, in England, whilst oral procedure plays an almost negligible role. Such a generalisation is dangerous, though it contains an element of truth. At the European Court a party is unlikely to be successful unless the written procedure relating to his case is well and soundly conducted, but the importance of the oral procedure that follows it should not be underestimated. It may further be noted that in two "special forms of procedure" (dealt with in Chapter 5) oral procedure may well assume a greater relative importance to written procedure. These are, intervention by a new party in a pending action and the procedure by way of "objection" or for a ruling on "some other preliminary point which does not involve raising the main issue" (*"Exception"* and *"Incident"*; *"Prozesshindernde Einrede"* and *"Zwischenstreit"*; *"exceptie"* and *"incident"*; *"eccezione"* and *"incidente"*; R.P. 91, *post*, pp. 274–275). The relative importance of oral procedure is enhanced because the intervener must accept the state of the action as at the moment the request to intervene is made (which may be at any time, and even immediately, before the opening of the oral procedure) and is, moreover, limited to making submissions aimed at either the support

or the rejection of the submissions of one of the parties to the principal action. In the case of an "objection", or application for a ruling on some other preliminary point, the relative importance of the oral procedure is enhanced because the exchange of written pleadings between the parties is limited to one exchange instead of the usual two (that is, there is a claim (*"demande"; "Schriftsatz"; "verzoek"; "domanda"*) and defence (*"défense; "Klage-beantwortung"; "verweerschriften"; "difesa"*) but not the normally ensuing reply (*"réplique"; "Replik"* or *"Erwiderung"; "verdere conclusien"* or *"repliek"; "replica"*) and further reply (*"duplique"; "Gegenerwiderung"; "dupliek"; "controreplica"*).

5. As a generalisation (but no more) it would be fair to say, with reference to the distinction between "accusatorial" and "inquisitorial" aspects of the procedure (see para. 2, *ante* p. 210) that the written procedure is "accusatorial" and, matters being left to the diligence of the parties, the Court has at most a passive role during this phase, whereas after the decision of the Court to order a measure by way of procedure of enquiry or the calling of evidence or, if none such is ordered, from the beginning of the oral procedure, the Court itself assume active control of the action, which in this phase is thus "inquisitorial". But it would be erroneous to suppose that the Court is merely dormant during the written procedure. It may, for example "at any moment" declare that the claim is inadmissible on grounds of public policy (*"ordre public"; "unverzichtbare Prozessvoraussetzungen"; "openbare Orde"; "ordine pubblico"*) (under R.P. 92, *post*, p. 275) and must therefore carefully examine the claim to ensure no such declaration is required. (An example of the application of R.P. 92 and the making of such a declaration is to be found in consolidated cases 31 and 33/62, R. Vol. VIII at p. 970.)

Parties. Their representation; agents legal advisers and legal representatives. The articles of the Court's Statutes treated below are the first in Title Three "Procedure" of the Statutes. They are dealt with at this point not only for that reason but because, though they are concerned with underlying aspects of all procedure and are therefore relevant to this chapter, they are not directly implemented by the Rules of Procedure with which it is concerned. (Their direct implementation is by Rules comprised in Title One, "Organisation" of the Rules of Procedure. For "agents, legal advisers and legal representatives", see R.P. 32–36 in Chapter 3, "Organiz-ation", *ante*, pp. 206–208.)

E.E.C. St. 17

The States and the institutions of the Community shall be represented before the Court by an agent appointed for each case; the agent may be assisted by a legal adviser who is a practising member of the Bar (*avocat inscrit à un barreau*) of one of the Member States.

E.A.E.C. St. 17

[*Identical with E.E.C. St.* 17.]

E.C.S.C. St. 20

The States and the institutions of the Community shall be represented before the Court by agents appointed for each case; the agent may be assisted by a legal representative who is appropriately qualified in one of the Member States.

Undertakings and all other natural or legal persons must be assisted by a legal representative who is appropriately qualified in one of the Member States.

The agents and legal representatives appearing before the Court shall have the rights and privileges necessary for the independent performance of their duties under conditions to be laid down in rules made by the Court and submitted for the approval of the Council.

The Court shall have, as regards legal representatives who appear before it, the powers normally accorded to Courts of law, under conditions which shall be laid down by the same rules.

University teachers being nationals of Member States, whose law gives them the right of audience shall have the same rights before the Court as are afforded by this Article to legal representatives.

Parties. A party (in the sense of a directly participating litigant) (*"la partie"; "die Partei"; "procesparti"; "la parte"*) before the Court may be one of four kinds:

(i) a Member State of the Community in question;

(ii) an institution of the Community in question;

(iii) a party, other than of the kind in (i) or (ii), who is by virtue of nationality (or presumably, of residence, and possibly of mere presence) within the nexus of legal relationships which is the Community in question (the sense in which "nexus of legal relationships" is here used, is explained in Chapter 1, *ante*, p. 15). A party of this third kind may be: "any natural or legal person" within the nexus of E.E.C.; "any natural or legal person" within the nexus of E.A.E.C.—such may in practice be principally the "undertakings" as defined in E.A.E.C. 196 (see *ante*, p. 36); or the "undertakings" or "associations of undertakings" so defined in E.C.S.C. (see in particular E.C.S.C. 80, *ante*, p. 48) or other natural or legal persons within the nexus of E.C.S.C.

(iv) "any other person" (*semble*, not within the Community nexus) who can substantiate a valid legal interest in making application by way of Request to the Court (see in Chapter 2, "Legality of Acts", comment "Any natural or legal person may, under the same conditions, appeal . . .", *ante*, p. 84) or in being admitted to intervene (as to intervention see *post*, p. 276) or to appear before the Court other than as intervener (*e.g.* as a third party claiming retrial, as to which see Chapter 5, *post*, p. 284) (*Cf.* also Regulation 17, 3(b), in Chapter 1, *ante*, p. 23.)

"Party" is sometimes used in a looser sense than that of a directly participating litigant. For example, R.P. 37 (1) (*post*, p. 220) referring to "as many copies" of every procedural document" as there are parties in the case" includes all those to whom such documents are to be communicated (see "Communication", *post*, p. 215).

Representation. ("Represented" (Eng.) is: *"représenté"; "vertreten"; "vertegenwoordigd"; "rappresentato"*). Representation is obligatory in respect of all written proceedings (by virtue of E.E.C. St. 17, E.A.E.C. St. 17 and E.C.S.C. St. 20, *ante*, p. 21). It is also obligatory in respect of oral argument before the Court (see E.E.C. St. 29, E.A.E.C. St. 30 and E.C.S.C. St. 28 paragraphs two and three, *post*, p. 249). The requirements as to representation of parties of the first two kinds listed in the comment "Parties" (*supra*) are the subject of paragraph one of E.E.C. St. 17, E.A.E.C. St. 17 and E.C.S.C. St. 20 (*supra*). Their distinctive feature is the provision for an "agent" (presumably inspired by the example of the International Court of Justice). Parties listed as the third kind in the comment "Parties" (*supra*) are represented as provided in paragraph 2 of the same Statutes.

A "practising member of the Bar" who either "assists" a party (as provided in paragraph one of the above Statutes) or "represents" one (as provided in paragraph two of the above Statutes) is required by R.P. 38(3) (*post*, p. 221) to deposit with the Registrar "credentials certifying that he is appropriably qualified in one of the Member States." This certificate will normally be issued by the authorities of the Bar to which he belongs. The member of the Bar concerned, to prove the capacity in which he acts before the Court, also requires a second certificate, signed by the Registrar (see R.P. 33(b), *ante*, p. 207, and Instructions to the Registrar, Article 9 *post*, p. 305). This certificate is also usable by the holder in respect of third parties with regard to the rights, privileges and immunities conferred on him (for summary of which see *infra*). An agent requires an official certificate issued by the State or institution which he represents, and a copy of it is furnished immediately to the Registrar by that State or institution (R.P. 33(a), *ante*, p. 207). A Member of the Bar representing a legal person constituted under private law (as to distinction between private law and public law, see in Chapter 2, E.E.C. 181 and equivalents, *ante*, p. 153) and comment "contracts between the Communities and their servants are contracts of public law" in Chapter 2 *ante*, p. 151) must provide written evidence of authority given by an authorized representation of such legal person (see R.P. 38 (5), *post*, p. 221).

Agents, legal advisers, and legal representatives. (*"Agents, conseils, avocats"; "Bevollmächtigte, Beistände, Anwälte"; "gemachtigden, raadslieden, advocaten"; "Agenti, consulenti, avvocati".*) Professors, as specified in E.E.C. St. 17 and equivalents, are legal advisers. They are not entirely on the same footing as agents or legal representatives in respect of the written procedure. Thus, every formal "procedural document" (see "Procedural Document," *post*, p. 216) must be signed by an agent or legal representative (R.P. 37 (1), *post*, p. 220) but, in the oral procedure, an agent, legal adviser, or legal representative (R.P. 58, *post*, p. 251) may plead.

The details of the privileges, immunities and facilities of these in respect of their work before the Court are contained in R.P. 32–36 (*ante*, pp. 206–208). They may be summarized as follows: their utterances and written statements, relating to the action or to the parties, made or produced before the Court or a judicial authority acting on behalf of the Court by virtue of a *"commission rogatoire"* ("letter of request", as to which see Chapter 6, R.P. 109(a), at *post*, p. 299) are privileged. Their papers may not be searched or seized. They are entitled to the exchange of money and to the freedom of movement necessary for fulfilling their task. Their entitlement to these rights is certified as explained in the last sentences of the preceding comment "Representation". These privileges, immunities and facilities are granted solely in the interest of the proceedings before the Court and may be withdrawn by the Court if it is of the opinion that such withdrawal is not contrary to that interest.

A legal adviser or legal representative whose behaviour before the Court, a section, or a judge is incompatible with the dignity of the Court, or who uses his rights to unjustified ends, may be excluded from the proceedings by an order (which see under R.P. 63–68, *post*, pp. 253 *et seq.*) of the Court or the Section, after the Advocate-General has been heard, and the defence of the interested legal adviser or legal representative assured. Such an order takes effect immediately. Professors entitled to plead before the Court are in the same position as agents, legal advisers, and legal representatives. (Free legal aid is available in certain circumstances (see R.P. 76, *post*, p. 264 and S.R.P. Chapter II (Articles 4 and 5) *post*, p. 301).)

In *Firma I. Nold KG* c. *Haute Autorité* (Case 18/57, R. Vol. V at p. 111) the Court overruled an objection as to the validity of the Request brought on the ground that it was signed by a member of the Bar of Frankfurt on Main who had been forbidden by that Bar to practise, though not disbarred. It did so on the ground that the law of the Land Hesse governing the profession of "barrister" and hence the professional status of the legal representative who had signed the Request provides in paragraph 107 (2) that withdrawal of the right to appear at the Bar does not affect the validity of legal acts performed by the "barrister".

Phases of Procedure. The articles of the Court's Statutes (*infra*) are dealt with at this point as are these so far dealt with in this Chapter, because they are not amplified in the Rules of Procedure.

E.E.C. St. 18

The procedure before the Court shall be in two stages: one written and the other oral.

The written procedure shall include communication to the parties, as well as to the institutions of the Community whose decisions are in dispute, of the formal Requests, statements of case, defences, and comments (*requêtes, mémoires, défenses, observations*) and replies (*répliques*), if any, as well as of all supporting documentary evidence and papers or of certified copies thereof.

Such communications shall be made by the Registrar in the sequence and within the time-limits laid down by the rules of procedure.

The oral procedure shall include the reading of the report presented by a judge acting as rapporteur, the hearing by the Court of agents, legal advisers and counsel and of the submissions (*conclusions*) of the advocate-general as well as the hearing, if appropriate, of witnesses and experts.

E.A.E.C. St. 18

[*Identical with E.E.C. St.* 18.]

E.C.S.C. St. 21

The procedure before the Court shall be in two stages: one written and the other oral.

The written procedure shall include communication to the parties, as well as to the institutions of the Community whose decisions are in dispute, of the Requests, statements of case, defences and comments and replies, if any, as well as of all supporting documentary evidence and papers or of certified copies thereof.

Communications shall be made by the Registrar in the sequence and within the time-limits laid down by the rules of procedure.

The oral procedure shall include the reading of the report presented by a Judge acting as Rapporteur and the hearing by the Court of witnesses, experts, agents and legal representatives and of the submissions of the Advocate-General.

The Procedure is both written and oral. An action necessarily passes through the written phase and the oral phase, in that order. If the Court, at the end of the written procedure, exercises its discretion to order a measure by way of "procedure of enquiry" or the "calling of evidence" (*"L'instruction"; "Beweisaufnahme"; "Instructie"; "Istruzione della causa";* R.P. 45–54 *post*, pp. 233–247) this, in effect, constitutes a third phase of procedure between the written and the oral.

"The written procedure shall include . . .". "Communication to the parties, as well as to the institutions of the Community whose decisions are in dispute . . .". See under "Such communications shall be made by the Registrar" (*infra*).

An Institution of the Community, or a Member State, directly a party to an action before the Court, will have communicated to it all necessary "procedural documents" (see "procedural document", *post*, p. 216). But E.E.C. St. 18, E.A.E.C. St. 18, and E.C.S.C. St. 21 require communication of a wide range of documents "to the institutions of the Community whose decisions are in dispute" (*i.e.* in issue between the parties).

An act of an Institution may be the subject of a reference (under E.E.C. and E.A.E.C.) to the Court by a tribunal of a Member State for a preliminary ruling on a point respecting that act in issue before such tribunal, and in that event, though the Institution is not a party to the case, E.E.C. St. 20 and E.A.E.C. St. 21 (which see *post*, p. 293) require the decision of the tribunal of the Member State making the reference to be "notified" to "the Member States and to the Commission, and also to the Council if the act the validity or interpretation of which is in dispute originates from the Council".

Communication is not identical with service (which see, this Chapter *post*, p. 266) or with notification (exemplified in the preceding paragraph) (see also Instructions to the Registrar, Article 3 in Chapter 6, *post*, pp. 302–303). Apart from what is to be found in E.E.C. St. 18, E.A.E.C. St. 18, and E.C.S.C. St. 21 no provisions are made in respect of Communication.

"Such communications shall be made by the Registrar . . .". There is no provision as to the manner or method of communication. Clearly, documents may be held at the Registrar's office at the disposal of the parties to an action who are at liberty to consult them there, as is provided for in respect of reports by experts and reports of oral procedure (R.P. 53 (2), *post*, p. 247). The Registrar may also communicate documents or certified copies of them to the parties through the post. But it should be noted that neither the Statutes nor the Rules of Procedure require parties to annex to the copies of their procedural documents (see "procedural document" *post*, p. 216) copies of the accompanying file. If such copies are necessary it would appear to be incumbent on the Registrar to provide them. (This view seems to be supported by the Instructions to the Registrar, Article 3 (3), *post*, p. 303.)

". . . Requests, statements of case, defences, comments, . . . , replies . . .".   This is not equivalent to a list of "pleadings" (in the meaning of English procedure) in the order in which they are to be served, but a general enumeration of the types of "procedural document" (see next paragraph) likely to be necessary in the course of the written procedure. The statement of case may accompany a request, a defence, a reply, or a further reply, or it may be made by other than one of the parties participating directly in the litigation in certain circumstances (such as those provided for in E.E.C. St. 20, paragraph two, see *post*, p. 293). Comments do not necessarily follow defences and precede replies (E.E.C. St. 20 paragraph two, *loc. cit.*, *supra*, for example, provides for written comments to be made at the same time as statements of case and, like these, to be made not only by the parties who are the directly participating litigants). The "procedural documents" which the parties litigating in an action before the Court are either bound or entitled to deliver, the order in which they must be delivered, and requirements concerning them are specified in R.P. 37 (1–5), 40 and 41 (for text of which see Section I, *post*, pp. 220 *et seq.*). As to the weight given by the Court to statements of case and comments see in Chapter 5, comment on ". . . written statements of case or written comments . . ." *post*, p. 295.

"Procedural document" (*"acte de procédure"*; *"Schriftsatz"*; *"processtuk"*; *"atto di procedura"*).   This is a term for a category of formal act or process, into which category the requests etc., enumerated in the preceding paragraph, certainly fall. The term though used is not, however, strictly defined anywhere in the Rules of Procedure, Statutes or Treaties, though, whatever connotation *"acte de procédure"* may have in the internal legal systems of France, Belgium or Luxembourg, the Rules of Procedure (R.P. 37 (1), *post*, p. 220) limit it to documents drawn up in one of the official languages of the Court signed by the agent or legal adviser of the party concerned. The R.P. do not draw a distinction between *"acte de procédure"* and *"pièce de procédure"*. (*"Pièce"* means "document".)   If *"acte de procédure"* had been used in the R.P. in the wider sense in which it is commonly used, so as to embrace oral acts as well as documentary acts, and *"pièce de procédure"* used by the R.P. for a documentary act only, it might have been preferable. In practice, it is readily appreciated at the Court that oral *"actes"* of the Bench or of the parties' legal representatives are in fact *"actes de procédure"*, but it is unfortunately not technically correct to call them so.

"The oral procedure shall include the reading of the report presented by a judge acting as rapporteur . . .".   This is (in point of time) the second report prepared by the reporting judge. Unlike the "preliminary report" (referred to in R.P. 44 (1), *post*, p. 232), which is directed to the question whether a measure by way of procedure of enquiry or the calling of evidence is necessary, it is, of course, not secret. It initiates the oral procedure. The Statutes provide for "the reading" of the report.

In practice this report is in duplicated typescript and made available to the judges and to the parties and their legal representatives at the latest by the day preceding that fixed for the hearing. The reading aloud of the report during the hearing may normally be dispensed with. On the day of the hearing copies of the report are available (together with notices intended primarily for the press) to the press and members of the public, at the entrance to the Court. (A typical heading is *"Affaires Nos.* 24–63 et 52–63.

Rapport presenté conformément à l'article 21 *Protocole sur le Statut de la Cour de la C.E.C.A.".* At the end of the report appear the words *"Luxembourg, le* 10 *octobre* 1963, *Louis DELVAUX, Juge Rapporteur."*)

The report provides a compact summing up of the development of the case to the end of the written procedure and, after setting out the parties, their legal advisers, addresses for service, and the relief sought, comprises (normally) four parts devoted to 1. The facts; 2. The submissions of the parties; 3. The legal arguments of the parties, and 4. The procedure (to date).

It may be noted that some reporting judges entitle their report "Report for the hearing" (*"Rapport d'audience"; Sitzungsbericht "Rapport ter terechtzittung"; Relazione d'Udienza*). The hearing here referred to is part of the oral procedure, which a hearing of witnesses, being part of the "procedure of enquiry" is not. In a case (18/63, 10 and 11 December 1963) where the hearing of witnesses was followed by the beginning of the oral procedure on the next day, the *"Rapport d'Audience"* was presented at the beginning of the second day (*i.e.* made publicly available in duplicated typewritten form on that day).

Report in respect of a "preliminary point of procedure". Where a party to an action has claimed, by way of what is termed "a preliminary point of procedure" (see R.P. 91, *post*, pp. 274–275), that the Court should rule on an "objection" or "some other preliminary point" without entering into the full inquiry into the main issues, the President fixes the time within which the other party may present in writing its grounds and submissions. Thereafter the procedure is oral, unless the Court otherwise determines (R.P. 91 (2) and (3), *post*, p. 275). Although neither the Statutes nor the Rules of Procedure require a report by the reporting judge in these circumstances, it is the practice of the Court for a report to be furnished, in the same way as if the substance of the main action were being dealt with. (The example inthe preceding paragraph of a typical heading to a Report, was in respect of an "objection of inadmissibility", see "admissibility" *post*, pp. 225–226.)

"...The hearing...of agents, legal advisers, and legal representatives". See Agents, legal advisers and legal representatives (*ante*, p. 213). As to witnesses see under E.E.C. St. 23 (*post*, pp. 235 *et seq.*).

"The submissions of the Advocate General". See Chapter 3, "Reasoned Submissions", *ante*, p. 190.

II. WRITTEN PROCEDURE (R.P. 37–44)

(*De la procédure écrite; schriftliches Verfahren; Van de schriftelijke behandeling; Della fase scritta*)

E.E.C. St. 19

Proceedings shall be instituted before the Court by a formal Request addressed to the Registrar. The Request shall contain the name and the *"domicile"* of the plaintiff and the status of the signatory, the name of the party against whom the Request is lodged, the subject matter of the dispute, the relief sought and a short summary of the main arguments on which the petition is based.

The formal Request shall be accompanied, where appropriate, by the act (*acte*) the annulment of which is sought or, in the case mentioned in Article 175 of this Treaty, by documentary evidence of the date on which an institution referred to in that Article was called upon to act. If these documents are not attached to the Request, the Registrar shall ask the party concerned to produce them within a reasonable period; in that case the rights of the party shall not lapse even if such documents are produced after the expiry of the time-limit set for the bringing of proceedings.

E.A.E.C. St. 19

[*Identical with E.E.C. St. 19, except that the second paragraph is related to E.A.E.C. 148.*]

E.C.S.C. St. 22

A matter shall be brought before the Court by a Request addressed to the Registrar. The Request shall contain the name and the residence of the party and the description of the signatory, the subject matter of the dispute, the submissions and a short summary of the grounds of fact and of law on which the application is based.

The Request shall be accompanied, where appropriate, by the decision the annulment of which is sought or, in the case of an appeal against an implied decision, by documentary evidence of the date of lodging of the request for action. If these documents are not attached to the Request, the Registrar shall ask the party concerned to produce them within a reasonable period, in that event the rights of the party shall not lapse even if such documents are produced after the expiry of the time-limit set for the bringing of proceedings.

"**A matter shall be brought before the Court by a Request addressed to the Registrar**". The Request (*"Requête"; "Klageschrift"; "Verzoekschrift"; "Istanza"*) originates the action.

Deposit with the Registrar of a Request in due form (as to which see (R.P. 38, paragraph 1 (a)–(e). "The requirements as to content of the request", *post*, p. 221) originates the action, provided the Court *prima facie* has jurisdiction. Preliminary matters concerning the form of the Request and the decision that *prima facie* the Court has jurisdiction are the responsibility of the Registrar.

"**The quality of the signatory (etc.)**". In practice, some correspondence may ensue between the Registrar and the petitioner to regularize the Request, as for example, where it is in due form except that it has not been signed by a lawyer admissible to practice before the Court and representing the petitioner. It happens in practice also, that petitions are addressed to the Court under the mistaken belief that it is also the European Court of Human Rights, so that the Registrar must return the petition explaining that the Court has no jurisdiction. (More subtle arguments regarding the Court's jurisdiction or competence may, of course, arise during the course of an action before the Court, but at this stage the concern, which is that of the Registrar only, is with *prima facie* jurisdiction). Petitions are in practice not infrequently received by the Registrar which are unacceptable because they appear to be the work of some one insane.

It "**shall be accompanied, where appropriate, by the (documentary) act** (*l'acte; "Akt"; "akte"; "atto"*) **the annulment of which is sought . . .**". This is an implicit reference to E.E.C. 173, E.A.E.C. 146 and E.C.S.C. 33 which make provision for supervision by the Court of the legality of certain acts of the Council and Commission of E.E.C. and E.A.E.C. or of the High Authority of E.C.S.C., and for their annulment on specified grounds (as to which see Chapter 2, "Legality of Acts", *ante*, p. 93; and as to acts of the above mentioned Institutions see respectively, in Chapter 1, "Council" and "Commission" under both E.E.C. and E.A.E.C. and "High Authority" under E.C.S.C. *ante*, pp. 20, 21, 40, 42, and p. 51).

"**Or . . . in the case mentioned in E.E.C. 175.** (The E.A.E.C. equivalent is 148 and that of E.C.S.C. is 35, *ante*, pp..119–120.)

"**Documentary evidence of the date on which an institution . . . was called upon to act . . .**". This is an express reference to the Treaty provision whereby the Council or Commission of E.E.C. or E.A.E.C., or the High Authority of E.C.S.C. may be proceeded against before the Court on the ground that, in violation of the Treaty in question, it has failed to act (as to which see Chapter 2, "Failure to Act", *ante*, p. 119, and, as to the acts concerned, references as in preceding paragraphs of this comment).

"**If these documents are not annexed to the Request . . .**". Or, in general, if the Request does not comply with the requirements of E.E.C. St. 19 (and also of R.P. 38 (2–6), which see *post*, p. 221) as to content, annexures and certain formal conditions, it may, on the invitation of the Registrar be "regularised" (R.P. 38 (7), *post*, p. 222).

"**Where regularisation is effected after the time-limit set for the bringing of proceedings**". This is two months, in the case of a claim under E.E.C. 173 and its equivalents in the other Treaties, "dating as the case may be, either from the publication of the measure concerned or from its notification to the complainant or, in default of this, from the day on which the latter learned of the said measure" (E.E.C. 173, E.A.E.C. 146 and E.C.S.C. 33 in Chapter 2, "Legality of Act", *ante*, p. 83). In the case of a claim under E.E.C. 175 and its equivalents in the other Treaties, it is two months from the failure of the Institution "to make its attitude clear" within two months of being "called upon to act", a total of four months from its being so called upon (E.E.C. 175, E.A.E.C. 148, E.C.S.C. 35 in Chapter 2, "Failure of Act", *ante*, p. 119.)

If the necessary documents are produced within the reasonable period determined by the Registrar, even though after the time limit for the bringing of proceedings, the applicant's rights do not lapse. (See R.P. 38 (7), *post*, p. 222 and Instructions to the Registrar, 5 (1), *post*, p. 303.)

At this stage, therefore, Requests are handled very much in an administrative manner, but when these preliminaries, if any, are completed the action is, in law, originated.

The "admissibility" of the claim presented in the Request depends in the first place on the applicant possessing the necessary "interest" and "quality" and the claim may be finally defeated at an early stage if either of these is shown to be absent. These aspects are not considered by the Registrar when the Request is deposited. "Admissibility" may be challenged on other grounds and at various stages of the action and by different procedural methods. "Interest" and "quality" are dealt with, together with the other aspects of "admissibility" (*post*, pp. 225–226).

R.P. 37

Paragraph 1

The original of every procedural document shall be signed by the agent or legal representative of the party concerned.

It shall be submitted with two copies for the Court and as many copies as there are parties in the case. These copies shall be certified by the party submitting them.

Paragraph 2

Within such time as is specified by the Court, Institutions shall furthermore produce translations of all procedural documents in the other official languages. The second subparagraph of the last preceding paragraph shall apply.

Paragraph 3

Every procedural document shall be dated. For the purpose of calculating time limits, only the date of lodging with the office of the Registrar of the Court shall be taken into consideration.

Paragraph 4

Every procedural document shall have annexed to it a file containing the supporting exhibits and documents, together with a schedule of these exhibits and documents.

Paragraph 5

If, by reason of the length of an exhibit or document, extracts only are annexed to the procedural document, then the exhibit or document in its entirety, or a complete copy thereof, shall be lodged with the Office of the Registrar.

"(1) The original of every procedural document ...". As to procedural documents in general see ". . . Requests, statements of case, defences, comments . . . replies . . ." (*ante*, p. 216).

"(4) Every procedural document shall have annexed to it a file containing the supporting exhibits and documents ...". Instructions to the Registrar, Article 14, (*post*, p. 306) appears to show that annexures to a procedural document may be delivered to the Registrar at a different moment of time from the procedural document itself.

Technical rules as to the evidential value (and consequent admissibility) of documents, such as are common in the national legal systems of the original six Member States of the Communities, are entirely absent from the Statutes, Treaties and Rules of Procedure, (except that the Registrar's record of a deposition of a witness or of a Court sitting, or recording in the register and noting of a procedural document, or similar, is expressed to constitute an "official record" ("*acte authentique*", "*öffentliche Urkunde*"; "*authenticke akte*"; "*atto autentico*";) (see under R.P. 47 (6) *post*, p. 243; under R.P. 53, *post*,

p. 247 and under R.P. 62 *post*, p. 252; also Chapter 3 under R.P. 15, *ante*, p. 195). While there is thus no legal limit to the evidence admissible, the forms in which proof may be established are precisely defined (see under "Procedure of Enquiry", R.P. 45 (2), *post*, pp. 234 *et seq.*).

The onus of proof falls on the party alleging a fact. The making of an offer of proof (as required by R.P. 38 (1) (e) *infra* and R.P. 40 (1) (d), *post*, p. 226) is in itself an implicit recognition of that position.

R.P. 38

Paragraph 1

The Request referred to in Articles 22 of the E.C.S.C and 19 of the E.E.C. and E.A.E.C. Statutes shall contain:

(*a*) the name and permanent address of the applicant,

(*b*) the description of the party against whom the Request is directed,

(*c*) the subject matter '*objet du litige*' of the dispute and a short summary of the grounds of fact and of law on which the application is based,

(*d*) the applicant's submissions,

(*e*) means of proof available where appropriate.

Paragraph 2

For procedural purposes, the Request shall specify an address for service in the town where the Court has its seat. It shall also indicate the name of the person who has been authorised to receive service of documents and who has agreed to do so.

Paragraph 3

The legal representative assisting or representing a party shall be required to submit credentials to the Office of the Registrar, certifying that he is appropriately qualified in one of the Member States.

Paragraph 4

The Request shall be accompanied, if necessary, by the exhibits specified in Article 22, Second Paragraph of the E.C.S.C. Statute and in Article 19, Second Paragraph of the E.E.C. and E.A.E.C. Statutes.

Paragraph 5

If the applicant is a legal person constituted under private law (as understood in the Communities) it shall attach to its request:

(*a*) its statutes;

(*b*) proof that the authority granted to its legal representative has been properly conferred by a representative authorised to grant it.

Paragraph 6

Requests submitted under Articles 42 and 89 of the E.C.S.C. Treaty, Articles 181 and 182 of the E.E.C. Treaty and Articles 153 and 154 of the E.A.E.C. Treaty shall be accompanied, as the case may be, by a copy of the clause conferring jurisdiction contained in the contract entered into by the Communities or on their behalf, or by a copy of the special agreement reached between the Member States concerned.

Paragraph 7

If the Request does not comply with the conditions enumerated in Paragraph 2 to 6 of this present Article, then the Registrar shall set the applicant a reasonable period in which to regularise the Request or to produce the exhibits mentioned above. Failing such regularisation or production within the period allowed, the Court shall decide after the Advocate General has been heard, whether as a result of the non-compliance with these conditions it must refuse to entertain the request as being bad in form.

Paragraph 1 (a)–(e). These requirements as to content of the Request duplicate as to (*a*)–(*d*) those laid down in E.E.C. St. 19 and equivalents (*ante*, pp. 217–218). A statement of the relief sought customarily figures in (*d*) "the applicant's submissions". Requirement (*e*), "means of proof available where appropriate", is additional to the requirements in the Statutes. There are thus five requirements in all as to the content of the Request in respect of the substance of the action. To these must be added, for procedural purposes (R.P. 38 (2) *ante*, p. 221) address for service in the town where the Court has its seat. R.P. 38 (5) (*ante*, p. 221) requires the Request to have certain documents annexed where the applicant is a legal person constituted under private law. (As to distinction between private law and public law see under E.E.C. 181 and equivalents in Chapter 2, *ante*, p. 153.) In *Meroni & Co. Erba Meroni & Co. Milan* c. *Haute Autorité* (Consolidated Cases 46 and 47/59 R. Vol. VIII at p. 801–2) the Court stated:

"In accordance with E.C.S.C. St. 22 and R.P. 38 (1) the request must indicate the object of the action and contain the submissions of the applicant. It is thus incumbent on the applicant to indicate the precise facts on which he relies to justify his claim and to formulate his submissions in an unequivocal manner. Failing such precision the Court would risk either ruling *ultra petita* or else omitting to rule on a count in the submissions. Moreover, failing such precision the right of the defendant to have to reply only to facts explicitly defined, and to have to refute only clear and precise allegations, would be disregarded.

In the present case the applicants have not complied with these duties, although the Court, during the oral procedure and in its order concerning the re-opening of the oral procedure, invited them to do so. As far as the facts are concerned on which they wish to base their claim, the applicants have restricted themselves to placing on the file a number of Parliamentary documents and to referring during the oral procedure to all the facts and arguments contained therein. But they have refrained from stating exactly what illegal elements, pointed out in these documents, constitute negligence, on the part of the competent services of the Community, which has caused them injury. If the Court were to hold admissible the contentions of the applicants made with such a lack of precision, it would deprive the defendant of a large part of the possibilities provided by the Rules of Procedure for it to present its defence with full awareness of what it was doing . . . ."

In *Société Fives Lille Cail et autres* c. *Haute Autorité* (Consolidated Cases 19, 19, 21/60, 2 & 3/61, R. Vol. VII at p. 588) the Court stated:

The defendant contends that the text of the Request does not, for lack of precision, make it possible to understand the content or the aim of the charge of "ultra vires" and of "infringement of the rules of law relating to the implementation of the Treaty" which might be capable of having as a consequence the annulment of the decision sought to be upset. Thus the imperative rules of E.C.S.C. St. 22 together with those of R.P. 38 laying down that the Request originating on action must contain "a short summary of the grounds of fact and of law on which the application is based", are said to have been disregarded.

It does not appear clearly from an examination of the contentions of the High Authority whether it intended to criticize, from the point of view of form, both the Requests in cases 2 and 3/61 and those in Cases 19 and 21/60. It is, however, incumbent on the Court to examine this question of its own initiative (*ex officio*) since the provisions governing the form of Requests do not merely affect the interest of the parties, but also the possibility for the Court to exercise its jurisdictional control.

As to the terms of the Requests, if it must be allowed that the grounds of law as they are couched in the Requests need not adhere strictly to the terminology and order of E.C.S.C. 33 paragraph 1, the presentation of these grounds in terms of their substance rather than by their qualification in law can suffice, provided nevertheless that it appears adequately from the Request which of the grounds set out in the Treaty is invoked. The merely abstract statement of grounds in the Request does not satisfy the requirements of the Statute and the Rules of Procedure. The terms 'short summary of the grounds of fact and law' used in the text of these, mean that the Request must state explicitly in what the ground consists, upon which the Request is based. The charge invoked must be firmly rested on the facts set forth. Such is not the case here. In fact, the applicants have restricted themselves to reproaching the High Authority with *ultra vires* (*excès de pouvoir*) and infringement of the rules relating to the implementation of the Treaty, without defining what constituted *ultra vires*, a general expression which may comprise all the grounds for origination of an action for annulment provided for in Article 33, and, moreover, without specifying the rule of law the infringement of which by the High Authority would justify an action at the Court. To refer to an undertaking in respect of the applicants and to an assurance given to them by the O.C.C.F. (the Joint Office of Scrap Consumers) or the U.C.F.F. (Union of French Scrap Consumers) on the occasion of the conclusion of deals in scrap, does not reveal an impersonal and general rule of law the infringement of which alone can permit recourse to the Court's jurisdiction to annul. It is only in the Reply that the applicants define the rule of law said to be infringed as the general principle governing the lawfulness of the cancellation of acts of the administration, a principle 'forming part of the body of rules relating to the implementation of the Treaty'. The cause for annulment thus stated had not been made clear either directly or by implication in the Requests originating the action. It constitutes, not an elaboration of a ground there set out, but an entirely new ground. The reference to it is out of time and, on that account, the Requests must be declared inadmissible."

The Court has overruled an objection to a Request signed by a German barrister (Rechtsanwalt) forbidden to practice, though not disbarred, by the Bar of Frankfurt on Main to which he belonged (see case 18/57 under "agents, legal advisers and legal advisers and legal representatives", *ante,* p. 214).

". . . Grounds of fact and of law . . ." (c) *("moyens; "Klagegründe";* *"aangevoerde middelen"; "motivi").* The requirement that the Request must contain a summary of these, duplicates the requirement of E.C.C. St. 19 and equivalents (see *ante,* p. 217). Grounds are the elements of fact and of law without which no reasonable (and reasoned) claim could be set up. In respect of the claim they afford the essential support, or what is termed in French its *"cause",* meaning its foundation in law (compare "cause of action" in English usage). Grounds thus provide the basis of the "argument" which in turn enables the development of the "submissions" *("conclusions"; "Anträge"; "conclusies"; "conclusioni").* Grounds, argument and submissions should be carefully distinguished. The last named contain two elements: the deductions from the grounds and argument, together with the decision it is submitted the Court should make (the "relief sought"). (Somewhat different in character are the submissions of the Advocate General, judicial in essence, and covering all aspects of the case, see Chapter 3, *ante,* p. 190). The distinction between grounds and argument is essential because, although the introduction of fresh grounds, once the Request and Defence are delivered, is severely restricted, new arguments are permitted. (See comment "fresh grounds" under R.P. 42 (2), *post,* p. 229.) Unfortunately, in the four original official languages the distinction, linguistically speaking, cannot always be clearly made (reference should be made to comment on *"(d)* the arguments of fact and law which are relied upon . . ." under R.P. 40 (1) and the comparative linguistic table therein contained, *post,* pp. 227–228). Compare also in Chapter 3 under R.P. 27 (3)" . . . opinion giving his grounds therefor *(ante,* p. 203).

"The submissions of the applicant" (d). In *Rudolf Pieter Marie Fiddelaar* c. *Commission C.E.E.* (Case 44/59 R. Vol. VI (11) at p. 1093) the Court stated:

" . . . According to R.P. 38 (1) (d) the submissions of the applicant must be contained in the Request. The submission referred to [earlier in the judgment—*author*] was presented for the first time in the written observations of the applicant in relation to the procedure of enquiry ordered by the Court on 20th June 1960. It is not contained by implication in the submissions formulated in the Request. This submission must therefore be considered to have been made too late, and because of that, to be inadmissible."

Exhibits accompanying the Request may be those specified in R.P. 38 (4) or (6) as the case may be. (Note the requirement of R.P. 37 (4), *ante,* p. 220 as to the file of supporting exhibits and documents to be annexed to every procedural document. Instructions to the Registrar Article 14 (*post,* p. 306) appear to suggest that annexures to a procedural document may be delivered to the Registrar at a different moment of time from the procedural document itself.)

Credentials of the legal representative assisting or representing a party are required by R.P. 38 (3) *(ante,* p. 221) to be submitted to the Office of the Registrar.

The form of the Request, according to custom but not compulsorily, is that of an address to the President and members of the Court.

Paragraph 6 "Contract entered into by the Communities". The English version omits reference to the fact that the contract may be of either public law *("contrat de droit public ou privé"; "des . . . öffentlichrechtlichen* *oder privatrechtlichen Vertrages"; "publiekrechtelijke of privatrechtelijke overeenkomst"; "contratto di diritto pubblico o privato"*). As to distinction between public law and private law, see *ante*, p. 153).

Paragraph 7 Regularization of the Request. Where this is not in accordance with R.P. 2–6, regularization may be made within "a reasonable period" determined by the Registrar. Where documents that should have accompanied the Request are accordingly produced within the "reasonable period", the rights of the applicant do not lapse even if their production occurs after the time limit set by the Treaties for the bringing of an application (see comment "Where regularisation is effected after the time limit", etc. *ante*, p. 219). But failure to produce such documents within the reasonable period may result in the formal inadmissibility (and therefore the lapse) of the Request (see comment "has agreed to entertain it" under R.P. 39, *infra*) being so decided by the Court after hearing the Advocate General. The Registrar's duties in respect of R.P. 38 (7) are specified in Instructions to the Registrar, 5 (1) (*post*, pp. 303–304).

R.P. 39

The Request shall be served on the defending party. In the case provided for in Paragraph 7 of the preceding Article, service shall be affected as soon as the request has been regularised or the Court has agreed to entertain it having regard to the formal requirements set out in the preceding Article.

Service of the request. Service may be registered post or by hand against receipt. (As to detailed requirements of service see R.P. 79, *post*, p. 266). "Service" is not "communication" or "notification"—see under "the written procedure shall include", *ante*, p. 215.

". . . Has agreed to entertain it . . .". "Admit it" would have been a preferable translation for *"aura admis la recevabilité"; ". . . Festellung, dazz . . . nicht . . . unzulässig ist"; ". . . ontvankelijk heeft geoordeeld"; "ne avra riconosciuto la ricevibilità".* The reason is that *"Recevabilité", "Zulässigkeit", "Ontvankelijkheid",* and *"Ricevibilità"* are terms of art, translated elsewhere in the Rules and Treaties as "admissibility". [In Italian, *"proponibilità"* is not identical with *"ricevibilità"*—see case 3/54 R. Vol. 1 at pp. 132–2.]

The concern of the Court with admissibility under R.P. 39 is limited to formal admissibility "having regard to the formal requirements set out in the preceding Article". When it pronounces on formal admissibility it assumes a responsibility which is in the first place that of the Registrar under R.P. 38 (and 39).

Admissibility in the substantive sense can be ruled upon only by the Court. The importance of admissibility in the case law of the Court is apparent from the fact that most of the Court's decisions, after setting out the facts and the arguments of the parties, devote the first part of the Court's examination of the law to the question of admissibility, not necessarily because it has been put in issue by one of the parties but because the Court of its own motion holds it necessary to do so. Admissibility may be a question of the necessary "interest" and "quality" being present in the applicant. If either of them is not present the application may be finally defeated at an early stage. But an application may be admissible in the sense that the necessary characteristics are present in the applicant to entitle him to present it, and yet be defeated on the ground of inadmissibility because the treaty Articles on which it is sought to base the application are held not to provide the necessary basis for it.

9

Interest and admissibility. In *Chambre Syndicale de la Sidérurgie de l'Est de la France et autres* c. *Haute Autorité* (Consolidated Cases 24, 34/58 R. Vol. VI (ii) at p. 598) the Court stated:

". . . the defendant argues that the claim is not admissible (as to its first and third counts) for lack of interest; that, since all the undertakings in the Community have an interest in seeing an end put as soon as possible to special internal tariff measures that are discriminatory in their nature, the applicants could not maintain that their personal position was different from that of the generality of iron and steel undertakings of the Community.

The applicants and the German undertakings which benefit from the tariff schedules that are the concern of this action are in competition, because they are engaged in the same productive activity, sell the same products, and obtain their supplies of mineral combustibles from the same mines. Consequently the decision it is sought to upset and which permits the continuance of reduced tariffs—which might have an effect on this competition—is of concern to the applicant undertakings in the sense of article 33, paragraph 2" (of E.C.S.C.).

Quality and admissibility. In *Groupement des Industries Sidérurgiques Luxembourgeoises* c. *Haute Autorité* (Consolidated Cases 7 and 9/54 R. Vol. II at pp. 83–88) the Court ruled concerning the quality of the applicant to "bring to the attention" of the High Authority, under E.C.S.C. 35 paragraph 1, its failure to act, and, on its continuing so to fail to act, to apply to the Court by Request for a ruling on the substance of the matter.

Capacity is distinct from quality. Where the capacity of a party to apply by Request is disputed, capacity will be determined by the Court on the basis of the internal law of the State which is the personal law of the applicant. Thus basing itself on German law, the Court held in *Firma I. Nold* c. *Haute Autorité* (Case 18/57 R. Vol. V p. 110) that a German company, of the type known as *"Kommanditgesellschaft"*, in liquidation, had the necessary capacity to maintain a suit at the Court, though not having a "member with unlimited liability" (*"unbeshränkt haftender Gesellschafter"*) and despite the fact the authority (mandate) to take proceedings was not conferred in writing (on the former "member with unlimited liability" who did in fact bring the proceedings).

Objection of inadmissibility. This is one example of a so-called preliminary point of procedure (see R.P. 91, *post*, pp. 274–275). If successfully raised such an Objection will result in the whole action being disposed of without full inquiry into the issues in the main action. But inadmissibility may be alleged by way of defence in the ordinary manner to an application, without recourse to the special procedure by way of Objection.

R.P. 40

Paragraph 1

During the month following service of the Request, the defending party shall submit a statement of defence, containing:

(*a*) the name and permanent address of the defending party;

(*b*) the arguments of fact and of law which are relied upon;

(*c*) the submissions of the defending party;

(*d*) means of proof available;

The provisions of Article 38 paragraphs 2 to 5 of these Rules shall apply.
Paragraph 2
The time limit allowed by the preceding paragraph may be extended by the President at the defending party's request and for good cause shown.

Acts of procedure subsequent to the Request. See, generally, comment on "... Requests, statements of case, defences, comments ... replies ...", *ante*, p. 216.
Defence. The statement of defence must be submitted within one month from service of the Request (R.P. 40 (1)), though this time may be extended by the President (R.P. 40 (2)).

"... (b) the arguments of fact and law which are relied upon".
(*"Les arguments de fait et de droit invoqués"; "die tatsächliche and rechtliche Begründung"; "de aangevoerde gronden, zowel feitelijk als rechtens"; "gli argomenti di fatto e di diritto invocati"*). This wording should be compared with that in R.P. 38 (1) (c), *ante*, p. 221. The word "arguments" appears here in the French, Italian and English text when the German and Netherlands versions (though not identical with the wording of the respective language in R.P. 38 (1) (c)) clearly refer to "grounds". The Netherlands version, indeed, here uses "*gronden*" and not "*middelen*" which appears in R.P. 38 (1) (c). The importance of the distinction between "grounds" and "argument" is relevant however, to steps in procedure *following* delivery of defence (see comment "fresh grounds" under R.P. 42 (2), *post*, p. 229 and case 2/54 therein cited). For the purposes of the latter, moreover, difficulties resulting from the apparent contradiction in wording between the original official languages, may be overcome in practice by the circumstance that an argument can only be developed on the basis of grounds. (See in particular comment "fresh grounds" under R.P. 42 (2) *post*, p. 229) and under R.P. 38 (c), comment " ... grounds of fact and of law ..." *ante*, p. 224.)

Grounds, arguments and reasoning. Besides the differences between grounds and arguments a further related concept requires to be distinguished, that is, reasoning (for example the reasoning of the Court that is required to figure in any judgment or the reasoning of the Judge expressing his opinion with a view to the collective formulation of a judgment). In respect of the three concepts (grounds, arguments, and reasoning) differing shades of meaning as between the four original languages have been acquired by words of identical origin. Alternatively, words of different origin have become accepted, in some languages, to express differences of concepts referred to in other languages by words of the same origin. This explains the choice of wording that has been made in four of the Rules of Procedure tabulated below.

	English	French	German	Netherlands	Italian
R.P. 27 (3)	Opinion (of a judge) giving his grounds therefor.	*Opinion en la motivant*	*begründete Auffassung*	*gevoelen met redenen omkleed*	*parere motivato*
R.P. 38 (1)	Grounds of fact and law.	*moyens*	*Klagegründe*	*middelen*	*motivi*

	English	French	German	Netherlands	Italian
R.P. 40	arguments of fact and of law	*arguments de fait et de droit*	*tatsächliche and rechtliche Begründung*	*Gronden zowel feitelijk als rechtens*	*argomenti di fatto o di diritto*
R.P. 63	grounds (in the sense of *reasoning*, author. Compare E.E.C. 190 and equivalents for reasoned decision of administrative bodies (*ante*, pp. 26, 46, 100). See for comparison wording of R.P. 76 *post*, p. 264 and of E.E.C. St. 33 and equivalents (*post*, p. 256)	*motivation*	*Entscheidungs-gründe*	*rechtsover-wegingen*	*motivazione*

(Among other points brought out by the above table may be noted: (i) the difficulty of expressing in Italian the distinction between grounds and reasoning (*motivi, motivazione*) and the confusion that may at first sight be caused by the use in French of apparently the same word for reasoning (*motivation*) as the Italian, though different words, in these two languages, are used for grounds (*moyens, motivi*); (ii) the Netherlands expressions differ in their origin for each of the three concepts (*middelen, gronden, rechtsover-wegingen*); (iii) in the German the same word (*grund*) is employed, with qualifying terms to express the precise concept.

"... (c) the submissions of the defending party ...". See "sub-missions" in comment "grounds of fact and of law ...." under R.P. 38 (c), *ante*, p. 224.

"The provisions of R.P. 38 (2–5) shall apply" (see *ante*, p. 221). These provisions are concerned with address for service, the credentials of the legal representative, the documents to accompany the Defence and the Statutes (and authority of legal representative) of a legal person constituted under private law.

All available arguments must be advanced together in the Defence, whether they be an "objection" ("*exception*"; "*Prozesshindernde Einrede*"; "*exceptie*"; "*eccezione*") on grounds of lack of jurisdiction of the Court, or of procedural irregularities (errors as to form or time-limits, etc.) or whether they be arguments on the main issue. But the defendant is not obliged to have recourse to the Special Procedure for objections and other preliminary points of procedure, provided by R.P. 91–92 (see Chapter 5, "Preliminary Points of Procedure", *post*, pp. 274 *et seq.*).

Judgment by default. This may be given if the defendant fails to deliver a statement of defence; though prior to giving judgment by default the Court is required to take certain steps (as to which see Chapter 5, "Judgment by Default and Re-trial", R.P. 94, *post*, p. 280 *et* p. 282).

R.P. 41

Paragraph 1

The request and the statement of defence may be supplemented by a reply from the applicant and by a further reply from the defending party.

Paragraph 2

The President shall fix a date by which these procedural documents shall be submitted.

Reply and further reply. These are required (R.P. 41(2)) to be delivered within the time limit fixed by the President of the Court. This time limit may be extended by the President (by virtue of R.P. 82, *post*, p. 269). The party concerned may waive his right of presenting a reply or further reply (by virtue of R.P. 44(1) (b), *post*, p. 232). The reply and further reply enable the parties to answer each other with more precise or complete explanations, and they therefore also permit the development of the grounds ("*moyens*") formulated in the request and defence, though in that respect only, without making it possible for the grounds ("*moyens*") to be added to, or opinions completed. This comment on reply and further reply is continued under R.P. 42, *infra*.

R.P. 42

Paragraph 1

The parties may also offer means of proof in the reply and in the further reply in support of their arguments. Reason shall be given for the delay in offering them.

Paragraph 2

The submission of fresh grounds of fact and of law during the proceedings shall be prohibited unless these grounds are based upon points of law and of fact which have been raised during the written procedure.

If, in the course of the written procedure, one of the parties raises a fresh ground as mentioned in the preceding paragraph, the President may, upon expiry of the normal procedural time limits, upon the report of the Judge acting as Rapporteur and after hearing the Advocate General, set the other party a time limit within which to reply thereto.

The decision on the admissibility of such ground shall be reserved until the final judgment.

"(1) . . . Means of proof". Means of proof additional to those offered in the request (by virtue of R.P. 38(1) (e), *ante*, p. 221) and in the statement of defence (by virtue of R.P. 40(1) (d), *ante*, p. 226) may be offered "in support of the arguments" in the reply and further reply. But since the proper place for the offer of means of proof is with the request or statement of defence, R.P. 42(2) requires reasons to be given for the delay in not presenting them until reply or further reply.

"(2) fresh grounds of fact and law". These are in general prohibited unless based on points of law and of fact which have been raised during the written procedure. This appears to mean that such points, on which fresh grounds are based, can only be such as are raised, for the first time, at some stage later than the request but not later than the further reply. (In the original rule (R.P. 29(3) now rescinded) of the Coal and Steel Community Court, fresh grounds were not permitted to be raised after delivery of the request. Thus in *Gouvernment de la République Italienne* c. *Haute Autorité* (case 2/54, R. Vol. I, pp. 73 *et seq.*) the High Authority, in its further reply asked the Court (p. 82, *loc. cit.*) "to declare inadmissible, if need be, in accordance with article 20 (3) of the Rules of Procedure, the fresh grounds contained in the reply." The Court held in one particular, however, that what had been advanced in the Reply was not a fresh ground, but "an argument, advanced in support of the ground based on infringement of the Treaty, put forward originally in the request, which could not be declared inadmissible" (*loc. cit.*, p. 99). Where, in the same case, a fresh ground (insufficiency of the reasoning ("*motivation*") of the High Authority's decisions sought to be invalidated) was not raised until the reply, the Court declared it inadmissible (*loc. cit.*, p. 100, paragraph 8). (See under R.P. 40 "(b) the arguments of fact and law which are relied upon", *ante*, p. 227). (Further cases on admissibility of fresh grounds, and the distinction between them and arguments, are *Société des Charbonnages de Beeringen et autres.* c. *Haute Autorité* (Case 9/55 R. Vol. II p. 323 at p. 352; *Firma 1. Nold K.G. etc.* c. *Haute Autorité*, Case 18/57 R. Vol. V, p. 89 at p. 114); *Hamborner Bergbau A.G. et autres.* c. *Haute Autorité*, (Consolidated cases 41 and 50/59 R. Vol. VI p. 989, submissions of Advocate General at p. 1029); in *Compagnie des Hauts Fourneaux de Chasse* c. *Haute Autorité*, (Case 2/57 R. Vol. IV p. 129) the Court stated (at p. 146 *loc. cit.*):

"It is necessary to distinguish between the introduction of fresh grounds during the procedure, on the one hand, and the introduction of new arguments on the other. In the present case the Court considers that the applicant has not introduced fresh grounds [but] has simply developed those contained in the Request by resorting to a number of arguments some of which were presented for the first time in the Reply."

In these circumstances there is nothing to prevent the Court examining them; in *Société Commerciale Antoine Vloebergs S.A.* c. *Haute Autorité* (Consolidated cases 9 and 12/60 R. Vol. VII p. 391) the Court held that arguments adduced, for example, to show the existence of a wrongful act or default in the performance of the Community functions ("*faute de service*") may be completed and developed in the course of the procedure.

E.E.C. St. 21

The Court may require the parties to produce all documents and to supply all information which the Court considers desirable. In case of refusal, the Court shall take judicial notice thereof.

The Court may also request Member States and institutions not being parties to the case to supply all information which the Court considers necessary for the proceedings.

E.A.E.C. St. 22

[*Identical with E.E.C. St.* 21.]

E.C.S.C. St. 24

The Court may request the parties, and their representatives or agents, as well as the Governments of Member States, to produce all documents and to supply all information which the Court considers desirable. In case of refusal, the Court shall take formal notice thereof.

The Court's power to order (*"demander"; "verlangen"; "versoeken"; "richiedere"*) the parties (and in E.C.S.C. St. their agents and legal representatives, and also the Governments of Member States) to produce documents or to supply information it considers desirable, as well as its power in E.E.C. and E.A.E.C. to request Member States or Institutions not parties to the action to supply information, extends to all phases of procedure.

The Court takes notice of refusal by any party to the action to comply with such an order. (There is no example of such a refusal ever having been made. But it is to be assumed that in "taking notice" the Court will presume that the information refused would be harmful to the argument of the party refusing.)

The Court is free to make its own assessment of the evidential value of documents submitted to it, except those the authenticity of which is recognized by Community law, which prove themselves. See R.P. 62 (1) "record", *post*, p. 252. It should be noted that "discovery of documents", effected as between the parties to an action, is not practised in Continental European legal systems. An order to the parties may be made by the European Court requiring them "to produce . . . documents and supply . . . information" directly to the Court itself (rather than to each other in the first place, as part of the procedure during which they prepare their respective approaches to the trial). The order therefore applies to all documents and information "which the Court considers desirable" and may thus be properly regarded less as involving a method of proof (of matters the parties have "offered to prove", as to which see R.P. 38 (1) (e), *ante*, p. 221 and R.P. 40 (1) (d), *ante*, p. 226) than as part of the "procedure of enquiry" (see *post*, p. 233) which the Court itself conducts by means of certain measures or which it directs the reporting judge (see Chapter, 3 *"rapporteur" ante*, p. 200) to conduct (E.C.S.C. St. 24 is in fact headed "Measures by way of Procedure of Enquiry"). If made, an order by the Court, requiring the production of documents and the supply of information, is, in point of time, made after the close of the written procedure (which occurs upon the delivery of the further reply, see "Termination of written procedure," *post*, p. 232) and following the preliminary report of the reporting judge (*"rapporteur"*, *loc. cit.*, *supra*). It is complementary to that written procedure. Other than by virtue of the Statutes such an order (for the production of documents and the supply of information) may be made by the Court by virtue of the Rules of Procedure as part of the procedure of enquiry.

E.C.S.C. St. 23

When recourse is had against a decision taken by one of the Community's institutions, it shall transmit to the Court all documents relating to the case before the Court.

Where a claim is against a decision of an Institution of the Coal and Steel Community, that Institution is required by E.C.S.C. St. 23 (*supra*) (which has no equivalent in the other Statutes) to transmit to the Court all documents relating to the case brought before it. The same applies to all minutes of proceedings relating to the contested decision (see Judgment in Case 2/54 R. Vol. 1 p. 79 at p. 87 for an example of an order of the Court requiring transmission of minutes by the High Authority). The Court may authorise the suppression of names in the minutes (see order in case 2–45, *loc. cit.*, *supra*).

An **"expert examination and report"** (*"expertise"*; *"Begutachtung durch Sachverständige"*; *"deskundigenonderzoek"*; *"perizia"*). This may similarly be ordered by the Court at any moment by virtue of the Statutes (and will be technically a measure of procedure of enquiry by virtue of R.P. 45(2) (d), *post*, p. 234). It seems unlikely that in practice there could be a formal measure of enquiry before the end of the written procedure.

E.E.C. St. 22

The Court may at any time charge any person, body, office, Committee or organ of its own choice with the duty of making an expert examination and report.

E.A.E.C. St. 23

[*Identical with E.E.C. St. 22.*]

E.C.S.C. St. 25

At any time the Court may entrust any person, body, office, committee or agency of its own choice with the duty of holding an enquiry or making an expert examination and report; for this purpose the Court may draw up a list of persons or bodies qualified to serve as experts.

R.P. 43

The Court may, after hearing the parties and the Advocate General and at any time, whether for the purposes of the written or oral procedure or for those of its final judgment, order several pending cases which relate to the same subject to be dealt with together, on the ground of their inter-connection. The Court may again separate them.

R.P. 44

Paragraph 1

After the submission of the further reply in defence referred to in Article 41, Paragraph 1 of these Rules, the President shall fix a date on which the Judge acting as Rapporteur shall present his preliminary report on whether procedure of enquiry on the case is required. The Court, after hearing the Advocate General, shall decide whether it will be necessary to take measures of Investigation.

The same procedure shall be applied:

(a) If the reply has not been submitted within the time limit fixed in accordance with Article 41, Paragraph 2 of these Rules;

(b) if the party concerned states that he is waiving his right of presenting a reply or further reply.

Paragraph 2

If the Court decides to open the procedure of enquiry and does not undertake this itself, it shall assign the matter to a Section.

If the Court decides to open the oral procedure without procedure of enquiry, the President shall fix a date for the opening of the oral procedure.

Termination of written procedure. This occurs, following delivery of the further reply (if any) upon the fixing by the President of a date for the preliminary report (R.P. 44(1)) of the judge acting as *rapporteur*. (See *"Rapporteur"* in Chapter 3, under E.E.C. St. 12, *ante*, p. 200).

Preliminary report of the Judge acting as *Rapporteur*. This report is considered by the Court in secret. It should not be confused with the second report which the same judge prepares for reading at the opening of the oral procedure (see comment "The oral procedure shall include the reading of the report presented by a judge acting as *rapporteur* . . ." under E.E.C. St. 18, *ante*, p. 216).

III. PROCEDURE OF ENQUIRY: CALLING OF EVIDENCE
(R.P. 45–54)

("De l'instruction"; "Beweisaufnahme"; "van de instructie"; "Dell'istruzione della causa")

Introductory. Difficulties of translation in the above title have been surmounted by the use of two phrases, the former corresponding to the literal meaning of the French, Netherlands and Italian, the latter to the German, original. What is involved in R.P. 45–54 is a procedure of enquiry carried out by means of the calling of evidence.

The Court itself, having heard the Advocate General, determines what (further) measures by way of procedure of enquiry it considers appropriate. The procedure of enquiry, strictly speaking, begins with the initiation of the written procedure (see R.P. 24(1), *ante*, p. 200). The purpose of the (further) procedure of enquiry (which is the subject of this section) is to establish certain facts held necessary for satisfactory adjudication in the action. The Court determines what measures shall be taken by means of an order (see under "Judgments", comment "Judgments and orders", *post*, p. 253) setting out the facts to be proved and served on the parties (R.P. 45(1), *post*, p. 234). The Court may decide that no measures by way of procedure of enquiry are required (as, for example, where the written proof in the form of documents annexed to procedural documents is sufficient (see under R.P. 37(4); "Every procedural document shall have annexed to it a file containing the supporting exhibits and documents . . . ," *ante*, p. 220; and under R.P. 38(4) "Exhibits accompanying the Request" *ante*, p. 221) or where documents produced following an order of the Court are sufficient (see under E.E.C. St. 21 and equivalents, *ante*, p. 230). While there are no technical rules as to the evidential value and admissibility of documents (with the exception of the Registrar's record—see R.P. 47(6), *post*, pp. 240, 242 and R.P. 62, *post*, p. 252) and thus no legal limit to the admissibility of "proofs", or what purports to be documentary evidence, the forms in which proof may be established in the procedure of enquiry are precisely defined (R.P. 45(2), *post*, p. 234).

Certain measures by way of procedure of enquiry may be taken by a section of the Court (see Chapter 3, Organisation, under E.E.C. 165, *ante*, p. 181) rather than by the whole Court. The assistant reporting judges may be required to participate in the procedure of enquiry (as to assistant reporting judge see Chapter 3, under E.E.C. St. 12, *ante*, p. 198). The Court (or

Section) proceeds, itself, to take the measures by way of procedure of enquiry the Court orders, or charges the judge acting as *rapporteur* so to do. The Advocate General takes part in these measures.

Section 1. "Measures for calling of evidence" (R.P. 45 & 46)
("Des mesures d'instruction"; "Allgemeine Bestimmungen"; "van de maatregelen van instructie"; "Dei mezzi istruttori").

R.P. 45
Paragraph 1

The Court having heard the Advocate General, shall determine what measures for calling of evidence it considers suitable, by an order setting out the facts to be proved. This order shall be served on the parties.

Paragraph 2

Without prejudice to the provisions of Articles 24 and 25 of the E.C.S.C. Statute, Articles 21 and 22 of the E.E.C. Statute and Articles 22 and 23 of the E.A.E.C. Statute, measures for calling of evidence include:

(*a*) the personal appearance of the parties;
(*b*) a request for information and production of documents;
(*c*) evidence by witnesses;
(*d*) expert examination and report;
(*e*) a visit to the scene.

Paragraph 3

The Court shall give effect to the measures for calling of evidence which it has ordered, or shall delegate this duty to the Judge acting as Rapporteur.

The Advocate General shall take part in the calling of evidence.

Paragraph 4

The right to submit evidence in rebuttal and to supplement the means of proof available shall be preserved.

"2 (a) The personal appearance of the parties". The Court itself may put questions to and examine the parties during the sittings that occur as part of the procedure of enquiry, as well as during the oral procedure proper. (See E.E.C. St. 29 and equivalents, *post*, p. 249).

No special requirement as to form exists in respect of the personal appearance of the parties, but a record of every sitting for the purpose is required by R.P. 53(1) *post*, p. 247.

Legal person or party. Where a party to an action is a legal person constituted either public or private law, as to the difference between which see under E.E.C. 181 and equivalents, *ante*, p. 153) the individual duly authorised by the legal person to represent it in dealings with third parties will be liable to appear personally when the Court sits, by virtue of R.P. 45(2) (a). A State appears by the department or body within the competence of which the subject matter of the action falls, saving the delegation of authority permitted by the internal law of that State (evidence of which may need to be furnished) and in accordance with the principles applying when a legal person is a party before the Court. The Board of a Company, if its Regulations are silent on the matter, will need to designate one (or more) of its members for the purpose of appearance in its name, unless the Court itself does so.

"Contradictory" nature of this measure of procedure of enquiry. The personal appearance of the parties is "contradictory" in the sense indicated at *ante*, pp. 209–210. It follows that all parties litigating in the action have a right to be present, as throughout all aspects of the procedure of enquiry (see R.P. 46(3), *post*, p. 237).

Presence of agents, legal advisers and legal representatives. Inasmuch as R.P. 46(2) (*post*, p. 237) specifically makes R.P. 56 and 57 (*post*, p. 250) applicable to procedure before the Section of the Court charged with the procedure of enquiry, and that R.P. 57 enables the President in the course of the hearing to put questions to the agents, legal advisers and legal representatives of the parties, it would seem that such also have a right to be present, and to ask the Court the questions they deem pertinent to be put to the parties.

The principles set out in the preceding two paragraphs also apply to the hearing of witnesses (see under "Hearing of witnesses", *post*, p. 243).

"2(b) a request for information and production of documents". This provision duplicates in respect of the procedure of enquiry that of the Statutes (see E.E.C. St. 21 and equivalents, *ante*, p. 230) relating to all phases of procedure. That being so, the request for information may appear to be less a method of proof strictly so called than a complement to the procedure, though the distinction is not of great practical importance. The production of documents is not subjected to any particular procedural requirements and the Instructions to the Registrar, article 7(2), (which see in Chapter 6, *post*, p. 305) indicate that, if necessary, production may be made during a sitting in open court.

It is to be presumed that, although the Rules of Procedure are silent on the matter, the documents and information produced as a result of a Court order under R.P. 45(1) and (2)(b) are to be communicated (see "communication" *ante*, p. 215) to the parties through the Office of the Registrar, in order that it may be possible for them, should they desire, to submit evidence in rebuttal (as entitled to do by R.P. 45(4), *supra*). It is the practice of the Court to communicate such documents and information, and a failure to do so would be inconsistent with the general principle of publicity of the procedure and of its contradictory character (*ante*, pp. 209–210) which latter prevents the Court from taking into consideration for the purposes of its judgment any document or information unknown to one or both of the parties.

"2(c) Evidence by witnesses". This provision implements the general provision for the hearing of witnesses, in the following Articles of the Statutes:

E.E.C. St. 23

Witnesses may be heard in the circumstances to be laid down in the Rules of Procedure.

E.A.E.C. St. 24

[*Identical with E.E.C. St. 23.*]

E.C.S.C. St. 28

[Contains as the first sentence of paragraph two a provision identical with E.E.C. St. 23.]

The Rules of Procedure devote a special section of the Chapter dealing with the procedure of enquiry and the calling of evidence to "The Summoning and Hearing of Witnesses and Experts" and reference should be made to this (*post*, p. 237).

"2(d) expert examination and report". This provision implements the general provision for expert examination and report, in the following Articles of the Statutes:

E.E.C. St. 22

[Printed on ante, p. 232.]

E.A.E.C. St. 23

[Identical with E.E.C. St. 22.]

E.C.S.C. St. 25

[Printed on ante, p. 232.]

"Holding an enquiry". This is not provided for in E.E.C. St. 22 and is equivalent to "evidence on commission".

". . . At any time . . .". These words occur in all three of the above Articles and appear to have as a result (certainly in E.E.C. and E.A.E.C.) that the obtaining of an expert examination and report may occur outside the procedural phase defined as the procedure of enquiry and calling of evidence, that is, it may occur during the written or even during the oral procedure. (Whether the same result, applying also alternatively to holding an enquiry, follows in E.C.S.C. is rendered to some extent uncertain by the fact that E.C.S.C. St. 25 appears under the general heading Measures by way of Procedure of Enquiry, but this heading could be read as not limited to the phase of procedure strictly so called).

Enquiry. Enquiry by the expert himself may be involved in making his examination prior to the preparation of his report.

Report. The Court is not bound by the expert's report. See *post* pp. 245–246.

"2(e) visit to the *locus in quo*". The order of the Court prescribing this must be served on the parties, in accordance with the general rule of R.P. 45(1) (*ante*, p. 234) and the parties may be present during the visit (in accordance with R.P. 46(3) (*post*, p. 237).

A record of the visit and of the findings of the Court in respect of it must be drawn up by the Registrar in accordance with R.P. 53 (*post*, p. 247).

It is not only for the purposes of a visit to the *locus in quo* that the Court (or its Sections), for one or more given sittings, may select a place other than that in which the Court has its seat (R.P. 25(3) *ante*, p. 200).

R.P. 46

Paragraph 1

The Section entrusted with carrying out the calling of evidence shall exercise the powers vested in the Court by Articles 45 and 47 to 53 of these Rules; the powers vested in the President of the Court shall be exercised by the President of the Section.

Paragraph 2

Articles 56 and 57 of these Rules shall apply to proceedings before the Section.

Paragraph 3

The parties may attend the calling of evidence.

"**(1)**... **by articles ... 47 to 53.** These Articles comprise the special section on the summoning and hearing of witnesses and experts, *infra.* 1

"**(2) Articles 56 and 57 ...**". The applicability of R.P. 56 and 57 to procedure before a Section results apparently in the right of the agents, legal advisers, and legal representatives of the litigating parties also to be present (see under R.P. 45(2)(a) "Presence of agents, legal advisers and legal representatives", *ante*, p. 235).

"**(3)**". The right of the parties to be present appears to follow from the contradictory nature of the procedure (see under R.P. 45(2)(a) "contradictory nature of this measure of procedure of enquiry", *ante*, p. 235).

Section 2.—"The Summoning and hearing of witnesses and experts" (R.P. 47-53).

(*"De la citation et de l'audition des témoins et experts"*; *"Ladung und Vernehmung von Zeugen und Sachverständigen"*; *"van de oproeping en het verhoor van getuigen en deskundigen"*; *"Della citazione e dell' audizione dei testimoni e dei periti"*).

The general provision in the Statutes for the summoning and hearing of witnesses and experts has been referred to previously (in section 1, 2(c), E.E.C. St. 23 and equivalents (respecting witnesses) *ante*, p. 235 and in (2) (d), E.E.C. St. 22 and equivalents (respecting experts) *ante*, p. 236). The Statutes also make general provision in respect of the following four matters: (a) defaulting witness; (b) oath of witness and expert; (c) evidence of witness or expert by letter of request; (d) violation of oath by witness or expert. These matters are the subject of a sequence of four Articles in the Statutes of E.E.C. and E.A.E.C. and are assembled in one Article of E.C.S.C. St. as follows:

E.E.C. St. 24

The Court shall have the powers generally possessed by courts of law as regards defaulting witnesses and may impose pecuniary penalties as shall be laid down by the Rules of Procedure.

E.A.E.C. St. 25

[*Identical with E.E.C. St. 24.*]

E.E.C. St. 25

Witnesses and experts may be heard on an oath taken in the form laid down by the rules of procedure or in the manner laid down by the domestic law of the witness or expert.

E.A.E.C. St. 26

[*Identical with E.E.C. St. 25.*]

E.E.C. St. 26

The Court may order that a witness or expert be heard by the judicial authority of his place of residence.

This order shall be sent for execution to the competent judicial authority in accordance with the rules of procedure. The documents obtained in pursuance of these letters of request shall similarly be sent to the Court in accordance with these rules.

The Court shall defray the expenses incurred, subject to the right to charge these expenses, where appropriate, to the parties concerned.

E.A.E.C. St. 27

[Identical with E.E.C. St. 26.]

E.E.C. St. 27

Each member State shall treat any violation of an oath by a witness or expert in the same manner as if the same offence had been committed before a domestic court dealing with a case in civil proceedings. When the Court reports such a violation the Member State concerned shall prosecute the offender before the competent domestic court.

E.A.E.C. St. 28

[Identical with E.E.C. St. 27.]

E.C.S.C. St. 28

The cause list shall be settled by the President.

Witnesses may be heard under conditions which shall be determined by the rules of procedure. They may be heard on oath.

During the hearings the Court may also examine the experts and the persons entrusted with the holding of an enquiry, as well as the parties themselves; the latter, however, may only address the Court through their representative or legal representative.

When it is established that a witness or an expert has concealed or falsified the facts on which he has testified or been examined by the Court, the Court shall be empowered to refer such lapse from duty to the Minister of Justice of the State of which the witness or expert is a national, in order to have applied to him the relevant penal provisions of the law of his country.

The Courts shall have as regards defaulting witnesses the powers generally given in such matters to Courts and tribunals, under the conditions determined by rules laid down by the Court and submitted for the Council's approval.

The Rules of Procedure implement the above general provisions of the Statutes as follows:

R.P. 47

Paragraph 1

The Court shall order the proof of certain facts by witnesses, either of its own volition, or at the request of the parties, after hearing the Advocate General. The order of the Court shall set out the facts to be established.

Witnesses shall be summoned by the Court, either of its own volition or at the request of the parties or of the Advocate General.

Application by one of the parties for the hearing of a witness shall indicate precisely the facts on which the witness is to be heard, and the reasons supporting the application.

Paragraph 2

Witnesses the hearing of whom is recognised to be necessary shall be summoned by means of an order of the Court which shall contain:

(*a*) the surname, Christian names, description and place of residence of the witnesses;

(*b*) an indication of the facts on which the witnesses are to be heard;

(*c*) where appropriate, mention of the arrangements made by the Court for reimbursement of expenses claimed by the witnesses, and of the penalties to which defaulting witnesses are liable.

This order shall be served upon the parties and the witnesses.

Paragraph 3

The Court may make the summoning of witnesses, the hearing of whom is requested by the parties, conditional upon deposit in advance with the Court pay office of a sum to cover the taxed expenses; the amount of this shall be fixed by the Court.

The Court pay office shall advance the sums necessary for hearing of witnesses chosen by the Court itself.

Paragraph 4

After verification of the identity of the witnesses, the President shall inform them that they will be required to certify their statements on oath.

Witnesses shall be heard by the Court after notice to the parties to be present. After each has given his evidence the President may, at the request of the parties or of his own volition, put questions to the witnesses.

Each of the Judges and the Advocate General shall also have this right.

Paragraph 5

After giving evidence, the witness shall take the following oath: "I swear that what I have said is the truth, the whole truth and nothing but the truth."

The oath may be taken in manner laid down by the law of the country of the witness concerned.

The Court may, with the agreement of the parties, excuse the witness from being sworn.

Paragraph 6

Under the President's direction, the Registrar shall draw up a record of each witness's evidence. After being read out this record shall be signed by the witness, the President or Judge acting as Rapporteur and the Registrar. It shall constitute an official record.

"Paragraph 1.—The Court shall order the proof of certain facts by witnesses . . .". (If, that is, following its consideration of the preliminary report of the judge acting as *rapporteur* (see *ante*, p. 233) it decides that such proof is necessary).

". . . Certain facts". (*"certains faits"; "bestimmte Tatsachen"; "bepaalde feiten"; "determinati fatti"*).

While there is no limitation, in the Statutes of the Court or the Rules of Procedure, on the power of the Court to order "proof by witnesses", R.P. 47(1) imposes the requirement that proof shall be of "certain" facts. What may be comprised within that expression is left to the discretion of the Court but it would seem that the Court will not order the proof by witnesses of any fact unless it is very material to a point at issue, although not perhaps necessarily conclusive as to that point. In this respect the Court would seem to enjoy a somewhat wider discretion than is practised by the relevant domestic courts and implicit in the French, Belgian and Italian Codes of Civil Procedure, in which the facts admitted to proof by witnesses are so admitted because they are conclusive on a point at issue. (The expression *"certains faits"* in the French means no more than "defined" or "given" facts (*"bestimmte Tatschen"*). It has, of course, a widely different meaning from *"faits certains"*, or "ascertained facts" which phrase is not used in the Rules of Procedure, and with which it must not be confused). It should be noted that R.P. 47(1) also requires the Court, in its order, to *"set out the facts to be established"*. The result is that the questions or facts as to which the testimony of witnesses is required must be precisely defined in the order. Hearsay evidence is not expressly excluded by the Rules of Procedure.

". . . Either of its own volition, or at the request of the parties, after hearing the Advocate General ("of its own volition"; *"d'office"; "von Amts wegen"; "ambtshalve"; "d'ufficio"*). This is an example of what may be regarded as the inquisitorial aspect of the procedure (see this Chapter *ante*, p. 210). It should be noted that alternatively the order may be made at the request of the parties.

The contents of the order. The (first) order may (and usually does) designate (by name, occupation (*"qualité"*), and address) the witnesses the Court itself selects to be heard, and sets out the questions on which their evidence is desired. Particular individual questions may be addressed to particular witnesses individually, or to a group of witnesses. Several questions may be addressed to one particular witness, or a group of witnesses. The order may invite the parties to designate witnesses they desire to be heard in respect of particular facts or questions defined by the Court in the same order; or alternatively, the parties may receive such an invitation by letter from the Registrar. It should be noted, however, that the Court is empowered (by R.P. 47(3), *ante* p. 239) to make the summoning of witnesses whom the parties desire to be heard dependent on the payment into Court of a sum of money of which it fixes the amount sufficient to cover the taxed costs of the attendance.

The order indicates that the witnesses will be heard at the beginning of the oral procedure on a date to be subsequently fixed.

The order may also invite the parties to deliver, within a specified time limit, a written report setting out relevant events related to a particular defined fact or event. It may further invite written replies to particular questions, which must be precisely set out in the order, addressed to all the parties, or, similarly, replies to particular questions addressed to the petitioner or to the defendant.

A second order of the Court is necessary (as is apparent from the preceding paragraph) as a consequence of the first. This second order is the subject of R.P. 47(2) (see comment, *infra*). It fixes the date for the hearing of the witnesses and orders them to attend thereat. It thus effectively constitutes the means whereby the witnesses are "summoned" (*"cités"; "geladen"; "opgeroepen"; "citati"*).

Paragraph 2.—The contents of the (second) order. The order summoning the witnesses is required by R.P. 47(2) to contain (a) the surnames, christian names, occupation (*"qualité"*) and residence of the witnesses; (b) an indication of the facts in respect of which they will be heard and (c) as needed, mention of the measures taken by the Court for the refund of the expenses borne by the witnesses (which measures are covered by R.P. 51(1) and (2), *post*, p. 246) and of the penalties for failure to attend. In practice, as noted above, much of these three matters may be covered by the first order, which is expressly or in effect subsumed in the second.

This (second) order designates the witnesses summoned by the Court at the request of the parties in response to the first order (see under Paragraph 1, *supra*) sets out the precise questions on which their testimony is required (and may repeat the names of witnesses, designated in the first order, which the Court itself requires to be heard, similarly setting out the precise questions on which their testimony is required).

It has been known for a third order of the Court, regarding the same hearing, to be made, substituting one witness in the place of another at the request of one of the parties and adding an additional witness by decision of the Court of its own volition.

In case 18/63 (hearing of witnesses 9th December 1963) there were nine witnesses of whom two were selected by the Court of its own volition. This case concerned a claim by a former employee against the E.E.C. Commission and it is of interest to note that the employee (who was present in Court throughout the hearing of witnesses and the ensuing oral procedure) was not called as a witness.

Objection to witness(es). Either of the parties may object to one or more of the designated witnesses on the grounds of "incapacity", or "unworthiness" (*"indignité"*), or for any other cause, within fifteen days starting from the service of the order summoning witnesses. Objection is made by a formal "procedural document" (see *ante*, p. 216) containing the reasons for the objection and offers of proof, (R.P. 50(1) and (2), *post*, p. 246).

(An example of "incapacity" might be that the witness was the superior of the party in a given administration, of "unworthiness" that the witness was a habitual drunkard). In the event of objection to a witness the Court decides whether it should overrule or uphold the objection (*"la Cour statue"; "ent-scheidet der Gerichtshof"; "beslist het Hof"; "la Corte provvede"*) (R.P. 50, *post* p. 246).

Paragraphs 4, 5 and 6.—The Conduct of the Hearing of Witnesses.
The only requirements of the Rules of Procedure respecting the conduct of the hearing are those set out in R.P. 47 (4) (5) and (6) covering the taking of the oath, the putting of questions to the witnesses, after they have completed their depositions, by or through the President of the Court (or Section) or by any judge or the Advocate General, and the drawing up of a record (*"procès verbal" "Protokoll"; "proces-verbaal"; "verbale"*), by the Registrar for signature by the witness after it has been read out to him. The practice of the Court in connection with these matters is not hard and fast but normally assumes the following pattern.

Witnesses wait together in a room outside the Court until called in one by one to make their deposition. After doing so each witness is shown to a different room outside the Court from the one in which he had waited. Normally, therefore, the witnesses do not meet during the sitting of the Court for the hearing, but, though not provided for in the Rules of Procedure, the Court has been known to require a "confrontation" of two witnesses, in order to check the statements of one against those of the other.

The witness stands immediately before the President of the Court, and nearer to him than the counsel for the parties, who have their desks some six feet behind, and to either side, of the witness. The witness cannot therefore observe the faces of counsel of either party, and the latter cannot observe the countenance of the witness, but can only see one side of his face from a position to the rear of it.

After verification of the identity of the witness he is told from the Bench that his statement will be under oath and required to give an assurance that he has no personal interest in the case (see "incapacity" under heading "Objection to Witness(es)", *ante*, p. 241). The witness is then asked for his statement in respect of the question or questions addressed to him in precise terms in the order(s) of the Court providing for the hearing (see "Contents of the Order", *ante*, pp. 240–241).

Since the Registrar is required to keep a record (as to its contents see "Instructions to the Registrar", *post*, p. 305) it frequently happens in practice that the President must ask a witness to suspend the flow of his oral statement, to enable this to be done, before continuing further. The Registrar draws up the record in one of the four official languages selected as "the language of procedure" (see under "Some practical features of the hearing. The language of procedure" *post*, p. 251). Complications may arise where that is not the native language of the witness. Accommodation is usually reached, but the witness is entitled to call for the service of an interpreter if he desires (to be sure of correctly understanding the record before he signs it, or during the course of his statement). It appears not infrequently to happen that the witness may make his statement in an official language of the Court other than the "language of procedure" (see *loc. cit., supra*) (and address it more particularly to the Judge present who has the same native language as his own) during which time the Registrar may listen to the witness's statement in a different language from the one in which he makes his record.

A request by a witness (a professional man) to be allowed to read out a written statement he had prepared on the question addressed to him in the Court's order was refused by the President (in case 18/63 on 10th December, 1963).

Questions put to a witness by counsel for the parties (in theory these are put to the witness through the President but in practice they are often put direct on the invitation of the President, who first asks his fellow judges and the Advocate General if they have any questions) may contain an element of the cross questioning familiar to the practitioner in the English Courts, but it seems clear that the President will disallow questions not directed to the illumination of the facts or questions precisely defined in the order(s) of the Court, or not aimed at discrediting or enhancing the value of the testimony. Questions may be put to the witness, by invitation of the President, by counsel for the parties virtually as the questions occur to them. There is no formal order (*e.g.* for the claimant first, for the defendant second, or vice versa).

It may happen that counsel for one (or both) of the parties has (have) a different native language from the witness, and where the President was of the same nationality as the witness (Italian, as in case 18/63 hearing of witnesses on 10th December, 1963) he summarised in Italian for the benefit of the witness questions put to the witness in French by counsel for the parties on the President's invitation.

At the conclusion of oral questions to the witness, and his answers to them, following his statement, the Registrar reads his record to the witness. The witness himself, or counsel for the parties, may request amendments of wording (such as may relate to the balance of emphasis, the general impression conveyed by the recorded statement, etc.) Such requests may cause a three cornered exchange between the President, the Registrar and counsel. From practice to date it is not clear how far the Court would be disposed to allow such requests to go, but it seems reasonable to assume that it would curb any excess. Requests for amendments will inevitably be noted by the Bench, and may presumably have a bearing on the eventual judgment.

When the reading of the record is terminated, the oath (R.P. 47(5) *ante*, p. 239) is read out to the witness by the President. Thereupon the witness takes the oath by saying the two words "I swear". He next signs the record of the Registrar.

A tape recording is made of all that is said in Court during the hearing of witnesses (as it is of all other phases of oral procedure). But it would seem that little direct use can be made of this, inasmuch as when the report of the Registrar has been signed by a witness (and signed by the President or the reporting judge and the Registrar) "it constitutes an official record" (R.P. 47(6), *ante*, p. 240). The effect of its being constituted an official record is that it alone may be used by the Court as the evidence of the witness. An "official record" (of whatever kind) is accepted by the Court as proving itself.

Perjury.—False testimony. The Statutes of the Court make general provision for the "formal report" ("*dénonciation*"; "*Anzeige*"; "*aangifte*"; "*denuncia*") by the Court of a witness who perjures himself, to the relevant judicial authority of Member States (see E.E.C. St. 27 and equivalents, *ante*, p. 238). Article 109 of the Rules of Procedure (which see *post*, p. 299) requires the making of supplementary rules of procedure relating (*inter alia*) to the formal report of perjured witnesses (see R.P. 6, R.P. 7, *post*, p. 302).

Defaulting witness. The Statutes of the Court confer upon it the above powers normally recognised in this matter as possessed by the Courts and tribunals (see E.E.C. St. 24 and equivalents under section 2, *ante*, p. 237), and specifically confer on the Court the power to impose fines. This provision is expressly duplicated in R.P. 48(2), *infra*.

R.P. 48

Paragraph 1

Witnesses who have been duly summoned are requested to obey the summons and attend the proceedings.

Paragraph 2

When a duly summoned witness does not present himself before the Court, the Court may impose upon him a penalty not exceding 250 accounting units of the European Monetary Agreement and may order the costs of fresh service of the summons to be borne by the witness.

The same penalty may be imposed upon a witness who, without good reason, refuses to give evidence or to be sworn.

Paragraph 3

If a witness upon whom a penalty has been imposed produces a valid excuse to the Court he may be relieved from payment of the penalty.

Paragraph 4

Enforcement of penalties imposed or of orders made under this Article shall be affected in accordance with the provisions of Articles 44 and 92 of the E.C.S.C. Treaty, Articles 187 and 192 of the E.E.C. Treaty and Articles 159 and 164 of the E.A.E.C. Treaty.

"**Paragraph 2. When a duly summoned witness does not present himself . . .**" the Court may, by virtue of R.P. 48(a), impose a penalty (*i.e.* a fine) (see "defaulting witness", *ante*, p. 243) and also "order the costs of fresh service of the summons to be borne by the witness". The decision imposing a fine is (*semble*) made by order. (See comment "Judgments, Orders" *post*, pp. 253–254). It may presumably form one order together with that ordering the costs of fresh service ("*réassignation*"; "*erneute Ladung*"; "*hij . . . opnieuw zal worden opgeroepen*"; "*rinnovazione della citazione*") to be borne by the witness.

"**Paragraph 4. Enforcement of penalties . . .**" ("*Exécution forcée des sanctions*"; "*Vollstreckung . . . der Strafen . . .*"; "*gedwongen tenuitvrerlegging . . . van . . . de sancties . . .*"; "*esecuzione forzata delle sanzioni*"). For the purposes of enforcement in a Member State (or where the order is by the Court of E.E.C. or E.A.E.C., in any State) of the penalty or order as to costs against a defaulting witness, (see paragraph 2, *supra*) this order is in effect made equivalent to a judgment of the Court by virtue of the provision of R.P. 48(4) whereby E.E.C. 187 and 192 (and equivalents in E.A.E.C. or E.C.S.C.) are made to apply to it (see "Enforcement of judgments", *post*, p. 255).

R.P. 49

Paragraph 1

The Court may order the making of an expert examination and report. The order appointing the expert shall specify the task of the expert and fix a time limit within which his report shall be submitted.

Paragraph 2

The expert shall receive a copy of the order together with all the documents and exhibits necessary for carrying out his task. He shall be placed under the orders of the Judge acting as Rapporteur who may be present during the expert's work and shall be kept informed of the progress of the expert in the task assigned to him.

Paragraph 3

At the request of the expert, the Court may decide to hear witnesses. This shall be carried out in accordance with the provisions of Article 47 of these Rules.

Paragraph 4

The expert may give his opinion only on the points which are expressly put to him.

Paragraph 5

After submission of the report, the Court may order the hearing of the expert, after notice to the parties to attend.

Paragraph 6

After submission of the report, the expert shall take before the Court the following oath:

"I swear that I have carried out my task conscientiously and with full impartiality."

The oath may be taken in the manner laid down by the law of the expert's country.

The Court may, with the agreement of the parties, excuse the expert from being sworn.

This is the principal Article of the Rules of Procedure setting out the requirements in respect of the examination and report of an expert (in implementation of R.P. 45(2) (d), see *ante*, pp. 234–236). The following points especially should be noted in regard to R.P. 49 and related Rules:

1. The Court order defines precisely the terms of reference ("*mission*") of the expert it designates, and fixes a time limit for the delivery of his report (R.P. 49(1)). The expert may express an opinion only on the points specifically submitted to him (R.P. 49(4)).

2. The expert is under the control of the reporting judge who must be kept informed of the progress of his task and who may be present during the carrying out of it.

3. On the application of the expert the Court may examine witnesses (by virtue of R.P. 49(3) and in accordance with the procedure as to such hearings prescribed in R.P. 47 (see *ante*, pp. 239 *et seq.*).

4. A party to the action may object to an expert (under the same conditions as he may object to a witness) on the grounds of incapacity, unworthiness or for any other cause (see "Objection to witness(es)" *ante*, p. 241). The Court must rule on the objection (R.P. 50(1) and (2), *post*, p. 246).

5. The expert may be heard, by order of the Court, in the presence of the parties, after the delivery of his report (R.P. 49(5)) which is in writing.

6. Examination of an expert (as of a witness) may be taken by letter of request (see *ante*, p. 235, and Supplementary Rules of Procedure articles 1–3

post, pp. 300–301) by the Court of its own volition or on the application of a party, by virtue of R.P. 52 (*infra*).

7. A report of each hearing of the expert (as of each hearing of a witness, as to which see "Conduct of Hearing of Witnesses", *ante*, p. 242) is drawn up by the Registrar, and when signed by the expert, the President and the Registrar, constitutes an "authentic act" (see R.P. 53, *post*, p. 247). As far as the expert's opinion is concerned only what is included in the report of the Registrar may be considered by the Court, together with the expert's report, in reaching its decision.

8. The question of legal liability of an expert for tort ("*faute*") causing damage to a party to the action (which principle of liability exists in, for example, the Belgian Code of Civil Procedure) has not been ruled on by the Court.

R.P. 50

Paragraph 1

If one of the parties should object to a witness or an expert for reasons of legal disability, disqualification, or for any other reason, or if a witness or expert should refuse to give evidence or to be sworn, the Court shall give a ruling thereon.

Paragraph 2

An object to a witness or an expert shall be taken within 14 days of the notification of the order summoning the witness or appointing the expert, by means of a written statement indicating the grounds for objection and the means of proof available.

R.P. 51

Paragraph 1

Witnesses and experts shall be entitled to reimbursement of expenses for travel and subsistence. An advance for these expenses may be granted to them from the Court pay office.

Paragraph 2

Witnesses shall be entitled to compensation for loss of earnings, and experts to fees for their work.

This amount shall be paid to witnesses and experts by the Court pay office after they have fulfilled their duties or tasks.

R.P. 52

The Court may, at the request of the parties or of its own volition, issue letters of request for the hearing of witnesses or experts, in manner to be determined by the Rules referred to in Article 109 of these Rules.

Evidence of witnesses by letter of request (*"commission rogatoire"*; *Ersuchen um Rechtshilfe"*; *"rogatoire commissie"*; *"rogatoria"*). This matter forms the subject of Supplementary Rules of Procedure (for text see Chapter 6, *post*, pp. 300–301) adopted at Luxembourg on 9th March 1962 made in execution of Articles 52 and 109 of the Rules of Procedure and provided for generally in E.E.C. St. 26.

R.P. 53

Paragraph 1

The Registrar shall draw up a record of every sitting. This record shall be signed by the President and by the Registrar and shall constitute an official record.

Paragraph 2

The parties may examine all such records as well as the expert's report in the Registrar's office and may obtain copies at their own expense.

"... **Official record** ..." (*acte authentique*"; "*öffentliche Urkunde*"; "*authentieke akte*"; "*atto autentico*"). Such a document proves itself. In general, technical rules as to the evidential value of documents, such as are common in the national legal systems of the original Six Member States of the Communities, are absent from the Rules of Procedure, Statutes and Treaties. The concept of "official record" or authentic act, embodies one such technical rule, and R.P. 15(3) (*ante*, p. 195) R.P. 47(6) (*ante*, p. 240) R.P. 53 and R.P. 62 (*post*, p. 252) exceptionally adopt it, but compare "texts ... shall be authentic ..." R.P. 31 (*ante*, p. 206).

Section 3.—"Closure of Procedure of Enquiry" (R.P. 54)
("*De la clôture de l'instruction*"; "*Abschlusz der Beweisaufnahme*"; "*van de sluiting der instructie*"; "*Della chiusura dell'istruzione*").

R.P. 54

Unless the Court decides to set a time limit within which the parties may submit written comments the President shall fix the date for the opening of the oral procedure after completion of the procedure of enquiry.

If a time limit has been set for the submission of written comments, the President shall fix the date for the opening of the oral procedure at the end of this period.

"... **A time limit within which the parties may submit written comments** ...". During this period a party may supplement (*i.e.* develop or complement) ("*ampliation*"; "*Erweiterung*"; "*nadere bewijsaanbiedingen*"; "*ampliamento*") his means of proof (in accordance with R.P. 45(4), *ante*, p. 234).

"... **The President shall fix the date for the opening of the oral procedure at the end of this period** ...". This is ambiguous in wording, but Court practice shows the proper meaning to be that the President does not fix the date for the opening of the oral procedure until the expiry of the time-limit for written comments. He then fixes the date of the opening of the oral procedure.

The fixing by the President of the date of the opening of the oral procedure closes the procedure of enquiry and calling of evidence. But it does not follow that no further measures of enquiry may be ordered, or that the re-opening and extension of any part of the procedure of enquiry may not be ordered (either of which is possible by virtue of R.P. 60, *post*, p. 252). Questions put by the judges or the Advocate General during the oral procedure, to the agents, legal advisers and legal representatives of the parties (by virtue of R.P. 57, *post*, p. 250) may also be considered, technically, as measures of "enquiry".

IV. ORAL PROCEDURE (R.P. 55–62)

(*De la procédure orale; Mündliche Verhandlung; Van de mondelinge behandeling; Della fase orale*)

General provision is made by the Statutes that "the oral procedure shall include the reading of the report presented by a judge acting as rapporteur, the hearing by the Court of agents, legal advisers and legal representatives and the submissions of the Advocate General, as well as the hearing, if appropriate, of witnesses and experts" (E.E.C. St. 18 and equivalents, see "Phases of Procedure," *ante*, pp. 214–215). Normally, the reading of the report by the reporting judge therein referred to is that of a written document available to the Judges, the Advocate General and the parties legal representatives and advisers. It takes place the day before the hearing proper begins (see comment "The oral procedure shall include the reading of the report presented by a judge acting as rapporteur *ante* p. 216).

Provision is also made with regard to four general aspects of the hearing by articles of the Statutes, not so far dealt with in this Chapter. They are set out under A, B, C and D, *infra*.

A. The Cause List

("*Rôle d'audience*"; "*Terminliste*"; "*Auditienblad*"; "*Ruolo d'Udienza*")

E.E.C. St. 31

The cause list shall be settled by the President.

E.A.E.C. St. 32

[*Identical with E.E.C. St. 31.*]

E.C.S.C. St. 28

[*Identical with E.E.C. St. 31.*]

See R.P. 55 and comment thereto (*post*, pp. 249–250). As to date and times of sittings etc., see Chapter 3, R.P. 25 (*ante*, p. 200).

B. Publicity of Hearing

("*Hearing*"; "*Audience*"; "*mündliche Verhandlung*"; ("*hearing*" and "*oral procedure*" are not distinguished in German) "*terechzitting*" "*udienza*")

E.E.C. St. 28

Hearings shall be in public unless the Court, of its own volition or at the request of the parties, shall, for substantial reasons, decide otherwise.

E.A.E.C. St. 29

[*Identical with E.E.C. St. 28.*]

E.C.S.C. St. 26

Sittings shall be in open court unless the Court should decide otherwise on serious grounds.

C. Questions put by the Court

Questions may be put by the Court to the experts, the witnesses and the parties themselves.

E.E.C. St. 29

During the hearings the Court may examine the experts, the witnesses and the parties themselves. Provided always that the parties may only address the Court through their representative.

E.A.E.C. St. 30

[*Identical with E.E.C. St.* 29.]

E.C.S.C. St. 28 paragraph 3

During the hearings the Court may also examine the experts and the persons entrusted with the holding of an enquiry, as well as the parties themselves; the latter, however, may only address the Court through their representative or legal representative.

The above Articles of the Statutes appear to indicate that a further attendance of witnesses or experts may be required other than by way of procedure of enquiry (*ante*, pp. 237 *et seq.*). In practice the Court often decides that witnesses should be heard not by the Section in charge of the procedure of enquiry but by the whole Court and therefore orders that the hearing of witnesses should take place as part (at the beginning) of the oral procedure.

D. Keeping of a Record of each Hearing

E.E.C. St. 30

A record shall be kept of each hearing, signed by the President and the Registrar.

E.A.E.C. St. 31

[*Identical with E.E.C. St.* 30.]

E.C.S.C. St. 27

[*Identical with E.E.C. St.* 30.]

The provisions regarding the above four aspects of this oral procedure are amplified and at some points modified, by the Rules of Procedure, as follows:

R.P. 55

Paragraph 1

Subject to the priority enjoyed by decisions referred to in Article 85 of these Rules, the Court shall deal with the cases before it in the order in which the procedure of enquiry has been completed. Where there are a number of cases on which the procedure of enquiry is completed simultaneously, the order shall be determined by the date of entry of the Request in the register of such Requests.

The President may, in view of special circumstances decide to give priority to a given case.

Paragraph 2

If the parties in a case on which the procedure of enquiry has been completed all agree to ask for the case to be postponed, the President may accede thereto. In default of agreement between the parties, the President shall refer the matter to the Court to decide.

This article amplifies E.E.C. St. 31 and equivalents (see "The Cause List," *ante*, p. 248). As to the Registrar's duties in respect of the Cause List see Chapter 6, *post*, p. 304.

R.P. 56

Paragraph 1

The hearing shall be opened and directed by the President, in whom shall be vested the maintenance of order in Court.

Paragraph 2

A decision to hear a case in camera shall entail a prohibition against publication of the proceedings at the hearing.

Paragraph 2 of this Rule amplifies E.E.C. St. 28 and equivalents (see "Publicity of Hearing," *ante*, p. 248).

The Court is in plenary session for the hearing, the work and authority of the Section having been terminated at the close of the procedure of enquiry and calling of evidence, immediately preceding the hearing. This is the logical outcome of R.P. 24(1) (*ante*, p. 200). The only hearing that may take place before a Section of the Court is one concerned with the claim of an employee or other agent of one of the Communities (R.P. 95 *post*, p. 283). As to the consequences of judges being in even number and as to quorum of judges see R.P. 26 (*ante*, pp. 201–202).

R.P. 57

The President may, in the course of the hearing, put questions to the agents, legal advisers or legal representatives of the parties. Each Judge and the Advocate General shall also have this right.

This Rule specifies persons to whom and the persons by whom questions may be put during the hearing, which persons are not enumerated in the Statutes (see "Questions put by the Court," *ante*, p. 249). It makes no specific saving for the experts, witnesses and the parties themselves, who, by virtue of the Statutes, may be questioned by the Court, but such saving is unnecessary. It should be noted, however, that parties may only address the Court (in reply to questions) through their lawyers (R.P. 58, *post*, p. 250) ("address the Court": "*plaider*"; "*verhandeln*"; "*pleiten*"; "*partecipare*" "*alla discussione orale*"). For the purposes of the hearing the legal adviser may thus be said to "represent" the party for whom he addresses the Court but he has no similar right of representation in the written procedure (see agents, legal advisers, and legal representatives, *ante*, p. 213).

R.P. 58

The parties may only address the Court through their agent. legal adviser or legal representative.

This rule must be read in relation with R.P. 57, *ante*, p. 250.

Some practical features of the hearing. "The language of procedure" (*"la langue de procédure"*; *"Die Verfahrenssprache"*; *"de procestaal"*; *"la lingua processuale"*); only one of the official languages of the Court (French, German, Netherlands, Italian) may be the language of procedure (R.P. 29(1), *ante*, p. 204. And see generally in Chapter 3, "Official Languages", R.P. 29 and 30, *ante*, pp. 204–206). The language of procedure is chosen by the original applicant, unless (a) the defendant is a Member State or a physical or legal person who is a national of a Member State, when the language of procedure is the official language of that State (or where there are more than one such, the one chosen by the applicant); or (b) the parties agree in asking the Court to adopt one of the other official languages; or (c) the Court or Section, following the desire of one party (though not if an institution of the Community) orders the use totally or partially of another one of the official languages. On a submission for a preliminary ruling the official language is that of the Member State of which the judicial authority is making the submission.

Witnesses and experts declaring that they are unable to express themselves adequately in one of the official languages. The Court or Section may authorise them to use another language. It is the task of the Registrar to ensure translation into the language of procedure (R.P. 29(4), *ante*, p. 205 and see comment "The conduct of the hearing of witnesses", *ante*, pp. 242–243).

An official language other than the language of procedure. This may be used by the President (of the Court or Section)) in directing the hearing, by the judges or Avocate General when asking questions, or by the Advocate General for his submissions. But the Registrar is required to ensure translation of all such use into the language of procedure (R.P. 29(5), *ante*, p. 205)

Anything said (or written) during the procedure before the Court or a Section is translated, under the supervision of the Registrar, at the request of a judge, the Advocate General or a party, into any of the official languages that such may request (R.P. 30, *ante*, p. 206).

Headphones, on which may be followed simultaneous translations into the three official languages other than the one in which the procedure in the case is being conducted, are installed at each individual seat in the Court. A practice has consequently grown up for the agents, legal advisers and legal representatives of the parties to provide the translators, immediately prior to the hearing, with a typed copy of the address to the Court about to be made (the *"plaidoyer"* or *"plaidoirie"*) in order to ensure a satisfactory translation.

At the conclusion of the hearing the Judges and the Advocate General will also have copies made available to them. As far as the latter, in particular, is concerned, this is thought to be very helpful, since he does not have necessarily a long time between the conclusion of the hearing and the date fixed for the delivery of his submissions (terminating the oral procedure). One week is a normal time allowed to him.

The fact that "hand outs" of addresses are thus used might be thought virtually to turn an oral hearing into essentially a written procedure. That is, however, not the case, for two principal reasons: First, the judges, who have no copy of the address at the time it is made, must therefore be orally addressed, even though from a prepared text. Second, during any address in the hearing, there are almost certain to be exchanges of questions and answers between the judges and the agents, legal advisers or legal representatives of the parties, or exchanges between the latter themselves.

The Registrar keeps a record of these two types of exchanges (as to contents of this record see "Instructions to the Registrar", *post*, p. 305) which is appended to the texts of the address(es) before they are made available to the Judges and the Advocate General.

R.P. 59

Paragraph 1

The Advocate General shall make his reasoned oral submissions, before the closing of the oral procedure.

Paragraph 2

After the Advocate General's submissions, the President shall declare the oral procedure closed.

Generally as to the Advocate General, see under E.E.C. 166 and equivalents in Chapter 3, *ante*, pp. 189 *et seq.*

Though, after the Advocate General's submissions, the President declares the oral procedure closed, it may be re-opened by virtue of R.P. 61, *infra.*

R.P. 60

The Court may at any time order the taking of a measure of enquiry, or require the re-opening and extension of any part of the procedure of enquiry. It may direct the Section or the Judge acting as Rapporteur to carry out these measures.

As to measure of enquiry and procedure of enquiry, see under "Closure of Procedure of Enquiry" (R.P. 54) comment on "The President shall fix the date for the opening of the oral procedure at the end of this period" (*ante*, p. 247).

R.P. 61

The Court may order the re-opening of the oral procedure.

R.P. 62

Paragraph 1

The Registrar shall draw up a record of every sitting. This record shall be signed by the President and by the Registrar, and shall constitute an official record.

Paragraph 2

The parties may examine all such records in the Registrar's office, and may obtain copies at their own expense.

The Statutes (E.E.C. St. 30 and equivalents, see under "Keeping of a record of each hearing" *ante*, p. 249) do not specifically charge the Registrar with making the record.

For requirements as to contents of the Registrar's record see Chapter 6, *post*, p. 305.

"... **Official record ...**". See, in comment "The Conduct of the Hearing of Witnesses" paragraph beginning "Since the Registrar is required to keep a record ... (*ante*, p. 242); comment "A record of each hearing" (*ante*, p. 249); under R.P. 53, "... Official Record ..." (*ante*, p. 247).

V. JUDGMENTS (R.P. 63–68)

(Des arrêts; Urteile; van de arresten; Delle sentenze)

Introductory. Consideration of decisions. Upon the closure of the oral procedure (R.P. 59, *ante*, p. 252) the Court (or the Section concerned) considers its decision in secret in the judges' council chamber before delivering judgment. Secrecy is imposed by the Statutes (E.E.C. St. 32 with which E.A.E.C. St. 33 and E.C.S.C. St. 29 are both identical): "The Court's consideration of its decisions shall be and shall remain secret". "Consideration of decisions" (*"le délibéré"*; *"Beratung"*; *"beraadslaging"*; *"deliberazione"*) is the subject of special rules; but since (though E.E.C. St. 32 and equivalents (*supra*) are contained in Title III, "Procedure", of the Statutes) both the Statutes and the Rules of Procedure deal with it primarily as a matter of organisation of the Court (respectively in their Title II and Title I), it is also treated in this book in Chapter 3, Organisation (see E.E.C. St. 15 and equivalents (*ante*, pp. 201–202) and R.P. 27 (*ante*, pp. 202–203). It may be noted here that judgments are arrived at by majority decision of the judges (R.P. 27(5) (*loc. cit.*). The rules governing "consideration of decisions" apply to judgments, and in some cases to orders of the Court. Judgments and orders therefore need to be distinguished.

Judgments and orders. Whereas, generally, a judgment is delivered in order to dispose of the action, many (and in practice most) orders ("order" *"ordonnance"*; *"Beschlusz" "beschikking"*; *"ordinanza"*) are made by the Court (or Section) at some point in the procedure prior to the judgment. (Such, typically, are orders made in respect of the procedure of enquiry or calling of evidence, *ante*, p. 233). Exceptionally, some decisions which are, like judgments, conclusive in respect of a particular issue (or issues) are made by order, if need be, following "consideration of decision" (see *supra*). There is set out below a list of instances in which the decision of the Court (or Section) is made by order. Those instances in which the order is comparable to a judgment, in the sense of being conclusive, are marked with an asterisk.

Instances where the Court (or Section) renders its decision by order. (The letters C to S indicate whether the decision is the Court's or a Section's. An asterisk indicates that the order is conclusive in the same sense as a judgment).

1. (C)* Rectification of judgment (R.P. 66(4), this section *post*, p. 259)
2. (S)* Free Legal Aid (see this Chapter, R.P. 76, *post*, p. 264)
3. (C)* Letter of Request (for evidence) (see Chapter 6, "Supplementary Rules of Procedure" *post*, p. 300).
4. (S)* Dispute on recoverable costs (see this Chapter, R.P. 74, *post*, p. 263).
5. (C or S)* Barring legal adviser or legal representative from the proceedings (see Chapter 3, "Organisation", R.P. 35(1), *ante*, p. 207).
6. (C) Taking of measure of enquiry, or re-opening and extension of procedure of enquiry (see this Chapter, R.P. 60, *ante*, p. 252).
7. (C) Expert's examination and report (see this Chapter, R.P. 49, *ante*, p. 244).

8. (C) Determine measures for calling of evidence (see this Chapter, R.P. 45, *ante*, p. 234).
9. (C) Proof of certain facts by witnesses (see this Chapter, R.P. 47(1), *ante*, p. 240).
10. (C) Summoning witness(es) (see this Chapter R. P. 47(2), *ante*, p. 239).
11. (C) Fresh Service of Summons on witness (see this Chapter, R.P. 48(2), *ante*, p. 244).
12. (C)* Admissibility of intervention (see Chapter 5, R.P. 93(3), *post*, p. 278).
13. (C) Re-opening of the oral procedure (see this Chapter, R.P. 61, *ante*, p. 252).
14. (C)* Striking a case from the register (see this Chapter, R.P. 77 and R.P. 78, *post*, p. pp. 265 *et* 266).
15. (C) (or President alone)* Decision in summary procedure in case of urgency (see Chapter 5, R.P. 86(1), *post*, p. 273).

Judgments have "binding force" but there is no similar provision in respect of orders. R.P. 65 (*post*, p. 259) provides that as from the day of its delivery (*"prononcé"*; *"Verkündung"*; *"uitspraak"*; *"pronuncia"*) a judgment has binding force (*"a force obligatoire"*; *"wird rechtskräftig"*; *"verbindende kracht"*; *"forza obbligatoria"*). The meaning of this would appear to be that on that day it acquires the force of law, in the sense of becoming binding on the parties and imposing obligations upon them with regard to their respective interests in the action. It is nowhere provided that orders shall have binding force, though it would appear that orders relating to certain matters at least (such as 4, 14 and 15 in the list in the preceding comment, *supra*) have binding force by necessary implication. Binding force is not, however, identical with "executory force" (see next paragraph).

"Executory force" of judgments. Whereas "binding force" (see preceding paragraph) is effective as between the parties to an action (making it impossible for them to dispute what is decided in a judgment having binding force), "executory force" is the quality necessary in a judgment before it can be enforced by, if need be, the instrumentality of someone else (see "execution (enforcement) of judgment", *post* p. 255). "Executory force" is expressly conferred on the Court's judgment by the treaties themselves (*"les arrêts" ont force exécutoire"*; *"Die Urteile ... sind ... vollstreckbar"*; *"De arresten ... zyn ... uitvoerbaar"*; *"Le sentenze ... hanno forza esecutiva"*) in the following articles:

E.E.C. 187

The judgments of the Court of Justice shall be enforceable under the conditions laid down in Article 192.

"... The conditions laid down in "E.E.C. 192 (see E.E.C. 192, *ante*, pp. 26–27

E.A.E.C. 159

[*Identical with E.E.C. 187 except that it refers to* E.A.E.C. *164 which corresponds to* E.E.C. *192, supra, and see E.E.C. 164, post,* p. 255

E.C.S.C. 44

The judgments of the Court shall be enforceable in the territory of Member States under the conditions laid down in Article 92 below.

This article confers upon judgments executory force "on the territory of Member States", a limitation omitted from E.E.C. 187 and E.A.E.C. 159 (*supra*). For text of E.C.S.C. 92, see *infra*.

"Execution, enforcement of judgments". The mechanism of enforcement consists of two elements: (i) the document comprising the judgment is, by virtue of the Treaties, made to constitute a document of title (*"forment titre exécutoire"*; *"sind vollstreckbare Titel"*; *"vormen executoriale titel"*; *"costituiscono titolo esecutivo"*) (see E.E.C. 192 and E.C.S.C. 92 paragraph 1, *infra*); (ii) execution is enforced with no other check (except what is necessary to check the authenticity of the document of title) in accordance with the rules of civil procedure in force in the State in whose territory it takes place. Both these elements are the subject of one Article of each Treaty as follows:

E.E.C. 192

[*Printed on* ante, *pp*. 26–27.]

See the comment immediately preceding.

E.A.E.C. 164

[*This omits paragraph one of E.E.C.* 192 *but is otherwise identical.*]

The resultant omission of the express provision that judgments "constitute title" for execution (*"forment titre exécutoire"* etc.) may be considered remedied by the reference to "title" in paragraph 2.

E.C.S.C. 92

Decisions of the High Authority which involve a pecuniary obligation shall have the enforceability of a Court judgment.

Enforcement in the territory of Member States shall be carried out by means of the legal procedure in force in each State, after the order for enforcement in the form in use in the State in whose territory the decision is to be carried out has been appended to the decision without other formality than verification of the authenticity of the decision. These formalities shall be carried out under the responsibility of a Minister designated for this purpose by each of the Governments.

Enforcement may be suspended only by a decision of the Court.

The first sentence of the second paragraph contemplates enforced execution "in the territory of Member States" only, a limitation omitted from E.E.C. 192 and E.A.E.C. 164 *supra*. Compare E.C.S.C. 44, *ante*, p. 254.

Stay of execution. See Chapter 2 "Jurisdiction", *ante*, pp. 179 *et seq.*, and Chapter 5 "Special Forms of Procedure", *post*, pp. 270 *et seq.*

Costs of enforcement. These are payable by the party against whom the judgment is enforced by virtue of R.P. 71. The costs which one of the parties has had to incur for the purposes of enforcement shall be refunded by the other party on the scale in use in the State where the enforcement takes place.

Procedural requirements in respect of judgments imposed by the Statutes. Two articles of Title II "Procedure" of the Statutes make general provision in respect of judgments as follows:

E.E.C. St. 33

Judgments shall be reasoned. They shall give the names of the judges responsible for them.

E.A.E.C. St. 34

[*Identical with E.E.C. St. 33.*]

"The Judgments shall be reasoned" (*"motivés"*; *"mit Gründen versehen"*; *"met redenen omkleed"*; *"motivate"*). Virtually identical wording is used in R.P. 76 (*post*, p. 264). Compare table of expressions in the four languages in comment "(b) the arguments of fact and law which are relied upon" under R.P. 40, *ante*, p. 227.

". . . The names of the judges responsible for them". See ". . . the names of the judges who took part . . ." under E.C.S.C. St. 30, *infra*, and compare R.P. 63, *infra*.

E.C.S.C. St. 30

Judgments shall be reasoned. They shall give the names of the Judges who took part.

". . . The names of the judges who took part". Compare "the names of the judges responsible for them" in E.E.C. St. 33 (*supra*). There may be no difference in practice but in principle a difference appears possible, and R.P. 27 (*ante*, pp. 202–203) does not eliminate the possibility.

E.E.C. St. 34

Judgments shall be signed by the President and the Registrar. They shall be read in open court.

E.A.E.C. St. 33

[*Identical with E.E.C. St. 34.*]

E.C.S.C. St. 31

Judgments shall be signed by the President, the Judge acting as Rapporteur and the Registrar. They shall be read in open court.

The requirements that the reporting judge should sign the judgment does not apply in E.E.C. or E.A.E.C. (*supra*).

A judgment has to be signed and read. It follows that there can be no such thing as a purely oral judgment. In E.C.S.C. this might at one time have seemed possible (see comment on R.P. 64(1), *post* p. 258). Probative force (*"force probante"*) pertains to the signed document, not to what is "pronounced" or read in Court. See R.P. 64, *post* p. 258.

R.P. 63

The judgment shall contain:

  a statement that it is delivered by the Court;
  the date of delivery;
  the names of the President and the Judges taking part;
  the name of the Advocate General;

the name of the Registrar;

particulars of the parties;

the names of agents, legal advisers and legal representatives
of the parties;

the submissions of the parties;

a mention that the Advocate General has been heard.

a brief summary of the facts;

the grounds on which the judgment is based;

the order of the Court, including a decision on costs.

"...The date of delivery...". See R.P. 64(3) and R.P. 65, *post*,
pp. 258–259. It may be noted that written statements of case and written
comments are not specifically required to be contained in the judgment,
though they are (procedural) facts and ought therefore (*semble*) to figure
in the "brief summary of facts" that is required. See in Chapter 5, under
E.E.C. St. 20, comment "... written statements of case or written comments
..." *post*, p. 295.

"...A decision on costs...". As to costs, see "Costs", *post*, p. 261.

The parties and their lawyers play no part in the drawing up of the judgment. The Court may act in accordance with the parties' submissions.
Though the parties and their lawyers play no part in the drawing up of
the judgment, where a party waives a right to make a submission in respect
of costs the Court may render judgment accordingly. Thus in *Gouvernement
de la République Française* c. *Haute Autorité* (case 1/54 R. Vol. 1 at p. 34) where
the Agent of the French Government declared that it had made "no submission in regard to costs", the Court acted in accordance with this and in
its judgment ordered each party to pay its own costs. Where the Court
thus adopts what is put forward by the parties the German expresses this as
"*Kenntnis nehmen von*" (but see next paragraph of this comment). The
Netherlands language similarly uses only one expression: "*acte nemen van*".
In the French and Italian the concept is expressed either subjectively or
objectively: "*prendre acte de*" and "*donner acte de*", "*prendere atto di*" and
"*dare atto di*" (the use of both expressions, in French and Italian, occurs
in the judgment, *loc. cit.*, *supra*).

Where, however, a party submitted to the Court in terms that it should
act in accordance with the fact that it reserved the right to bring another
action before the Court for damages against the High Authority, and give
judgment accordingly, the Court held the submission inadmissible (*Société
Nouvelles des Usines de Pontlieue Aciéries du Temple (S.N.U.P.A.T.)* c. *Haute
Autorité* (Consolidated Cases 42 and 49/59 R. Vol. VII at p. 143). The
terms expressing the application to the Court "to act in accordance with"
this fact were in the original languages in the objective form as follows:
"... *la requérante demande*... *à la Cour de lui*... *donner acte*... *de ses ré-
serves*..."; "*la ricorrente ha*... *chiesto all Corte di*... *darle atto che essa si
riserva*"; "*Die Klägerin beantragt ferner, ihr zu bestätigen, dasz*... *sie sich
vorbehält*". It will be noted that in the German "*ihr zu bestätigen*" corresponds
to the objective form of "*donner acte*" and "*dare atto*" whereas in case 1/54
(*loc. cit.*, first paragraph this comment, *supra*) the same expression ("*Kenntnis
nehmen von*") was used for both "*donner acte*" and "*prendre acte*".

The party had submitted not only that the Court should act in accordance
with the fact that it (the party) reserved the right to bring another action
but also in accordance with the fact that it was its (the party's) "intention to
request the consolidation of the new action with the present case". To have
admitted the second part of the request would in any event have run counter

to the principle that judgments are rendered with a view to concluding the action (see, "Judgments and orders", *ante*, p. 253). This was indeed one, but only one, of the grounds on which the Court rejected the two-fold submission. The French text of the Court's reasoning on this point is here quoted for convenience:

> "11—QUANT À LA RECEVABILITÉ DES CONCLUSIONS SUPPLÉMENTAIRES
> DE LA REQUÉRANTE
>
> Attendu que la requérante demande en outre à la Cour de lui donner acte . . . de ses réserves d'introduire devant la Cour un nouveau recours en dommages-intérêts contre la Haute Autorité, pour faute de service, en réparation du préjudice subi par elle à la suite des dérogations sus-visées, et de lui donner acte également de ce qu'elle a l'intention de solliciter la jonction de ce nouveau recours au present litige;
>
> attendu que la requérante n'a pas établi qu'elle a un intérêt légitime à présenter de telles conclusions et que la Cour ne voit pas davantage l'existence de pareil intérêt;
>
> qu'en effet le droit d'agir de la requérante ne saurait en aucun cas dépendre du fait que la Cour lui ait préalablement donné acte de son intention d'en user;
>
> que la jonction du litige futur et du litige actuel, qui est tranché par le présent arrêt est inconcevable;
>
> que, dès lors, faute d'intérêt, ces deux chefs du présent recours sont irrecevables."

R.P. 64

Paragraph 1

The judgment shall be delivered in open court, after notice to the parties to attend.

Paragraph 2

The original of the judgment, signed by the President, by the Judges who took part in its consideration and by the Registrar, shall be sealed and deposited in the Registrar's office; a certified copy of it shall be served on each of the parties.

Paragraph 3

The Registrar shall make a note on the original of the judgment of the date on which it was delivered.

This Rule implements in part the requirement of E.E.C. St. 34 and equivalents (*ante*, p. 256).

Paragraph 1. The judgment shall be delivered in open Court . . ."
(*"rendu en audience publique"*; *"in öffentlicher Sitzung verkündet"*; *"ter openbare terechtzitting uitgesproken"*; *"pronunciata in pubblica udienza"*). See *ante*, pp. 256–257). What is delivered in open Court is a signed document read aloud. A purely oral judgment cannot exist. Some of the doubts on this point that might have been caused by the wording of the original E.C.S.C. Rules of Procedure, now rescinded, have been removed by a change of wording (*e.g.* in the French, *"rendu"* replaces *"prononcé"*). Following delivery in open Court an entry signed by the President and Registrar is required to be made at the foot of the original that the judgment (or order) has been so read (by virtue of "Instructions to the Registrar", Article 6, *post*, p. 304). In that Instruction

the German and Netherlands versions describe "read" by the same word as used for "delivered", *"verkundet"* and *"uitgesproken"*, but the French and Italian change to *"lu"* and *"letto"*. In E.E.C. St. 34 and equivalents (*ante*, p. 256) only the Netherlands uses the same expression *"uitgesproken"*. The others are *"lus"*, *"verlesen"* and *"lette"*. The judgment in writing proves itself in subsequent proceedings without further evidence.

Paragraph 3. "... delivered". In all the languages except French the same word is used as in R.P. 65 (*infra*). The French uses *"rendu"* and in R.P. 65 *"prononcé"*.

R.P. 65

The judgment shall have binding force from the date of its delivery.

"The judgment shall have binding force . . ." See comment "Judgments have binding force", *ante*, p. 254.

". . . Delivery . . ." See comment . . ."delivered" under R.P. 64(3), *supra*.

R.P. 66

Paragraph 1

Without prejudice to the provisions relating to the interpretation of judgments, clerical errors and mistakes in reckoning or patent inaccuracies may be corrected by the Court, either of its own volition or at the request of one of the parties, within a period of 14 days from delivery of the judgment.

Paragraph 2

The parties, duly notified by the Registrar, may submit written comments within a time limit set by the President.

Paragraph 3

The Court shall reach its decision in the Judges' Council Chamber, after hearing the Advocate General.

Paragraph 4

The original of the order making the correction shall be annexed to the original of the judgment which is corrected. A note of this order shall be made in the margin of the original of the judgment which is corrected.

Paragraph 1. "... the provisions relating to the interpretation of judgments ..." As to procedure, see Chapter 5, "Interpretation of Judgments", *post*, pp. 291 *et seq.*; as to jurisdiction see Chapter 2, *ante*, p. 61.

Paragraph 1. ..."clerical errors and mistakes in reckoning or patent inaccuracies may be corrected by the Court either of its own volition or at the request of one of the parties ..."

...**"Patent inaccuracies ..."** (*"inexactitudes évidentes"*; *"offenbare Un-richtigkeiten"*; *"klaarblijkelijke onnauwkeurigheden"*; *"evidenti inesattezze"*). There must presumably be no possibility of doubt as to the material nature of the inaccuracy, but it would seem that such can be considered "patent" by reference not only to the text itself. An example of inaccuracies appearing obvious to the Court is in *Mannesmann A. G. et autres* c. *Haute Autorité* (Consolidated Cases 4 13/59 R. Vol. VI (1) at p. 329). The Court's decision is made by order (R.P. 66(4), *supra*) (*c.f.* "Judgments and orders", *ante*, pp. 253–254). For an example of such an order see *Mannesmann A. G. and Ors.* c. *Haute Autorité* (*loc. cit., supra*). For an example of an Order of the Court rejecting the claim of a party for rectification of a judgment see *Société Fives Lille Cail elé.* c. *Haute Autorité* (Consolidated cases 19, 21/60 and 2, 3/61 R. Vol. VII at pp. 630–1). The order making the correction is annexed to the original of the judgment which is corrected (R.P. 66(4), *supra*). (As to jurisdiction see also Chapter 2, *ante*, p. 61).

R.P. 67

If the Court has omitted to give a ruling, either on one count in the submissions or on the matter of costs, the party intending to rely upon this shall approach the Court by way of a Request within one month of service of the judgment.

The Request shall be served on the other party and the President shall set him a time limit within which he may submit his written comments.

After submission of these written comments and after the Advocate General has been heard, the Court shall decide at one and the same time whether the application can be entertained and whether it is well founded.

"... **One count in the submissions** ..." (*"un chef isolé des conclusions"*; *"einzelner Punkt der Anträge"*; *"een afzonderlijk punt van de conclusies"*; *"un capo isolato delle conclusioni"*). The judgment of the Court concludes with the operative part (*"le dispositif"*) based on the reasoning which immediately precedes it (*"la motivation"*). It is possible that in one sentence of the operative part a ruling on more than one count in the submissions (by way of claim or defence of the parties) can be given, without direct reference to all such counts severally. The absence of specific mention in the operative part of the judgment of one count in the submissions would presumably not suffice to found a claim by way of Request, since in the preceding part of the judgment giving the reasoning of the Court, all the submissions of the parties should have been taken into consideration. Only if that is not so in respect of a single count (which furthermore is not met in the operative part) will a claim under R.P. 67 lie.

"... **Or on the matter of costs** ..."   As to costs, see *post*, p. 261. The Court has no power to proceed on its own volition to remedy an omission to give a ruling.

"... **the Court shall decide** ..."   Presumably, it decides by judgment complementing the judgment containing an omission to rule.

The judgment or order terminating the case must contain a ruling on costs (R.P. 69, "Costs", *post*, p. 261).

R.P. 68

The Registrar shall see to the publication of official Court law reports.

These reports are referred to throughout this book by the abbreviation "R" (for *"Recueil de Jurisprudence"*).

VI. COSTS (R.P. 69–74)
(*Des dépens; Prozeszkosten; Van de proceskosten; Delle spese*)

R.P. 69
Paragraph 1

The Court shall give a ruling on costs in the judgment or order terminating the case.

Paragraph 2

The losing party shall pay the costs, if application has been made to this effect in the submissions.

If there are several losing parties the Court shall decide how the costs are to be apportioned.

Paragraph 3

The Court may leave each party to bear its own costs wholly or in part if the parties fail respectively on one or more counts, or for exceptional reasons.

The Court may order one of the parties, even the winning one, to refund to the other party the costs which the former has caused the latter to incur and which the Court considers to have been frivolous or vexatious.

Paragraph 4

A party who withdraws from the case shall be ordered to pay the costs, unless this withdrawal is justified by the attitude of the other party.

In the absence of a submission from the other party on this point, the parties shall bear their own costs.

Paragraph 5

Where it decides not to proceed to judgment the Court shall make such order as to costs as it thinks fit.

Paragraph 1. "The Court shall give a ruling on costs . . ." This provision duplicates that of E.E.C. St. 35, E.A.E.C. St. 36 and E.C.S.C. 32. Where the Court omits so to rule, application to it to do so may be made under the provision of R.P. 67 (*ante*, p. 260) but where no application is made by a party the Court has no power to remedy the omission of its own volition.

Paragraph 2. "The losing party shall pay the costs . . ." (See *Meroni et autres* c. *Haute Autorité* (Consolidated Cases, 14, 16, 17, 20, 24, 26 and 27/60 R. Vol. VIII judgment at p. 341–342). In *Comptoirs de vente du Charbon de la Ruhr "Geitling"* etc. c. *Haute Autorité* (Consolidated Cases 16, 17, 18/59. R. Vol. VI (i) at p. 65) the Court stated:

"By the terms of R.P. 69(2) the losing party shall pay the costs. In the present case the applicants lost on admissibility. However, the fact that, in the reasons given [by the High Authority] for decision 17–59, recital No. 7 was drafted in such a clearly imperative way, might normally give the impression that it represented the taking up from that moment of time of a clear position, and thus was in fact a decision. This may have led the applicants to bring the present action and has caused them frivolous costs. Consequently the costs of the action must be borne in part by the defendant . . ."

Paragraph 3. "The Court may leave each party to bear its own costs . . ." (*"compenser les dépens"; "die Kosten . . . gegen einander aufheben"; "de proceskosten . . . compenseren"; "compensare . . . le spese"*). See *Niederrheinische Bergwerks-Aktiengesellschaft* (R. Vol. VII, judgment at pp. 91–92). In *Meroni & Co. Erba, Meroni & Co. Milan* c. *Haute Autorité* (Consolidated Cases 46 & 47/59. R. Vol. VIII at p. 807) the Court stated:

"The applicants have failed . . . but they were led to (bring the action) because they did not know, or might not have known, that the Court would be prepared to try, without holding them barred by prescription, appeals introduced after the Compensation accounts had been closed. This lack of knowledge, which can not be held against the applicants, led them to bring their actions for compensation at the moment they thought appropriate. This circumstance constitutes an exceptional reason, within the meaning of R.P. 69(3) for leaving each party to bear part of the costs."

Each party was ordered to bear its own costs.

In *Meroni & Co. Acciaieria di Roma (FERAM)* etc. c. *Haute Autorité* (Consolidated cases 5, 7, 8/60 R. Vol. VII at p. 215) the Court ordered costs against the High Authority except those incurred subsequent to the notification of the revocation of its decisions against which the claim was brought.

Paragraph 3. ". . . costs . . . which the Court considers . . . frivolous or vexatious". Where a party applied by two Requests when one would have sufficed, the costs of one Request were awarded against the applicant (*"Société métallurgique de Knutange* c. *Haute Autorité* (Consolidated Cases 15/59 and 29/59 Vol. VI (1) judgment at pp. 28–29). In *Comptoirs de vente du Charbon de la Ruhr "Geitling" et autres* c. *Haute Autorité* (Consolidated Cases 16–18/59 R. Vol. VI (1) judgment at pp. 55–57) the applicant had applied by a Request which turned out to be frivolous but the applicant had reason to suppose otherwise. The Court awarded a measure ($\frac{1}{2}$) the costs against the defendant, although not admitting the applicant's Request. In *Meroni & Co. et autres* c. *Haute Autorité*, Consolidated Cases 5, 7, 8/60 R. Vol. VII, judgment at pp. 213–214 considers R.P. 69 (2), (3), (4) and (5).

Paragraph 4. "A party who withdraws from the case . . ." See "Withdrawals" R.P. 77–78 (*post*, pp. 265–266).

R.P. 70

In the proceedings referred to in Article 95, paragraph 1, of these Rules, the costs incurred by the institutions shall be borne by them, without prejudice to the provisions of Article 69, paragraph 3, second sub-paragraph of these Rules.

For an example of costs being shared between the defendant (High Authority) and the unsuccessful applicant, see *Raymond Elz.* c. *Haute Autorité* (Consolidated Cases 22 and 23/60 R. Vol. VII judgment as to costs at pp. 377–378). The case also exemplifies the principle that the awarding of costs does not necessarily involve fixing their amount in terms of money. If the amount of recoverable costs is disputed the Section may rule (see R.P. 74, *post*, p. 203).

R.P. 71

[*Printed at* ante *p.* 255.]

R.P. 72

The Court shall make no charge in respect of proceedings before it, subject to the following provisions:

(*a*) if the Court has incurred expenses which might have been avoided it may, after the Advocate General has been heard, order the party who has caused these expenses to refund them.

(*b*) the cost of all copying and translation work carried out at the request of one of the parties, considered by the Registrar to have been abnormal, shall be paid for by this party on the basis of the scale of charges referred to in Article 15, paragraph 5 of these Rules.

"(b) the cost of all copying and translation work ... considered abnormal ... on the basis of the scale referred to in ..." The charges are set out in Instructions to the Registrar (Article 20):

"Article 20

The Registrar's fees shall be as follows:

(a) For an office copy of a judgment or order, a certified copy of a procedural document or record, an extract from the Court register, a certified copy made under Article 72(b) of the Rules of Procedure: 30 Lux. francs per page.

(b) For a translation made under Article 72(b) of the Rules of Procedure: 200 Lux. francs per page.

These fees shall be for the first copy, each subsequent copy being charged at the rate of 5 Lux. francs per page or part of a page."

R.P. 73

Without prejudice to the provisions of the preceding Article, the following shall be regarded as recoverable costs:

(*a*) sums due to witnesses and experts under Article 51 of these rules;

(*b*) expenses necessarily incurred by the parties for the purpose of the proceedings, in particular travel and subsistence and remuneration of an agent, legal adviser or legal representative.

R.P. 74

Paragraph 1

If there is dispute on the recoverable costs, the Section to which the case has been assigned shall, at the request of the party concerned, after hearing the other party's comments and the Advocate General's submissions, make an order, against which no recourse shall be available.

Paragraph 2

The parties may, for the purpose of enforcement, request an office copy of the order.

"... **Dispute on the recoverable costs ...**" This may arise because the judgment is not required to fix liquidated costs but only the proportion in which they are to be borne. (See R.P. 69, *supra*). If need be, therefore, the liquidated amount has to be determined by a special order of the Section.

Order against which no recourse shall be available. This is the form of the Section's decision on the application.

Paragraph 2. ..."office copy of the order". This now has to be requested. In the rescinded Rules of Procedure it was incumbent on the Court to supply the order.

VII. FREE LEGAL AID (R.P. 76)

(*"De l'assistance judiciaire gratuite"*; *"Armenrecht"*; *"van de toelating om kosteloos te procederen"*; *"Del gratuito patrocinio"*)

R.P. 76

Paragraph 1

If one of the parties finds himself partially or wholly unable to meet the cost of the proceedings, he may at any time ask for the benefit of free legal aid.

The application shall be accompanied by full information showing that the party concerned is in need, including a certificate from the competent authority in support of his contention of lack of means.

Paragraph 2

If the application is made prior to the proceedings which the party making it intends to institute, it shall give a brief account of the purpose of those proceedings.

The application need not be made through a legal representative.

Paragraph 3

The President shall appoint a Judge to act as Rapporteur. The Section to which the the latter belongs shall decide, after considering the written comments of the other party and after the Advocate General has been heard, whether free legal aid should be granted wholly or in part, or whether it should be refused. It shall consider whether the case is not clearly ill-founded.

The Section shall make an order without giving reasons, against which no recourse shall be available.

Paragraph 4

The Section may at any time, either of its own volition or on request withdraw the benefit of free legal aid if the conditions which led to its being granted have changed during the course of the proceedings.

Paragraph 5

In the event of free legal aid being granted, the Court pay office shall make advances to cover expenses.

The decision as to costs shall order deduction to be made in favour of the Court pay office of sums paid out by way of free legal aid.

These sums shall be recovered by the Registrar from the party ordered to pay them.

Paragraph 1 "... **he may at any time ask for the benefit** ..." That is, before or after the action is originated. (As to origination see, *ante*, p. 218).

Paragraph 2 "... **the application need not be made through a legal representative**". (*"La demande est dispensée du ministère d'avocat";* *"Der Antrag unterliegt nicht dem Anwaltszwang"; "Het versoek kan zonder bijstand van een advocaat worden ingediend"; "Per la presentazione della domanda non e prescritta l'assistenza di un avvocato"*). See "agents, legal advisers and legal representatives" (*ante*, pp. 213–214). This presumably applies to an application made "at any time" (see paragraph 1, *supra*).

Paragraph 2 "The Section shall make an order without giving reasons against which no recourse shall be available". (without giving reasons—*"non motivée"; "ohne Angabe von Gründen"; "miet met redenen omklede"; "non motivata"* virtually identical wording is used in E.E.C. St. 33 and equivalents, *ante*, p. 256).

Compare expressions tabulated in comment "arguments of fact and law which are relied upon", *ante*, pp. 226–227.

VIII. WITHDRAWALS (R.P. 77, 78)

(*"Des désistements"; "Aussergerichtliche Erledigung und Klagerücknahme"; "van de afstand van instantie"; "della rinuncia agli atti"*)

R.P. 77

If, before the Court has given its decision, the parties come to an agreed settlement of their dispute and inform the Court that they withdraw claims, the Court shall order the case to be struck from the register.

This provision shall not apply to proceedings specified in Articles 33 and 35 of the E.C.S.C. Treaty, Articles 173 and 175 of the E.E.C. Treaty and Articles 146 and 148 of the E.A.E.C. Treaty.

"... **The parties** ... **inform the Court that they withdraw claims**"... (*"renoncent à toute prétention"; "auf die Geltendmachung ihrer Ansprüche verzichten"; "van haar vordering afzien"; "rinunciano ad ogni pretesa"*). The parties must agree (including presumably any intervener) before a claim can be withdrawn. Withdrawal represents a waiver of all legal right and claims based thereon. It transcends the action. Not so the wish to discontinue (in R.P. 78, *infra*) which operates solely in respect of the proceedings in the present action.

The result, however, as far as the Court is concerned, is the same. It must "order the case to be struck from the Register" (*"ordonne la radiation de l'affaire du registre"; "die Streichung der Rechtssache im Register an"; "de doorhaling van de zaak in het register"; "la cancellazione della causa del ruolo"*).

Since the order terminates the case the Court must rule on costs in the order (by virtue of R.P. 69, *ante*, p. 261). The order "is served" (*infra* on the parties (*infra*); ("... articles 33 and 35 of the E.C.S.C. Treaty etc.", see these in Chapter 2 under "Legality of Acts" (*ante*, p. 89) and "Failure to act" (*ante*, p. 120)).

R.P. 78

If the applicant in the case gives written notice to the Court that he wishes to discontinue, the Court shall order the case to be struck from the register.

"... **Wishes to discontinue** ..." ("*entend renoncer à l'instance*"; "*nimmt der Kläger ... die Klage zurück*"; "*afstand wenst te doen van instantie* ..."; "*intende rinunciare agli atti*"). This operates solely in respect of the action and does not constitute a waiver of all legal rights, (*cf.* R.P. 77, *ante*, p. 265). The result as far as the Court is concerned is the same (see under R.P. 77, *loc. cit.*). One party, in practice the applicant, may discontinue under R.P. 78. But for a withdrawal of claims under R.P. 77 (*loc. cit.*) there must be prior agreement between the parties. Discontinuance in accordance with R.P. 37 (*ante*, p. 220) is effected by "procedural document" deposited with the Registrar. It is communicated to the opposing party who is restricted to making submissions as to costs and cannot resist the discontinuance.

Discontinuance (or withdrawal) in respect of one only of several heads of claim in the submissions. This is possible by virtue of R.P. 78. In *Comptoir de Vente du Charbon de la Ruhr "Geitling" et autres* c. *Haute Autorité* (Consolidated Cases 16, 17, 18/59 R. Vol. VI (1) p. 45) the applicant wished to discontinue in respect of the eighth only of the eight heads of claim in the submissions. The defendant undertook during the oral procedure to bear the costs of this eighth head of claim. The Court admitted this agreement to discontinue (judgment, paragraph 2, at p. 67, *loc. cit*). The headnote to the reported case reads on this point: "The submissions of the applicant claiming the quashing of a decision (of the High Authority) which had not been cancelled with retroactive effect, but only abrogated, continue to have point in respect of the period between the entry into force and the cancellation of the decision; they have not become without object, but if the applicant subsequently declares to the Court that he considers them to be without object, this declaration has the character of a discontinuance."

Discontinuance in respect of some but not all of the defendants. In *Firma I. Nold K.G.* c. *Haute Autorité* (Case 18/57 R. Vol. V p. 89 at p. 100) the applicant discontinued in respect of all the defendants other than the High Authority (they were presumably wrongly joined in the first place). The discontinuance was accepted by those defendants and by the Court which "by order ... directed the removal of the case from the files so far as the said defendants were concerned".

IX. SERVICE (R.P. 79)

("*Des significations*"; "*Zustellungen*"; "*van de betekeningen*"; "*Delle notifiche*")

Service is distinct from both communication and notification (see this Chapter under "the written procedure shall include ... communication" *ante*, p. 215). But distinction between service communication and notification is not, however, consistently made in all four original treaty languages. Thus in "Instructions to the Registrar" (*post*, p. 303) the French refers to "*significations, notifications et communications*"; the German to "*Zustellungen*", "*Bekanntgaben und Mitteilungen*"; the Netherlands to only "*betekeningen en mededelingen*"; the Italian to only "*notifiche e comunicazione*".

R.P. 79
Paragraph 1

It shall be for the Registrar to see that service required by these Rules of Procedure is effected at the address for service of the addressee, either by despatch by registered post of a copy of the document to be served, acknowledged by written receipt, or by delivery by hand against receipt.

Copies of the document to be served shall be made and certified to be copies of the original by the Registrar, save where they come from the parties themselves in accordance with Article 37, paragraph 1 of these Rules.

Paragraph 2

The Post Office receipt on despatch and the acknowledgement of receipt by post or by hand shall be annexed to the original of the document.

Service is the responsibility of the Registrar. (See R.P. 79(1), *supra* and "Instructions to the Registrar" *post*, p. 303). The date of service is the date of receipt or of the signature for receipt through the post, of the procedural document. Every service is entered in the record of the Registry (Instruction 14) (*post*, p. 306).

"Address for service..." (*"domicile élu"*; *"chosen domicile"*). In the case of a legal person, the delivery at its registered office (*"siège statuaire"*) into the hands of an employee must be considered sufficient, and no argument could subsequently be sustained on the basis that the procedural document delivered did not reach the competent authorities (see judgment of 10th December 1957 R. Vol. III p. 183).

Service of procedural documents. "The parties shall be served with the procedural documents and the other documents relating thereto" ("Instructions to the Registrar", *post*, p. 303. As to procedural documents in general see under "requests, statements of case, defences, comments ... replies" *ante*, p. 216). In addition to the more usual procedural documents (request, defence, reply, further reply, etc.) required to be served, attention may be called to other examples where service is necessary: The request for intervention is served on the parties (R.P. 93(3), Appendix, *post*). A copy of the judgment is served on each of the parties (R.P. 64(2), *ante*, p. 258). The application for judgment by default is served on the defendant (R.P. 94, *post*, p. 280). The order of the Court setting out the facts to be proved is served on the parties (R.P. 45(1), *ante*, p. 234) and the order of the Court as to the hearing of witnesses is served on the parties and on the witnesses (R.P. 47(2), *ante*, p. 239).

X. TIME LIMITS (R.P. 80–82)
(*"Des délais"*; *"Fristen"*; *"van de termijnen"*; *"Dei termini"*).

R.P. 80
Paragraph 1

The procedural time limits provided for by the E.C.S.C., E.E.C. and E.A.E.C. Treaties, the Statutes of the Court and these Rules of Procedure, shall be reckoned by excluding the day of the date of the procedural step as from which time starts to run.

Time limits shall not be suspended during Court vacations.
Paragraph 2
If the date of expiry of the time limit falls on a Sunday or on an official holiday, such expiry shall be postponed until the end of the next working day.

The list of official holidays drawn up by the Court shall be published in the Official Journal of the European Communities.

Paragraph 2 ". . . official holidays".
Rules of Procedure, Appendix I provides:
"Having regard to Article 80 paragraph 2 of the Rules of Procedure requiring the Court to fix the list of official holidays;
DECIDES:
Article 1
The list of official holidays within the meaning of Article 80 paragraph 2 of the Rules of Procedure is fixed as follows:

> New Year's Day
> January 23
> Easter Monday
> May 1
> Ascension Day
> Whit Monday
> August 15
> November 1
> December 25
> December 26

Article 2
The provisions of Article 80 paragraph 2 of the Rules of Procedure refer solely to the official holidays mentioned in Article 1 of this Decision.
Article 3
This Decision which shall be Appendix I to the Rules of Procedure shall enter into force on the same day as the Rules of Procedure to which it is annexed.
It shall be published in the Official Journal of the European Communities."

As to the Court vacations see in general R.P. 28 (*ante*, p. 203) and as to official public holidays of the place where the Court "has its seat", see R.P. 28(3), (*loc. cit.*).

R.P. 81

Paragraph 1
The time limits fixed for the institution of proceedings against some measure taken by an institution shall commence, in the case of notification, from the day following that on which the person concerned has received notification of the measure in question or, in the case of publication, on the fifteenth day after the publication of the measure in the Official Journal of the European Communities.

Paragraph 2

Periods of grace allowed on account of distance shall be determined by a decision of the Court published in the Official Journal of the European Communities.

This provision derives from E.E.C. St. 42. E.A.E.C. St. 43 and E.C.S.C. St. 39 (identical with E.E.C. St. 42).

Paragraph 2 . . . "Periods of grace allowed on account of distance . . ." Rules of Procedure Appendix II provides:

"Having regard to Article 81, paragraph 2 of the Rules of Procedure relating to periods of grace allowed on account of distance;
DECIDES:
Article 1

Except where the parties have their usual residence in the Grand Duchy of Luxembourg, the procedural time limits shall be increased by reason of distance, as follows:

In Belgium	2 days
In Germany, Metropolitan France and the Netherlands ...	6 days
In Italy	10 days
In the other Countries of Europe	15 days
In other Countries	one month

Article 2

This decision which shall constitute Appendix II to the Rules of Procedure shall enter into force on the same day as the Rules of Procedure to which it is annexed.

It shall be published in the Official Journal of the European Communities."

R.P. 82

Time limits set in pursuance of these Rules may be extended by the authority which laid them down.

"Time limits set in pursuance of these Rules may be extended". This is not so for time limits provided for by the Statutes or Treaties. "In pursuance of these Rules" the President may set time limits (see R.P. 41(2), *ante*, p. 229; 42(2), *ante*, p. 229; 66(2), *ante*, p. 259) or a Section may do so (see R.P. 46(1), *ante*, p. 236; R.P. 95(1), *post*, p. 283); or the Registrar may do so (R.P. 38(7), *ante*, p. 222).

Special Forms of Procedure (R.P. 83–108)

(Des procédures spéciales; besondere Verfahrensarten; Van de bijzondere procedures; Dei procedimenti speciali)

"Special Forms of Procedure" is the heading of Title Three of the Rules of Procedure, and the eleven chapter headings into which the title is sub-divided are treated in the present chapter of this work under the same headings and in the same order, in eleven sections, *seriatim*, below. In each of the eleven sections, where applicable, the articles of the Court's Statute(s) constituting the general enactment providing the basis for the particular provisions of the Rules of Procedure, are treated first.

I. "SUSPENSION OF ENFORCEMENT AND OTHER INTERIM MEASURES BY WAY OF SUMMARY PROCEDURE IN CASE OF URGENCY". (R.P. 83–90)

("Du sursis et des autres mesures provisoires par voie de référé"; "Aussetzung des Vollzugs oder der Zwangsvollstreckung und sonstige einstweilige Anordnungen"; "Van Verzoeken tot opschorting van executie en ter verkrijging van andere voorlopige maatregelen in kort geding; "Della sospensione dell'esecuzione e degli altri provvedimenti urgenti mediante procedimento sommario")

E.E.C. St. 36

The President of the Court shall have power to decide certain matters by means of a summary procedure, which shall depart, to the extent necessary, from some of the rules contained in this Statute. This summary procedure, the details of which shall be determined by the rules of procedure, shall apply to applications for suspension of operation, as provided for in Article 185 of this Treaty, or to the prescribing of interim measures pursuant to Article 186, or to suspension of enforcement in accordance with Article 192, last paragraph.

In the event of the President being prevented from carrying out his duties, his place shall be taken by another judge in accordance with the rules of procedure.

The decision of the President or of his alternate shall be provisional and shall in no way prejudice the decision of the Court on the substance of the case.

E.A.E.C. St. 37

[*Identical with E.E.C. St. 36.*]

E.C.S.C. St. 33

[*Identical with E.E.C. St. 36.*]

"...By means of a summary procedure..." The summary procedure, which is based on the enabling provision of E.E.C. St. 36 and its equivalents, may be invoked in respect of any of the three types of matter enumerated in the same articles of the Statutes, that is to say: (i) the obtaining of suspension of enforcement of an administrative act (E.E.C. 185 and equivalents) of an institution; (ii) the application of provisional measures by virtue of E.E.C. 186 (and equivalents) and (iii) the stay of execution of a judgment or order of the Court itself (in accordance with E.E.C. 192, final paragraph and equivalents). Though, from the substantive point of view, stay of execution of a court decision is different from suspension of enforcement of an administrative act (so that in Chapter 2, the former is treated on *ante*, p. 177 and the latter on *ante*, p. 158), they are assimilated for procedural purposes (see R.P. 89, *post*, p. 273). That the expression "suspension of enforcement" should be used in the Rules of Procedure (as in the heading to this section) to cover both is not only convenient, but also reflects the fact that in the original Treaty languages a verbal distinction between enforcement and execution is made, in the Title of the Section, only in the German ("*Vollzug*" and "*Zwangsvollstreckung*"). In the other languages, "*executie*" (Netherlands) and "*esecuzione*" (Italian) is used to embrace both concepts, while in the French no noun at all is inserted after "*sursis*" (suspension) to express them. (It may be noted that in E.E.C. St. 36 in respect of an administrative act suspension of enforcement is "*sursis*" (with no noun, in the French), "*Aussetzung*" (with no noun, in the German), "*opschorting*" (with no noun, in the Netherlands), "*sospensione*" (with no noun, in the Italian), whereas, in respect of a court decision, the expressions are "*suspension de l'exécution forcée*"; "*Aussetzung der Zwangsvollstreckung*"; "*schorting van de gedwongen tenuitvoerlegging*"; "*sospensione dell' esecuzione forzata*").

R.P. 83

Paragraph 1

Any application for suspension of enforcement of some measure taken by an institution, made in pursuance of Article 39, second Paragraph of the E.C.S.C. Treaty, Article 185 of the E.E.C. Treaty and Article 157 of the E.A.E.C. Treaty shall only be admissible if the applicant has made this measure the subject of proceedings before the Court.

Any application relating to one of the other interim measures referred to in Article 39, third paragraph of the E.C.S.C. Treaty, Article 186 of the E.E.C. Treaty and Article 158 of the E.A.E.C. Treaty shall only be entertained if it comes from one of the parties in a case before the Court and if it relates to that case.

Paragraph 2

The applications referred to in the preceding Paragraph shall specify the subject matter of the dispute, the circumstances

giving rise to urgency and the grounds of fact and of law showing *prima facie* justification for the granting of the interim
measure requested.

Paragraph 3

The application shall be made in a separate document and
following the procedure laid down in Articles 37 and 38 of these
Rules.

In *Barbara Erzbergbau AG et autres* c. *Haute Autorité* (Consolidated Cases
3–18, 25, 26/58. R. Vol VI (i) at p. 466) the President of the Court in his
Order of 11th April 1960 stated:

"During the present procedure it is not necessary to decide whether an
intervener is entitled to claim the suspension of enforcement of a decision
and in what circumstances. It is sufficient to hold that in deciding whether
the claims are well founded it is not necessary to take into account the
Request to intervene brought by the Land of Baden-Würtemberg in case
8-58 [one of the cases consolidated].

The claims for suspension of enforcement were introduced less than
six weeks before the 10th May 1960, the date on which the judgment in
the main action will be published. The applicants invoke in support the
fact that the Federal Government has now resolved to carry out the
decisions of the High Authority of the 9th February 1958, which for a
long time it had been obliged to do, as appears from the Court's judgment
of 8th March 1960 in case 3/59. From the time the above mentioned
decisions were taken the applicants could have expected to see them
carried out, and after they had been carried out they might have brought
a claim for suspension of enforcement which might have been sustainable.

In principle it is for the applicant to judge the opportuneness and
expediency of bringing a claim for suspension of enforcement, and to
decide in which phase of the procedure this claim shall be presented.

However, there are obvious objections to allowing such a claim when
it is introduced after the close of the written procedure and after the oral
procedure on the issues in the main action, at a moment when the Court
has already begun its consideration of the judgment in the main action.
Moreover, as the defendant has also observed, it should be noticed that
for certain undertakings the carrying out of the decision of 9th February
1958 does not involve immediate disadvantageous consequences, and that
it only results in partial tariff increases for most of the other undertakings.

It is true that that constitutes a disadvantage for the undertakings
which are the object of these measures; but, as the applicants maintain,
it is not clear why these tariff modifications could not be made retrospec-
tive. The preceding considerations make the rejection of the claim
inevitable. It is not necessary to order the measures by way of procedure
of enquiry that the applicants propose . . .".

R.P. 84

Paragraph 1

The application shall be notified to the other party, and the
President shall set a short time limit within which that party
may submit written or oral comments.

Paragraph 2

The President shall decide whether to order that the procedure
of enquiry should be opened.

The President may decide to grant the application even before the other party has made comments. Such decision may be later varied or revoked, even of the Court's own volition.

R.P. 85

The President shall decide himself or refer the decision to the Court.

In the event of the absence, or inability to attend, of the President, the provisions of Article 7, Paragraph 2 of these Rules shall apply.

If the application is referred to the Court it shall adjourn all cases and give a decision, after hearing the Advocate General. The provisions of the preceding Article shall apply.

R.P. 86

Paragraph 1

Rulings on such an application shall be given by reasoned order against which no recourse shall be available. This order shall be immediately served on the parties.

Paragraph 2

The enforcement of the order may be made subject to the provision of security by the applicant, the amount and the nature of which shall be fixed having regard to the circumstances.

Paragraph 3

The order may appoint a date from which the interim measure will cease to be applicable. Failing this, the measure shall cease to have effect as from delivery of the judgment terminating the case.

Paragraph 4

The order shall be only temporary in nature, and shall in no way prejudice the Court's decision on the substance of the case.

R.P. 87

On the application of one of the parties, the order may at any time be varied or revoked by reason of a change in circumstances.

R.P. 88

Rejection of an application for an interim measure shall not prevent the party who made it from making another application based on fresh facts.

R.P. 89

The provisions of this Chapter shall apply to an application for suspension of enforcement of a decision of the Court or of some measure taken by another institution, submitted under Articles 44 and 92 of the E.C.S.C. Treaty, Articles 187 and 192 of the E.E.C. Treaty and Articles 159 and 164 of the E.A.E.C. Treaty.

The order granting the application shall fix a date on which the interim measure shall cease to have effect.

R.P. 90

Paragraph 1

The application referred to in Article 81, third and fourth Paragraphs of the E.A.E.C. Treaty shall contain:

(*a*) the names and permanent addresses of the persons or undertakings subject to inspection;

(*b*) particulars of what is to be inspected and the aim of the inspection.

Paragraph 2

The President shall give his ruling by order. The provisions of Article 86 of these Rules shall apply.

In the event of the absence, or inability to attend, of the President, Article 7, Paragraph 2 of these Rules shall apply.

As to the jurisdiction by virtue of E.A.E.C. 81 to which this article relates see Chapter 2, *ante*, pp. 176 *et seq.*

II. PRELIMINARY POINTS OF PROCEDURE (R.P. 91, 92)

(*Incidents de Procédure; Prozeszhindernde Einreden und Zwischenstreit; Van de incidenten; Degli incidenti*)

In practice, objections raised by a party on the ground of inadmissibility of an action ("*exceptions d'irrecevabilité*") and examination by the Court itself of its own volition of the admissibility of an action in the light of the public policy ("*ordre public*") of the Community, are the matters with which the Court is most frequently concerned under the above heading. (A glance through the headnotes of decided cases in the Official Reports shows how on nearly every occasion the question of admissibility is expressly dealt with in the Court's judgment, either because it has been raised by a party or the Court has paid attention to it on its own initiative. In certain circumstances the Court is expressly required by its own Rules of Procedure to examine the admissibility of an action. This occurs in respect of judgment by default (see *post*, pp. 280 *et seq.*) where prior to judgment the Court must make such an examination, though this is not by way of a "preliminary point of procedure" in the technical sense under discussion in the present section).

As to the grounds on which a Request may be held inadmissible see Chapter 4, under "Request" *ante*, pp. 218 *et seq.* Disputes as to the authenticity of a document or an act ("*acte*") are also the possible subject-matter of an application under this heading.

"Preliminary points of procedure" is thus not synonymous with "interlocutory proceeding" in English practice though objections raised by a party are in fact interlocutory in the English sense, in that without full inquiry into the issues in the main action the court rules on the objection. This may, in consequence, dispose of the main action also. (See Case 21, 26/61 quoted in Chapter 2, under E.C.S.C. 35 "It is not permissible by the device . . .", *ante*, pp. 124 *et seq.*). The heading in the original authentic language either fails to comprise what it is taken to comprise in the domestic practice of the State concerned ("*incidents de procédure*" has a wider connotation in French civil law than in community practice, embodying arguments which enlarge the issues in the action or matters concerned with proof; "*Van de incidenten*" has similar defects as a heading in the Netherlands language) or is partly a descriptive title conveying the nature of what is comprised withing the heading (as in the German: "*Prozeszhindernde Einreden und Zwischenstreit*"). The real meaning of the heading can therefore only be fully appreciated by reference to the practice of the Court in relation to it.

R.P. 91

Paragraph 1

If one of the parties should apply to the Court for a ruling on an objection or some other preliminary point which does not involve raising the main issue, he shall make his application in a separate document.

The application shall contain a summary of the grounds of fact and of law on which it is based, the applicant's submissions and, annexed thereto, documents relied upon in support.

Paragraph 2

Immediately after the lodging of the document making the application, the President shall set a time limit within which the other party may set out his grounds and submissions in writing.

Paragraph 3

Unless the Court decides otherwise, the remainder of the procedure shall be oral.

Paragraph 4

The Court shall, after hearing the Advocate General, rule on the application or else reserve it to be dealt with as part of the main issue.

If the Court rejects the application or reserves it, the President shall set new time limits for the case.

"... **In a separate document** ..." ("*par acte séparé*"; "*mit besonderem Schriftsatz*"; "... *een afzonderlijke akte*"; "*con atto separato*"). The reference is to an act of procedure in the technical sense, that is a "procedural document" (see "Procedural document", *ante*, p. 216).

Paragraph 2. It will be noted that the procedure under R.P. 91 is limited to one interchange of submissions between the parties. There is no equivalent to the reply (*réplique*) and further reply ("*duplique*") which may follow the request and defence.

Paragraph 4. In *Entreprise Plaumann & Co., Hamburg, c. Commission C.E.E.* (Case 25/62, R. Vol. IX, at p. 221) "the defendant applied to raise an objection of inadmissibility against the present Request; ... by order of the Court ... the said objection was reserved to be dealt with as part of the main issue".

R.P. 92

The Court may at any time of its own volition consider whether there exist bars to proceedings which are matters of public policy ("*ordre public*"); it shall give its ruling following the procedure laid down in Article 91, Paragraphs 3 and 4 of these Rules.

III. INTERVENTION
("De l'Intervention"; "Streithilfe"; "Van de voeging of tussenkomst";
"l'intervento")

Intervention is provided for in the Statutes of the Court as follows:

E.E.C. St. 37

The Member States and the institutions of the Community may intervene in cases before the Court.

The same right shall appertain to any other person who shows that he has a valid interest in the result of any case referred to the Court, except in cases between Member States, between institutions of the Community or between Member States and institutions of the Community.

Submissions contained in the application to intervene shall be limited to supporting the case of one of the original parties to the case.

E.A.E.C. St. 38

[Identical with E.E.C. St. 37.]

E.C.S.C. St. 34

Natural or legal persons who show that they have a valid interest in the result of a case before the Court may intervene in that case.

Submissions contained in the application to intervene shall be limited to supporting or rejecting the case of one of the parties.

The intervener must limit himself to supporting the submissions of the party in whose favour he intervenes (or, alternatively only in E.C.S.C., to seeking the rejection of the submissions of the party against whom he intervenes—see E.C.S.C. St. 34, *supra*, and Case 1, *post*, p. 278).

Time limit for application to intervene. "The Request to intervene must be presented at the latest before the opening of the oral procedure" (R.P. 93 (1), Appendix, *post*). (In the earlier Rules of Procedure, now amended, the application was required to be made "before the close of the written phase" of the procedure).

Moment for initiating intervention. It has been suggested that in E.E.C. and E.A.E.C., where the intervener is limited to supporting the submissions of either the applicant or the defendant in the main action (see E.E.C. St. 37 and E.A.E.C. St. 38, *supra*), intervention cannot be made until these submissions are complete, that is to say, if need be until either the reply of the applicant, or the further reply of the defendant, has been delivered. The point has not been judicially decided and is perhaps not free from doubt, but the better view appears to be that intervention in support of the applicant can be made at any time after delivery of the Request; and in support of the defendant at any time after delivery of the Defence, in either case up to the moment the President declares the oral procedure open. In an E.C.S.C. case (see 1, *post*, p. 278) the Court, basing itself on the second paragraph of E.C.S.C. St. 34 (*ante*, p. 276) which permits intervention seeking the rejection of a party's submissions, held an intervention against the applicant admissible, though the applicant sought a declaration of the inadmissibility of the intervention on the ground that the Request for intervention was presented, with the intention of supporting the defendant, before the defendant had delivered his submissions.

Capacity to apply to intervene. As in respect of a Request originating the main action, the capacity of the applicant to intervene is (if disputed) determined on the basis of the national law which is the applicant's personal law (see *Nold* c. *Haute Autorité*, R. Vol. V, p. 85, referred to under "Capacity is distinct from quality", *ante*, p. 226).

Formal requirements for request for intervention. Reference should be made to the details set out in R.P. 93(2) (Appendix, *post*). Provision is there made that the would-be intervener must be represented in accordance with the usual requirements for representation of any party before the Court (as to which see "Parties, representation" *ante*, pp. 211–214). R.P. 93(2) (d), (*post*, p. 278) requires a statement of the reasons establishing the legal interest of the would-be intervener in the ultimate judicial decision regarding the case. This matter is examined in the immediately following paragraph. A single request is sufficient even where more than one legal person, exercising different activities, seek to intervene. (This was impliedly determined by the Court in its order of the 19th February 1960 in the case of *Gouvernement du Royaume des Pays Bas* c. *Haute Autorité*, R. Vol. VI (ii) at p. 757).

The party applying to intervene (other than a Member State or a Community Institution) must have a legal interest in the ultimate decision. E.E.C. St. 37, E.A.E.C. St. 38 and E.C.S.C. St. 34 require that a legal interest in the ultimate decision must be substantiated by a would-be intervener other than a Member State or Community Institution (whose interest is held by some authorities to be always presumed) but there is no requirement that such would-be intervener must also in principle be qualified to originate a principal action before the Court should the eventuality arise.

Whether or not the necessary legal interest exists, forms the subject of a pronouncement of the Court immediately following the application to intervene. (In contrast, the interest of the party whose Request originates the principal action—though considered in much of Continental European doctrine not to differ in legal essence from that required in an intervener—is normally not pronounced upon by the Court until its judgment on the issues in the whole action is delivered).

"Any person" may intervene. In *Confédération Nationale des producteurs de fruits et légumes etc.* c. *Conseil C.E.E.* (Consolidated Cases 16 & 17/62, R. Vol. VIII at p. 940) the Court stated:

"It follows from E.E.C. St. 37 paragraph two that any person other than the Member States and the Institutions of the Community can intervene in actions in which the opposing parties, as in the present case, are private parties and a Community Institution, on condition that the said person demonstrates a justified interest in the outcome of the action. The expression 'any person', couched in as wide terms as possible, also comprises associations such as the intervening party".

(Compare the category "natural or legal persons", in E.E.C. 173, *ante*, p. 84, and see under E.C.S.C. 33, *ante*, pp. 91–93).

The nature of the requisite legal interest in an intervener. This is illustrated by the cases (see *infra*, 1–5).

Intervention may have been possible for third party claiming re-trial. (As to meaning of "third party" in this context, see *post*, p. 284). See quotation from *Breedband N.V.*, etc. under R.P. 97(1) (c), *post*, p. 286.

Time for parties to main action to present comments on the intervention. The parties are granted a period of time by an order of the President of the Court (R.P. 93(3), Appendix, *post*). The intervener has no right of reply to these comments. Any such reply is irregular and must be excluded from the documents filed in the case. (See the order made 19th February 1960 in *Gouvernement du Royaume des Pays Bas* c. *Haute Autorité*, R. Vol. VI Pt. 2 at p. 757).

Decision as to admissibility of the intervention. The Court has a discretion to rule on the admissibility of the intervention with or without hearing oral argument. In practice oral argument tends to be dispensed with, except where objections to the intervention appear deserving of full discussion by the opposing parties. The decision is made by order of the Court after the Advocate General has been heard (R.P. 93(3), Appendix, *post*). The opinion of the Advocate General is not made known to the parties or the would-be intervener (which seems somewhat unsatisfactory, particularly in contrast to the procedure governing the presentation of the Advocate General's submissions in public audience at the close of the oral procedure in the main action).

Procedure following order admitting intervention. If the intervention is admitted, communication is made to the intervener "of every procedural document served on the parties" to the main action (R.P. 93(4), Appendix, *post*). The intervener must accept the action as it stands at the moment of the intervention, and the time within which he may present "in writing his grounds in support of his submissions" is that fixed by order of the President of the Court, (R.P. 93(5), Appendix, *post*). Whether the admitted intervener, though bound to accept the action as it stands at the moment of the intervention, may adduce reasons or objections different from those relied upon by the party in whose support he intervenes is not altogether free from doubt, though some decisions of the Court affirm the autonomy of the intervener (see *infra*). There seems clearly, however, to be nothing to prevent the intervener from adducing his own offers of proof. R.P. 38(1) (e) (*ante*, p. 221), for example, is made applicable to the request to intervene by R.P. 93(2) (Appendix, *post*).

Intervention and the language of procedure. R.P. 29 (*ante*, pp. 204, *et seq.*) applies.

In *De Gezamenlijke Steenkolenmijnen in Limburg* c. *Haute Autorité* (Case 30/59 R. Vol. VII at p. 94) the Court, in its Order of 18th February 1960, stated:

". . . It is only as from the moment that he is admitted to intervene that the intervener is obliged to use the language required for the procedure in the main action, without prejudice to the application of R.P. 29(2) (c)".

Costs of intervention proceedings. R.P. 69–75 (*ante*, pp. 261 *et seq.*) apply.

Cases on nature of legal interest in intervener.
1. Order of 24th November 1955 in Consolidated Cases 7 and 9/54 R. Vol. II at pp. 143 and 191.

2. Judgment of 10th May 1960 in Consolidated Cases 3 to 18 and 26/58 in R. Vol. VI Part 1 p. 357.

3. Judgment of 15th July 1960 in Consolidated Cases 24 and 34/58 in R. Vol. VI Part 2 at p. 553.

4. The requisite interest where there is more than one intervener is illustrated in *Gouvernement du Royaume des Pays Bas* c. *Haute Autorité* (Case 25/59 R. Vol. VI. (ii), order of 19th February 1960 at p. 789). The Netherlands Government had sought to annul a decision of the High Authority which charged the Government with failing to carry out an obligation imposed by the Treaty (to publish prices and tariffs for the transport of coal and steel products by road) and prescribed the measures to be taken in execution of that obligation. The interveners were Dutch transport undertakings and steel users. The Court distinguished the two aspects of the controversy: the international aspect, namely the relations between States and the High Authority, and the community aspect, limited to the interpretation of the Treaty. It admitted the intervention only in respect of the second aspect, recognizing the interest in the ultimate decision of the interveners in their function as transport concerns or consumers of the products transported, who would bear the consequences of any obligation imposed on the Government to enforce publication of tariffs and prices of transport.

5. In *Société Nouvelle des Usines de Pontlieue Aciéries du Temple (S.N.U.P.A.T.)* c. *Haute Autorité* (Consolidated Cases 42 and 49/59 R. Vol. VII p. 101) a French Company originated an action against the High Authority in respect of decisions exonerating a Dutch and an Italian undertaking from the payment of dues on scrap imported into the Community. The Court admitted the intervention of the two undertakings, holding their interest obvious, inasmuch as, were the French company successful, the defendant would have been obliged to revoke the concession made to them.

Case on moment for initiating intervention. In the case referred to in "5" (*supra*) a Dutch undertaking had intervened, submitting that the Request of the applicant should be rejected, before the defendant had delivered its further reply. The applicant raised an objection of inadmissibility arguing that since the intervener's intention was to support the defendant's submissions, the intervention should have been delayed at least until these were presented. The Court dismissed the objection and allowed the Request for intervention, invoking the second paragraph of E.C.S.C. St. 34 (*ante*, p. 276). The Court's orders were dated 20th January and 6th May 1960 (but are not printed in the Official Reports.)

Cases on independence of intervener as to arguments different from those of party in whose support he intervenes. In *De Gezamenlijke Steenkolenmijnen in Limburg* c. *Haute Autorité* (Case 30/59 R. Vol. VII at p. 37) the Court stated:

"The Request by way of intervention of the Government of the Federal Republic of Germany was declared admissible by order of the Court dated 18th February 1960.

Though in its statement in intervention the Government of the Federal Republic of Germany supports the submissions of the defendant, it uses arguments contrary to those of the defendant and arguments against which the latter expressly takes up a position.

The applicant considers that since R.P. 93(5) obliges the intervener to accept the action at the state in which it exists at the moment of intervention, the intervener was no longer at liberty, at the time it intervened—after delivery of the Further Reply—to raise a fundamental argument which is in contradiction to those of the party the intervener is supposed to be supporting.

However, the applicant does not wish to invoke R.P. 93(5) in order that the Court shall not be prevented from examining the case made out in the Request (to intervene).

The question must be examined *ex officio* by the Court.

By the terms of E.C.S.C. St. 34 the submissions in the request to intervene can have no other object than the support of the submissions of one party or their rejection. The Government of the Federal Republic of Germany supports in its intervention the submissions of the defendant. The arguments it adduces, though different from those of the defendant, are directed towards the rejection of the submissions of the applicant. The procedure of intervention would be emptied of all content were the intervener to be prohibited from using every argument which had not been used by the party it supports. In these circumstances the arguments put forward by the Government of the Federal Republic of Germany in its intervention are admissible."

In the same case, Advocate General Lagrange had submitted that there was a distinction between "new reasons and objections" (grounds) on the one hand and "new arguments" on the other. "Generally speaking the intervener is not permitted to put forward a new ground and set up a new objection by virtue of the fact that the principal party must remain dominant in the action . . . otherwise, in support of the submissions to which he adheres, the intervener is at liberty to put forward any argument, of fact or of law, which seems to him expedient, even if this were to be out of line with—or indeed in opposition to—those of the principal party. In view of the special interest which he must substantiate, he must be permitted to present his own view independently." (R. Vol. VII at p. 66).

The Judgment of 22 March 1961 in *Société Nouvelle des Usines de Pontlieue Aciéries du Temple* c. *Haute Autorité* (Consolidated cases 42 and 49/59 R. Vol. VII at p. 145) is to similar effect as the above. "The interveners have set up objections of inadmissibility of which the defendant did not avail himself. The right to do so cannot be denied to the interveners, given that such objections and arguments are directed to the rejection of the submissions of the applicant."

IV. JUDGMENTS BY DEFAULT AND RE-TRIAL (R.P. 94)

(*"Des Arrêts par défaut et de l'opposition"*; *"Versäumnisurteil und Widerspruch"*; *"Van de Arresten bij verstek gewezen en het verzet"*; *"Delle sentenze in contumacia e dell' opposizione"*)

R.P. 94

Paragraph 1

If the defending party, having been duly notified, does not reply to the Request in the manner and within the time limit laid down, the applicant may apply to the Court to give judgment is his favour.

This application shall be served on the defending party. The President shall fix a date for the opening of the oral procedure.

Paragraph 2

Before giving judgment by default the Court, after hearing the Advocate General, shall consider the admissibility of the Request and shall verify whether the formalities have been properly observed and whether the submissions of the applicant appear to be based on good grounds. The Court may order measures by way of procedure of enquiry to be carried out.

Paragraph 3

Judgment by default shall be enforceable. The Court may however suspend enforcement until it has given a ruling on a claim for retrial submitted in pursuance of paragraph 4 below, or it may make enforcement conditional upon the provision of security the amount and nature of which shall be fixed having regard to the circumstances; this security shall be released if no claim for retrial is made or if the claim is rejected.

Paragraph 4

Recourse may be had against a judgment by default by means of a claim for retrial.

The claim shall be lodged within one month from date of service of the judgment; it shall be submitted following the procedure laid down in Articles 37 and 38 of these Rules.

Paragraph 5

After service of the claim for retrial, the President shall set a time limit for the other party to submit his written comments.

The procedure shall follow the provisions of Article 44 *et seq.* of these Rules.

Paragraph 6

The Court shall give its ruling by a judgment against which no recourse by way of retrial shall be available.

The original of this judgment shall be annexed to the original of the judgment by default. A note of the judgment given on the retrial shall be made in the margin of the original of the judgment by default.

This Rule implements the Statutes (for text of which see Chapter 2, *ante,* p. 177) as follows:

E.E.C. St. 38

[*Printed on* ante, p. 177.]

E.A.E.C. St. 39

[*Identical with E.E.C. St.* 38.]

E.C.S.C. St. 35

[*Printed on* ante, p. 177.]

The wording appears to exclude the possibility of judgment by default where the application is not to the full jurisdiction (see Chapter 2, *ante,* p. 177).

Paragraph 1 ". . . in the manner and within the time limit laid down . . ." (R.P. 94, para. 1).

One month from the service of the request on the defendant is allowed by R.P. 40(1). The time may be extended. (See generally in Chapter 4 "Acts of Procedure subsequent to the request", *ante*, pp. 226–227).

Paragraph 1 ". . . application shall be served on the defending party . . ." (R.P. 94, para. 1). That the defendant is entitled to be served with the application may justify an extension under R.P. 40(2) of the time for him to present a defence.

Paragraph 2. "Before giving judgment by default, the Court . . .". It is required by paragraph 2 to do four things: (i) hear the Advocate General; (ii) consider the admissibility of the Request (*cf.* examination of admissibility as a Preliminary Point of Procedure *ante*, p. 225); (iii) verify the proper observance of formalities; (iv) verify whether the submissions of the applicant appear to be based on good grounds. The Court may also order measures by way of procedure of enquiry.

The wording in the fourth requirement (*supra*) ("appear to be based on good grounds"; "*paraissent être fondées*"; "*begründet erscheinen*"; "*gegrond voorkomen*"; "*appaiono fondate*") suggests that the Court is empowered to dispense with measures by way of procedure of enquiry and adjudicate on a *prime facie* basis. In practice, the Court does in fact decide on a *prime facie* basis. The situation is different from that where the parties by mutual agreement seek an order of the Court removing the case from the register (see R.P. 77, *ante*, p. 265).

Failure of the defendant to the request is thus not equivalent to acquiescence in judgment against himself. Moreover, a defendant may have recourse against a judgment by default by means of a claim for retrial (see Paragraph 4, *infra*).

Paragraph 3. "Judgment by default shall be enforceable". Such a judgment has "executory force" (as to which see "Executory force", *ante*, p. 254).

Paragraph 4. "Recourse may be had against a judgment by default by means of a claim for retrial". The effect of a claim for retrial ("*opposition*", "*Widerspruch*" "*verzet*", "*opposizione*") is to reverse the position of the parties as applicant and defendant respectively, and the implication of the requirement of R.P. 94(4), second sentence (*ante*, p. 281) is that the claim must be made in the usual form of a request. It has been suggested that the written procedure must stop upon the delivery of written comments by the applicant in the original action (within the time limit set by the President in accordance with R.P. 94(5), first sentence), but this is inconsistent with the delivery of a further reply as referred to in R.P. 44(1), made applicable by R.P. 94(5), second sentence. In general, procedure on a claim for retrial follows the usual pattern. It may be noted that judgment on a claim for retrial (if the claim is admitted) necessarily involves judgment in the original action. (It may also be noted that a claim for re-trial, unless the claim is rejected, in fact necessitates two decisions of the Court: (1) to admit the claim, and (2) to pass judgment on it. In practice, unless it rejects the claim, the Court will be likely to merge the two decisions into one, admitting the claim and giving judgment on it. For though there is nothing to prevent the Court, if it so desires, from inviting the parties to argue separately the question of the admissibility of the claim, it is difficult to separate the question of admissibility from the main issues raised by the claim—more so than, for example, in the case of intervention.)

Paragraph 6. "The Court shall give its ruling by a judgment . . .".
It is not given by an order (as to difference see "Judgments, Orders", *ante*, pp. 253–254).

Intervention in procedure by default. No distinction is made by the Statutes, in respect of intervention, between actions *inter partes* or *ex parte*. It presumably follows that intervention in procedure by default or on a claim for retrial may be made subject to the conditions governing intervention in general (see this Chapter, comment under E.C.S.C. St 34, *ante*, pp. 276 *et seq.*).

The provisions of the Statutes and of the Rules of Procedure leave no room for uncertainty as to the position where the intervener wishes to support the submissions of the original applicant, but are less clear (because of the divergence between E.C.S.C. St. 34 and E.E.C. St. 37 and E.A.E.C. St. 38, analysed under "III Intervention", *ante*, pp. 276 *et seq.*) as to the position where an intervener wishes to seek the rejection of the original application although the defendant is taking no part in the proceedings. Intervention by a third party where a defendant is claiming retrial must of course be distinguished from a claim for retrial by a third party. The latter is provided for in a special section of the Rules of Procedure (see *post*, p. 284).

V. PROCEEDINGS BY SERVANTS OF THE COMMUNITIES
(R.P. 95, 96)

("*Des recours des agents des communautés*"; "*Klagen von Bediensteten der Gemeinschaften*"; "*Van de beroepen van de ambtenaren der Gemeenschappen*"; "*Dei ricorsi dei dipendenti delle comunità*".)

R.P. 95
Paragraph 1
Proceedings instituted by an official or other servant of an institution against the institution shall be judged by a Section appointed each year for this purpose by the Court, unless the matter be one to be dealt with under the summary procedure in case of urgency.

The provisions of these Rules shall apply to proceedings before such Section. The powers of the President of the Court shall be exercised by the President of the Section.
Paragraph 2
The Section may refer the case to the Court for decision.

In *Alberto Campolongo* c. *Haute Autorité* (Consolidated Cases 27, 39/59 R. Vol. VI (ii) at p. 841) Advocate General Roemer said:
. . . "According to R.P. 95(1) the general rules of procedure apply also to the actions brought by servants of the Communities. According to E.C.S.C. St. 22, the Request must contain an indication of the object of the action and the submissions. R.P. 38(1) repeats this requirement. Thus the Request must indicate precisely the subject-matter and a short summary of the grounds of the action and the relief sought of the Court. Later extensions of the claim are not permitted. That results, *a contrario*, from R.P. 42(1, 2), whereby in certain circumstances and even after delivery of the request, the applicant can still make other offers of proof and introduce new grounds. No exception to this principle is laid down for

the procedure in full jurisdiction [as distinct from jurisdiction to annul] which can no doubt be considered as embracing actions by servants of the Communities. Here too the judge is bound by the submissions of the parties as formulated in the Request. It is only if the Request contains a claim which seeks to replace an administrative decision by a decision of the Court that the latter can take consequential action. The extension of the submissions in a subsequent statement must therefore be considered inadmissible . . ."

VI. EXCEPTIONAL FORMS OF RECOURSE (R.P. 97–100)

("*Des voies de recours extraordinaires*"; "*Ausserordentliche Rechtsbehelfe*"; "*Van de buitengewone rechtsmiddelen*"; "*Dei mezzi straordinari di ricorso*")

A. "Claims by a Third Party for Retrial"

("*De la tierce opposition*"; "*Drittwiderspruchsklage*"; "*Van het derden-verzet*"; "*Dell' opposizione di terzo*")

The Statutes of the Court provide the basic authority, on which the procedural requirements rest, as follows:

E.E.C. St. 39

The Member States, the institutions of the Community and any other natural or legal persons may, in cases and under conditions to be determined by the rules of procedure, claim as third parties (*tierce-opposition*) a retrial of cases decided without their having been heard, where such judgments are prejudicial to their rights.

E.A.E.C. St. 40

[*Identical with E.E.C. St. 39.*]

E.C.S.C. St. 36

Natural or legal persons and any of the Community's institutions may, in cases and under conditions to be determined by the Rules of Procedure, claim as third-parties a retrial of cases decided without their having been heard.

Broadly speaking the three articles of the three Statutes (*supra*) lay down the same principle, that after judgment given in an action to which they were not a party, certain persons may claim retrial of the action, expressly if "the judgment prejudices their rights" (in E.E.C. St. and E.A.E.C. St.) and impliedly if it does so in E.C.S.C. St. (since the relevant rule of procedure (see R.P. 97 1(b), *post*, p. 285) requires the claimant to "indicate in what way the judgment objected to prejudices" his rights).

The specific mention of "Member States" in E.E.C. St. and E.A.E.C. St. which is absent from E.C.S.C. St. is purely a matter of wording, since in E.C.S.C. St. the Member States are of course within the category of "legal persons".

"Any . . . natural or legal person . . .". The addition of the word "any" in E.E.C. St. and E.A.E.C. St. to the wording of E.C.S.C. St. probably effects no change of principle. But, insofar as it stresses that the category

of natural or legal person is not subject to limitation, it supports an argument
that applicants need not be nationals of (or even resident, or merely present
in) one of the Member States. See in Chapter 4, comment on Parties,
ante, p. 212; in Chapter 1, comment on "establish among themselves a
community", *ante*, p. 15 and in Chapter 2, comment following "Any
natural or legal person may, under the same conditions, appeal . . .", *ante*,
p. 84.

Rights. The rights which an individual may defend by third party
claim for retrial appear to include the prerogatives enjoyed by such individual in the exercise, as the servant of the Community, of the privileges
and immunities established (by the relevant Protocol annexed to the Treaty,
see Chapter 1, *ante*, pp. 29–32, 47, 56) in favour of the Community. The
Court has expressly recognised the existence of "subjective rights" vested in
the Community's servants, in the following passage:
> "The privileges provided for in the protocol confer subjective rights
> on the beneficiaries, as is clearly shown by the German and Netherlands
> equivalents of the term "privilege" ["*Vorrechte*", "*voorrechten*"—"*rechte*",
> "*rechten*", mean "rights", *author*]; it is usual to suppose that a material
> right has as a corollary the possibility for the beneficiary of enforcing
> it himself by an action at law rather than by an intermediary". (In *Jean
> E. Humblet* c. *Etat Belge*, Case 6/60 R. Vol. VI (2), p. 1125 at pp. 1149–
> 1150).

The rights which a Member State or an Institution of the Communities,
being persons of public law, may defend by third party claim for retrial
include the "powers" and legal prerogatives of such Member State or
Institution.

Interest in the claimant is a necessary condition for the bringing of a
claim for retrial, as it is for the bringing of an action (as to interest see
Chapter 4, "Procedure", *ante*, pp. 219–220 and 226).

R.P. 97

Paragraph 1
The provisions of Articles 37 and 38 of these Rules shall be
applicable to a claim by a third party for retrial and in addition
the claim shall:
(a) specify the judgment objected to;
(b) indicate in what way the judgment objected to prejudices
the rights of the third party making the claim;
(c) indicate the reasons why the third party making the
claim has not been able to take part in the case.
The claim shall be made against all the parties in the case.
If the judgment has been published in the Official Journal of
the European Communities, the claim shall be submitted within
two months of that publication.
Paragraph 2
Suspension of enforcement of the judgment object to may be
ordered on application of the third party making the claim.
The provisions of Part 3 Chapter 1 of these Rules of Procedure
shall apply.

Paragraph 3

The judgment object to shall be varied to the extent to which the third party's claim is allowed.

The original of the judgment given on the retrial shall be annexed to the original of the judgment objected to. A note of the judgement on the retrial shall be made in the margin of the judgment objected to.

Paragraph 1(c). "... to take part in the case". The possibility for a third party claiming retrial to have intervened in the main action is an important consideration for the Court. In *Breedband N.V.* c. (1) *'Société des Aciéries du Temple,* (2) *Haute Autorité, etc.* (Consolidated Cases 42 and 49/59 Claim by a Third Party for Retrial, R. Vol. VII p. 275 at p. 303) the Court "examined in what circumstances the third party claiming retrial could "have participated in the main action" and stated:

"A good administration of justice and the security of legal relationships ("*la sécurité des relations juridiques*"; "*Rechtssicherheit*"; "*rechtszekerheid*"; "*certezza delle relazioni giuridiche*") imply the necessity of avoiding that persons interested in the outcome of a case pending before the Court should be admitted to establish their rights after judgment determining the matter in dispute has been given. It is precisely in order to meet this necessity that E.C.S.C. St. 34 gives third parties whose interests are involved in the case pending before the Court, the means of intervening of their own initiative provided that their submissions have no other object than the support of the submissions of a party or their rejection. Therefore R.P. 97(1) (c) provides for the admissibility, both of the third party claiming retrial, who having been called upon to take part in the main action was for valid reasons unable to do so, and also of all those who were not in a position to intervene in the main action in accordance with E.C.S.C. St. 34 and R.P. 93.

Therefore it is necessary to examine whether the third party could have intervened of its own initiative in this action in the circumstances provided for in E.C.S.C. St. 34. The present third party claim for retrial is directed against the part of the judgment ruling on case 49/59, the object and submissions of which were published in the Official Journal of the European Communities of the 19th November 1959. Such publication has as its purpose to put third parties in a position to know of actions brought at the Court ... the third party claiming retrial has shown a justified interest ... but has not "indicated", in the meaning of R.P. 97 (1) (c) the reasons why he did not participate in the main action. The present claim is therefore inadmissible ...".

(The passage here quoted from the judgment was re-iterated virtually verbatim by the Court in *Gouvernment du Royaume de Belgique* c. *Société Commerciale Antoine Vloeberghs et Haute Autorité,* Consolidated Cases 9 and 12/60 Third Party Claim for Retrial R. Vol. VIII at pp. 353–354).

Paragraph 1 "... against all the parties in the case ..." (Compare R.P. 37(1), "as many copies as there are parties in the case", *ante*, p. 220, and see p. 212). The English translation appears to embrace all parties, that is those indirectly as well as directly involved in the action, but the original languages ("*toutes les parties au litige principal*"; "*sämtliche Parteien des Hauptverfahrens*"; *tegen alle partijen in het hoofdgeding*"; "*tutte le parti della causa principale*") appear to be restricted to parties directly involved.

Paragraph 2 "Suspension of enforcement of the judgment objected to . . ." The "stay of execution" of a judgment is treated, as to jurisdiction, in Chapter 2 (*ante*, p. 177) and, as to procedure, in this Chapter, "Suspension of enforcement and other interim measures by way of summary procedure (*ante*, pp. 270 *et seq.*).

Paragraph 3 "The original of the judgment given on the retrial". Decision on the retrial is by judgment, not by order (as to the distinction see Chapter 4, *ante*, pp. 253–254).

B. Reconsideration by the Court of its Own Judgment
(R.P. 98–100)

("*De la révision*"; "*Wiederaufnahme des Verfahrens*"; "*Van de herziening*"; "*Della revocazione*")

The jurisdiction of the Court to reconsider its own judgment is conferred in identical terms by E.E.C. St. 41, E.A.E.C. St. 42 and E.C.S.C. St 38 (for the text of para. 1 of St. 38 see *post*, p. 289). The Statutes provide that application for reconsideration may be made only on the grounds that a fact has been discovered likely to prove of decisive importance *and* that fact was unknown to the Court and to the party applying for reconsideration before the judgment of which reconsideration is sought. The Statutes provide that no application for reconsideration may be made after the expiry of ten years from the date of the judgment, and to this time requirement the Rules of Procedure add another, that application must be made within three months from the day when the applicant becomes acquainted with the new fact (see immediately *infra*).

Paragraph 2 of these Statutes is as follows: "The procedure for reconsideration shall open with a ruling by the Court expressly finding that a new fact exists, recognising that it fulfils the criteria required to lead to a reconsideration and holding the application for a reconsideration to be entertainable accordingly."

R.P. 98

Reconsideration shall be applied for at the latest within three months from the day on which the applicant came to know of the fact upon which the application for reconsideration is based.

R.P. 99

Paragraph 1

The provisions of Articles 37 and 38 of these Rules shall apply to an application for reconsideration which shall in addition:

(*a*) specify the judgment objected to:

(*b*) indicate the points on which the judgment is objected to;

(*c*) set out the facts in which the application is based;

(*d*) indicate the means of proof tending to show that there are facts which justify a reconsideration and that the time limit laid down in the preceding Article has been observed.

For text of R.P. 37 and R.P. 38 see *ante*, pp. 220–222.

Paragraph 2

The application for reconsideration shall be made against all the parties to the judgment the reconsideration of which is sought.

R.P. 100

Paragraph 1

Without prejudice to the main issue the Court shall rule on the admissibility of the application by judgment given in the Judges' Council Chamber after hearing the Advocate General and after consideration of the written comments of the parties.

Paragraph 2

If the Court declares the application to be admissible, it shall proceed with the consideration of the main issue and give judgment thereon in accordance with the provisions of these Rules.

Paragraph 3

The original of the judgment given on reconsideration shall be annexed to the original of the judgment which was reconsidered. A note of the judgment given on reconsideration shall be made in the margin of the judgment which was reconsidered.

Paragraph 1 "... the Court shall rule ... by judgment ...". It does not do so by order (as to the distinction see Chapter 4, *ante*, pp. 253–254).

"...Judgment given in the Judges' Council Chamber ..." It is, as required by the Statutes (for text see *ante*, p. 287), the first step in the procedure of reconsideration. Since the Court rules on the admissibility of the application by reasoned decision, its decision is a judgment, not an order, and is final on the point. Though the Rules of Procedure do not expressly provide for procedure of enquiry or calling of evidence, nor for an oral hearing, it would seem to be essential for the Court to be able to order enquiry and the calling of evidence in order to make certain that a new fact genuinely exists.

Paragraph 2 is concerned with the issues, and procedure under this paragraph follows the usual course provided for in the Rules of Procedure. In effect the case is re-opened, if need be *ab initio*. (This circumstance is indicated in the wording of the German heading to this section: "*Wiederaufnahme des Verfahrens*"). Thus the defendant in the reconsideration procedure may seek to prove other new facts to counter the effect of the new fact on which the application is based. A fresh exchange of comments will be necessary, followed by a fresh hearing.

Time limit. Claim for reconsideration of a judgment must be made within ten years from the date of the judgment of which reconsideration is sought (E.E.C. St. 41, E.A.E.C. St. 42 and E.C.S.C. St. 38, for provisions of which, see *ante*. p. 287). As to time limits in general see Chapter 4, R.P. 80–82, *ante*, pp. 267–269.

In *Acciaieria, Ferrieria di Roma* c. *Haute Autorité* (Case 1/50 R. Vol. VI (i) at pp. 362–3) the Court stated:

"*Grounds.*—By the provisions of E.C.S.C. St. 38 paragraph two and R.P. 100(1) the Court must first rule on the admissibility of the application by judgment given in the Judges' Council Chamber. The claim was made within the appointed time and in due form. The applicant alleges infringement of R.P. 29 and 30, supporting his contention with the fact that in case 23/59 the defendant had deposited with the Registry, at the direction of the Court, documents drawn up in languages other than the language of procedure which were not translated into the latter with a view to their being communicated to the applicant. The applicant would thus not have been in a position to refer to documents which might have furnished him with arguments in support of his contention. By the provisions of E.C.S.C. St. 38(1) 'Application for a judgment to be reconsidered may be made to the Court only on the ground of discovery of a fact likely to prove of decisive importance and which, before judgment was delivered, was unknown to the Court and to the party which applied for reconsideration'.

The documents in question were deposited with the Registry before the close of the oral procedure and consequently were within the cognizance of the Court before it rendered judgment. By the production of a document drawn up in one of the official languages of the Community it is not only its physical existence but also its content which is brought to the cognizance of the Court. Indeed, like all the institutions of the three Communities the Court is quadrilingual by virtue of a presumption *juris et de jure*. The provisions concerning the language of procedure cannot be regarded as being of public policy (*'ordre public'; 'zwingendes Recht'; 'openbare orde'; 'ordine pubblico'*)

(a) because the language of procedure is that of the applicant, unless the defendant is one of the Member States of the three Communities or a legal person subject to the jurisdiction of one of the Member States;

(b) because both on the joint application of the parties and on the application of a single party and without the consent of the other party being necessary, the Court can authorise the use of an official language other than the language of procedure.

That therefore the first fundamental condition required by E.C.S.C. St. 38 (the discovery of a fact unknown not only to the party that applies for re-consideration, but also to the Court) is not met in the present case ..."

VII. APPEALS AGAINST DECISIONS OF THE ARBITRATION COMMITTEE (R.P. 101)

(*"Des recours contre les décisions du comité d'arbitrage"; "Klagen gegen Entscheidungen des Schiedsausschusses"; "Van het Beroeptegende beslissingen van de Arbitrage-Comissie"; Dei ricorsi contro le decisioni del collegio arbitrale"*).

Limits of the Court's jurisdiction. The Statutes of the Court make no special provision for appeals the subject of this section. But E.A.E.C. 18, in conferring on the Court jurisdiction to adjudicate on such appeals, limits the jurisdiction to (i) the formal legality of the decision, and (ii) the interinterpretation placed by the Committee on the provisions of the E.A.E.C. Treaty (see Chapter 2, "Jurisdiction," *ante*, pp. 171 *et seq.*). It should be noted that, contrary to the principle generally followed in the Treaty, the effect of such an appeal is to suspend the enforcement of the Arbitration Committee's decision, pending the Court's adjudication on the issues (*loc. cit., supra*).

R.P. 101

Paragraph 1

The Request instituting the appeal referred to in Article 18, second Paragraph of the E.A.E.C. Treaty shall contain:

(*a*) the name and permanent address of the applicant;

(*b*) the description of the person signing the Request;

(*c*) particulars of the Arbitration Committee's decision against which appeal is made;

(*d*) particulars of the parties;

(*e*) a brief summary of the facts;

(*f*) the grounds of fact and of law and submissions of the applicant.

Paragraph 2

The provisions of Article 37, Paragraphs 3 and 4 and of Article 38, Paragraphs 2, 3 and 5 of these Rules shall apply.

In addition a certified copy of the decision objected to shall be annexed to the Request.

Paragraph 3

As soon as the Request has been lodged, the Registrar shall ask the Registrar's office of the Arbitration Committee to forward the file on the case to the Court.

Paragraph 4

The procedure shall be in accordance with Articles 39, 40, 55 *et seq.* of these Rules.

Paragraph 5

The Court shall give its ruling by judgment. If it quashes the Committee's decision the Court shall, if appropriate, remit the case back to the Committee.

"The request introducing the appeal ..." "Appeal" is a generic term (being a rendering of *"recours"* (Fr.), *"beroep"* (N.), *"ricorso"* (It.), and less distinctively, of *"klage"* (G)) and is the one used in E.A.E.C. 18 (*loc. cit., supra*) conferring jurisdiction. Specifically, the appeal is introduced by Request (*"requête"* (Fr.); *"Klageschrift"* (G.); *"verzoekschrift"* (N.); *"istanza"* (It.)).

Since this is a Request initiating a "Special form of procedure" the normal requirements as to the contents of a Request (R.P. 38(1), *ante*, p. 221) are replaced by R.P. 101(1) (a) to (f) (*supra*). In particular, it may be noted that no provision is made for a statement of "means of proof available where appropriate"; and, for the same reason the Court has no power to order procedure of enquiry or the calling of evidence (R.P. 45–54, *ante*, pp. 233 *et seq.*, are not applicable).

"... A certified copy of the decision objected to ..." This is required by R.P. 101(2) (*supra*) to be annexed to the Request, which also makes R.P. 37 (3) and (4) and R.P. 38 (2), (3) and (5) applicable (for relevant texts see *ante*, pp. 220 and 221). Hence, this special form of procedure thus follows normal procedure as closely as possible (see also R.P. 101(4), *supra*). But R.P. 41 (for text see *ante*, p. 229) is not made to apply, so that the written procedure does not embrace the possibility of a reply or further reply. The oral procedure begins immediately (there is no provision for a date to be fixed by the President) following entering of the defence, and is in accordance with R.P. 55 *et seq.* (as to which see *ante*, pp. 248 *et seq.*).

"The Court shall give its ruling by judgment". It does not do so by an order (as to the distinction see Chapter 4, *ante*, pp. 253–254).

"... **If it quashes the Committee's decision the Court shall, if appropriate, remit the case back to the Committee**" (R.P. 101(5)). This is closely similar to the effect of a judgment of the Court quashing an administrative act E.A.E.C. 149, E.E.C. 176, E.C.S.C. 34). But, if the decision of the Arbitration Committee is looked upon as a judicial rather than an administrative decision then, to the continental European lawyer, the role of the Court in respect of it will be readily comparable to that of a Court of Cassation, which does not function as an appellate tribunal inquiring into all the issues, any more than the European Court does in this special form of procedure.

VIII. INTERPRETATION OF JUDGMENTS (R.P. 102)

(De l'interprétation des arrêts; Auslegung von Urteilen; van de interpretatie van arresten; "Dell'interpretazione delle sentenze)

E.E.C. St. 40

In case of difficulty as to the meaning or scope of a judgment, it shall be for the Court to interpret such judgment upon the request of any party or any institution of the Community which shows that it has a valid interest therein.

E.A.E.C. St. 41

[Identical with E.E.C. St. 40.]

E.C.S.C. St. 37

[Identical with E.A.E.C. St. 41 and E.E.C. St. 40.]

Two conditions for the admissibility of a claim for interpretation of a judgment. These are laid down by the Statutes (*supra*): (i) there must exist a difficulty as to the meaning and scope of the judgment, and (ii) the claimant must be able to establish an interest in having the difficulty resolved. "It is sufficient, in order for a difficulty within the meaning of E.C.S.C. St. 37 to exist, that the parties in the action [decided by the judgment to be interpreted] give different meanings to the text of the judgment to be interpreted" (*per* the Court in *Associazione Industrie Siderurgiche Italiane (ASSIDER) c. Haute Autorité (Interpretation of Judgment No.* 2/54), Case, 5/55 R. Vol. I at p. 278. The Court drew attention to the fact that:

"the expression difficulty is general; it is not so narrow as the expression '*contestation*' which figures in the French text of article 60 of the Statute of the International Court of Justice". As to which parts of the text of the judgment may be the object of interpretation, the Court held (*ibid,* p. 278): "Obviously it can only be those parts which express the judgment of the Court on the dispute submitted to it *i.e.,* the operative part ['*le dispositif*'] and, amongst the reasons, those which form the basis for the operative part and which on that account are essential . . . . The Court cannot be called upon to interpret the passages which give assistance in completing or explaining these essential reasons.

In the event of a number of Requests, made against a single decision of the High Authority where as a result of one of them the decision is annulled, the applicants who delivered the remaining Requests may be considered as "parties" to the proceedings within the meaning of E.C.S.C. St. 37, but on the express condition that the applicant has invoked, in his prior Request, the same ground of claim as that for which the judgment to be interpreted has annulled the decision, or, as in the present case, has declared the Request well founded. All these parties are entitled to ask for interpretation of the judgment of nullity or of the judgment declaring one of the other Requests well founded . . .".

The Court exercises its discretion freely. It has held that where several applications have been brought against a single decision and, as a consequence of one of them, the decision is annulled, each of the claimants in the other applications has the right to seek interpretation of the judgment, to the extent that it has ruled on the legal question they have raised.

R.P. 102

Paragraph 1

An application for interpretation shall be submitted in accordance with the provisions of Articles 37 and 38 of these Rules. It shall also specify:

(*a*) the judgment in question;

(*b*) the provisions, the interpretation of which is sought.

The application shall be made against all the parties involved in that judgment.

Paragraph 2

The Court shall give its ruling by judgment after giving the parties facilities to submit their comments and after hearing the Advocate General.

The original of the interpreting judgment shall be annexed to the original of the judgment so interpreted. A note of the interpreting judgment shall be made in the margin of the judgment so interpreted.

Rectification of a judgment (in respect of clerical errors etc.). In some ways it is analogous to interpretation and may be applied for by virtue of the provisions of R.P. 66 (*infra*). See Chapter 4, *ante*, pp. 259–260.

Decision is by judgment not order. The Court's decision on the interpretation is made by judgment, not by an order (R.P. 102(2)). (As to the distinction see Chapter 4, *ante*, pp. 253–254.)

R.P. 66

Paragraph 1

Without prejudice to the provisions relating to the interpretation of judgments, clerical errors and mistakes in reckoning or patent inaccuracies may be corrected by the Court, either of its own volition or at the request of one of the parties, within a period of 14 days from delivery of the judgment.

Paragraph 2

The parties, duly notified by the Registrar, may submit written comments within a time limit set by the President.

Paragraph 3

The Court shall reach its decision in the Judges' Council Chamber, after hearing the Advocate General.

Paragraph 4

The original of the order making the correction shall be annexed to the original of the judgment which is corrected.

A note of this order shall be made in the margin of the original of the judgment which is corrected.

Reference may be made to the order of the Court in *Mannesmann A.G. et autres* c. *Haute Autorité* (Consolidated Cases 4/59 to 13/59, R. Vol. VI (1) at pp. 342–343) involving the application of R.P. 57 of the original rules, now amended, of 4th March 1953, which is not substantially different from R.P. 66 of the Rules now in force.

IX. PRELIMINARY RULINGS (R.P. 103)

("*Des décisions à titre préjudiciel*";
"*Vorabentscheidungen*";
"*Van de prejudiciele beslissingen*";
"*Delle decisioni in via pregiudiziale*")

There are considerable differences in respect of the Court's jurisdiction in questions of preliminary ruling as between E.E.C. and E.A.E.C. on the one hand and E.C.S.C. on the other. These differences originate in the Treaties themselves (E.E.C. 177, E.A.E.C. 150, E.C.S.C. 41, which see in Chapter 2, "Preliminary Ruling", *ante*, pp. 132, 140, where the jurisdictional aspects are fully treated).

In addition to these jurisdictional differences there are also procedural differences which result from the circumstance that E.C.S.C. St. contains no special provisions for preliminary rulings comparable to those of E.E.C. St. and E.A.E.C. St., which are as follows:

E.E.C. St. 20

In cases provided for under Article 177 of this Treaty, the decision of the domestic court which suspends its proceedings and refers a case to the Court shall be notified to the Court by the domestic court concerned. Such decision shall then be notified by the Registrar to the parties in the case, to the Member States and the Commission, and also to the Council if the act the validity or interpretation of which is in dispute originates from the Council.

The parties, the Member States, the Commission and, where appropriate, the Council are entitled to submit statements of Case or written comments to the Court within two months of such notification.

E.A.E.C. St. 21

[*Identical with E.E.C. St.* 20.]

"**In cases provided for under Article 177 . . .**" ("under Article 150" in E.A.E.C. St.). This is a reference to the Court's jurisdiction "to give preliminary rulings (*décisions à titre préjudiciel*) concerning: (a) the interpretation of the Treaty; (b) the validity and interpretation of acts of the Institutions of the Community; (c) the interpretation of the statutes of any bodies set up by an act of the Council, except where these statutes provide otherwise", in issue before a domestic court of a Member State (see Chapter 2, "Preliminary Ruling," *ante*, pp. 130 *et seq.*).

11

"...The decision of the domestic court which suspends its proceedings". In *Société Bosch* c. *de Geus* (Case 13/61 R. Vol. VIII p. 89) the Community Court was requested for a preliminary ruling in a judgment of the Court of Appeal of the Hague setting out the circumstances in which the point of treaty interpretation arose before it and formulating the request in the words

"... la Cour, *avant de poursuivre l'examen* de ces griefs, demande à la Cour de Justice de la C.E.E. de se prononcer sur ce point, conformément à l'article 177 du Traité". [author's italics]

The Hague Court by the reference to E.E.C. 177 thus "suspended its proceedings". The plaintiff before the Hague Court took this judgment to the Dutch Court of Final Appeal (Court of Cassation), however, contending that the Hague Court was in error in referring to the Community Court. In respect of this appeal to the Dutch Court of Final Appeal two opposing arguments were advanced, before the Community Court, by the parties to the original action in Holland. The plaintiffs contended that before deciding the point submitted to it by the Hague Court, the Community Court should await the judgment of the Dutch Final Court of Appeal, on the ground that by the Dutch code of Civil Procedure (article 398, last paragraph) the effect of appealing to the Court of Final Appeal is to stay the execution of the judgment appealed against (with the result that the suspension of the proceedings ordered by the Hague Court was not legally effective for the purposes of E.E.C. St. 20). The defendants (in the original action) contended on the other hand that in accordance with E.E.C. St. 20 the proceedings before the Hague Court were suspended by the mere fact of the reference made by that Court to the Community Court. On this point the Community Court, finding that the parties had presented their comments in application of E.E.C. St. 20 paragraph two, held that:

"the national law of the Court which requests a preliminary ruling, and community law, constitute two distinct and different legal orders ... just as the Treaty (of E.E.C.) does not prohibit the national Court of Final Appeal from giving judgment on the appeal, but leaves the examination of its admissibility (*"recevabilité"*) to internal law and to the appreciation of the national judge, so the Treaty requires no more, for the Community Court to have jurisdiction, than that there should exist a request within the meaning of Article 177 (E.E.C.) without there being any necessity, for the Community judge, to examine whether the decision of the national judge has acquired the force of *res judicata* according to the provisions of his national law". (*Société Bosch* c. *de Geus, loc. cit., supra*. See also in Chapter 2, comment under paragraph 2 of E.E.C. 177, *ante*, pp. 132, 136–137).

"...Shall then be notified (*"communiqué"*) by the Registrar...". See, in general, Communication under E.E.C. St. 18 (*ante*, p. 215).

"... To the parties in the case, to the Member States ... originates from the Council". As under the provisions of E.E.C. St. 18, E.A.E.C. St. 18 and E.C.S.C. 21 (*ante*, p. 214) communication is required to be made not only to the parties in the case, but also to the Member States, etc. Under E.E.C. St. 20 it is required to be made to the Member States as well as the Institutions from which the act in dispute (in issue) originates. There are presumably never more than two "parties in the case" (in the strict sense) in any action before the Court, but R.P. 37(1) (*ante*, p. 220) speaks of the delivery "of two copies" (of all acts of procedure) "for the Court and as many copies as there are "parties *en cause*", as if there could be more. (This presumably is intended to make provision for third parties whose interests may be affected by the judgment and for Community Institutions and Member States).

"... **Written statements of case or written comments** ...". E.E.C. St. 20 and E.A.E.C. St. 21 require these to be lodged, by the persons they entitle to do so, within two months of notification by the Registrar that the Court has received notification of the decision of a tribunal of a Member State invoking the Court's jurisdiction to give a preliminary ruling. (It may be noted that the Court will not necessarily treat such statements or comments in the same manner as, or give them the same weight as, the Request, Defence, Reply and Further Reply, together with their supporting statements or comments. Thus, in Consolidated Cases 73–4/63 some of the written comments, put in by virtue of E.E.C. St. 20, were summarised in the part of the judgment setting out the facts, but not treated in detail or even referred to in the reasoning or the operative part. It appears normally to be the case, on the other hand, in actions not concerned with a preliminary ruling, but directly *inter partes*, that comments and statements are at least referred to with approval or disapproval in the Court's treatment of its reasoning. In the preliminary ruling case 13/61 (R. Vol. VII p. 100), however, one statement was referred to in the Court's reasoning (although four such were not mentioned). The explanation of the treatment accorded statements of case and comments may lie at least partly in the fact, that not being submissions, they are not positively required to feature in a judgment of the Court, as are the latter (see in Chapter 4, "Judgments", especially R.P. 67, *ante*, p. 260, regarding the Court's omission to rule). (See also, in general, comment on "... requests, statements of case, defences, comments ... replies ..." in Chapter 4, *ante*, p. 216.)

R.P. 103

Paragraph 1

In cases falling under Article 20 of the E.E.C. Statute and Article 21 of the E.A.E.C. Statute, the provisions of Article 44 *et seq.* of these Rules shall apply after submission of written statements of case or written comments as provided in the aforesaid Articles 20 and 21.

The same provisions shall apply in default of such submission within the time limit fixed by the aforesaid Articles 20 and 21, or if the parties, the Member States, the Commission or, as the case may be, the Council declare their intention not to make any such submissions.

Paragraph 2

In cases falling under Article 41 of the E.C.S C. Treaty, the decision to refer the matter shall be served on the parties in the case, the Member States, the High Authority and the Special Council of Ministers.

Within a time limit of two months dating from the day of such service the interested persons mentioned in the preceding paragraph shall have the right to submit written statements of case or written comments.

After submission of these, or in default of such submission within the period laid down in the preceding sub-paragraph, the provisions of Article 44 *et seq.* of these Rules shall apply.

"**... The provisions of article 44** *et seq.* **of these Rules ..."** (paragraph 1). For the text of these see *ante,* pp. 232 *et seq.* The effect of this provision of R.P. 103 is that procedure follows the normal pattern laid down for actions as from the stage when the further reply (in this case the statements or comments) has been lodged, starting with the fixing by the President of the date for the presentation of the preliminary report of the reporting judge, the procedure of enquiry and the calling of evidence if so ordered, and the oral procedure followed by judgment.

X. SPECIAL FORMS OF PROCEDURE UNDER ARTICLES 103 TO 105 OF THE EUROPEAN ATOMIC ENERGY COMMUNITY TREATY (R.P. 104–105)

("*Des procédures spéciales visées aux articles* 103 *à* 105 *du traité C.E.E.A.*";
"*Verfahren gemäss Artikel* 103 *des E.A.G. Vertrags;*
"*Van de bijzondere procedures bedoeld in de artikelen* 103 *tot* 105 *van het Verdrag E.G.A.*";
"*Dei procedimenti speciali previsti degli articoti* 103, 104, 105 *del trattato C.E.E.A.*").

The jurisdiction conferred on the Court by, and the general purport of, E.A.E.C. 103–105, is examined in Chapter 2, "Preliminary Opinion", etc., *ante,* pp. 163 *et seq.*

R.P. 104

Paragraph 1
In cases falling under Article 103, third paragraph of the E.A.E.C. Treaty, the Request shall be submitted in four certified copies. It shall be served on the Commission.

Paragraph 2
The Request shall be accompanied by the draft agreement or convention concerned, comments made by the Commission to the State concerned and all other documents in support.

The Commission shall submit its comments to the Court within a time limit of ten days, which may be extended by the President after the State concerned has expressed its views.

A certified copy of the aforementioned comments shall be notified to that State.

Paragraph 3
Immediately after the lodging of the Request, the President shall appoint a Judge to act as Rapporteur.

Paragraph 4
The decision shall be taken in the Judges' Council Chamber after the Advocate General has been heard.

If they so request the agents or legal advisers of the State concerned and of the Commission shall be heard.

R.P. 105

Paragraph 1

In cases falling under Article 104, last paragraph and Article 105, last paragraph of the E.A.E.C. Treaty the provisions of Article 37 *et seq.* of these Rules shall apply.

Paragraph 2

The Request shall be served on the State to which the person or undertaking belongs against whom the Request is made.

XI. OPINIONS (R.P. 106, 107, 108)

(*"Des avis"; "Gutachten"; "Van de adviezen"; "Dei pareri"*)

Recourse to the Court for it to act in an advisory capacity is provided for in E.E.C. 228 and E.C.S.C. 95(4), for the text of which and comment thereon see Chapter 2, "Preliminary opinion", *ante,* p. 163 for E.E.C. and p. 167, for E.C.S.C.

Procedure in respect of such advisory activity is regulated by the following rules.

R.P. 106

Paragraph 1

If an application for a preliminary opinion referred to in Article 228 of the E.E.C. Treaty is submitted by the Council it shall be served upon the Commission. If the application is submitted by the Commission, it shall be served upon the Council and the Member States. If the application is submitted by one of the Member States, it shall be served upon the Council, the Commission and the other Member States.

The President shall set a time limit within which the institutions and Member States on whom the application has been served shall be able to submit their written comments.

Paragraph 2

The opinion may deal with either the compatibility of the proposed agreement with the provisions of the E.E.C. Treaty, or the power of the Community or one of its institutions to enter into that agreement.

R.P. 107

Paragraph 1

Immediately after the submission of the application for a preliminary opinion referred to in the preceding Article, the President shall appoint a Judge to act as Rapporteur.

Paragraph 2

The Court shall deliver a reasoned opinion in the Judges' Council Chamber, after hearing the Advocates General.

Paragraph 3

The opinion signed by the President, the Judges taking part in its consideration and the Registrar shall be served on the Council, the Commission and the Member States.

R.P. 108

When the opinion of the Court is required under Article 95, fourth paragraph of the E.C.S.C. Treaty, an application shall be submitted to it jointly by the High Authority and the Special Council of Ministers.

The opinion shall be given in accordance with the provisions of the preceding Article. It shall be notified to the High Authority, the Special Council of Ministers and the European Parliamentary Assembly.

For examples of opinions see (i) *demande d'avis* ("application for a preliminary opinion") introduced by the High Authority and the Special Council of Ministers of E.C.S.C., 4 February 1960 in respect of the procedure for treaty revision under E.C.S.C. 95 (3 and 4) (R. Vol. VI(i) at p. 93) and the opinion ("*avis*") itself (at p. 107); and (ii) *demande d'avis* ("application for a preliminary opinion") introduced by the same parties as above in respect of the procedure for treaty revision under the same articles (R. Vol. V, p. 533) and the opinion (*avis*) itself (at p. 551).

Final Provisions
(R.P. 109–112 etc.)

I. RULES OF PROCEDURE: FINAL PROVISIONS

The Final Provisions of the Rules of Procedure (R.P. 109–112 *infra*) make provision for supplementary rules (see *infra*) on three defined matters, repeal the Rules of Procedure of the Court of Justice of E.C.S.C. (now the same body as the Court of the other two Communities (see Chapter 3, "Organisation of the Court", *ante*, p. 180) and provide for their own publication in the Official Journal of the Communities.

R.P. 109

Subject to the application of Article 188 of the E.E.C. Treaty and Article 160 of the E.A.E.C. Treaty and after consultation with the governments concerned the Court shall draw up, insofar as it is concerned, supplementary Rules providing for:

(*a*) letters of request;

(*b*) application for free legal aid;

(*c*) formal report by the Court, in accordance with Article 28 of the E.C.S.C. and E.A.E.C. Statutes and Article 27 of the E.E.C. Statute, of perjury by witnesses and experts.

"... (a) letters of request ...". For the text of Supplementary Rule regarding these see S.R.P. 1 (1–3) *post*, pp. 300–301. See also Chapter 4, "Evidence of witnesses by letter of request" (*ante*, p. 246).

"... (b) application for free legal aid ...". For the text of the Supplementary Rules regarding these see S.R.P. 4 and 5, *post*, p. 301.

"... (c) formal report ... of perjury ...". For the text of Supplementary Rules regarding these see S.R.P. 6 and 7, *post*, p. 302.

R.P. 110

Upon entry into force of these Rules the following shall be repealed:

(*a*) The Rules of the Court of Justice of the European Coal and Steel Community, adopted on the 4th March 1953 and published in the Official Journal of the European Coal and Steel Community on the 7th March 1953;

(*b*) The additional Rules of the Court of Justice of the European Coal and Steel Community adopted on the

31st March 1954 and published in the Official Journal
of the European Coal and Steel Community on the 7th
April 1954;

(c) The Rules of the European Coal and Steel Community
Court of Justice on costs, adopted on the 19th May 1954
and published in the Official Journal of the European
Coal and Steel Community on the 26th May 1954;

(d) The Rules of Procedure of the European Coal and Steel
Community Court of Justice for disputes referred to in
Article 58 of the Service Regulations for Personnel of
the Community, adopted on the 21st February 1957 and
published in the Official Journal of the European Coal
and Steel Community on the 11th March 1957.

II. APPENDICES

R.P. 111

The provisions of these Rules shall not apply to proceedings
begun before their coming into force.

R.P. 112

These Rules, drawn up in the official languages, shall be
published in the Official Journal of the European Communities
and all four texts shall be authentic.

The Appendices to the Rules of Procedure are as follows:

Appendix I

[*Printed on* ante, *p.* 268.]

Appendix II

[*Printed on* ante, *p.* 269.]

III. SUPPLEMENTARY RULES OF PROCEDURE

S.R.P. Chapter I

LETTERS OF REQUEST

Article 1

Letters of request shall be issued by means of an order; this
order shall contain the names, forenames, description and
addresses of the witnesses or experts, shall state the facts on
which the witnesses or experts are to be heard, name the
parties, their agents, legal representatives or legal advisers
together with their address for service and shall set out briefly
the subject of the dispute.

The order shall be notified to the parties by the Registrar.

Article 2

The Registrar shall forward the order to the Minister of
Justice of the Member State on whose territory the witnesses or

experts are to be heard. Where applicable it shall be accompanied by a translation in the official language or languages of the Member State to which it is addressed. The Minister of Justice of the Member State shall transmit the order to the judicial authority competent under its law.

The competent judicial authority shall give effect to the letters of request in accordance with the provisions of its law. Having completed its action, the competent judicial authority shall forward to the Minister of Justice the order containing the Letters of Request, the documents obtained in pursuance thereof and a detailed statement of expenses. The Minister of Justice shall forward these documents to the Registrar of the Court.

The Registrar shall be responsible for having the documents translated into the procedural language.

Article 3

The Court shall defray the expenses of the Letters of Request subject to the right to order their payment, where appropriate, by the parties.

Letters of request result from the procedure of enquiry and the calling of evidence that may be ordered by the Court following the close of the written, and immediatly prior to the oral, procedure (see R.P. 45(2) at *ante*, p. 234; also R.P. 109, *ante*, p. 299).

S.R.P. Chapter II

FREE LEGAL AID

Article 4

The Court shall, in the order deciding entitlement to free legal aid, order that a legal representative shall be appointed to assist the party concerned.

If the party does not make his own choice of legal representative, or if the Court considers that this choice should not be endorsed, the Registrar shall forward an authenticated copy of the order and a copy of the request for legal aid to the competent authority of the State concerned as shown in Annex I. With the proposals put forward by that authority before it, the Court shall itself proceed to appoint a legal representative to assist the party.

Article 5

The Court shall advance the expenses.

It shall adjudicate on the legal representative's disbursements and fees; on Request, the President may order that he receive an advance.

The provisions of this Chapter are in implementation of R.P. 76 (*ante*, p. 264); see also "(b) application for free legal aid . . .".

S.R.P. Chapter III

REPORTS OF PERJURY ON THE PART OF WITNESSES OR EXPERTS

Article 6

The Court, after hearing the Advocate General, may decide to report to the Minister of Justice of the Member State within the jurisdiction of whose courts criminal proceedings fall to be taken, any false evidence given by a witness, or any false statement made by an expert, on oath before the Court.

Article 7

The Registrar shall be responsible for transmitting the decision of the Court.

Such decision shall set out the facts and circumstances on which the report is founded.

See "Perjury" in Chapter 4 (*ante*, p. 243); also "(c) formal report . . . of perjury . . .", *ante*, p. 299.

IV. INSTRUCTIONS TO THE REGISTRAR

These are formulated by the Court on proposals put forward by the President (see R.P. 14, *ante*, p. 193).

SECTION I. FUNCTIONS OF THE REGISTRAR'S OFFICE

Article 1

Paragraph 1

The Registrar's Office shall be open to the public on Mondays to Fridays from 10 a.m. to 12 noon and from 3 p.m. to 6 p.m. and on Saturdays from 10 a.m. to 12 noon except on those official holidays listed in Appendix I to the Rules of Procedure.

When the Registrar's Office is closed, procedural documents may properly be placed in the Court's letter box, which shall be cleared daily when the Registrar's Office is opened.

Paragraph 2

When the Court or a Section holds a sitting in open court the Registrar's Office shall always be opened to the public 30 minutes before the sitting is due to begin.

Article 2

The Registrar shall be responsible for the keeping of the court files relating to pending cases and shall arrange that they be constantly kept up to date.

Article 3

Paragraph 1

The originals of judgments, orders and decisions shall be drawn up under the responsibility of the Registrar who shall submit them for signature to the appropriate members of the Court.

Paragraph 2

The Registrar shall ensure that any service, notification or communication provided for in the European Coal and Steel Community, European Economic Community and European Atomic Energy Community Treaties, in the European Coal and Steel Community, European Economic Community and European Atomic Energy Community Statutes and also in the Rules of Procedure shall be made in accordance with the provisions of the latter; he shall attach a registered letter, signed by him, to the copy of the document to be served, notified or communicated, specifying the case number, register number and a summary statement of the nature of the document. A copy of this letter shall be attached to the original document.

Paragraph 3

The parties shall be served with the procedural documents and the other documents relating thereto.

If only one copy of bulky documents is deposited with the Registrar's Office, the Registrar, after consulting the judge acting as Rapporteur, shall inform the parties by registered letter that they may be seen at the Registrar's Office.

With regard to the distinction in paragraph 2 between service, notification and communication see Chapter 4, "Service", *ante*, p. 266 and Chapter 4, "Communication", *ante*, p. 215.

Article 4

Paragraph 1

A receipt shall be given, on request by the party concerned, for any procedural document lodged with the Registrar's Office.

Paragraph 2

Failing express authorisation from the President or the Court, the Registrar shall refuse to accept, or as the case may be, shall immediately return, under registered cover, any procedural or other document not provided for in the Rules of Procedure or not in the procedural language.

Paragraph 3

If a procedural document is deposited with the Registrar's Office on a different date from its entry in the register, mention of this shall be made on the procedural document.

Article 5

Paragraph 1

The Registrar after consultation with the President and the judge acting as Rapporteur, shall take all necessary steps to ensure the application of Article 38(7) of the Rules of Procedure.

He shall set the time limit provided for in the said Article by registered letter with acknowledgment of receipt.

Should the person concerned not comply with the request of the Registrar, the latter shall refer the matter to the President of the Court.

Paragraph 2

The request to the Registrar's Office of the Arbitration Committee provided for in Article 101(3) of the Rules of Procedure, shall be sent by registered letter with acknowledgment of receipt.

The file shall be returned to the Registrar's Office of the Arbitration Committee after the Court has pronounced judgment or after the case has been struck from the Court Register.

As to regularisation of the Request, see Chapter 4, "The Request", *ante*, pp. 218–220.

Article 6

Paragraph 1

An entry shall be made at the foot of the original that the judgment or order has been read in open Court; this entry, in the procedural language, shall be as follows:

"Read in open Court at . . . . , on the . . . .
                    Registrar   President
                    (signature)   (signature)"

Paragraph 2

Marginal entries in judgments referred to in Articles 66(4), 94(6), 97(3), 100(3) and 102(2) of the Rules of Procedure shall be made in the procedural language; they shall be initialled by the President and the Registrar.

As to judgments and orders see Chapter 4, R.P. 63, etc., *ante*, p. 253.

Article 7

Paragraph 1

Before each sitting in open court, whether of the Court or of a Section a cause list shall be drawn up by the Registrar in the procedural language.

This list shall contain:
    the date, hour and place of the sitting;
    particulars of the cases to be called;
    the names of the parties;
    the names and descriptions of the agents, legal advisers and legal representatives of the parties.

The cause list shall be put up at the entrance to the Courtroom.

Paragraph 2

The Registrar shall draw up a record, in the procedural language, of each sitting in open court.

This record shall contain:

the date and place of the sitting;

the names of the judges, Advocates-General and Registrar in attendance;

particulars of the case;

the names of the parties;

the names and descriptions of the agents, legal advisers and legal representatives of the parties;

the names, forenames, descriptions and permanent addresses of witnesses or experts heard;

particulars of evidence produced at the sitting;

particulars of exhibits put in by the parties during the sitting;

the decisions of the Court or Section or of the President of the Court or Section, given at the sitting.

Should the oral procedure in the same case require several successive sittings, one record only need be drawn up.

Paragraph 1. As to the provisions of the Statutes and of R.P. 55 in respect of the Cause list see Chapter 4, "Cause List" under "Oral Procedure", *ante*, p. 248.

Paragraph 2. As to the record see in Chapter 4 "The conduct of the Hearing of Witnesses" especially sentence beginning "Since the Registrar is required . . .", *ante*, p. 242, and ". . . Official record . . .", *ante*, p. 247.

Paragraph 2. ". . . evidence produced at the sitting . . ." see in Chapter 4, "The Procedure of Enquiry", R.P. 47(2) (b), *ante*, p. 239; and in Chapter 4, "The Oral Procedure", *ante*, pp. 248 *et seq.*

Article 8

The Registrar shall ensure that the persons or bodies entrusted with an enquiry or the making of an expert examination and report, shall, in accordance with Article 49 of the Rules of Procedure, have all necessary means for the performance of the task entrusted to them.

As to enquiry and expert examination and report see Chapter 4, *ante*, pp. 234 *et seq.*, and under "Procedure of Enquiry: Calling of Evidence".

Article 9

The credentials for which provision is made in Article 33(b) of the Rules of Procedure shall be transmitted to the legal adviser or legal representative as soon as the date for the opening of the oral procedure has been fixed, or, at the request of the person concerned, at any other time following the lodging with the Registrar's Office of the authority containing such person's nomination, should this be necessary for the proper conduct of the proceedings.

Credentials shall be drawn up by the Registrar.

Article 10

In accordance with Article 32 of the Rules of Procedure, an extract from the cause list shall be communicated in advance to the Minister for Foreign Affairs of the State in which the Court is sitting.

"In accordance with R.P. 32".   R.P. 32 deals with a letter of request of the European Court to a judicial authority (Court) in a given State.

". . . In which the Court is sitting".   That is, the Court of Justice of the European Communities.

Section 2.   Keeping the Register

Article 11

The Registrar shall be responsible for keeping up to date the register of cases submitted to the Court.

Article 12

When the Request instituting an action is registered, a serial number shall be ascribed to the case, followed by the year and accompanied by mention either of the applicant's name or of the subject-matter of the Request. Cases shall be referred to by this number.

Summary proceedings shall be given the same number as the main proceedings, followed by the letter "R".

Article 13

The pages of the register shall be numbered in advance.

It shall periodically be certified and initialled by the President and the Registrar in the margin of the last entry made.

Article 14

Steps in the proceedings and procedural documents relating to cases submitted to the Court shall be entered in the register and, in particular, the exhibits lodged by the parties and service effected by the Registrar.

Annexes to procedural documents shall be entered when they are lodged separately from the principal document.

Article 15

Paragraph 1

Entries shall be made consecutively and in the order of production or performance of the procedural document or step to be registered.

They shall be numbered in consecutive and continuous sequence.

Paragraph 2

Registration shall be effected immediately after the procedural document has been lodged at the Registrar's Office.

Where the document originates from the Court, registration shall be made on the same day as the document is drawn up.

Paragraph 3

The entry in the register shall contain the necessary information for identification of the document and in particular:

the date of registration;

particulars of the case;

the nature of the document;

the date of the document.

It shall be made in the procedural language; numbers shall be entered in figures and standard abbreviations shall be permitted.

Paragraph 4

Where alterations are deemed necessary these shall be made in the margin and initialled by the Registrar.

Article 16

The serial number of the registration shall be shown on the first page of any procedural document issuing from the Court.

Mention of the register entry shall be made on the original copy of any procedural document lodged by the parties in the form of a stamp bearing the following wording, in the procedural language:

"Entered in the register of the Court of Justice under
No . . . .
Luxembourg, the . . . ."

This statement shall be signed by the Registrar.

SECTION 3. SCALE OF FEES OF THE REGISTRAR'S
OFFICE AND COURT FEES

Article 17

The Registrar's fees set out in this Section shall be the only such fees to be charged.

Article 18

Payment of Registrar's fees shall be made either in cash at the Court Pay Office or by bank transfer to the Court's bank account in the demand for payment.

Article 19

Where the party liable to pay Registrar's fees has been granted legal aid, the provisions of Article 76(5) of the Rules of Procedure shall apply.

Article 20

The Registrar's fees shall be as follows:

(*a*) For an office copy of a judgment or order, a certified copy of a procedural document or record, an extract from the Court register, a certified copy of the Court register. a certified copy made under Article 72(b) of the Rules of Procedure: 30 Lux. frances per page.

(*b*) For a translation made under Article 72(b) of the Rules of Procedure: 200 Lux. francs per page.

One page contains a maximum of 40 lines.

These fees shall be for the first copy, each subsequent copy being charged at the rate of 5 Lux. francs per page or part of a page.

Article 21

Paragraph 1

Where, pursuant to Articles 47(3), 51(1) and 76(5) of the Rules of Procedure, an advance is requested from the Court Pay Office, the Registrar shall require the submission of details of the expenses in respect of which the advance is requested.

Witnesses shall be required by him to provide documentary evidence of their loss of earnings and experts to provide a note of their fees.

Paragraph 2

The Registrar shall authorise payment by the Court Pay Office of sums due under the previous paragraph, such payment to be vouched by a signed receipt or proof of transfer.

Where he deems the sum requested to be excessive he shall have power to reduce this sum on his own authority or to spread payment over a period.

Paragraph 3

The Registrar shall authorise repayment by the Court Pay Office of the expenses of Letters of Request payable in accordance with Article 3 of the Supplementary Rules to the judicial authority specified by the Minister referred to in Article 2 of the said Rules, in the currency of the State concerned, such payment to be vouched by proof of transfer.

Paragraph 4

The Registrar shall authorise payment by the Court Pay Office of an advance as specified in Article 5, second Paragraph of the Supplementary Rules, in accordance with the provisions of Paragraph 2, second sub-paragraph above.

Article 22

Paragraph 1

When sums paid in respect of free legal aid are recoverable as provided in Article 76(5) of the Rules of Procedure, such sums shall be claimed by registered letter signed by the Registrar. This letter shall specify, in addition to the sum to be reimbursed, the method and time limit allowed for such reimbursement.

The same provisions shall apply in cases coming within Article 72 (*a*) of the Rules of Procedure and Article 21(1), (3) and (4) of these Instructions.

Paragraph 2

In default of payment of the sum claimed within the time limit allowed by the Registrar, the latter shall request the Court to make an immediately enforceable order which he shall have enforced as provided in Articles 44 and 92 of the European Coal and Steel Community Treaty, 187 and 192 of the European Economic Community Treaty, and 159 and 164 of the European Atomic Energy Community Treaty.

Section 4. Court Publications

Article 23

The Registrar shall be responsible for Court publications.

Article 24

Official law reports shall be published in the official languages and shall consist, unless otherwise decided, of judgments of the Court with the submissions of the Advocates General, and opinions given and orders made in the summary procedure during the course of the calendar year.

Article 25

The Registrar shall be responsible for publication in the Official Journal of the European Communities:

(*a*) Of notices concerning Requests instituting proceedings, pursuant to Article 15(6) of the Rules of Procedure;

(*b*) Of notices relative to a case being struck out of the register;

(*c*) Unless decided otherwise by the Court, of the order contained in any judgement or provisional order;

(*d*) Of the Composition of the Sections;

(*e*) Of the appointment of the President of the Court;

(*f*) Of the appointment of the Registrar;

(*g*) Of the appointment of the Assistant Registrar and of the administrative officer.

FINAL PROVISIONS

Article 26

These Instructions, drawn up in the official languages, shall be published in the Official Journal of the European Communities, all four texts being authentic.

Appendix

It is considered that readers may find it convenient to have set out without annotation the text of R.P. 93 which makes provision for Intervention. The Rule is fully discussed in the main part of the work. Other Articles of the Treaties and Rules of Procedure etc. which did not appear to require detailed annotation in the main part of the work are set out below for convenience of reference.

All the above Articles are arranged in this Appendix in the same sequence as the Chapters of the main part of the work to which they relate, with appropriate headings and cross references, as follows:

CHAPTER 1.—THE TASK OF THE COURT

European Economic Community. The task of the Community is to establish a Common Market. See *ante*, pp. 16, 27.

E.E.C. 8

1. The Common Market shall be gradually brought into existence during a transitional period of twelve years.

This transitional period shall be divided into three stages of four years each; the length of each stage may be modified in accordance with the provisions set out below.

2. A group of measures, to be simultaneously initiated and carried through, shall be allotted to each of these stages.

3. Transition from the first to the second stage shall be conditional upon a finding that the objectives specifically laid down in this Treaty for the first stage have been essentially achieved, and that, subject to the exceptions and in accordance with the procedures provided for in this Treaty, all obligations have been met.

This finding shall be unanimously reached by the Council on a report by the Commission at the end of the fourth year. Provided always that a Member State may not prevent unanimity by relying upon the non-fulfilment of its own obligations. Failing unanimity, the first stage shall be automatically extended by one year.

At the end of the fifth year, the Council shall make its finding subject to the same conditions. Failing unanimity, the first stage shall be automatically extended by a further year.

At the end of the sixth year, the Council shall make its finding by qualified majority vote on a report by the Commission.

4. Within one month of the last-mentioned vote any Member State which voted in a minority, or, if the required majority vote was not obtained, any Member State shall be entitled to call upon the Council to appoint an Arbitration Board whose decision shall be binding upon all Member States and upon the institutions of the Community. The Arbitration Board shall consist of three members unanimously designated by the Council on a proposal by the Commission.

If the Council has not made such appointments within one month of being called upon to do so, the members of the Arbitration Board shall be appointed by the Court of Justice within a further period of one month.

The Arbitration Board shall appoint its own Chairman.

The Board shall deliver its award within six months of the Council vote referred to in the last sub-paragraph of paragraph 3.

5. The second and third stages may not be extended or curtailed except in accordance with a decision of the Council acting unanimously on a proposal of the Commission.

6. Nothing in the preceding paragraphs shall cause the transitional period to last more than fifteen years after this Treaty comes into force.

7. Save for the exceptions or derogations provided for in this Treaty, the expiry of the transitional period shall constitute the final date for the entry into force of all the rules provided for and for the completion of all the measures involved in the establishment of the Common Market.

European Economic Community. Powers are conferred on the Commission to ensure that effect is given to rules laid down by the Council. See *ante*, p. 23.

(Council) Regulation 17, Article 16

Penalties

1. The Commission may, by means of a Decision, impose on undertakings or associations of undertakings penalties of from fifty to one thousand units of account per day of delay, reckoning from the date fixed in its Decision, in order to oblige them:

(*a*) to put an end to an infringement of Article 85 or Article 86 of the Treaty in conformity with a Decision taken pursuant to Article 3 hereof;

(*b*) to discontinue any action prohibited under Article 8 (3);

(*c*) to supply completely and truthfully any information which it has requested by a Decision taken under Article 11 (5);

(*d*) to submit to any investigation it has ordered by a Decision taken pursuant to Article 14 (3).

2. When the undertakings or associations of undertakings have fulfilled the obligation which it was the object of the penalty to enforce, the Commission may fix the final amount of the penalty at a figure lower than that which would result from the initial Decision.

3. The provisions of Article 10 (3) to Article 10 (6) shall apply.

CHAPTER 2.—THE JURISDICTION OF THE COURT

Community liability in tort under E.C.S.C. 40. "Wrongful act or default in the performance of its functions" (professional secrecy); see *ante*, pp. 145, 146.

E.C.S.C. 47

The High Authority may collect the information necessary to carry out its tasks. It may have any necessary checks made.

The High Authority shall not disclose information which is of the kind covered by the duty of professional secrecy, and in particular information about undertakings and about their business relations and how their costing is made up. With this reservation, it shall publish such data as may be useful to Governments or to any other parties concerned.

The High Authority may impose fines and periodic penalty payments upon those undertakings which evade the obligations imposed on them by decisions made in pursuance of this Article, or which knowingly furnish false information. The maximum amount of such fines shall be 1 per cent of the annual turnover and the maximum amount of such payments shall be 6 per cent of the average daily turnover for each day's delay.

Any violation by the High Authority of the duty of professional secrecy which has caused damage to an undertaking may be the subject of proceedings for compensation before the Court under the conditions provided for in Article 40.

CHAPTER 5.—SPECIAL FORMS OF PROCEDURE

Intervention. Time limits and formal requirements for request for intervention are set out. See *ante*, pp. 276, 277, 278.

R.P. 93

Paragraph 1

A Request to intervene shall be submitted at the latest before the opening of the oral procedure.

Paragraph 2

The Request shall contain:

  (*a*) particulars of the case;

  (*b*) particulars of the parties;

  (*c*) the name and permanent address of the intervener;

  (*d*) a summary of the reasons showing that the intervener has a valid interest in the outcome of the case, save as provided in Article 37 of the E.E.C. Statute and Article 38 of the E.A.E.C. Statute;

  (*e*) submissions tending to support or oppose the case of one of the original parties to the suit;

  (*f*) means of proof available and in an annex documents in support thereof;

  (*g*) specification by the intervener of an address for service in the town where the Court has its seat.

The intervener shall be represented in accordance with the provisions of Article 20, first and second paragraphs of the E.C.S.C. Statute and Article 17 of the E.E.C. and E.A.E.C. Statutes.

The provisions of Articles 38 and 39 of these Rules shall apply.

Paragraph 3

The Request shall be served on the parties to the case. After giving them facilities to submit their written or oral comments the Court shall, after hearing the Advocate General, make an order.

Paragraph 4

If the Court allows the intervention, every procedural document notified to the parties shall be communicated to the intervener.

Paragraph 5

The intervener shall accept the case as he finds it at the time of his intervention.

The President shall set a time limit by which the intervener shall submit in writing the grounds of fact and of law supporting his submissions, and also the time limit within which the original parties to the case may make their replies.

Proceedings by servants of the Communities. See *ante*, pp. 283, 284.

R.P. 96

Paragraph 1

Where an application under the summary procedure in case of urgency, is made in proceedings falling within Article 95 Paragraph 1 of these Rules of Procedure and the President of the Court is absent or unable to attend, he shall be replaced by the President of the competent Section.

Paragraph 2

Without prejudice to his power to refer the matter to the Court, given in Article 85 of these Rules, the President may refer the application under summary procedure to the competent section.

Index

MEMBER STATES—(*contd.*)
   Court of Justice, cases before, intervention
      in, 276
   economy of, disturbances in, review of
      justification of High Authority in
      connection with, 126
   E.C.S.C. High Authority, claim by, 71
   E.E.C., claim by, 74
   representation before the Court by agent,
      211

MUNICIPAL LAW
   Community Law, relation between, 3, 4,
      59
   E.E.C. relation between, 29
   jurisdiction where
      E.A.E.C. a party, 29
      E.C.S.C. a party, 5, 7, 58
      E.E.C. a party, 29

N

NON-MEMBER STATES
   E.E.C. and, agreements between, 33

NUCLEAR FUEL
   E.A.E.C., activity, as, 36, 37

O

OFFICERS OF THE COURT. *See
   under* JUDGE *and* ADVOCATES-GENERAL

P

PENALTIES
   appeals against, 81
   monetary, 80, 312
   patent rights as to, 81
   payment, periodic, 80
   review of by Court of Justice, 78–83

PRECEDENCE
   community law, meaning in, 8, 138
   English law, comparison with, 9
   French law, comparison with, 9

PRELIMINARY OPINIONS
   Court of Justice of, 163 *et seq.*

PRIVATE INTERNATIONAL LAW
   E.E.C. contractual liability of, 28
   E.E.C. tortious liability of, 28

PRIVATE PARTIES
   actions by, before the Court, 66

PRIVILEGES
   E.A.E.C. of, 46, 175
   E.C.S.C. of, 56, 175
   E.E.C., 29, 175

PROCEDURE. *See also* SPECIAL FORMS OF
   PROCEDURE
   "acte", as part of, 218
   agent, representation by, 211, 213
   basic characteristics, 209, 210
   cause list, 248
      settlement of, President by, 238
   comments, 216
   costs, 261–264
      decision on, 257
   decision, as part of, 218
   defences, 216
   document, 216
   documentary evidence in, 219
   evidence, calling of, 233 *et seq.*
      measures for, scope of, 234
   examination by Court, 249
   exhibits to be annexed to documents, 220
   expert opinions, 234 *et seq.*
   hearing, publicity of, 248
   judgment, default, by, 228
      delivery of, 258
      execution and enforcement of, 255
      nature of, 253 *et seq.*
      orders distinct from, 253
      reasoned, 256
   language, 251
   legal advisers, 213
   legal aid, free, 264, 265
   legal representatives, 213
   official language, 251
   oral, 214, 215, 248
      reopening, 252
   party, nature, 212
   perjury, 243
   phases, 214
   questions put by Court, 249
   reasoned oral submissions in, 252
   Registrar, functions, 214 *et seq.*
   replies, 216
   reports of hearing, Registrar, kept by, 249
   representation by agent, 211
   representation, why necessary, 213
   requests, 216
      contents, 221 *et seq.*
      court by, 230 *et seq.*
      serving, 225
   service, 266, 267
   statement, case of, 216
      defence, contents of, 226
   time limits, 267–269
      proceedings, as to, 219
   withdrawals, 265, 266
   witnesses, 233 *et seq.*
      defaulting, 243
   written, 214–233, 247
      importance, 210
      request, institution of proceedings by
         217

R

REGISTRAR
   administration of Court of Justice, 198, 203
      appointment, 192
   authority, 193
   documents, care of, 196
   fees scale, 307